THE EXQUISITE CORPSE OF ASIAN AMERICA

SEXUAL CULTURES

General Editors: José Esteban Muñoz and Ann Pellegrini

Titles in the series include the following:

The Exquisite Corpse of Asian America

Biopolitics, Biosociality, and Posthuman Ecologies

Rachel C. Lee

NEW YORK UNIVERSITY PRESS
New York and London

NEW YORK UNIVERSITY PRESS
New York and London
www.nyupress.org

References to Internet websites (URLs) were accurate at the time of writing.
Neither the author nor New York University Press is responsible for URLs
that may have expired or changed since the manuscript was prepared.

ISBN 978-1-4798-1771-9 (hardback) — ISBN 978-1-4798-0978-3 (pb)

For Library of Congress Cataloging-in-Publication data, please contact
the Library of Congress.

New York University Press books are printed on acid-free paper,
and their binding materials are chosen for strength and durability.
We strive to use environmentally responsible suppliers and materials
to the greatest extent possible in publishing our books.

Manufactured in the United States of America

10 9 8 7 6 5 4 3 2 1

Also available as an ebook

CONTENTS

An insert of color images follows page 138.

Introduction

Parts/Parturition

Part to Whole

Cut your arm. Cut.
See. You feel no pain
'cause you already so-wa inside
. . . .
spread the cut you just made
before the blood get hard . . . .
Then we write her name . . . .
—Lois Ann Yamanaka, *Saturday Night at the*
Pahala Theater, 1993

With respect to the human parts, organs, fetuses and embryos you are viewing, Premier . . . cannot independently
verify that they do not belong to persons executed while
incarcerated in Chinese prisons.
—language to be posted by "Body Worlds" exhibitor,
Premier Entertainments, by order of the New York State
Attorney General's Office, 2008

Lois Ann Yamanaka's poem series, "Parts," included in *Saturday Night
at the Pahala Theater*, launches a bitter complaint against women's
work of cleaning, cooking, and raising children. Written in the blazon
tradition—but one that *declines* to sanctify a female subject through
praising a single body part[1]—interior poems of the series titled "The
Brain," "The Face," "The Nostril," and "The Foot" highlight its speaker's

own corporeal burdens—her "splitting headache"—and the bodily harm she will visit upon others if they delay their domestic chores: "Want me / to punch / your face in? / . . . Now get / your ass / in your room / and fold / all the laundry. / Then iron / your father's shirts" ("The Face," 66). Section 3, "Girl in Parts," relays the speaker's hostile response to her daughter's divulgence of being raped: "Why you had to tell me this? / . . . Don't you ever talk / about this again" (73). In the crudely titled "The Crack," the speaker commands the girl—her daughter, presumably—to shut her mouth and seal her other lips, the labia: "you going think / you popular / but all they thinking / is you spread fast" (71). The focalized body parts shift from those of the mother to those of the daughter, with both of these female subjects lacking ownership of their bodies.

While these stanzas directly conjure parental disapproval as key to carving up the "girl in[to] parts," the divisive social structuring of Hawai'i's plantation economy implicitly contributes to this state of affairs. After overthrowing Hawai'i's Queen Lili'uokalani in 1893, American missionaries and businessmen turned these Pacific Islands into an archipelago of fruit and sugar plantations. Pursuing a strategy of divide and conquer, plantation owners recruited workers from different nations, counting on linguistic and ethnic differences to prevent collective labor organizing. At the same time, plantation overseers needed a language to command their multilingual workforce. Local pidgin English—assembled from Japanese, Native Hawaiian, Portuguese, Tagalog, and Chinese elements—grew out of these conditions. Written in this local dialect, Yamanaka's poetic apostrophe (i.e., direct address to a person or thing, often absent) brings into being the female body through this historically specific "language of command." Providing its own theorization of writing in relation to embodiment and the biological body, the poem's discourse—its series of imperatives—performatively instantiate this daughter or "you" as a divisible corporeality.

While the conjured person or thing ("girl in parts") addressed in this poem stays consistent, the speaker in the final poem of this series, which includes the excerpt quoted in the epigraph, switches from a mother to a teenage peer—a "14-year-old friend" who details an act of self-cutting. This action also places the apostrophed subject in the domain of clinical health. Even though this final poem, titled "What the

Hands Do about All of these Parts / Advice from a 14-Year-Old Friend,"
shifts its speaker from adult parent to adolescent pal, there is no lessening of the logic of fragmentation. The hospital, rather than the household, now provides the lexicon for processing this divisibility:

> Take the needle. Take it. . . .
> Push um deep, the needle,
> till you see the white part
> of your meat. Spread um—
> . . . .
> Kind of gray, yeah the feeling?
> Going away, the pain inside,
> 'cause you getting numb.
> Your whole body not throbbing yet?
> I remember the first time
> I did this. Felt so good . . .
> [when] the blood started dripping
> . . . .
> . . . Tasted like rust.
> . . . .
> My father took me emergency that day.
> That was the first time
> I seen him cry.
> No. No need towel.
> Lie down. Let the blood
> drip on the sidewalk.
> Then we write her name
> with the blood
> and when dry,
> . . . .
> . . . she going know
> How much you love her.

In relation to continuing debates in Asian Americanist criticism on
whether representational fullness constitutes the ideological goal of the
field,[2] Yamanaka's poem teases with the promise of self-enacted expression (what the hands can decisively do), but in the end neither reveals

the hidden essence of the addressed girl (the confessional testimony is only of her "friend") nor allows for a reading that affirms writing as the fulfillment of agency or autonomy. The addressee of the blazon is still commanded by another to physical action—to "cut," "push," and "spread" rather than to "fold all the laundry"—but these actions incorporate a notion of surgical opening up, body modification, and bioavailability as the avatars of agency. So too, a clinical intervention—the trip to the emergency room—provides the vehicle of parental recognition, such that the techniques of the hospital mediate the wounding and the eliciting of caring and affection.

To assign an ultimately defiant logic to the poem seems especially difficult to do, making it an uneasy fit with the relishing of "resistance" and "justice" in U.S. minoritarian critical contexts (see Nguyen; Chuh). The writing of "her name" at the poem's conclusion does not liberate the daughter from the anatomical carving up of the first three parts, and only partially points to the criminal agent who should be brought to justice—e.g., the first-person speaker doling out "pain in parts": the mother figure is fingered, so to speak, but the plantation economy is not. The writing—constituted by the repurposing of bodily fluids as ink— merely expedites the circulation of several sensations and sentiments, the primary one nominated as "love." Furthermore, the main significance of the poem may lie not in the closed loop between two putative whole (humanist) "Asian American" subjects—the parent and daughter—but in the distribution of affects and effects that the cutting generates, which brings me to my final point, for now, in relation to this work.

Even though the poetic series enumerates body parts, it does not profile them racially as much as instrumentally, sensually, and affectively. In the scalar shift from anatomical catalogue—brain, face, feet, nostril— to a more molecular circulation of bodily sensations and affects—the taste of "rust," the proprioceptive imbalance of feeling "trippy . . . your whole body . . . throbbing" (75), the stark visuality of "the white part / of your meat," and the crossed sensations of the "icy" numbness and "gray, yeah the feeling" (75)—we seem to have lost a body conventionally identifiable as an Asian American, racialized one. To impute an Asian American quality to this poem's contents, aesthetics, or importance in literary criticism would seem both audaciously unfounded and absolutely necessary for Asian Americanist critique, a necessary first step to explore the limits—as well as continuing salience—of racial analysis at a time when being biological means something not altogether recognizably humanist (with humanism's assumptions of the human subject defined by his or her organismal form, enlightened rationality, self-possession, and capacity of liberal consent and choice). To clarify this claim, let me turn to another instance where body fragments and assertions of Asian American political significance have become intertwined.[3]

* * *

If Yamanaka's poem offers one literary instance that theorizes the act of writing in relation to the cutting, tearing, and disassembling of the human body, the court-ordered language, generated with respect to the contemporary cadaver exhibits popularly known as Body Worlds, provides another.[4] Since 1998, these entertainments have drawn over thirty-five million visitors worldwide,[5] to science museums and other tourist sites, to view plastinated cadavers, posed in striking arrangements of partial dissection and intactness. These anatomical displays have spawned court cases, legal settlements, and congressional legislation in New York, California, Pennsylvania, and Washington, D.C. The intense feelings conjured by these corpses arguably derive from their violating notions of the human: their breaching of somatic integrity—exemplified in a flayed specimen's holding his "coat" of skin in his hand—and their flagrant use of human tissues in profitable displays. Significantly, one means of recomposing a wholeness from these alienable parts has been to disclose a speculated relation between the carved-up tissues and a certain life narrative connected to Chinese—i.e., ethnonational—personhood. The court-mandated language (quoted in the epigraph) serves judicial ends, by bringing these profitable entertainments under government regulation via the discursive "return" of plastinated parts to the prior(ity of) persons—the human source materials for these exhibits. In this case, writing—as informational publicity about the hidden identities of these bodies as executed Chinese prisoners—acts as an interdiction, designed to outrage potential visitors and thereby obstruct the flow of profits to the exhibitors. (The purported aim behind the strategy of embroiling the entertainment companies in lawsuits, however, is to stop the routine cutting of unidentified corpses in Dailan's "mummification factories.")[6]

Significantly, the legal furor over Body Worlds in the case of California did not begin as a cadaver-trafficking scandal but as a health scare when visitors noticed liquid droplets pooling on these anatomical specimens (in the majority of the exhibits no barriers exist between visitors and the displays). While later dismissed as liquid silicone, the leaking fluid first caused concern because of what the larger public generally knew about biological processes (e.g., that of postmortem bacterial feeding on human tissue that manifests as cadaver putrefaction). Skepticism, in short, initially greeted the promise of the new technology—plastination—to debiologize, so to speak, that is, halt the bacterially assisted processes of decay. Only later did attention turn to the specific dodgy quality of Chinese manufacture in the production of these shows. These educational displays, purportedly "[making] anatomy fun," underscore the intimacy of the leisure classes' entertainments with "cheap" transnational labor and more gruesomely the military-imprisonment complex that repurposes the "waste" of capital punishment into an educational resource.

An Asian American assemblywoman, Fiona Ma, from San Francisco, played a key role in drafting legislation to scrutinize these entertainments' procurement practices. Her sleuthing relied on racial profiling—the discernment that these bodies were of Asian descent, combined with the discovery of their assembly in Dailan—and a self-proclaimed insider knowledge regarding Chinese beliefs: "Chinese people are very superstitious about death. . . . They believe in full-body burials. They don't believe in organ donations, and some people don't even believe in giving blood. So, automatically, I thought that something was wrong with the show."[7] Here, a well-intentioned postmortem defense of the racial subject—indeed, the very defense helps conjure the racial dimensions of the cadavers—also plays upon processes of ethnicization that impute an insufficient, lesser modernity onto a "foreign" population, to recall Rey Chow's argument in *The Protestant Ethnic*. In this case, the "superstitious" Chinese fail to adopt a laissez-faire attitude toward their postmortem fates, an attitude crucial to supporting modern miracles in medicine that rely upon a cosmopolitan biosociality (circulation) of cadaver parts.

Both Yamanaka's "Parts" and the Body Worlds exhibits confront their audiences with the human body as fragment, and, relatedly, with the idea of corporeality as divisible and biology as plastic and manipulable. In what follows, I argue that *Asian Americanist critique and certain strains of bioethics have made ethical, political, and moral claims vis-à-vis these body parts; and they have done so through a distinctive rhetorical move that putatively returns the extracted body part to the violated racialized whole—a move that naturalizes a prior state of organic intactness and individuality to that racialized body.* (As this chapter proceeds, I clarify that what is at stake in racial analysis and what might be valuably embraced in these same studies is not so much the cohering of fragments into a singular whole, but the conceptual and discursive tool of a qualified personification.)[8] Here, I inquire whether literary criticism and performance studies can still remain humanist if they think in terms of distributed parts rather than organic structures, or, more exactly, turn fragment and substance into patterns—circulations of energy, affects, atoms, and liquidity in its accounting of the soma. Is the primary technique and value of Asian Americanist literary and cultural criticism that of conserving the boundary between a liberal humanist subject (qua coherent, complex, interiorized self—e.g., character of depth) and an alienating world of economically and biologically exploitative parasites? The nonconsilience of the critical paradigms offered by scholarship in a posthuman, biotechnical vein, and in an Asian Americanist critical vein, can reveal much about the limits of each.

One of the stories I will tell has to do with the types of writing we characterize as Asian Americanist critique. It has traditionally been associated with claims like the one forwarded by Fiona Ma wherein writing exposes an injustice or breach in ethics, thereby seeming to correct the injurious act (in Ma's case, the Body Worlds exhibit's overreliance on Chinese corpses). The mandated written supplement to be posted by Premier Entertainment—the *mea culpa,* as it were—becomes the performative agent of justice. By the turn of the twenty-first century, the field finds itself flirting with and embracing the position of the Yamanaka poem: rather than moving toward projecting a whole onto these operable fragments, it relishes the affects circulating—the ballistic force—from these tactile cuts, tears from context, and plastic transformations. The field has yet to square its relishing of the fragment with its anxiety about it, and remains worried over theoretical incoherence.

A caveat: I do not claim that Yamanaka's poem is the theoretical, political, or aesthetic advancement over the discursive presumptions and practice of the legal settlement vis-à-vis Body Worlds. Rather, my aim here is more modest. It is to establish that the mining of a preoccupation with human fragments and posthuman ecologies in the context of Asian American cultural production and theory is a particularly useful endeavor at this moment; and that its particular usefulness emerges, paradoxically, due to the amplified sense of the designation "Asian American" as a fictional (discursive) construct—only ambivalently, incoherently, or "problematically" linked to the biological body.

Relishing the Fragment

> What Asian American works of imagination manifest in full is a plethora of seemingly separate threads. . . . [Their] literary studies . . . [have] no single unifying grand narrative . . . no single linguistic Other . . . on which to hinge a counter-tradition of stylistics. (Lim, et al. ii, i)

The concern over the fragmentation of the Asian American body politic as well as the jockeying over the scholarly methods and ideological approaches of Asian Americanist study have been consistent preoccupations since the field's inception.[9] Whether tilted negatively—as a lament over incoherence—or positively—as a celebration of heterogeneity and invented ethnicity—the unanchored quality to Asian America's constituent parts has been a *prima facie* tenet of the field. Take for instance these words by Frank Chin, published in the 1970s, as compared with two pronouncements in the 1990s that, respectively, upbraid and applaud the nonessence at the core of this racial identification:

> Unlike the blacks, we have neither an articulated, organic sense of our American identity nor the verbal confidence and self-esteem to talk one up from our experience. . . . We have no street tongue to flaunt and strut the way the blacks and Chicanos do. . . . (Chin 1976, 557)

All the time hungry, [our] every sense [has been] out whiffing for something rightly ours, chameleons looking for color, trying on tongues and
clothes and hairdos, taking everyone else's, with none of our own. (Chin
1972, 59)

Asian-Americans couple fear of nullity with an awareness of perpetually
inauthentic, heterogeneous role playing: of having too many identities.
(Buell 187)

[Asian America] inhabits the highly unstable temporality of the "about-
to-be." . . . [T]here is no literal referent for the rubric "Asian American."
(Koshy 1996, 315, 342)

The final quotation from Susan Koshy's "The Fiction of Asian American Literature" (1996) emphasizes the "artificiality" of this ethnic rubric
in order to draw attention to the field's theoretical weakness, while the
penultimate quotation, from Frederick Buell just two years earlier, casts
Asian Americans' "weak ethnicity"—defined by a self-consciousness of
both the fractious plurality troubling this pan-ethnic identity, and the
imitative stylings of other, stronger racial and ethnic formations—as
its unique innovation. For Buell, Asian American ethnics deconstruc-
tively cite and perform primordial ethnic ties, proleptically instantiating the poststructuralist approach to race and ethnicity as outlined, for
instance, in Henry Louis Gates's *Signifying Monkey*.[10] As suggested by
the quotation in the epigraph from a 2004 issue of *Studies in the Literary Imagination*, the sentiment that Asian Americanist literary studies
consists of fragmented, separate "threads" still reverberates in the early
years of the twenty-first century.[11]

A more recent variation on this thesis suggests that without a solid
historical periodization or formalist singularity at its core, Asian Americanist critical practice becomes stabilized by an implicit recourse to a
biological rationale. For instance, in a 2007 special issue of *Representations*, Colleen Lye writes,

If in the early days of legitimation "Asian American literature" had to
confront a skepticism that there might be too few justifying texts, today

the field's integrity is perhaps even more challenged by the vertigo of too many possibilities. . . . [In this] embracing [of] pluralism and cosmopolitanism . . . how can we guard against an ever-greater dependency on biological notions of identity to help us order our epistemological projects. Maximal inclusiveness can mean that we fall back upon a minimal definition of "Asian American" that we might not want to have[, namely,] the delineation of [the Asian American] archive by a biologically based definition of authorial identity.[12]

While Lye's bid for a more rigorously historicist, formalist, or aesthetic rationale to guide Asian Americanists' grouping of texts is commendable, what gives one pause is the additional worry voiced here concerning the field's commission of a foundational theoretical error tied to its implicit selective principle: its anchoring in a problematic biology (as distinct from cultural or national background) of the authors.[13] To put it more polemically, if in the past racial significance was assigned by way of profiling the body of the author, then what is needed in the twenty-first century is something more like an anonymous or pseudonymous approach in which the "immanent" qualities defining the object(s) of analysis, themselves, regardless of authorship, would recognizably contour them as Asian American.[14] Voiced here, in other words, is the hope for a more discursive or artifactual location of Asian American/ist technique or encounter.

Indeed, the reigning modus operandi of race studies has been to emphasize the social construction rather than biological essence of race, figuring the former as historically variable in contrast to the supposed inert contours of the latter (presuming biology as fixed immanence rather than also a fluid historical process).[15] Precisely this context presented as a curiosity the very cultural texts that form the bulk of this book's inquiry: given that race has been acknowledged not as biological but as a discursive (legal-juridical) construction and as an outgrowth of historically variable political-economic formations, how is it then that Asian American artists, authors, and performers keep scrutinizing their body parts? Were Asian American artists simply not as intellectually sophisticated as the Asian Americanist critics, the latter already aware that race was not biological? Dimissing this hypothesis as too simplistic, I initiated this book in part to take seriously these artists' concern with embodiment, body parts, and perspectives that see and feel multiple scales of biology simultaneously.

The dismissal of an always problematic "biological" framing of race is one reason the field of Asian Americanist Studies has, for the most part, avoided an engagement with the developing interdisciplines of biocultures, medical humanities, and posthuman studies.[16] These studies neither accept the wholesale reduction of biological materiality (whether in petri dishes or in normate contours of the sentient organism) to mere discourse or code; nor do they ignore that biological processes and structures remain phenomenologically apprehended and functionally altered through human inventions, including language, medical technology, kinship networks, family dynamics, the economy, and various apparati of governmentality. So if the evocation of the biological is not about research in biology or biocultures today, what exactly might be its rhetorical utility for Asian Americanist Studies? One answer already intimated is that the biological has become a shorthand for something like fixity, lending a contrastive fluidity (and historical specificity) to the field's meta-narrations of either its perpetual incoherence or its evolving complexity.[17] Another answer is suggested by Arun Saldhana: he places the overemphasis on power relations such as race as discursive formations, rather than ontological and phenomenological ones, in the wider context of a modern epistemology that has dichotomized nature and culture. He notes that while postcolonial, race, and feminist studies have gone down a discursive (social constructionist) route, biotech "mocks that effort" to dichotomize the two—nature is always already culturally altered; culture is always already composed of material nature.[18]

The field of Asian Americanist literary and cultural criticism has not been immune from the move to an increasingly more discursive (and arguably disembodied),[19] metacritical reflection on "Asian Americanness," one that destabilizes historical or live bodies as the field's referent to emphasize the textual composition—in law, ethnography, historical archives, film, and the like—of the Asiatic racial form. For instance, taking seriously poststructuralism's emphasis on the arbitrariness of signs and the failure of representation to capture some prior reality (an anterior, prediscursive subject), Kandice Chuh advocates a "subjectless Asian Americanist critique" in which the critic, "rather than looking to complete the category 'Asian American,' to actualize it by such methods as enumerating various components of difference (gender, class, sexuality, religion, and so on) . . . [might instead] critique the effects of the various configurations of power and knowledge through which the term comes to have meaning" (10–11). Chuh demands an alternative view to the field's equation of justice and liberation with the fullness of subjectivity, and questions the tacit endorsement of cultural pluralism as the driving logic of Asian Americanist cultural critique. The discursive turn (away from human referents) has also become articulated as a "new" critical attention to form and aesthetics—e.g., studies such as those offered by Christopher Lee, Joseph Jonghyun Jeon, Josephine Park, Timothy Yu, Rocio Davis, and Sue Im Lee. Asian Americanists are in search of the properly discursive grounds of the field's coherence: e.g., in form and aesthetics, in ideology, in structural position vis-à-vis political economy, and so forth, that would provide a less "essentialist" approach to Asian American literature, artifacts, and practices.[20] The relishing of these fractured approaches is directly in proportion to the disaffection from the stolidity of the biological. (But is anyone really doing a biological reading of Asian American texts, and if so, what would that look like?)[21]

To be sure, my project is not arguing for literature and performance's reflection of the "reality" of Asian American human referents; nor is it eschewing formal analyses; nor is it a call to arms for more Asian Americanists to enter the field of biology—though it is responsive to calls within the field of biocultures for humanists to familiarize themselves with critical studies of science,[22] and it is also informed by a particular feminist-inflected branch of Science and Technology Studies (STS) regarding tissue culturing, assisted reproductive technology, metabolism, the neuroenteric system, immunology, transplantation surgery, and the origin of species, as they each ruminate over the traffic in and plasticity of body parts. Moreover, lest my brief overview above be mistaken as a critical dismissal, this tilt of the field toward a more discursive reflection on Asian Americanness very much informs the ground of my thinking. I want to know, or at least pose the question for collective exploration, whether the anxiety regarding Asian Americanness as a biological category is, to put it somewhat crudely, an anxiety about a fixed embeddedness to race or an anxiety about the shifting (posthuman) meanings of being biological.

The Political Economy of Asiatic Biologies

One example of recent scholarship that connects the thinking about the Asiatic body and its biology (aka its nutritive requirements) to wider critiques of modernity and postmodernity is Eric Hayot's "Chinese Bodies, Chinese Futures." Hayot notes the way a particular abject figure in the late nineteenth century—the coolie—prefigures the ideal type of laborer for modernity (i.e., Fordist capitalist production), one who can subsist only on rice, rather than meat, and is resented for this culturally specific lowering of the threshold of labor's cost. The spare nutritive requirements of this biological body are thus resented not only for the future deprivation they imply to eaters of meat but also because of the seeming "indifference [to suffering]" (122) that the coolie also represents—which is to say, the surprising resilience of this biology to withstand harsh conditions:

> The coolie's ability to endure small levels of pain or consume only the most meager food and lodging represented an almost inhuman adaption to contemporary forms of modern labor. . . . An "absence of nerves," remarkable "staying qualities," and a "capacity to wait without complaint and to bear with calm endurance" were all features of Chinese people in general described by Arthur Smith in his 1894 *Chinese Characteristics*, the most widely read American work on Chinese in the late nineteenth and early twentieth centuries. . . . The coolie's biologically impossible body was the displaced ground for an awareness of the transformation of the laboring body into a machine. . . . [H]is ability to endure (in work and in life) permitted him [to write all day, or stand from morning until dusk] without succumbing to exhaustion or boredom.[23]

Hayot's analysis underscores the "impossible biology" of the coolie's body—and its alignments with both "past and future, animal and superhuman" capacities—as that which makes "the suffering of [industrial] modernity" as well as the "possible end to suffering via indifference" palpable in the late nineteenth and early twentieth centuries.[24] Similarly, in Donna Haraway's analysis of late-twentieth-century information capital—"cyborg" technology shadowed by its original military aims—the update to the coolie is the so-called nimble-fingered Asian female, the "Southeast Asian village women workers in Japanese and U.S. electronics firms"[25] who likewise make intelligible the contradictory disequilibriums of post-Fordist, transnational capital and its flexible modes of production. One speculative question that this book pursues is the genealogical links between these resented and racialized biologies (qua "nature-cultures")[26] preferred by Fordist and post-Fordist production and the similarly impossible biologies of cellular matter—tissue culture able to survive *in vitro*, that is, without the nutrition or "lodging" provided *in vivo* by the organism—whose very displacement facilitates the extraction of surplus values on behalf of contemporary biotech and for-profit medicine.

Toward the conclusion of his analysis, Hayot imagines the sophisticated Asian Americanist challenge to his own somatic focus and its "anthropomorphic aperture":

> Work in Asian American studies has consistently thought of race as located most fundamentally in a set of human minds and human bodies. [Colleen] Lye argues, to the contrary, that the structures that make the Asiatic a figure for (and index of) globalizing labor markets suggests that race is not a human concept but an economic one, that the "form" governing its representation and even its phenomenological experience owes more to the movements of capital than to the white perception of otherness.[27]

"De-anthropomorphization" becomes the neologic mouthful Hayot coins to refer to Lye's approach:

> Lye's forceful de-anthropomorphization of the concept of race . . . thus leads us to a broader theory of the disappointments of what one might call anthropomorphic desire, that is, of the disappointments produced by the awareness that an originary fantasy of the body's personal and human simplicity can only be thought in relation to such larger and more inhuman concepts as transnationalism, diaspora, globalization or the history of the means of production.[28]

Clearly, Hayot desires that the "animal and superhuman" biology of the coolie, rather than being reduced to a mere menacing fiction constructed by whites (like Arthur Smith), be understood as a material effect of capitalist production—of capitalism's search for endless surplus and the consequent lowering to the utmost limits the costs of labor. But by the same token, it is also striking how political economy and historical materialist critique in the tradition of Marx are very much wedded to an anthropomorphic aperture and to human (labor)'s centrality to wealth production (Cooper 2008, 6–7). Thus, even when speaking of a context where human fragments produce surplus value in tissue economies, as is the case with cellular and metabolic processes, Eugene Thacker—drawing on Marx—relies on an anthropomorphic aperture, if for nothing else than to limn distortions and displacements of the organismal form as the (scale of) biology now capitalized in our contemporary biopolitical moment. My dwelling at some length on Hayot's qualifications to his own illuminating reading of how "Chinese bodies" functioned as central racialized symbols of the tiered biologies capitalized in industrial, Fordist production offers a concrete example of the way in which the rhetorical pose pitting Asian Americanist theory against the biological—here, evoked as the "anthropomorphic aperture"—has led to, if not a total avoidance, then much hesitation in thinking precisely about how research on the biological and biosociality might richly inform the field.

Fragmented Biologies

To recapitulate, one story repeatedly gestured toward in current accounts of Asian Americanist cultural criticism argues for the exciting possibilities of discursive and formal analyses, ostensibly to keep the field from the twin evils of, first, getting scattered in its "too many possibilities" and, second, falling back upon a naïve biological or strategic essentialism as the grounds of its coherence. In my redubbing of that same story, the bugaboo of biological essentialism is pushed aside for a different biological anxiety, one emphasizing biological personhood not as fixed or singular but as multiform and distributed across time spans and spatial ecologies. To tell that story, let me turn to the way fragmentation has become a more literal concern for scholars dealing with tissue culturing, immortal cell lines, and transplantation. For these scholars, a complex dance between personification and pluriform, distributed manifestations of a singular organism (that can live multiple lives and exceed the temporality of the mortal human life span) is being mapped.

Tissue culturing—the capacity to grow and combine cells outside the body—was first accomplished with nonhuman biologies (amphibian nerve fiber, avian cardiac tissue) in the first decade of the twentieth century.[29] It was not until the late 1940s that "living human tissue was for the first time drawn into biomedical research on a large scale" and in relation to the search for a polio vaccine:

> Although taken for granted today, it is not at all inevitable that human cells should be perceived as factories whose productive and reproductive capacities could be harnessed to make large volumes of cells and biological molecules. In the course of this fundamental shift in the role of living human tissues in biomedical research . . . the living human as research subject was fundamentally reorganized—distributed in space and time in previously unimaginable ways.[30]

Science and technology scholar Hannah Landecker traces the story, or more precisely stories, of the standard human cell line HeLa and its racialization. In 1951, HeLa was dubbed "immortal," meaning having the capacity to "continue growing and dividing unperturbed by [its] artificial environment."[31] This immortality of the cell line contrasted the curtailed life span of Henrietta Lacks, after whom HeLa took its name, the historical person who died of cervical cancer eight months after undergoing a tissue biopsy at John Hopkins University Hospital—the source of this still widely used mo cell line. (Without Lacks's knowledge or consent, the biopsied tissue was sent to the research laboratory of George and Margaret Gey.)

In terms of the specific racialization of HeLa, Landecker deconstructs geneticist Stanley Gartler's pronouncement at a cell tissue and organ culture conference in 1967 (a decade and a half after HeLa's initial distribution as a stable "immortal" or mo cell line) that HeLa had contaminated the supposedly distinct eighteen cell lines in use at various labs. Prior to Gartler's lecture—that is, in mid-1950s popular science articles—the press spoke of the HeLa cells as originating from "a young Baltimore housewife," an "'unsung heroine of medicine named

Helen L.," with race absent as a qualifier.[32] Gartler mounted an argument that linked eighteen distributed and supposedly differentiated cell lines in various labs to a single donor specified as an African American woman—the cells promiscuously infiltrating other cell lines and thus appealing to the "worst fears" of miscegenation in Gartler's audience.[33] As Landecker's careful review of his research protocols demonstrates, Gartler unnecessarily evoked Negro ancestry, and implicit rhetorics of the one-drop rule, to make his point. In the 1990s and 2010s, the story of HeLa again features the anchoring figure of the African American subject, Henrietta Lacks, but this time figured primarily as an economic persona, with "Lacks's family [unable to] collect, because nobody ever patented the cells and thus it is difficult to pin down either past or present profit. . . ."[34] In 2010, journalist Rebecca Skloot renewed interest in HeLa by publishing to significant acclaim the trade book *The Immortal Life of Henrietta Lacks*; while literary scholar Priscilla Wald, in her 2012 presidential address to the American Studies Association, most recently evoked HeLa to contour the difficulty in naming "the specific malfeasance" with regard to Henrietta Lacks.[35]

Landecker's tracing of HeLa's discursive circulation as at times angelic housewife, at other times aggressive black woman, and then as dispossessed financial stakeholder, underscores three important points about the conjuring of the anthropomorphic dimensions of these biological tissues. The first is a reiteration and spin of Landecker's own assertion that personification, as a discursive strategy, isn't surprising given that these cell lines are proxies for humans:

> Cell lines are made to stand in for persons . . . functioning in the laboratory as proxy theaters of experimentation for intact living bodies. . . .
> Their identification as "living" and "human" entities cannot fall from them, because it is this origin that gives them commercial and scientific value as producers of biological substances for use by humans and their validity as research sites of human biology.[36]

And yet, their fragmented form, or radical exteriorization of heretofore invisible biological (life) processes, is at the core of their being preferred in laboratory practice: tissue culture provides a more palatable practice than vivisection as conventional means to view and experiment on living biological processes. While we might assume that personification works to dignify the human by returning the part to the whole, personifications can also be used to extend racism, as Gartler's example makes clear—not only by returning the part to the whole but also by placing that whole within an agonistic (threatening) dialectic, or placing that whole within a classification system: the superhuman, aggressively invasive and prolific survivor rendering the regular (unmarked aka white) human as radically dependent, frail, and under assault. Reviewing journalistic coverage of both the HeLa cell line and a UCLA patent filed in 1981 on a cell line using biopsied tissue from John Moore's spleen, Wald likewise notes that the anthropomorphizing of cell lines fuses persons "with the characteristics of [their] cells" to denigrate or sanctify those persons.[37] The point to be registered is that personifications are neither necessarily politically progressive nor theoretically regressive; and the same could be said of depersonifications or deanthropomorphizations.

The second is that in none of these personifications is human personhood imagined as self-directed or self-determining in ways that can resist the biosociality and biomaterial circulation into which the person's body parts are ushered. Thus, even in Landecker's own analysis, Lacks is contoured as a kind of silent subaltern: "at the establishment of this cell line exists a moment of irredeemable silence. Lacks's illness and treatment in 1951 at John Hopkins took place in an institutional, cultural and scientific setting that had no room in it for heroic agency or any other expression of personal will on [Lacks's] part, even the simple act of donation."[38] In other words, this sort of qualified personification—one arguably at the core of racial studies (and studies of alienated labor)—is one emphasizing an always already suspended agency, a social and historical condition of alienated distance from any primordial humanness prior to a corporeal estrangement in society.[39]

Third, personification becomes part of a narrative of public scandal when particular circulations (and the integrity of their conduits, the logic of their channels) are called into question. When Gartler spoke at the Conference on Cell Tissue and Organ Culture, he was calling into question the integrity of the differentiated cell lines whose specific properties—as proxies for "breast cancer or colon cancer or amnion cells" rather than HeLa cervical epithelial tissue[40]—were crucial to their research use and proprietary value. Likewise, when news stories emphasized that Lacks's surviving family members had not been informed of the wide use of their female relative's biopsied tissue, the circuits of capital formation into which scientific research had been translated were similarly called into question. This tripping up[41] of a taken-for-granted circulation (i.e., traffic in biomaterials), I would hypothesize, needs the conjuring of a person to be wounded (a victim); or, put another way, scandal needs the scale of "the person" to be scandalous.

At the same time, personification as a discursive strategy doesn't necessarily have to work in conjunction with a scandalous, public exposure leading to a cessation or hiccough in circulation. That is, it can be used to contour as temporally receding but also fundamentally still relevant certain anthropocentric humanist values. Here's where Eugene Thacker's work in *The Global Genome* is useful. Thacker coins the term "biomaterial labor" to name the living entities—such as the HeLa cell line, but also nonhuman, mammalian bioreactors and model organisms[42]—generating surplus value in labs and bio-distribution centers: biology itself is conceived of as a factory where "labor power is cellular, enzymatic, and genetic" (45). The uniqueness of this labor, however, lies for Thacker not in its microscopic scale or its merging of the technological (culture) and the biological (nature), but in its seeming to elude—and thus force the limits of—a Marxist analysis with its anthropomorphic personification of the alienated laborer: "[though] biology is ceaselessly made to work, and biological life activity is constantly producing, yet the *seller of labor power* is absent from the production formula" (46; italics added).[43] Thacker's intervention into biotech is precisely to gauge these estrangements of biology—these "estranged biologies" that cannot "sell" temporal slices of themselves (36)—in relation to the alienated worker of Marxist theory (the "human reproaches" to the system of capitalism),[44] rather than as categorically more similar to inorganic matter (raw materials).

In its own tale of partial persons qua biomaterials inserted into biological exchanges or value production, science and technology studies (STS) conjures up fictitious and real persons and organismic scales that help us to understand comparatively, even as a form of inverted synecdoche, the industrial enrollment of biological living materials (such as mo cell lines or an extracted, lymphokine-producing spleen).[45] These latter distributed, temporally uncontained morphologies may prove the form and scale upon which present and future biopolitical strategies as well as their critiques are mounted. STS of tissue economies stress biology's already substantial nonpersonified forms, with biotech literally profiting from a view that distinguishes human biological materials from persons (thereby allowing the former to qualify as patentable inventions). If there is a common critical purpose to this scholarship in STS, it is to adopt a view not commensurate with biotech itself (its progress narrative that prizes first and foremost profitable biovalue) (Landecker 2000; Thacker; Squier 2000; Cooper 2008; Rajan; Reardon and Tallbear).[46] In doing so, they perform the scale of the anthropomorphic organism as a still crucial heuristic and ethical tool—and one would be hard pressed to call this a strategically essentialist tactic.

In light of the above research on tissue economies, we might nuance then the traditional strengths of Asian Americanist criticism, framing its earnest attempts to personify alienated labor power or to endow technologies of living matter—going under the name "coolie" or "immigrant"—with personhood, not as theoretically naïve, but as precisely what makes the field resonant and useful at this current moment. Taking the human organism, thus far, as its preferred scale, Asian Americanist scholarship also concerns itself with a form of traffic, interestingly, in the legal-political (and social, civil) category of the not-quite-human: immigrant, coolie, neocolonial, transnational laborer, sex worker, call center operator, etc. Scholarship within the field looks to culture not only as that which facilitates this traffic—the exchanges of these biologies into surplus value—but as that which also registers disruptions and contradictions in these lives of the not-quite-human, suborganismal, and trafficked (upon which I will elaborate shortly). To be clear, I'm not arguing that humanism—if understood as a recentering of the normative, bourgeois subject of rights—is the answer, but that we cannot begin to understand the focus on form, aesthetics, affect, theme, autonomy (and all those other things supposedly lending the field coherence outside of "biology") without understanding the cultural anxieties around being biological in an era that is reconceptualizing the body in informational, molecular, and posthuman terms.

Affect and Agency's Avatars

Not only for scholarship in STS but also in the overlapping field of the anthropology of medicine, humanist methods of thick description and textured readings still provide valuable avenues for attending to the lifeways glossed over by tissue economies. For researchers like Nancy Scheper-Hughes and Lawrence Cohen who study the effects of transplantation technologies on the Third World/Global South (Brazil and India, respectively), an anthropomorphic aperture—one centering human organismal life—is crucial to hearing the point of view of those aggressively recruited into giving up their organs and thus counterbalancing the dominance of the views espoused by the biotech, pharmaceutical, and for-profit medical industries.[47] Calling attention to how transplantation recipients are scrupulously followed by their doctors, who know little about the providers of these spare parts, Scheper-Hughes lambasts the construction of two unequal populations: "[Organ givers] are an invisible and discredited collection of anonymous suppliers of spare parts; [organ receivers] are cherished patients, treated as moral subjects and as suffering individuals [whose] names . . . biographies and medical histories are known."[48] For these ethnographers of poor populations of the global South capitalized by kidney brokers, a humanist attention to "local ethical dialects"[49] of those aggressively recruited into giving up their organs provides a methodological alternative to top-down formulations of professional bioethicist panels that construct "abstract normative principles—autonomy, beneficence, and distributive justice"—and by doing so, rule out or divert attention to the less codified dissent of vernacular voices.[50]

These ethical dialects are constituted, as Lawrence Cohen shows in his careful research on the perpetual debt economies of Chennai slums, by a verbal emphasis on sacrifice for the family—to get a spouse out of debt being the overwhelming rationale, among Cohen's largely female subjects, for selling a kidney. In addition, kidney sellers make recourse to a gestural technique of flashing one's nephrectomy scar "where it hurts"—also described as the place "where he [the husband] hits me. There. When I don't have any more money."[51] Taking aim at arguments rationalizing kidney selling as a "win-win" situation (my life saved from kidney failure, your life saved from mounting debt), Cohen challenges the truncated scenario upon which such "ethical" arguments rely. He urges a capacious listening to what kidney sellers say when asked if they would donate again: "[T]he question is not whether the statement 'I would do it again' is coerced . . . speech [to the ethnographer] but rather what happens if one keeps listening: 'I would have to.'"[52] This phrase, "if one keeps listening" is repeated: "If one keeps listening, beyond the desire that sets the market in motion, one regains the temporal specificity lost in these transactional analyses: 'I would have to. That money is gone and we are in debt.' . . . Operable women are vehicles for debt collateral—and bear the scar."[53] Cohen's rejection of official bioethicists' focus on the "primary" transaction of the patient-donor exchange attends to what bioethicists relegate to second-order phenomena: contexts of gender and the perpetuity of debt. Thus, Cohen listens to the women repeatedly speak of tubal ligation as an operation they have prior to the kidney donation, which, he argues, demonstrates "the prior operability of [their] bodies. The operation here is a central modality of citizenship, by which I mean the performance of agency in relation to the state. It is not just an example of agency; it is agency's critical ground."[54] Both Cohen and Scheper-Hughes argue that the truncated view, the disembedding of the sale of the organ from the larger debt conditions motivating the agreement, leads to bad ethics—an ethics that paves the way for organs to enjoy a fluidity and liquidity, an ease of movement across bodies, labs, and practices. To contravene this bad ethics, these ethnographers propose local and, indeed, anthropocentric stories as means of combating the aggressive recruitment of organ donors from the Third World/Global South. They would mitigate the crisis-level social disequilibriums that become intensely realized as both the "collateralization of poor populations" (Cohen) and, borrowing from Michel Foucault, the biopolitics or biosociality of race: the creation of a population whose demise and limited lives are required to promote the enhanced, limitless lives of others—a figuration I shorthand elsewhere as "Life (Un)Ltd."[55]

Though ineffective in putting an end to their conditions of indebtedness, the kidney donors' actions—which include not only donation but also the visual flashings of the nephrectomy scar—seek another kind of public airing as to the value of their organs. The spectacular emphasis on this fleshly seam marking both the kidney's transfer elsewhere

and its biovalue as a function of its alienation feeds into a highly cir-
cumscribed notion of agency seeming to lie more in the organ's than in
the person's capacities. While most might balk at this implied wholesale revision of "agency" (as in, How can one call the condition of being
anatomically dissected a form of "agency"?), my point is precisely that
the difficulty of accounting for such events as either "gifts" or "coerced
exchanges" may mean that agency, as such, is too purified a conceptual
term, and yet one in which race, gender, sexuality studies, and other
identitarian fields are highly invested.

In terms of subject matter, Cohen's work distinctly falls within the
purview of a transnational Asian Americanist critique. Yet no one has
construed his work in this way or linked him genealogically to the field
of Asian Americanist Studies. My point, here, is to use the possibility of
doing so to open up further questions (and dialogue across area studies) as to the continuing importance or not of Asian Americanist scholars' emphasizing minor (and qualified) acts of agency and resistance,
which in Cohen's scholarship valuably morph into attempts at publicity
and the sacrificial gift of donating a kidney as an "avatar of agency."[56] In
his 2002 publication *Race and Resistance*, Viet Thanh Nguyen argued
that critics' examination of Asian American literature overemphasized
these texts' "resistance" to both capitalism and its normative racial
values. Nguyen exposed the possible bad faith of the professional-
managerial class of Asian Americanist intellectuals: their complicity
with capital while stressing an overt fidelity to radical outsiderness.
What Nguyen diagnosed as a specific ideological homogeneity in Asian
Americanist Studies, however, was only specifying to that particular
field what is more endemic to left criticism more generally—the mining of the possibilities of alternatives: counter-Empire or posse (Hardt
and Negri 2000), performative excess or camp (Butler 1989; Case),
and (as suggested above) avatars of agency through scandalous publicity. Thus, even while various scholars have not directly taken Nguyen's
findings to task by overtly reclaiming resistance as still key to understanding minority literature, much work in this vein continues. Rather
than locating "resistance" in a humanist subject, this work emphasizes
the necessity of a dialectical approach (Koshy 2001; Lowe) that stresses
human history as an unfolding of, let's say, a certain progress narrative (e.g., modernist rationality as emancipation, freedom, efficiency)

and the antagonism or counter to that narrative, so that this interplay of opposing forces is inevitable, the driving force of history. For Lisa Lowe and David Lloyd, a dialectical analysis allows for a focus on alternative rationalities, "social formations in time with but in antagonism to modernity [with globalization as the latest phase of modernity],"[57] rather than a relentless emphasis on the determining forces of capitalism and bureaucratic rationality.

Nguyen's argument regarding an ideological homogeneity of the Asian Americanist literary field can be seen as part of a broader meta-critical reflection within identity-based fields on the trap of figuring representations as both socially determined and in excess of that determination. Rather than "subversion" or "gender trouble," "resistance" was the word Nguyen chose, but it has morphed into "supplement," "haunting," and "affect." Thus, while "resistance" was the noble, heroic name given to a kind of purified antagonism that representations by Asian Americans might index, "melancholia," "irritation," "animateness," "zaniness," "anxiety," and "envy" (the first deftly explored by Anne Cheng and David Eng, the latter five drawn from Sianne Ngai's *Ugly Feelings* and *Our Aesthetic Categories*) all conceptually broaden the terrain of still antagonistic but limited agency with which we might think through the conditions of possibility for Asian American cultural productions. In short, if, in some earlier moment of Asian Americanist Studies, agency was mistaken for a sovereign-like power seized by the autonomous subject and bearer of rights (think the call to "empower" the people), the postmodern revamped placeholder for a now "suspended agency"[58] takes the scattered forms of discoordinated antagonisms, which have a corporeal correlative in the discoordinated cognitions or affective sensations of body parts, with embodiment here imagined as a technical-organic hybrid. These discoordinated antagonisms, as defined by Antonio Negri and Michael Hardt, can strike directly at the highest levels of power, following their claim that "the new . . . social movements" are defined not by their horizontal capacity to link up into a singular movement or wave but "by the intensity that characterizes them one by one."[59] Citing Tiananmen, Intifada, and Chiapas, among others, these theorists of Empire and Multitude nonetheless still focus on collectivities (aggregates) as their vanguard icon of discoordinated antagonisms. Another emphasis on the distributed intelligence and dynamic affects of body parts is provided by Elizabeth Wilson in her provocative theorization of "gut feminism."

Wilson speaks of the false divide in trauma theory, psychoanalysis, and the like, of the separation and hierarchy of psychic (mental, cognitive) over somatic (aka exo-cerebral) phenomena. "After normal psychic structures have been violently destroyed by trauma," Wilson states, the "primordial psychic power" in the organic substrata itself "begins to think," as in the gag reflex. Wilson's project is part of a larger argument with the ideational or discursive body supplanting the anatomical or biological body in both psychoanalytic and feminist scholarship (see chapter 3 on Margaret Cho for a fuller account of Wilson's work). She suggestively draws out the primitive psyche of the stomach and neighboring viscera (enteric nervous system) as an example of a motive capacity existing in the so-called peripheral anatomy—the psyche of our biological parts distributed beyond the brain.[60] Her excurses into the psychic capacities and distributed intelligence of the peripheral body parts (their registration of mood),[61] in short, point not simply to a waning of formerly robust—because centralized or coordinated— forms of "agency." Rather, her dwelling on the gut's digestive and ruminative (i.e., pondering) processes bespeaks a positive turn away from simplistic approaches marked by "an overriding concern with . . . causal primacy . . . as if determination is a singular, delimited event."[62] Recognizing the distributed agencies of body parts, in other words, represents a mode of inquiry attuned to a more complex, networked notion of bodily intelligences, proceeding from the amphimixed[63] capacities (the phylogenetic and ontogenetic pasts) of our biological parts.

One of the concrete effects of the above claims is apparent in the very design of this book. The table of contents indicates in the left-hand margin the one or more body parts that act as the springboard for each of the chapters, translating into the two-dimensional limits of the page the distributed somatic structure of this book's form and content. Throughout the chapters, I also adopt a horizontal or lateral method of reading and interpretation—one abjuring the vertical buildup toward a singular message or outcome and indebted to other cultural studies scholarship that models alternatives to a linear historicism. Particularly helpful has been Kathryn Bond Stockton's notion of "sideways growth," which she specifically names as a queer mode of accretion. More recently, Karen

Cardozo and Banu Subramaniam have outlined a method quite similar to my own in their emphasis on methods attuned to both vertical and "horizontal/lateral" processes (the latter modeled on gene exchanges among biological organisms) as key to understanding Asian/America as a multispecies assemblage. Additionally, I've drawn heavily from the expertise and methods of performance studies scholarship, itself a hybrid of anthropological and theatrical modes of inquiry (Schechner and Turner; Kirschenblatt-Gimblett; Roach; Foster 2002; Kondo 1997; Shimakawa; Phelan 1993; D. Taylor). My training as a literary scholar and performance studies critic also means that, in the stories unfolding in the following chapters, I remain especially attuned to the qualitative dimensions of affects, kinesthetics, tactilities, and distributed bodily agencies, through which events of particular import to Asian Americanist Studies, race studies, and postcolonial scholarship unfold.

In short, the contouring of Asian American works offered here is more phenomenological and topological than ideologically revealing or historically determinist. My work offers a methodological model of transversal crossings unfaithful to traditional genealogies of disciplined inquiry, as in the putting together of body parts (the cadavers in the Body Worlds exhibits), a literary text (Yamanaka's poem), and critical scholarship (STS research on transplantation surgery and tissue culture) in ways that may, at first, appear jarring. The aim of this type of transversal[64] thinking across platforms is not to expose a hidden truth but paradoxically to cultivate an openness to the wonders of the aleatory, the chance-event, and the insight of the accidental networked through unacknowledged amphimixis.[65]

By citing in my book's title a surrealist figure of contingency and chance (namely, the *cadavre exquis*), I am part of a group of thinkers who are not trying to predict the ends or foreclose the future of Asian Americanist critical inquiry and Asian American cultural production to a set of enactments most faithful to the original, revolutionary ideals. Instead, my contouring of a method of Asian Americanist cultural critique on the exquisite corpse is meant to cultivate an affective interest along a vibration of sufficient intensity linked to what feminism and queer theory have called a "politics of the open end" (Spivak). This politics finds wanting the teleological certainties offered in both the idea of the past always repeating itself (e.g., capitalism and the law of the father as all-encompassing and forever) or the complete reversal of the past (glorious revolution ending in utopia, the withering away of the state and the emerging of the classless society; or *jouissance* through writing the body). While these assertions of open-endedness to which I have alluded aim at the unpredictability of the future (at temporal uncertainty), the openness of the exquisite corpse, to my mind, also contains a dispositional, affective charge—the practice of scholarly analysis and art in a spirit of intense, but also generous, engagement that is distinct from an "odious control [that] does not work all that well."[66] Edification, rather, occurs by way of something unsought, by acknowledging the limits of willed agency and direct pursuit, and through cultivating "a state of expectation and perfect receptivity" that paradoxically is a function of resigning oneself to learning "in snatches."[67] This receptivity to the aleatory and multiply contingent has affinities, too, to a "sideways" and lateral mode of analysis and exploration, one that is skeptical toward knowledge economies that prize only the straightest, most direct (instrumentally efficient) routes toward presupposed (rather than open) ends.

The current round of affect theory, in a more technoscientific vein, speaks of affect as a level of engagement that is distinct from the semantic component of an event, and that works almost inversely to the fixing of an event, spectacle, memory, or process in conventional semantic understanding (Clough; Massumi). Affective intensity is a function of something ineffable, the suspension of meaning, which we might also see as the potentiality of plural, indeterminate meanings. Andre Breton's characterization of the surrealist *jeux* as playful exercises "in the definition of something not given," in the bringing "out into the open a strange possibility of thought, which is that of its pooling," and in its effects of establishing "striking relationships . . . remarkable analogies . . . [and] an inexplicable factor of irrefutability"—are intimations of the intensity and engagement (or, to use Breton's phrase, the "entertaining" aspect) to be had through semantic suspense. The exquisite corpse, then, is a bid for a cross-wired attention to cultural productions in terms of that critical mode's affective capacity, its capacity to bring "about something . . . unexpected."[68]

Surrealist Scales and Transversal Accidents

In the above excurses, I have referred to biosociality. One meaning of biosociality is that we're networked through biopower's imperative to live (to generate and optimize life). As several critics writing after Foucault note, there is a crucial mystification—a disavowal of violence—at the heart of modern biopower (Mbembe; Agamben; Bull; Braidotti 2007). Describing biopower as the "ascendancy of life over death," Rey Chow characterizes this "imperative to live [as] an ideological mandate that henceforth gives justification to even the most aggressive and oppressive mechanisms of interference and control in the name of helping the human species increase its chances of survival, of improving its conditions and quality of existence."[69] Chow notes that civilizing procedures directed at colonial and minority populations, and, in the extreme, massacres of the same, are both part and parcel of the imperative to optimize the life of the species through "racist genocide": "Killing off certain groups of people en masse is now transformed . . . into a productive, *generative* activity undertaken for the life of the entire human species."[70] As Achille Mbembe notes, an outright coercive "necropolitics" that unapologetically exercises power by dealing out death is merely the flip side of biopower. Dovetailing Chow's and Mbembe's observations with Lawrence Cohen's, one might note that biopower works, yes, through the compressed intensity of massacre (killing fields) but also through an incorporative and slow—bit by bit, scar by scar—vivisection, and through the recruitment or simple taking of biopsied tissues and organs (as in the case of Henrietta Lacks). Race studies has typically understood biopower in terms of ethnics', natives', and subalterns' occupying the position of *zoe* (or bare animal and cellular life) as opposed to *bios* (politically recognized life, narrated life lived by a historical organism). In chapter 1, using the examples of Ruth Ozeki's *My Year of Meats*, Greg Bear's *Blood Music*, and Kazuo Ishiguro's *Never Let Me Go*, I outline these authors' own puzzling out of whether the chromatic schema of the five races will become displaced by the nonisomeric categories of *bios/zoe* or whether a transliteration between the two is more likely.

I wish to extend in particular the Asian Americanist understanding of biosociality as also the living of oneself electively as fragments—as

cuttable and extractable bags of parts—and as highly attuned to operability as the critical ground of agency and citizenship. The ways in which
artists take up their concern with being biological are manifold. Being
biological becomes a dance in response to a dentist's chance description
of an immigrant's teeth (as in the work of Taiwanese American dancer
Cheng-Chieh Yu), a comic screed on the exploding vagina at the scene
of birth (a consistent feature of Margaret Cho's stand-up comedy), a
tango with mental disability from a temporarily able-brained caretaker's
perspective (danced in Denise Uyehara's performances), and a complicated character system and set of nested plots that together allegorize
the parasitic and commensal entanglements humans have with microorganisms (that which I explore vis-à-vis Amitav Ghosh's speculative
fiction). Additionally, my project takes seriously the claims of Hardt
and Negri (in *Empire*) on the topological folds of contemporary institutions of governmentality. If in the past power was effected through
enferments (containments like the prison, the school, and the army),
in our current moment—as Hardt and Negri, following Gilles Deleuze,
argue—the prison is best conceived not as a locally bounded site (from
which there could be an "outside" called freedom) but rather the prison
is everywhere and experienced as "a play of degrees and intensities."[71]

Hardt and Negri's spatial reconceptualizations of power (force flows)
have repercussions for our notions of private space and public space,
especially in the context of somatic sociality, where the supposed private sphere of the body, and the intimacies of grooming, hygiene, and
nutrition, become sites of an intense wagering of the will to health (the
will to optimize life). The flip side of this notion of the "private" soma
already "public" is a kind of nonscandalous quality to nakedness or
exposure—a kind of diffuseness of the pornographic so that the very
qualities or limits of obscenity become themselves fluid. The emphasis
on the limits of exposure (of the critical method of hidden-exposed,
which Eve Sedgwick aligned with the paranoia of detection) also takes
the form, throughout the following chapters, of a metacritical conversation regarding the stakes of an Asian Americanist emphasis on justice/
equilibrium against a more tactile, affective intensity of interest to be
had by more transversal, circuitous immersions.

One might very well ask the question, Why study biosociality in contexts specifically "Asian American" or racial? Why not study the literary

and cultural manifestations of distributed embodiment more generally? Wider cultural studies of biosociality are a main influence on this study, works such as Melinda Cooper's *Life as Surplus*, Susan Squier's *Liminal Lives*, Priscilla Wald's *Contagious*, Ed Cohen's *Body Worth Defending*, Donna Haraway's *When Species Meet*, Judith Roof's *Poetics of DNA*, Kim Tallbear's *Native DNA: Tribal Belonging and the False Promise of Genetic Science*, Charis Thompson's *Making Parents: The Ontological Choreography of Reproduction*, Lynn Margulis and Dorian Sagan's *Acquiring Genomes*, and Hannah Landecker's *Culturing Life* and her research on American metabolism, to name a few. My study in many ways places conventionally conceived works in the Asian Americanist canon—those either created by Asian Americans or depicting Asiatics and orientals to the American public—in conversation with that literature. However, the real force of placing Asian American cultural texts and Asian Americanist cultural study in relation to the question of the biological at this moment lies in the peculiarities of the Asian Americanist critical field's current theoretical articulation of its weakness as an immanent discursive formation and its overreliance on the biological. In essence, I am not arguing with the adage that Asian Americans have no common language, history, and so forth, to call their own. I am saying that precisely because of these noncommonalities, the question of biology looms larger, making the anxiousness of biological embodiment in Asian Americanist contexts a ripe arena of study and opening up the question of what being biological (bioavailable, biosupplementable, clinically carved up, etc.) means for race, gender, queer, and disability studies more generally.

The aim here is not to rescue an anthropomorphic aperture or the organism's integrity but to negotiate the tripartite scales of biosociality—the scale of the person, the scale of the microbe, and the scale of the population.[72] And as stated earlier, the larger stakes of this project also lie in the question of whether humanistic inquiry can still remain humanist if it thinks about embodiment more in terms of distributed parts and patterns of circulation—of energy, affects, atoms, and liquidity in its accounting of the soma. Going the other way (in a cautionary note to the fetishizing of everything reconceived as information flows), my argument is also that we would be wise not to throw out personification and the anthropomorphic aperture as valuable critical frameworks—frameworks through which the distributed, multiscalar biologies of a simultaneous human and posthuman moment are registered. Put another way, synchronic racial and postracial epistemologies become valuable heuristics to comprehend such plural embodied phenomenologies. The critical interest in personifications (as they occur in literature, performance, new media, and theoretical contexts) does not compute to an old-fashioned focus on persons rather than things, or assertions of pathetic fallacies on a reality of machinic flows, aka (ecological) systems. Indeed, my work in this book cleaves to a methodology that precisely attends to an order of thinking that "stands on a bridge," a phrase borrowed from Monique Truong's *Book of Salt* to describe one character's as-yet-undecided cleaving to either a territorially nationalist or a deterritorialized exilic politics. The standing on a bridge undertaken in *The Exquisite Corpse of Asian America* involves straddling the humanist, organismal structure of bodies and a proposed "future" but really contemporary moment of distributed and symbiogenetic[73] materiality where the enzymatic, cytoplasmic, metabolic, and regulatory activities of cross-species biologies coassemble with other chemical, informatic, and toxic force flows. Race scholars need to entertain the possibility but also not rush to conclude that thinking biologies in this nonautonomous, nondiscrete way (one that sees organisms as multispecies collectives) may so transform what we think of as race that these biologies' genealogies to past and current racial theory become unintelligible.

Femiqueer Embodiment and Ethics

Though up to this point I have highlighted the critical race studies, postcolonial, STS, and humanistic (affect/aesthetic) influences on the analyses that follow, I would be remiss not to underscore the terrain of feminist and queer embodiment studies as the gestational milieu of this project, and indeed, all of my scholarship to date. In thinking through Asian American body projects and embodied acts, I have drawn inspiration from works focused on body parts highly charged in the history of gendering: the vagina, the (bound) feet, and the breast (by way of Margaret Cho, Ruth Ozeki, Cheng-Chieh Yu, Londa Schiebinger, and Sarah Lochlann Jain). But even as such body parts have been flashpoints for thinking about "women's difference," it has been the more recent turns in feminist theory toward questioning bodily matter as the very grounding of feminism's project that have been more influential on my work. One way of understanding feminist theory's importance to this project lies in the initial centering and then vexing of the stable category woman, who would be both the subject and the object of women's studies. Feminist theory continues to grapple with "biological foundationalism," the grounding of its political projects and interrogatory practices in a natural, pre-given bodily fact, a grounding that smuggles in the idea that women across cultures are a natural affinity group.[74] This premise not only allows for Western feminists to overlook the distinct formations of gendering humanity in various locations but also allows feminism to mystify its political premises as a coalitional formation.

Feminists of color were crucial to the critique of woman as a natural category across times and spaces, and this project continues in that line of work, stressing, to quote Norma Alarcon, that "in cultures in which 'asymmetric race and class relations are a central organizing principle of society,' one may also 'become a woman' in opposition to other women"[75]—and that a feminism that relies upon a too narrow focus on woman's subordination risks understating or ignoring how men of color as a group may likewise be oppressed by (white) patriarchy or, if "patriarchy" is too outmoded a notion, then how men of color can be oppressed by masculinist neoliberal corporate logics. This project is also indebted to the historical preoccupation of women of color artists with the "body . . . as site [to contest] pornographic ethnography . . . the tradition of exhibiting 'real' human objects that goes back to Columbus's importation of 'New World' natives to Europe for purposes of scientific study and courtly entertainment."[76] If as Ella Shohat asserts, "the only visibility allowed people of color was the hyperbolized pathological visibility of the auction block, the circus, and the popular scientific exposition,"[77] the Asian American artists, writers, and performers examined here expressly negotiate with the pathological visibility of Asian Americans in the political sphere, the entertainment professions, the medical field, and domestic service, even as they also emphasize a kind of ubiquitous, civilian-enacted racial profiling at present that affects Americans of East Asian versus Southeast and South Asian descent, unevenly.

During the period of this book's composition, object-oriented feminist scholarship informed by the "new materialisms" coalesced in signal publications such as Jane Bennett's *Vibrant Matter* and Diana Coole and Samantha Frost's edited volume, *New Materialisms,* both appearing in 2010. Coole and Frost, for instance, offer a cogent review of how the false cleaving of "language, consciousness, subjectivity, agency, soul . . . imagination, emotions, values, meaning, and so on" from "biological material [and] the inertia of physical stuff" led from the 1970s onward to the rise of "radical constructivism" and a decline (they use the word "demise") of traditional materialist frameworks indebted to structural Marxism (2). Influenced by the work of Spinoza filtered through Gilles Deleuze, the new materialisms eschew the view that sees inorganic matter as without agency, instead regarding matter as "active, self-creative, productive, unpredictable" (9). While many of the following chapters harmonize with this new materialist perspective, it is also the case that ethnic studies, in contrast to feminist studies, did not see the demise of historical materialism as method (with Marx remaining *de rigueur* reading in the field). Moreover, it is unclear the extent to which the new materialists[78] themselves take seriously the theoretical work of those working at the nexus of postcolonial, race, and queer studies as they have engaged in similar projects of emphasizing nonhuman actants (D. Nelson; Morton; Tallbear 2012; Chen 2012).

At the intersection of queer theory– and feminist-inflected inquiries into science, medicine, and technology (what I call the "femiqueer"), groundbreaking challenges to the (gendered) body's naturalness emerged in the 1990s. This strand of querying gender stresses the historicity of the category "woman" and the relatively recent grounding of sex difference (in the eighteenth century) in the "truth of the body." For instance, Thomas Laqueur famously called attention to the one-sex theory of the body, wherein what we now think of as women's distinctive sex organs were merely less-developed versions of men's, located inside their bodies. Contesting the naturalness of dimorphic gender, scholars of the intersexed and of transgender point to figures such as the hermaphrodite that give lie to the claim that there are only two (male and female) sexes, posing alternatives such as the "five sexes," and highlighting the naturalness of anatomical sex as a backformation from the culturally constructed idea of binary gender.[79] Informed by queer

theory's rootedness in but also nonisometry with the fuller representation of gay, lesbian, and trans- bodies, this study introduces counterintuitive notions of queer reproductive infrastructures when thinking, for instance, of the hyper-hetero (cross-species) seeding grounds
of microbiological parasites requiring two or more host bodies (see
chapter 4).

Inspiration for my expanded notion of queer sites of reproduction
and kinship comes from both STS scholar Charis Thompson's work on
assisted reproductive technologies and in vitro fertilization (IVF) and
biologists such as Joan Roughgarden and Lynn Margulis' revisions to
sexual selection theory and the origins of sex. According to Thompson, the plurality of potential parents enabled by egg donorship, sperm
donorship, and gestational surrogacy allows, for instance, for the sister of a potential male parent (or, put more crudely, he who is trying
to procure an infant) to act as gestational surrogate employed by her
brother (for an embryo formed from her brother's sperm and a donated
egg). The incestuous connotations of this sister's birthing her brother's
child, however, remain deeply troubling to the state and those engaged
in such arrangements, with Thompson drawing out how both the legal
language restricting the channeling of certain egg-sperm combinations
and patients' conversations on how they understand the new kinship
formations of which they are a part struggle to keep intact a narrative
of linear cognatic descent—that meaning of "heteronormativity."[80] Kinship becomes a technological, biological, and discursive choreography
that, at the present moment, is haunted as much by the prospect of too
much "hetero" intimacy (xeno-assemblages) as by the prospect of too
much "homo" intimacy (incest). That this queer troubling of narratives of kinship occurs as much within privileged domains of high-tech
heteronormative reproduction as within gay, lesbian, and transgender
spaces, I argue, has implications for what archives and methods we
count as queer enough.

In Roughgarden's *Evolution's Rainbow* and *The Genial Gene*, this biologist draws upon observable physiology and behavior of nonhuman
animals (the wider natural world) and offers evidence of the inadequacy of thinking binary gender (she points to species of birds that, for
instance, have two phenotypal males and two phenotypal females), and
in turn, the inadequacy of the theory of sexual selection along the lines

offered by neo-Spencerian thinkers such as Richard Dawkins (but continuing to be misnamed "Darwinian sexual selection theory"), which
figures coy females selecting genetically superior males as the engine
driving survival of the fittest. In *The Genial Gene*, she takes aim at the
underlying competitive engine imputed to natural selection, arguing
that survival involves as much resilience in gregariousness and coop-
eration as it does competitive interaction. For her part, Lynn Margulis, whether or not intentionally, queers notions of sex in defining it
simply as transversal (or horizontal) gene transfers that can happen by
way of cosmic radiation as much as intergamete exchange. Summariz-
ing Margulis and Sagan's *Origins of Sex*, Myrna Hird distinguishes sex
(genetic recombination—crossing of genetic materials across nuclei,
cell membranes, and organisms) and reproduction (the accumulation
of more matter):

> [S]ex is "any process that recombines genes (DNA) in an individual
> cell or organism from more than a single source. . . . [It] may occur at
> the nucleic acid, nuclear, cytoplasmic, and other levels." Sex may occur
> through cosmic irradiation, virus and symbiont acquisition, or exposure
> to ambient chemicals. Reproduction, by contrast, is the process that aug-
> ments the number of cells or organisms. . . . Sexual reproduction [the
> augmenting of numbers of organisms via the recombination of genes
> rather than asexually—as in sporulation, budding, mitosis, fragmenta-
> tion, etc.] is a minority practice among species on earth.[81]

These evolutionary and micro-biologists' insights on the varieties
of reproduction and the nonisometry of sex with strictly interorganismal gamete exchange leave expansive areas to be reckoned with
in queer theory. Indeed, what Laura Hyun Yi Kang calls "trenchant
interdisciplinarity," whereby biology and women's/gender/queer studies mutually unsettle each other's founding presumptions and favored
methods—precisely through serious cross-engagement—still remains
largely unassayed.[82] Admittedly, my study here remains more multi-
disciplinary than trenchantly interdisciplinary; however, in bringing an
exquisite corporeal method, one informed by STS, race studies, femiqueer theory, and the aleatory, to the work of Asian American cultural
production, my own gamble is that Asian Americanist critique will

emerge as a particularly hospitable site for further cross-disciplinary experiments, along the lines contoured in this book, yielding insights important to feminist, gender, and queer studies as much as race, post-colonial, and American studies.

* * *

Allow me now to return to my opening reading of Yamanaka's "Parts" and to recapitulate that the rhetorical moves of the poem go increasingly inward, to the embodied experience of self-cutting, to the circulation of sensations and feelings (dizzy, grey, numb, icy) that end in the gratuitous expenditure of the apostrophed subject's biomaterials, her spilled blood, as insufficient guarantor of a reciprocated feeling (love). Blood is the species of this exchange and it takes the semiotic form of the writing of "her name." While the poem doesn't take on the "tissue" point of view of platelets or inhabit the "molecular" scale of coagulative processes, it nonetheless taps into a twisting of the interior and exterior—of embodying this distortion, this condition of extremity juxtaposed to philia (love). The poem fails to deliver justice or equilibrium figured as the battering voice of the first three parts met by a counterpunch (e.g., "I accuse you, mother!" followed by a declaration of freedom and autonomy). Nor does it offer a more tender reconciliation, where the daughter's self-cutting would elicit a maternal escort to the hospital. In this instance, rather than moving toward balance or homeostasis, poesis amplifies crisis and vitality qua continual disequilibrium. While we might think of this emphasis on extreme modes of survival in brutish conditions as flouting rather than satisfying the Asian Americanist emphasis on a desirable justice in the future, there is also another way to approach this emphasis on disequilibrium, but it involves a recursive loop in reading Yamanaka's poem both nonracially and racially.

For purposes of heuristic clarity, we might think of this disequilibrium first as a universal (nonracial) portrait of the suffering brought on by late capitalist biopolitics where alienation occurs not simply at the site of labor (production) but across vitality itself (reproduction, health, nutrition, etc.). Recalling both Eric Hayot's and Colleen Lye's analysis of the coolie's function as an ambivalent figure registering the shocks of modernity (its equivalence with suffering, where the coolie also offers a possible way out of suffering vis-à-vis indifference), we might ask—in the context of Yamanaka's poem—"Who or what becomes the 'Asiatic' figure that can bear the shocks of post-Fordist biopolitics—financialization of life itself?" In the apostrophed subject's self-cutting, we find a sort of answer. Her recourse is to her own biomaterials: her blood—and her fluid openness—become the bioavailable vehicles that can bear suffering with a kind of nervelessness or through the deliberate solicitation of the body's own organically produced anesthetics. In this latter reading, it both matters and doesn't matter if we figure the poem's apostrophed subject as Asian, for in a sense, the Asiatic racial form that in the past, by way of the population aggregate of "Chinese," worked as a conduit for modernity's disequilibriums has morphed in the biopolitical present into the generativity and plasticity of bodily fluids, organs, cells, molecules—these can "suffer" with indifference.

Attempted in the above reading, then, is an analysis of race in relation to a poem where there isn't necessarily a warrantable Asian character. Reading late-nineteenth- and early-twentieth-century American naturalist literature, Colleen Lye introduced this method of considering "examples of racial figuration even when it does not take the shape of a racially identified character."[83] My analysis here extends her method to turn-of-the-twenty-first-century poetry and human specimen exhibits, the latter of which represents the extension of the natural history diorama enabled by taxidermy to the preservation and scientific display of the human enabled by plastination.[84]

My analysis of racial figuration with respect to Yamanaka's poem occurs through an engagement with its thematic concerns with bioavailability and biological materials, rather than by equating its stylized use of local Hawaiian pidgin as the obvious racial marker (which might be called a linguistic essentialism). While at the outset I emphasized this poem's defying the kind of Asian Americanist reading exhibited in Fiona Ma's efforts vis-à-vis the Body Worlds exhibits—a reading referring to racialized physiognomy in order to pursue the project of justice—here I suggest that the poem's lack of a similar Asiatic anatomical detail doesn't necessarily mean that a racialized framework isn't a tenable heuristic device. That is, only if we think race bespeaks a relation of two humanist wholes (one colored and one white) can we not see race operative in this poem. But what if we were to revise race to include the realm of biopolitical social relations exacted not simply in the state's relation to the citizen but in the management of health mediated by the site of the family and peer "advice," as well as lived in the alienated, instrumental use of one's biomaterials, as well as lived across the technosomatic interface of poesis and the body of the reader?

The point, then, is not simply to answer in binary (1, 0, match, no match) whether Yamanaka's poem of bodily fragments is an Asian American one. My ambition is rather to intensify certain investments—in justice/equilibrium, in the anthropomorphic aperture, in humanist antagonistic agency—that become felt in the gut while probing these works' own conflicted relation to the salience of race in understanding and theorizing contemporary biopolitics and biosociality. How (many ways) does race qua "species-being" come to matter in the more or less universal condition of living the self as fragments, or to put it another way, as several surreal scales of organization, morphogenesis, and temporality?

Will race or racial personifications still circulate as vehicles to sensually and cognitively grasp posthumanness as a condition of estranged and dispersed biologies? This question of race's continuing salience cannot be determined in advance. Metacritically, I would frame my own endeavor here as an effort to enroll and ally studies of race, particularly those genealogically linked to the Asian Americanist field, as crucial platforms to understand that biosociality. My success or not in doing so will form part of the answer to that question as posed in some future discussion. But for now, it is certainly clear that critical cultural interventions into tissue economies and estranged biologies of the current moment might have fruitful sponsors within the postcolonial and racial studies fields. It is this sponsorship that I wish to encourage as a developing possibility.

1

How a Critical Biopolitical Studies Lens Alters the Questions We Ask vis-à-vis Race

Jane Takagi-Little, the heroine of Ruth Ozeki's novel *My Year of Meats* (1998), produces documentary infomercials that sell "the American way of life"—that is, the daily intake of beef, chicken, or pork—to Japanese housewives. Working for a U.S. livestock conglomerate called Beef-Ex, Jane includes minority races, lesbians, immigrants, the disabled, and untraditional families in these televisual features of representative Americans who lovingly cook with meat, thereby undermining the Japanese equation of Americans with robust Anglo-Saxons and white ethnics. Yet when she finds herself interviewing a family living on a cattle ranch and injecting their livestock with hormones in order to make ends meet, she has an "Aha!" moment. Is making more multicultural the social, political, and economic spheres of American life the most important work to be done in pursuing social justice?

The head cattle rancher, Gale, explains how maximizing profits means shortening fattening times by accelerating growth through hormone injections. This process restricts cattle movement, requiring antibiotics because the close quarters breed disease, and also leads to aborting heifers "when they get accidental bred [because] you can't have pregnant heifers in a feedlot. All they do is eat, eat, eat, and never gain" (263). As the vulnerable human face of these feedlot practices, Gale's five-year-old niece, unintentionally exposed to the hormone Lutalyse, has grown fully mature breasts on her small body. While this five-year-old's altered life cycle qua reproductive precocity appears treatable, Ozeki drives home the tragic stakes of these chemical contaminations in Jane's own struggles with a prior exposure to synthesized estrogen while *in utero*. Her mother took diethylstilbestrol (DES) while pregnant—prescribed by her midwestern doctor to prevent miscarriage in this "delicate" Japanese lady (156)—resulting in Jane's own malformed uterus and infertility. Ozeki's readers also learn that Jane's father has died of cancer because his work in postnuclear Japan exposed him to lingering environmental radiation after the Nagasaki and Hiroshima bombings.

Within this storyline, Ozeki's protagonist changes. She begins to perceive politics as encompassing more than democratic, more-inclusive cultural representation. Politics also includes the terrain of biology and ecology—of health, diet, and environment as they affect the reproduction and vitality of the population. Jane finds herself steeped in the biopolitical. Her documentary infomercials end up altering the bodily habits and life course of a Japanese housewife named Akiko, with Jane effectively molding Akiko's anatomy and desires. Her research on the efficiencies of the cattle industry, achieved through abortifacients and other hormone injections, doubles as research on her own (embryonic) medical history, with biopolitics here pointing to the entanglement of various populations—livestock and humans, cows and women.[1]

Broadly speaking, Asian American texts have been valuable to a revisionist U.S. literary canon precisely because of their testament to the active racial exclusion of Asians. Belying the promise of color-blind political equality, this exclusion occurs through legal bars to immigration, educational segregation, labor stratification also known as "glass ceilings," criminalization as enemy aliens and spies, and social and psychic wounding through harmful stereotypes. The fields of postcolonial, world, and U.S. literatures have yet to theorize Asian American cultural production in a sustained manner for what it tells us about biopolitics, modern modes of governmentality, and the somaticization of social and political traumas. This first chapter begins that process by considering how a critical biopolitical studies approach shifts the critical aims and insights afforded by Asian American cultural production. In the next section, I will define biopower—clarifying its relation to anatomopolitics, biopolitics, and necropolitics—before mapping the critical interactions between Asian American cultural production and a critical biopolitical studies framework.

Pastoral Governmentality and Necropolitics

A certain enigmatic imprecision characterizes the terms "biopolitics" and "biopower," an imprecision deriving from Michel Foucault's ongoing endeavor to refine these ideas.[2] Foucault distinguishes modern biopower from the favored technique of sovereign power in the *ancien regime*. Whereas the sovereign displays his spectacular power by way of "murderous splendor" (e.g., the gruesome public execution of enemies and offending subjects by tearing their bodies asunder), modern biopower operates by way of "distributing the living in the domain of value and utility. Such a power has to qualify, measure, appraise and hierarchize"—that is, to document, rank, and make visible subject bodies, rather than display itself spectacularly in its power to execute at will.[3] The techniques of modern biopower shift from gruesome spectacle toward a statistical aggregating and comparing of populations, together with disciplinary procedures aimed at individuals enacted to increase health, well-being, and vitality.[4] This biopower normalizes certain desires, "the historical outcome of a technology of power centered on life."[5] In those who have extended Foucault's schema, biopower is sometimes used as an umbrella term for two kinds of manifestations of power, a disciplinary "anatomo-politics of the human body" and a regulatory "biopolitics of the population."[6] But sometimes "biopolitical" simply stands as the adjectival form of biopower (a point to which I return).[7]

According to Nikolas Rose, a pastoral eugenics, policed by citizens and not the state, characterizes biopower in "advanced liberal" societies.[8] Rose describes this style of governance as interpersonal decision making,

> not organized or administered by "the state" [but taking] place in a plural and contested field traversed by . . . ethics committees . . . researchers . . . employers and insurers . . . biotech companies [and] self-help organizations. . . . Best [described as] *relational* . . . [this pastoral mode] works through . . . the affects and ethics of the guider [and] the guided. . . . These new pastors of the soma espouse the ethical principles of informed consent, autonomy, voluntary action and choice, and non-directiveness.[9]

For Rose, the prenatal consult—where one is given information on genetic-risk profiles and never coerced overtly into making eugenic rather than dysgenic decisions—epitomizes the pastoral quality that pressures the living to conform to ideals of optimized health and well-being.

As background for understanding how Asian American literary authors respond to and reflect upon this form of governmentality, let me briefly draw upon historical and ethnographic narratives to review how Asian Americans and Asians subject to U.S. imperialism have been regulated by biopower. Focusing on late-nineteenth- and early-twentieth-century Asian immigration to the United States, historians Joan Trauner and Nayan Shah elucidate the overt medical scapegoating of the Chinese. The labeling of these immigrants as carriers of small-pox and tuberculosis justified quarantines, invasive inspections of living spaces, and calls for the wholesale razing of the "pestilent" dens of Chinatown. According to Alexandra Minna Stern, the graphic images of "contagion and constitutional malaise" initially associated with Chinese men—portraits of them as effeminate, enervated, or "spotted with suppurating pustules [and] ugly lesions"—spread their biopolitical effects to other Asian communities:[10]

> Medicine and public health molded the adaptation of Asian immigrants to the West, from the health inspections and psychological exams they endured on Angel Island to the antiprostitution and antivice campaigns waged by Progressives in Chinatowns or the public hygiene angles of the Americanization campaigns that were promoted from inside and outside of Chinese, Japanese, and Filipino communities.[11]

While Stern privileges the immigrant paradigm in limning the specific ways biopower shapes successive waves of Asians to America, historian Claire J. Kim looks at imperial archives from the late nineteenth to early twentieth centuries reporting on the medical circuits through which the Philippines and Hawai'i came under official U.S. rule. According to Kim, Asian and Pacific Islander bodies became subjected to American biopolitical schemes not simply as *immigrants* biomedically assessed, sanitized, and clinically normed as they landed on American shores but as *tropical subjects* never having traveled from their archipelagic homes but targeted for "saving" by American philanthropic institutions aimed at improving global health (see also Warwick Anderson). Through "paternalistic missions to save colonial lives endangered by . . . infectious disease,"[12] American medical men associated with the Rockefeller Foundation's International Health Commission turned U.S. extraterritorial possessions such as the Philippines and Hawai'i (other extant U.S. territories include Guam, American Samoa, the Northern Mariana Islands, Puerto Rico, and the U.S. Virgin Islands) into living laboratories for the devising of "novel" techniques for epidemic control.[13] Such advanced biopolitical techniques would then make their modernizing way back to the metropole.

C. Kim notes as well the historiographical revisions demanded by such a critical biopolitical studies lens. Histories by Asian Americanists of Hawai'i and other tropical territories formerly colonized or administered by the U.S. understandably focus on labor history, since the large Asian immigrant presence in these islands emerged through plantation owners' importing of Asiatic labor (Yun, Jung). Noting, however, that "labor history in Hawai'i . . . has tended to overlook matters of reproducing family, sexuality, and gender as central features of the plantation regime in favor of attention to the contradictory formations of race and class that often divided workers," C. Kim argues that a "critical interimperial framework" (one congruent with what I call a critical biopolitical studies approach) remains a necessary intervention:

> Sugar plantation laborers were constantly subjected to underlying gendered and sexual protocols that were tied to policies of U.S. settler colonialism and efficient agricultural production. Access to sexual reproduction and family formation was also crucial to the ethnic and racial hierarchy in Hawai'i after its adoption of U.S. immigration and naturalization laws in 1900, classifying Asians as aliens ineligible for citizenship.[14]

Writing as well on the nonidyllic history of the mostly colored, polyethnic workforce on Hawai'i's plantations, literary scholar Stephen J. Sumida notes that "since native Hawai'ians were grievously diminished in number by exposure to disease foreign to them before the arrival of Captain Cook and his crew in 1778," white plantation owners in the nineteenth and twentieth centuries sought in Chinese, Japanese,

Filipinos, and Koreans—presumptive "cognate races" to the Kanaka Maoli of Hawai'i—"peoples both to labor on the plantations and to repopulate the islands" (Sumida 133). A critical biopolitical studies framework, in short, shows the inseparability of the erotic (and the reproductive), the environmental, the epidemiological, and the economic, suggesting as well that literacy in key concepts refined by scholarship in feminist/gender studies and queer theory remains necessary to a robust critical biopolitical studies.

Tackling a more recent instance of medical policing involving a restructuring of intimate relations, Anne Fadiman's *The Spirit Catches You and You Fall Down* (1997) reports on a Hmong family's frustrating encounter in the 1980s with the Merced County Medical Hospital while seeking treatment for their toddler Lia's epilepsy. Because they misunderstood the regimen and objected to the side effects, Lia's parents failed to administer the prescribed anticonvulsants to their daughter, prompting physician Neil Ernst to put Lia in foster care. While genuine concern prompts Ernst's call to Child Protective Services, he also wants the proud and superstitious Hmong to admit that Western medicine knows some things better than they. Here we see how a well-intentioned, pastoral mode of medical authority colludes with bans on immigration, xenophobia, and the criminalization of Asian groups. As another doctor attending to Lia puts it, "[Lia's parents] seemed to accept things that to me were major catastrophes as part of the normal flow of life. For them, the crisis was the *treatment,* not the epilepsy" (Fadiman 53). Fadiman's even-handed portrait limns this tragedy as both biomedical (the recurrence in Lia of ostensibly preventable *grand mal* seizures) and familial (the wresting of the child from her doting parents). A quintessential portrait of the refugee-immigrant experience of a part-benevolent, part-tyrannical system of biopower, the narrative stresses a sorrowful mix of clashing protocols of care, with no clear or single blameworthy agent.

While Rose stresses the pastoral quality of modern anatomopolitics, others such as Mbembe and Chow (both mentioned in the introduction), as well as Malcolm Bull and Rosi Braidotti, would regard an overemphasis on biopower's emotional circuits, its pastoral "relational" mechanisms, as having the potential to mystify the violence at the core of contemporary biopower. To them, "necropolitics" is merely the flip side of biopower. As Chow puts it, the ideological mandate to live and thrive "gives justification to even the most aggressive and oppressive mechanisms of interference and control in the name of helping the human species increase its chances of survival."[15] According to Jodi Kim, the period Americans call the Cold War (1947–1991) illuminates this point. While this era saw the United States and the Soviet Union engaged in a guarded but technically "peaceful" standoff, "hot wars" raged in Asia—in Korea, Vietnam, Cambodia, and Laos—in which U.S. troops were involved in the massive slaughter of Asians. In the name of protecting Americans' thriving way of life (the surplus comforts provided by democratic capitalism), the United States justified its outright necropolitics—its (assisted) killing of purported Communist sympathizers within nonaligned nations, so as to prevent the latter from falling, in domino fashion, to Soviet control. The orphaning of Asian populations resulting from these wars also meant that further biopolitical effects would follow—the thriving traffic in Korean adoptees to the United States being one such effect, with Korean mothers feeling compelled to give their children up for a putative better life following the "imperative to live."

As we can see, some critical confusion characterizes biopower and biopolitics partly because, while Foucault first differentiated these terms—making biopolitics and anatomopolitics subsets of biopower—the terms "biopower" and "biopolitics" are often collapsed in usage. As distinct from "anatomopolitics," "biopolitics" refers to a more *top-down managerial perspective employing a calculative logic in assessing population-aggregates comparatively*, with particular scrutiny paid to "the size and quality of the population; reproduction and human sexuality; conjugal parental and familial relations; health and disease; birth and death."[16] Because of its emphasis on aggregates, biopolitics more easily harmonizes with sociological analyses focused on "race." At the same time, literary accounts, especially if thickly described (to borrow a term from ethnographic fieldwork), owe much of their richness to the scale of anatomopolitics—referring to the corporeal entrainment of individual bodies and "the subjectivizing processes [whereby the individual shapes her] notions of the self and how [she] should want to behave."[17] Focusing on the radical feminist health movements of the 1970s, STS scholar Michelle Murphy specifies these subjectivizing, anatomopolitical processes as learned "procedural scripts" establishing "protocols" on "'how to' do something" (2012, 25). While Foucault stresses the spread of these protocols as a tactic furthering the docility of bodies, Murphy emphasizes that grassroots groups also disseminate such know-how, so as to challenge professional clinicians' monopoly on scientific knowledge and tool-use. Anatomopolitics, in other words, can involve the democratization of techniques, such as the opening of the vagina for cervical self-examination through use of the plastic speculum (which Murphy portrays as a protocol crucial to the grassroots women's health movement of the 1970s). Technologies formerly restricted to the space of the clinic are "seized" and redeployed at home.[18]

Literature, replete with what the sciences call "narrative method" (Reissman), offers an ample view of the subjection of the individual body—i.e., the scale of anatomy, choreographies of embodiment, and techniques of the self—prompted by state institutions, grassroots organizations, and the "capillary" influences of civil society, such as those intoned in do-it-yourself (DIY) pamphlets or friends' shared tips on diet and exercise. Chang Rae Lee's *Native Speaker* (1995), for instance, offers excruciating detail on the corporeal retraining of its protagonist, Henry Park, who, upon arriving in the United States, revises his lingual and bodily habits, a testament to this character's cultural assimilation, yes, but also to anatomopolitics—to the long-lasting effects of "health inspections and psychological exams" molding the adaptation of Asian immigrants to the United States. Thus when we think of the grid of biopower as challenged or depicted in literary representation and performance, a combined attentiveness to both poetic detail on the scale of individual bodies and psyches and extrapolation of these individual instances to the context of a dichotomous (eugenic/dysgenic, unmarked/marked) populational divide potentially yields rich insight speaking back to biopower's tenacity, efficacy, and perverse logic. Comprehending modern biopower requires, in short, attending to its combination of a "pastoral" relational style and a profiling, aggregating mode that carves out blunt distinctions among populations. At the same time, in comparison to the various ways in which taxonomies of race have fluctuated and emerged fairly recently (in the seventeenth and eighteenth centuries) and have, arguably, had their most trenchant articulation in a critical vein vis-à-vis contexts of U.S. racialization

(Silva), biopolitics as a critical lens offers a simpler heuristic that is both more transhistorical and transcultural (applicable to ancient as well as modern times, and descriptive of the metropole as well as the colony). Biopower qua biopolitics involves the aggregation, even if only retrospectively, of life into two big categories—*bios*, or politically worthy life, and *zoe*, or bare, animal life (e.g., as outlined by Georgio Agamben with regard to late antiquity). The point, however, is not to settle which framework, critical race studies or critical biopolitical studies, will emerge as the longer lasting in scholarly and political discussion; rather, the aim here is to illuminate their entanglement as background for comprehending Asian American cultural productions at the turn of the twenty-first century.

Animal Life

To reiterate, biopower qua biopolitics involves the aggregation of life into two big categories—*bios* or politically worthy life, and *zoe* or bare, animal life (Agamben). Didier Fassin and Mark Jerng (2008) have suggested that *bios*, i.e., life lived through "a body (not only through cells)" (Fassin) and in all its contingent historical particulars, is intimately wedded to narration and therefore is resonant and relational to other life narratives—literary genres of narrated life. In contrast, *zoe*, or "life itself," refers to "the universal organization of matter" (Fassin 47–48) and has mainly been the province of bioscience's manipulations and the focus of Science and Technology Studies (STS). While for Fassin *zoe* is the bare vitality of cells, scholars expressly engaged in race studies have traditionally understood *zoe* as unprotected animal life. Cultural critic Ed Cohen, historian Robert Lee, and transdisciplinary animal studies critic Mel Chen have tracked the nineteenth-century pathologizing of South Asians in the subcontinent and East Asian migrants to the United States through, respectively, their association with cholera and their metaphoric collapse in popular songs into rats, mice, and fleas (upon which they are claimed to feast).[19] More recently, news coverage of the early-twenty-first-century SARS (Severe Acute Respiratory Syndrome) scare drew on these earlier intimate conjoinings of Asiatic peoples and nonmammalian life (here birds) to raise fears of Asians as microbe carriers—as petri dishes for the crossing over of avian viruses to humans.[20]

The process whereby the human is reduced to the insect, rodent, bird, or microbe—what I will be calling *"zoe*-ification"—remains a persistent method of rendering fellow humans as a race or "species-being" apart. As suggested at the outset of this chapter, the critical biopolitical lens I wish to develop within and through Asian American cultural productions intervenes into *zoe*-ification by adopting a hospitable regard toward the intertwinement of nonhuman and human populations.

The canon of Asian American literature has reflected in a variety of ways upon mechanisms of *zoe*-ification, for instance, by testifying to Filipinos' bewilderment at Anglo-Americans' equating them with "monkeys" (Carlos Bulosan's *America Is in the Heart* [1943]); by hyperbolically playing upon the disgust of whites at Asians' trophic incorporation of monkeys and dogs (Maxine Hong Kingston's *Woman Warrior* [1976], Jessica Hagedorn's *Dogeaters* [1990], and R. Zamora Linmark's "They Like You Because You Eat Dog" in *Rolling the R's* [1995]); and by depicting empire's expansion into the Pacific Islands as a drama of native species (animals and humans) either rendered as the sexual prey of imported feral pigs or becoming subject to decomposing diseases such as leprosy and scabies brought in by European travelers (Lois Ann Yamanaka's *Heads by Harry* [1999] and *Blu's Hanging* [1997]). More recently, Asian diasporic literary considerations of *zoe*-ification occur through the tearing and sundering of bodies (their disaggregation into useful parts), harkening back, interestingly, to the fragmenting violence of the sovereign in the *ancien regime*. This form of *zoe*-ification finds expression in memoirs and films that figure Asians, and other people of the global South, as those whose organs and children (former parts of themselves) are alienable, easy to disentangle from their natal milieu either to serve as transplanted tissues extending the lives of those who can buy or otherwise procure organs (Karen Tei Yamashita's *Tropic of Orange* [1997], Kazuo Ishiguro's *Never Let Me Go* [2005], and Yiyun's Li's *Vagrants* [2009]); or to live anew as transnational adoptees raised in the privileged sectors of American modernity (see J. Kim 2010; Jerng 2010; and L. Briggs 2012).

It would be a mistake, however, to reduce the field's contemplation and tropology of the animal to that which literalizes how imperialist racial mechanisms dehumanize the Polynesian, Malay, Hindu, and Mongol. For instance, Sanjay Nigam's *Transplanted Man* proposes racialized minorities' affinities to experimental lab animals, in one of its subplots regarding an insomniac mouse named Johnny Walker, whose sleep disorder is on the same spectrum as that afflicting the South Asian human protagonist, also a sleepwalker, Dr. Sonny Seth. Here the emphasis is less on any continuity between white supremacy and the disregard for animals used in scientific research and more on how bench experiments, nursing, and doctoring—all ostensibly devoted to improving life—vie with the profit motive and the disequilibrium of mass migrations (i.e., the time-space compression of virtual and real travel) that create constant conditions of clash, crisis, and stress among micro- and macro-organismal populations, a stress we shorthand as illness. To cite another example, Amitav Ghosh's postcolonial science fiction, *The Calcutta Chromosome* (discussed at length in chapter 4), places the human—embodied as South Asian and North African migrants—within an ecology of machines, arthropods, and parasite protists (eukaryotic microorganisms) with which humanity compares and distinguishes itself. The novel looks to a future moment in which the anxiety driving the will to affirm boundaries between machine and human and between protist (formerly protozoan) and human will be tempered by a delirious, even "ecodelic" openness (a term borrowed from Rich Doyle) to the generative threshold of "becoming"—a refiguring of the (human) subject as inseparably entangled with other species, or put another way, as itself an ecology of networked plant-machine-protoctist-and-animal symbionts.

An Asian Americanist analysis of various literary and performative depictions of cross-species assemblages must also take into account the class-situated and non-normate embodied relations of certain populations that prime them to "working across the human-other divide" (Martin). Ruminating on the comfort of the upper-class British involved in the raising of prize dogs who are said to resemble their human owners, Emily Martin writes,

> an ease about one's security in the social hierarchy might produce a certain ease about boundary crossings of new kinds. . . . Those in the elite strata in the United States . . . are becoming more "English" in the sense that they feel both a certain security of class position and simultaneously experience a willingness to explore across divides into the nonhuman.[21]

At the same time, Martin notes that crossing boundaries with other species is not a new phenomenon but has been a normate worldview in communities that are less anxious about (inter)dependency, such as the handicapped, or that recognize the agency of nature, such as indigenous tribes: "Perhaps it was the dominance of the ideology of individualism in the West that shut our ears to ways our identities never were single."[22] The point to be registered is that openness to cross-species assemblages is simply one iteration of Asian American and Pacific Islander engagements with "bare" animal life (*zoe*), and not the more "advanced" ethical stance in comparison to articulations that prioritize social justice on behalf of those human-animals who have been degraded either by Anglo-Europeans' social disdain and economic exploitation of racial-immigrant others or by settler-colonialists' failure to honor treaties recognizing the sovereignty of indigenous tribes.

Then there is *bios*. Taking Mark Jerng's claim that *bios*, as life lived through a body in all its contingent historical particulars, remains resonant and relational to other literary genres of narrated life, we might consider how responses to *zoe*-ification also occur by way of the formal strategies of Asian American authors.[23] Asian American literature's recourse to the *bildungsromane* and autobiographical forms—the quintessential genres of narrating (autonomous liberal) personhood—can be seen as a means of establishing Asian immigrants and their children as just like other protected citizens (*bios*), at least in the narratological form of their life course, if not in the actuality of their legal status and civil treatment.[24] However, this is not to understate the proliferation within Asian American cultural production of non-*bildung* forms and aesthetic projects that reckon with *zoe*-ification not through counterfactual, literary assertion of the proper life-course (*bios*) but through questioning the very discursive and lexical techniques that nominate a life-form as either worthy of remembrance (meriting songs, ballads, and epics) or as numerical cypher—e.g., #65 out of 100.

Chinese Canadian poet Larissa Lai precisely draws the reader's attention to the porous borders between animal life (*zoe*) and the lives of mnemonically worthy hominids (*bios*) in her thirty-three page poem "Ham," published in *Automaton Biographies*. The eponymous subject of Lai's poem is the NASA chimpanzee whose successful suborbital travel by rocket in 1961 occasioned his renaming in both biblical and acronymic fashion. Though H-A-M calls to mind the outcast black son of Noah, the appellation refers to the *H*olloman *A*irforce *M*edical Center in New Mexico, the intermediary dwelling site of the astro-chimp after his being taken captive from Africa (Haraway 1989, 137–38). According to Donna Haraway, the primate, whose official name at Holloman was #65, only received the alphabetic name upon the determination of his safe descent back to earth because if "the mission had to be 'aborted,' the authorities did not want the public worrying about the death of a famous and named, even if not quite human astronaut" (Haraway 1989, 138). Yet, #65's handlers at Holloman couldn't help themselves from crafting a non-numerical but no less dehumanizing sobriquet for the chimpanzee: "Chop Chop Chang."

Renarrating U.S. cosmonautical history from the perspective of this H/ham, Lai bestows the simultaneously Orientalized and blackened chimp with sardonic wit and hipster cleverness: "i was there first / . . . / all ambition / my nutrition's an addition / to staightjacket neck-ring shock restraint / I'm tainted / almost human but not white / 98.5 percent checks out for biomedical verisimilitude" (91). Noting that banana pellets to sate him while in flight were only an afterthought, the chimpanzee speaking this dramatic monologue knows his voyager status as captive cargo rather than helmsman or paying customer. Nevertheless, Ham brazenly reminds the human audience that "your future [is] the power of my now . . . / my space / ya dig?" (91).

Despite Ham's tongue-in-cheek braggadocio on being the "emperor of the final frontier" (91), Lai's poem allows a more sobering truth to unfold by rehearsing the instrumentality of chimpanzee bodies to virological research at the Coulston Foundation laboratories in Alamogordo, New Mexico. Because the human audience's "future" follows the "now" (or prior path) of the hominid Ham, the comic voice of the primate taunts the human audience that "ha ha / *poke's on you* / tidy insertion / . . . / in case of contact with mad cow know how / kowtow in the go-down" (118; italics added). "You" as much as the captive chimpanzee have already succumbed and will continue to bear the pokes, prods, and insertions of both science's and the microbial world's (aka viruses') fantastic voyages through inner space. The poetic voice here suggests that the bioavailable labor involved in such parasitic or symbiotic events will require a corporeal resilience and set of skills akin

to those internalized by Asians in learning to greet a guest politely—
a skill set still denigrated, however, as a servile bow (the "know how
[of a] kowtow"). As suggested by "Ham," the salient, antiracist human
mission at the turn of the twenty-first century may be one of *lessening
anxiety* with regard to cross-species intimacies (i.e., poking insertions),
a task homologous with the unlearning of a denigrating attitude and
xenophobia toward Asians. In the end, Lai might be credited with moving #65 toward a greater narrative focalization, though in a trajectory
not entirely commensurate with becoming the singular "one" versus
the background "many" (Woloch). The poem instead renders the white
man's role in voyages of discovery a minute part of the broad arena of
animal adventures.

To reiterate the earlier point, a great deal of scholarly attention has
been devoted to Asian American novel-length works, *bildungsromane*,
and first-person memoirs and the way that they stylistically reckon
with *zoe*-ification through a rejection of Asian Americans' beastly categorization. As suggested in the foregoing reading, other forms such
as poetry, performance, and art might be productively engaged for the
demands they place on their audiences to consider other political directions of artistic endeavor not commensurate with returning the part
(particularized marked subject of difference) to the whole (the nationally recognized subject of rights).

New Microscopic Markers of Difference;
or, A Thousand Tiny Races

At the turn of the twenty-first century, the biosciences' repatterning of
life at the molecular level has raised the question of whether epidermal
racial categories will continue as operative terms in population management, as key channels of distributing structural economic violence,
and as salient boundaries in civil society. In the current diagram of
biopower, markers of difference tied to molecular information include
populations clustered around high cholesterol levels, mutations in the
BRCA1 or CDH1[25] gene, positivity for HIV, and so forth. As hypothesized by Paul Gilroy, because they are often not evident in surface phenotype, microscopic markers of difference present critical race theorists

with the possibility that the biosciences might afford positive avenues to challenge racist epistemologies and the material legacies grown out of comparative racialized anatomy:

> [In the recent past the] idea of race favored . . . the scale of comparative anatomy. . . . Our situation is demonstrably different. The call of racial being has been weakened by another technological and communicative revolution, by the idea that the body is nothing more than an incidental moment in the transmission of code and information, by its openness to the new imaging technologies, and by the loss of mortality as a horizon against which life is to be lived. . . .[26]
>
> At the smaller than microscopic scales [of imaging technologies] that open up the body for scrutiny today, "race" becomes less meaningful, compelling, or salient to the basic tasks of healing and protecting ourselves. We have a chance, then, to recognize the anachronistic condition of the idea of "race" as a basis upon which human beings are distinguished and ranked. . . . If "race" is a useful way of classifying people, then how many "races" are there? It is rare nowadays to encounter talk of a "Mongoloid race."[27]

Interestingly, Gilroy's contemplation of the continuing significance of racial taxa established by way of comparative anatomy concludes with a speculative note that the salience of race and the number of races are themselves unstable. Is he suggesting that this number might shrink to a stark two (black/white, *zoe*/*bios*)? While Gilroy leaves open-ended how many races there currently are, his question concludes with a singular detail: the falling into disuse of the "Mongoloid" category. One might recall here that Mongolian (not Mongoloid, the latter meaning "resembling a Mongolian" and used as a derogatory term for those with Down's Syndrome) was one of Johann Blumenbach's widely adopted five-fold chromatic schema first proposed in 1781—Caucasian (white), Mongolian (yellow), Ethiopian (black), American (red), Malayan (brown)[28]—and also one of Georges Cuvier's (1769–1832) big three—Caucasian, Mongolian, and Ethiopian.[29] These epidermal, phenotypal notions of race have origins in taxonomy, important to the inauguration of the field of biology itself, which is not to overstate the latter's distinction from natural history as much as to call attention to textual (binomial nomenclature, maps, trees) and laboratory techniques (including microscopy) as key to that distinction.[30]

Gilroy does not argue that "new hatreds" are not coming into being; rather, he claims that these "new hatreds are created not by the ruthless enforcement of stable racial categories but from a disturbing inability to maintain them."[31] Today, those working in a critical race studies vein ponder the degree to which a growing literacy in population groupings tied to molecular patterns will lend themselves to fashioning a social and material landscape of lesser institutional racism or only reinforce stratifications of race by simultaneously making "race" operational for niche marketing of pharmaceuticals (Duster) or for assessing health insurance rates, while disabling those working to revisit and mitigate the lingering effects of racial violence from evoking "race" as a term of political and material significance (Omi).[32] As Dorothy Roberts put it in 2011, despite President Bill Clinton's declaration, upon the completion of the Human Genome Sequencing Project, that the latter had proved "'human beings, regardless of race, are 99.9 percent the same' . . . [the subsequent expectations] of the demise of race as a biological category were premature. Instead of hammering the last nail in the coffin of an obsolete system, the science that emerged from sequencing the human genome was shaped by a resurgence of interest in race-based genetic variation."[33] While biological science has only multiplied the number of ways of microscopically differentiating potential populations, the resultant effects of that multiplication may not be the overthrow of Blumenbach's or Cuvier's scientifically specious, but heuristically facile (i.e., legible) racial schemas, but the enhancement of their affective, psychic importance and, thereby, materializations in legal, clinical, commercial, and civil social contexts.[34]

Allow me to dwell further on this somewhat counterintuitive point. Partly because it reassures its users as to the purported legibility of bodily surfaces to the naked human eye, epidermal notions of race persist despite genomic (aka microscopic) evidence to the contrary, e.g., that greater genetic variability exists between individual members of the same racial group than across supposedly distinct racial groups. While the modifier "epidermal" alludes most notably to the visibility of the skin (its pigmentation and oiliness) as site of racial legibility, for raciologists of the seventeenth through the eighteenth centuries, the salient gross anatomical markers were as much cranial profiles—nose and lip shape, hair type/texture, and whole body physique or "stature" (e.g., tall and lithe or squat)—as assessments of skin type.[35] In its historical moment of emergence, the authority of these epidermal notions of race derived from their descriptive (empirical) character, rather than from recourse to a storied/mythic justification of a certain hierarchical order of things. This racial mode of classification founded on physical traits, in other words, "marked a rupture with . . . the explanation of . . . human variety in the world in terms of a biblical genealogy"[36]—that is, in terms of an older mode of primary differentiation based on nonbelief or illiteracy in a sacred text and, relatedly, inability or unwillingness to speak the "civilized language"—accompanied by a concomitant designation of the sounds others make as noisy "barbar" sounds (as in the designation "barbarian").[37]

Describing and categorizing on the basis of visual evidence, raciology not only privileged the ocular sense but also followed the same logic of carving up the world into autonomous, self-evident entities, disentangled from their embeddedness in extant power relations and spiritual-storied milieu.[38] Raciology both partially disassembled and overlaid prior cultural (e.g., custom-based, religious, linguistic, and political) modes of differentiating peoples, with natural historians and natural philosopher-theologians (i.e., early biologists), then, reassembling "life" along lines of gross morphological resemblance.[39] While purporting to be scientific and objective, residual "great chain of being" thinking, according to microbiologist Lynn Margulis, nonetheless persisted, often blinding biologists—from the eighteenth through the early twenty-first centuries—from perceiving resemblances within and across the largest taxon groups that would argue against a hierarchical ranking of species.

Margulis uses the "great chain of being" to refer to religious thought across the Greek and Judeo-Christian systems, in which "the chain joined a panoply of gods at the top to, in descending order, men, women, slaves, animals, and vegetables . . . a substratum of rocks and minerals [occupying] the lowest link."[40] Her critique is aimed not primarily at the Cuviers and Blumenbachs, but rather at her late-twentieth-century contemporaries and their resistance to acknowledging morphologically, behaviorally, and genetically that (fused) bacteria are the evolutionary ancestors of all nucleus-bearing cells. All eukaryotic organisms (animals, plants, fungi, and protoctists) are multispecies assemblages; their cells themselves are symbiogenetic organisms.[41] Contesting notions of "less" or "more" evolved, "higher" or "lower" forms of life, Margulis states,

> All beings alive today are equally evolved. All have survived over three thousand million years of evolution from common bacterial ancestors. There are no "higher" beings, no "lower animals," no angels, and no gods. . . . We *Homo sapiens sapiens* and our primate relations are not special, just recent: we are newcomers on the evolutionary stage. Human similarities to other life-forms are far more striking than the differences.[42]

In short, the tendency to overlay a "progressive" or "advancing" tag on phenomena that have appeared more recently on a linear temporal schema still colors both racial and evolutionary classification with a perfidiousness based on religious value systems but also in more secular and scientific settings on species-arrogance and species-segregation.[43]

A critical race studies project in our current moment demands recognition of "new hatreds," proceeding in and through the biological body, without becoming hamstrung in the false requirement of having to pass the newness of those hatreds through an exact overlap with the "older raciology" in order to comment on them. My own project of STS-inflected critical inquiry hypothesizes the affective importance and persistence of older categories of race precisely because of the unsettling of the biological domain by both new technologies such as phylogenetics that, counterintuitively, have the potential to promote deeper awareness of biological populations' interspecies, cross-kingdom entanglement (as does Margulis) and new clinical and cosmetic surgical techniques that make more plastic and revisable phenotypal (external) markers of difference. Asian Americanist scholars, as part of the larger community of critical race theorists, remain highly suspicious of preemptory gestures toward scientifically ushering in a postrace society and thereby politically affirming it (Omi).[44] An Asian Americanist method would more likely insist that biopolitics at this moment creates micro-scale risk factors as new markers of difference *and*, by correlating those new markers to gross anatomical markers read off the body's surface (age, weight, gender, and race/ethnic ancestry among them), reasserts as well the salience of gross anatomical markers such as race.

The Turn of the Twenty-First Century as Racial-Postracial

As Ed Cohen and Roberto Esposito argue, at the heart of biopolitical logic is a paradox: to make or cultivate life, one deadens (other) life or strategically alienates parts of the self. To use a botanical metaphor, biopolitics is the logic of pruning the *nonselected* parts of the socius (or biological organism) so that the *selected* remainder can thrive. For race critics, the challenge has been to explore the extent to which populations (Foucault's "species-being") destined for such pruning are congruent with older classifications of race, or whether indeed race—as synecdoche for exploited, expendable bodies and bodily parts/habits— must make room for finer articulations of how disabled, diseased, or virally positive, impoverished, imprisoned, and otherwise debilitated classes are constituted as the new "aliens" at the center of a, perhaps, postrace era.

Greg Bear's award-winning science fiction, *Blood Music* (1986), both confirms and negates a postracial horizon promised by biotechnology's changes to biology—to the scale of protein, enzyme, and mineral interactions instead of phenotype as that to which society assigns primary socio-political meaning. Here, we return to *zoe* as cellular biology, as "the universal organization of matter" of STS scholars' concern (Fassin), with biopower referring to direct political and technological interference to "bare life" qua cellular processes. Literary contemplations of this *zoe* do not remain the province exclusively of Asian American authors, but, as we shall see, an Asian Americanist critical method of interrogating such texts while primed to their persistent Orientalism can afford key critical insights.

In *Blood Music*, a coding genius, Vergil Ulam, endows his white blood cells with intelligence. These intelligent cells, dubbed "noocytes," rapidly accelerate their learning curve, accomplishing stages of increasing self-organization manifest as transformations to their host's body: Vergil becomes disease-free, more efficient and healthy, as well as sexually virile. Reorganizing Vergil's tissual, skeletal, vascular, and nervous systems, the noocytes eventually dissolve his organismal form. Because they are cellular, the noocytes can travel, via perspiration, to connect with and transform other bodies. They go on to merge into a pliable brown biomass that can morph into anthropomorphic and geometric shapes (even the shape of the prior Vergil or a city-scape). The humans undergoing these final mutations lack anxiety because the noocytes slowly communicate through nonverbal means, to the cortex and other cells, the harmonious feeling of being choreographed into this coursing fluidity—this feeling described as "a music in the blood."

However, Bear's novel also details the fear of those watching their loved ones undergo these transformations. The obstetrician Edward Milligan—not having reached the "music in the blood" stage—equates his wife Gail's and his own transformation by the noocytes to being "topped off with a trillion Chinese" and, in an earlier short story, through nightmares of Gail's rape by a city (loc. 1755, 1373, 4374). Intimate and Orientalized violations provide the iconography of othering— of projecting elsewhere what is a proximal and, indeed, autologous biology: the "alien" unknown noocytes are one's own white blood cells. The intelligent cells are not genetically a distinct species-being, just as the 1.3 billion Chinese of China and Edward Milligan are both "homo sapiens." The cell is not the beastly animal (a species-being apart), but it is also not *bios*. *Zoe*-ification, here, manifests itself as concern with the alienness of one's own cells and anxiety regarding cellular autonomy and agency.

Most significantly, conjuring one's own cells, now micro-chemically amplified in intelligence, as "a trillion Chinese" bespeaks a somaticization into the aggregate level of population, that is, *into a biopolitical lexicon*. Provoking fear are relations of governance no longer clearly controlled by a top-down hierarchy led by the state or the brain but pastorally reorganized along more diffuse pathways of tissual and cellular interactions—a swapping if you will of the cerebral cortex as command and control center for a more distributed and collectivized agency of cells, though not without their own downstream and upstream directionality, order, and hierarchy (Bear, loc. 1261–63, loc. 3317–25). More simply put, the noocytes talking to one's brain cells and convincing them to rebirth as healthier, if microscopic, forms of streaming intelligent cells exemplifies the pastoral relationality that is taking over our bodies all the time and at a scale we cannot see.

The putative "Asiatic" distributed mass actions assigned to the noo-cytes make legible, through a biopolitical metaphor, the dynamism of a shift from an older mode of biopower—the hierarchical and spectacu-lar tactics of singular sovereign agents—to a contemporary biopower dubbed neoliberal, pastoral, relational, capillary, invisible, and distrib-uted, in sum, *not quite "known"* as of yet—*still alien conceptually even as we live it.* Bear's fiction avails itself of the "older" racial classifications—the biopolitics of population aggregates—then to translate into a famil-iar geopolitical and Orientalist idiom his readers' affective attitude toward and understanding of both bioscience's intervention on the level of cellular processes and biopower's aspects as both "pastoral" and intrusive.

Ambivalently delivering on a postracial horizon, then, Bear's fiction uses the vivid metaphor of "a trillion Chinese" even as, across the book's unfolding, the chromatic schema of the five races (red, yellow, black, white, brown) gives way to only one color—brown. The entire human species dissolves into the brown biomass excepting a few "slow" indi-viduals, their syndromes never named, whose brains work differently and who thereby do not choose the "music" of this coursing, collec-tive vitality. We might regard Bear's Orientalist citation of a racialized aggregate (the alien Chinese) simultaneous with his recourse to the brown sameness of all biological matter as a comment on the biotech-nologically transforming social world in which we find ourselves, one that is betwixt and between racial and postracial lexicons.

Likewise concerned with these matters, Kazuo Ishiguro's *Never Let Me Go* (2005) destabilizes the primacy of "chromatic" classifications of populations (Koshy 2001)—what Gilroy calls the "old raciology"—in the formation of new biological categories.[45] Rather than drawing on Orientalism as a mechanism to crystallize fears regarding instabil-ity in the current contours of human adult organismal form, however, Ishiguro's novel conveys the perspective of the minoritized bioavail-able subject, even as that subject appears not to correspond to a vis-ibly racial other. Set in a late 1990s British boarding school where stu-dents from preschool age understand their fates as organ donors who will die before the age of thirty, *Never Let Me Go* deconstructs race in a most unusual way. Ishiguro deliberately characterizes his main characters, the Hailsham students, as clones—biologically identical to "normals"—making clear that their categorization as "other," a distinct species-being whose tissues exist literally to extend the lives of others, is primarily socially constructed. The Hailsham students are figured as both biological similars—cloned and therefore genetically identical— to the nonsubjected population and, simultaneously, biologically alien to that same population due to the clones' mode of reproduction— ontogenesis through somatic cell nuclear transfer rather than hetero- sexual gamete exchange.[46] In other words, their difference falls into that same paradoxical figuration of race difference: genetically groundless yet still an embodied, epigenetic difference entwined with cultural hab- its of eating, histories of segregation and impoverishment, and other socially contingent factors that form the environment of gene expres- sion. As Becky Mansfield observes in the context of food advisories warning poor people of color of their increased methylmercury expo- sure (linked to decreases in intelligence), precisely because they eat greater quantities of fish than "typical" (read: as in the white middle- class diet), "far from dissolving race in favor of individualization, epi- genetic biopolitics" can result in "a transformation and even intensifica- tion of racialization" (Mansfield 355).[47]

At the same time, an epidermal notion of race, whose force and util- ity derives its function from the purported legibility of bodily surfaces, is not absent from Ishiguro's novel. Quite late in the narrative, Miss Emily, the former head of Hailsham, brings such a notion of race into this not-so-futuristic world. Believing that the retired schoolmaster can broker a deferral of their scheduled deaths, the novel's first-person narrator, Kath H., and her lover, Tommy, seek an audience with Miss Emily. At this hearing, Kath and Tommy are informed that she has qui- etly observed their prior forays seeking her out: "'Once not so long ago, I [Miss Emily] passed you sitting on that bench out there, and you cer- tainly didn't recognise me then. You glanced at George, the big Nigerian man pushing me. Oh yes, you had quite a good look at him, and he at you. I didn't say a word, and you didn't know it was me'" (256–57). "Race" is figured visually in the Nigerian eldercare attendant, whose phenotype and origins in a former British colony are key to his figura- tion as a racial other, glimpsed in an instant and named in relation to his servitude.

According to Miss Emily, George's appearance draws Kath's gaze. The incident localizes race: Kath, thus far racially unmarked in the narrative, stares at "the big Nigerian," who stares back. Why does he have a good look at Kath: is it merely because she stares at him, or does he intimate some fellow feeling? If we are to presume Kath's cloning from a normative pale-skinned Briton—as we might surmise from the 2010 movie adaptation (dir. Mark Romanek) featuring actresses Carey Mulligan as Kath H., Keira Knightley as Ruth, and actor Andrew Garfield as Tommy D.—then the species-being into which the Hailsham students have been aggregated remains phenotypically indistinct from the (white British) norms. That is, the clones' "species-being" is not commensurate with race read off the body's surface—the "old raciology" tied to the visual scale of epidermal phenotype. Instead, the markers of the clones' difference are undetectable by way of gross morphology or even microscopic (DNA molecular) detection; this difference is instead tied to processional markers—by the *manner* of reproduction.

But what do we make of George's glancing back? Here, the conditions of this "racial" encounter's retelling become most significant: it is Miss Emily who ascribes to Kath H. and "George the Nigerian" a volley of stares, precisely because Kath herself—not being literate in the racial schema of the wider world from the isolated confines of Hailsham—would not process George's phenotype as socially significant. To be a Hailsham student is to be biopolitically other but invisibly so, more like the closeted lesbian (see Carroll) or the uncultured cockney white than the visibly racial other; and also to be versed in this *invisible difference as the one that matters*. Through Miss Emily's monologue, Ishiguro compares the racializing mode of phenotypal marking to the neoracializing mode of cloned or ontogenetic marking, placing these minoritized patterns on a continuum rather than figuring the latter as a subsumption of or radical break with the former. Miss Emily's narration *constructs* a reciprocal recognition between the two types of species-being. Here, Ishiguro offers an allegory of the temporal overlap but distinctive nonisometry between biopolitical techniques of distinguishing populations via racial phenotype (and histories of colonial occupation keyed to comparative differences in gross anatomical *forms*) and potent techniques of distinguishing individual bodies by mode or *processes* of ontogenesis—via ART (assisted reproductive technologies), via cloning, and via adoption—rather than by any genetic distinctiveness.

Here, it is useful to underscore Alexandra Minna Stern's observation on the shift in eugenics across the twentieth century, from an endeavor overtly racialized prior to and through World War II—i.e., bent on eliminating poor stock figured as immigrants, darker-skinned people, and other biological "defects" (e.g., those with mental disabilities, a subject to which I return in chapter 5)—to one more circumspect about its racial-cleansing dimensions, targeting instead sexuality and sexual perversity through the demonizing of homosexuals, liberated women, et cetera. In other words, part of the shift was in terms of a product-oriented versus process-oriented approach to eugenics. In racialized eugenics, the species-being to be ameliorated and optimized was epitomized by the Nordic-Germanic breed with their disciplined bodies, while in contemporary eugenics, the positive contours (behaviors and traits) of the elect aggregate population are left open ended with attention paid instead to managing the channels of intimacy, intercourse, embryogenesis, gestation, childrearing, and such.

From an evolutionary understanding of race as a national grouping or kin resemblance produced by way of geographic, social, or legal barriers that across centuries have placed limits on exogamy, race becomes a phenomenological and processural determination. Kath H.'s narration makes clear that the Hailsham students live their difference as an ontological and ontogenetic one—they were made differently, even if they are genetically identical to their human possibles. They are experientially racialized by being raised in segregated ghettoes, compared to insects,[48] and cultivated only so as to provide their makers (the uncloned) an efficient bioemporium that advantageously supplies its own hospice-like infrastructure (before donation, all the clones apprentice as "carers" providing the nursing support for those undergoing organ removal). Public health and temperance is the unquestioned norm for the students/clones. In contrast to being (1) pathologized as sources of contagion and disease (i.e., racialized as biological defects with inferior "germ plasm") or (2) disdained as bad medical subjects (i.e., racialized like the Hmong as unscientific thinkers), the Hailsham students are differentiated by their abundant bioavailability and model health. Indeed, by being so obedient to medical surveillance and highly

assimilated to a biopolitical regime of which they are not the beneficiaries, they act akin to model minorities (but in the arena of public health).

On this point, Karen Shimakawa's discussion of "the model minority" figuration of Asian Americans is especially illuminating: "as radically other/foreign to U.S. Americanness as [the U.S. judiciary has]
insisted Asianness is, there has been a consistent, simultaneous rhetoric
(both legal and cultural) of 'melting pot'/'multicultural' inclusion that
envisions Asians as assimilable (or unavoidably assimilated) to U.S.
Americanness."[49] Thus, Shimakawa turns to the psychoanalytic concept
of abjection and to "the oxymoronic term" "model minority," both of
which bespeak the embracing of the minority "as exemplary of the correct embodiment of [privileged personhood/life/*bios*] even as it marks
that group out as distinguishable from 'normal[ity]'. . . by virtue of its
racialized minority status."[50] In Ishiguro's novel, the engendering of the
student/clones' distinct species-being occurs through their performative compulsions toward "the will to health" even as they are destined
for death. This neoracialization is lived/performed as the (stoic) capacity to accept the paradox at the core of biopolitical logic: that "[k]illing
off certain groups of people en masse is . . . a productive, *generative*
activity undertaken for the life of the entire human species."[51]

To reiterate the earlier question, then, "If contemporary biotech
opens up new divisions of populations based not on gross anatomy but
on oftentimes invisible risk factors, does this mean current races will be
superseded by neoraces?" The foregoing readings of *Blood Music* and
Never Let Me Go represent one sort of Asian Americanist response to
that question, one that ultimately affirms the tenacity of biopolitical
modes of aggregating life into a privileged bio-supplementable sector
(epitomized by organ recipients) and a bare bio-available one (epitomized by organ donors). Ishiguro's literary treatment of the structural
ambivalence inherent to biopolitics intensifies pathos at this bioavailable class's limited agency: its "model minority" efforts and performance
can do nothing to the binary structure of *bios* and *zoe*. Also, to recall
Shimakawa's argument, Asianness continually marks the frontier of
Americanness with the criteria of exclusion constantly shifting but the
compulsion to exclude and abject—to draw a boundary—remaining
consistent. Asian American and postcolonial cultural production has

just begun to produce literary imaginings of alternatives to the current biopolitics. Its enunciation as the pruning of the nonselected parts for the betterment of the whole is presented as an inevitable generation and proliferation of minor populations and characteristics (biological traits, bodily habits, and intimacies) destined for killing off. From one perspective, biopolitics construed in this way means that there will always be a necropolitical underbelly of "the imperative to live." Asian Americanist and other critical undertakings wed to a notion of justice will be morally and epistemo-ideologically enjoined to analyze and theorize that underbelly.

On Cosmological and Biospheric Speculations

Earlier I claimed that the biopolitical speaks both to (1) the disciplining of bodies through pastoral, well-intentioned directives on bodily habits and diet; and to (2) the entanglement of the reproductive futures of various populations, such as livestock and humans. Let me clarify now that the second characterization of biopolitics is a counterintuitive one. As rehearsed above and reflected upon as literary tragedy, biopolitics operates through a logic that carves up life into localized and bounded sectors and lets die the nonmodern, nonoptimal biologies, a logic foundational to the idea of enhancing life. This "carving up" epitomizes the epistemology of the clinic.[52] As recapitulated by Cindy Patton, the nineteenth-century clinic was both "a new 'carving up' of things and the principle of their verbalization in a form which we have been accustomed to recognizing as the language of a 'positive science.'"[53] Epitomizing that new "carving up," physicians' interaction with patients shifted over the course of the eighteenth century so that the key question "Where does it hurt?" displaced the more opened-ended query "What is the matter?" in the inauguration of doctoring and treatment. While one can imagine responses to the latter including references to imbalances in the world and the cosmos, "Where does it hurt?" narrows the field of interest to the clinical subject's body. This new clinical gaze was decidedly noncosmological and pridefully so: its novelty, in other words, was staked on a proclaimed (but, we might add, mystified) lack of an overarching theory (e.g., humoral or immunity theory) and "its abandonment of systems";[54] medical discourse was reorganized along the lines of clinical empiricism, with the idea that phenomena would surface as visible, observable evidence.

What insights could be yielded if race critics' interest in biopower and biopolitics started with a critical eye not just toward the management of species-beings (races), but toward the techniques outlined by Patton above—a set of practices wedded to assessing and manipulating human-bodies-and-world primarily in a disentangled and localized manner? An alternative to modernist biopower, in other words, may also lie in a retrieved cosmological orientation (with chapter 4 elaborating further on this retrieved cosmological orientation) in which the extracted part is returned not to a political community of liberal rights-bearing subjects but instead to a planetary commons of entangled biological life.[55] The species comprising this entanglement face each other instrumentally and unevenly, as well as interdependently and reciprocally.

On the level of ideology, Ozeki's *My Year of Meats* offers a good example of the type of fiction that wends its way toward a planetary approach. Its protagonist, Jane, discovers that governmentality works not simply through representative politics (having a voice in the electorate, having visibility in the media) but by seeping into the endocrine and lymph of global populations in an entangled system of capitalism, animal husbandry, gross consumption, empiric expansion, militarism, and atomic science. That system is toxic not only to distant others on another continent, trampled as casualties of war but also to those "at home"—the entire ecosystem thrown out of equilibrium. The terrain of racial justice narrated by Ozeki has shifted from hope in representative democracy and equal distribution of rights and opportunities to something more along the lines of not quite knowing whether an Asian American politics amplifies ecological disequilibrium. Do we want the democratization of meat (of nutritive riches for all), or do we want more responsible husbandry and maintenance of current ecosystems—rather than heading "faux dumb" into future biological mutations linked to hormonal exposure that produce infertility surprises? Ozeki's novel leaves her reader in a whole earth, a less divided-up world of thinking not so much about justice but about how to caretake entangled populations beyond the narrowly defined species-being to which Asian Americans have thought themselves to belong.[56]

2

The Asiatic, Acrobatic, and Aleatory Biologies of Cheng-Chieh Yu's Dance Theater

As the lights come up, an absurd creature stands before you: half folding chair from the waist up and half human from the waist down. With arms outstretched, this creature blindly toes its way forward. On the back wall looms a diagram that this creature cannot see: double rows in a semicircular arch—a dental chart—that resembles as well an amphitheater's seating chart, something to help you, the theatergoer, find your moorings. With this opening tableau, Taiwanese American dancer Cheng-Chieh Yu inducts her audience into the theater, in this case also the mouth—an archway for contesting ideologies about the body's racial and gendered nature, its comeliness, and its interface with technology.

In the first silent minute of *My Father's Teeth in My Mother's Mouth*[1] (hereafter referred to as *My Father's Teeth*), the metal-headed figure (later revealed as Yu) attempts to sit down on a chair, then wanders barefoot into metal shards—dental instruments—scattered downstage right. In this pantomime, the dancer reflects back the audience's own dance as they enter the performance space, seeking their assigned places, finding their (possibly wrong) seats, and encountering jagged material from which they may have to gingerly back away. Yu lifts the chair from atop her head, unfolding and propping it at a 45-degree angle among the metal debris, one of the chair's legs resting on an upright soda can. As the prosthetic remnant of the fleshly dancer, the chair has its legs tilted open, like a jaw hinged wide for clinical inspection or, from another perspective, like the bottom half of a woman braced for a gynecological exam. The image on the back screen switches to that of a Renaissance portrait, the slide closely cropped to reveal a slice of the nose and jaw. Dwarfed by these blown-up images of body parts, Yu grabs a freestanding can, shaking it above her head. Its rattling sound cues up a recorded Laotian folk song, putting an end to the silent opening movement. The dance begins again.

This chapter explores traveling performers, gender ambiguity, and the cosmetic construction of bodies through an examination of dancer Cheng-Chieh Yu's *Bowl Problems, My Father's Teeth,* and *She Said He Said, He Said She Said.* I attend to Yu's humorous playing with her own spectacular body—its being endowed with an extraordinariness due not simply to her skill as a modern dancer but also as a function of a U.S. racialized and gendered history that figures spectatorship of Chinese women as edifyingly entertaining. Linking this dance concert to an earlier showcasing of Chinese femininity—P. T. Barnum's American Museum exhibition of a "Chinese lady," Afong Moy, in 1834—I first argue that Yu's dance theater, likewise, puts the Chinese woman on display in America, but via the dental chart's (qua modern biopower's) universal scrutiny of oral health (the gaze appears less ethnological and more anatomopolitical). Second, I contour medical-dental theater and the ethnological showcase as entwined somatic theaters upon which Yu's choreography draws. Both traditions function as collectivizing occasions for the entertaining conveyance of an anatomical lesson, but each inculcates and relies upon distinct modes of sympathetic witness. Third, I trace the movements of Yu's body across her dance, reading also for their story of medical technique, from surgical pushing and pulling (barbaric extraction) to recombinatory dicing and reading (alluding to the technologies of assisted reproduction and regenerative medicine).

"Dance is often said to be a way of expressing the unspeakable," writes Joseph Roach in his development of the idea of the kinesthetic imagination.[2] As announced by the title of the work, the central image of Yu's performance is the mouth, and Peter Melville's set design makes the stage a simulacrum of an open maw. Despite its constitutive role in speech, the mouth—especially if unhampered by structural defects—remains a taken-for-granted speaking tool, its own materiality receding as attention is directed to the verbal meanings issuing from it. Across her work, Yu has grappled with the privileged place accorded to speech, verbalization, and textuality over and against dance and choreography. In the collaborative work *She Said He Said, He Said She Said* (2005), Yu

Fig. 2.1. Johnny Tu and Cheng-Chieh Yu in *She Said He Said, He Said She Said* (Highways Performance Space, 2005). *Photo by Fred Ho.*

and a male partner, Johnny Tu, position themselves in front of standing microphones, mutely pantomiming a politician or professor emphatically holding forth (see http://vimeo.com/73720943). As the choreography unfolds, the performers recast their microphones as partners in a four-way contact improvisation.

In the 2003 performance of *My Father's Teeth*, Yu also diminishes the singular importance of speech as both a privileged mode and a privileged metaphor for self-expression. She performs, without speaking, the body's multiple conscriptions by discourses of genetics, gender, straightness, and exoticism. As the teeth come into rattling prominence, the dancer reflects both on the cultural construction of a well-turned, speaking apparatus and, as we shall see, on the economic fetish of somatic (germinal) disassembly and reassembly. In this 2003 multi-media production, Yu stages the mouth as a trap of reproductive and national ideologies through which the body is formulated according to a straight aesthetics, referring literally to the lining up of white teeth but also to the instilling of a germinal reproductive mandate, and to the demand for a singular correspondence between bodies and nations. Though speech is not wholly absent (a recorded tape of a consultation with Yu's dentist overplays one section of the dance), the performance's main means of "expressing the unspeakable" is through its highly compressed use of props, through sound and visual effects, and through Yu's choreographed movements on stage, inflected as they are with a sensibility both graceful and absurdist.

Starting with a prior performance called *Bowl Problems,* first performed in 1999, Yu's artistic endeavors have been part of a triangular international nexus of diplomacy and strategic alliance involving the United States and the "two Chinas"—the People's Republic of China (PRC) and the Republic of China in Taiwan (ROC), the latter two negotiating issues of national sovereignty, singularity, and legitimate governance through discourses about traveling performers. Through my discussion of *Bowl Problems,* I clarify the transnational dimensions of the artist's feminist dance theater, which include the purported Chinese bodily capacity not so much to endure pain and suffering with calmness (as Hayot has traced in *The Hypothetical Mandarin,* and as partly discussed in the introduction), as to wow with its plasticity and flexibility.[3] I then turn to the way in which modern orthodontics provides Yu the occasion to reflect upon the historical overlap of ethnological and medical theaters as well as their increasing schism from the mid-twentieth century onward—a period, arguably, no longer as concerned with national rivalry and national projects of health. As Nikolas Rose argues in *The Politics of Life Itself,* neoliberalism's pastoral modes of biopower have rendered the will to health a more private affair in the late twentieth to early twenty-first centuries. Here, I inquire into the continuing salience of Asiatic biologies to make intelligible a contemporary biopower executed via anatomopolitics in two aspects: (1) the disciplined pursuit of personal health and cosmetic optimization; and (2) the cultural inculcation toward a particular gendered unfolding of one's life story. Finally, from the spectacularly crude technique of tooth extraction to the microscopically refined technique (and sub-cellular scale) of recombinatory dicing and reading, the movements of Yu's body across her dance adumbrate the course (and loci) of medical innovation. As if working around the double bind of both being denied and being gifted with the compassionate witness of her Western audi-ence, Yu's choreography, I argue, concludes with an image of (seeming) self-governance and autotelic generativity (though also undercut by a slide emphasizing somatic disintegration). This dancing medical the-ater performs the Asian (American) woman suspended in a stage of nascent transformability.

Circuses and Sympathy

From 1990 through 2010, Yu established herself as an accomplished choreographer with a politically inflected, comic sensibility. In 1999, in response to a commission from the Taipei Theater in New York, Yu created the irreverent *Bowl Problems*, featuring four Asian women dressed in traditional acrobat attire, who performed a variation on that entertaining staple, the Pagoda of Bowls. A theatrical pamphlet pub-lished in 1982 from Beijing announces that this "graceful and [skillful] balancing act" goes as far back as the Han Dynasty (206 BC–220 AD): 2,000-year-old tombs contain brick carvings "showing a handstand fig-ure with a pagoda of bowls."[4] After the Communist Revolution in 1949 and in light of the modernizing energies of the Cultural Revolution, however, traditional entertainments, such as Pagoda of Bowls, were also subject to critique and revision in the PRC (more on this in a moment). Given these circumstances, performers such as the Li Tong Hua Acro-bats (李棠華特技團), a troupe founded in 1945 in Shanghai but rees-tablished with the Nationalist government in Taiwan after 1949, sought to safeguard "Chinese" national culture through the preservation of tra-ditional folk arts, e.g., acrobatics.

Scandalously breaching into this realm of Chinese tradition, Yu cre-ated the irreverent *Bowl Problems*. With plastered smiles that are more grim than grinning, the four female "acrobats" in this piece execute a few simple moves—throwing, catching, and balancing bowls—then the vessels begin dropping to the floor. In a hilarious sequence, two women

Fig. 2.2. Publicity shot for *Bowl Problems* (2004). *Photo by Peter Melville.*

stack their bodies back-to-back, head to the other's toe, so that the
head of one and the legs of the other together simulate a contortionist's
single body, her legs looped over her ears. The ensemble of Taiwanese
and Korean American artists cast in this performance offers the audience only a poor copy of a "real" Chinese acrobatic troupe, a failing and
phony re-creation of its pyramid aesthetics—its stacks of both persons
and dishes.

Yu was inspired to create *Bowl Problems* as a rejoinder to presumptions about her skills based on superficial typecasting by American
choreographers: "When I was living in New York, there were a lot of
foreign dancers who were really good. And there I was . . . looking like
this [gesturing toward her face], and I had one choreographer pull my
leg up [past the head] saying 'Let's see those amazing Chinese moves.'"[5]
As a witty response to such racial stereotyping, *Bowl Problems* shows
the ensemble first extending, however fraudulently, the stock image of
their amazing Chinese moves, but then as the bowls start to fall, the
amazement of the audience is not so much dashed as transferred to the
structure of the entertainment itself. Instead of the wondrous sight of
extraordinary bodies, then, the audience is treated to the astonished

witnessing on the part of the performers themselves: their incredulousness is directed at both their corporeal (in)capacities and their placement within an entertainment not structurally dissimilar from a dog and pony show. From another perspective, *Bowl Problems* shines a spotlight on the limberness of youth prolonged across time, producing the perpetually girlish Chinese acrobat. At this time in her late thirties to early forties, Yu exploits the comic potential of what happens when such idealized, uniform femininity cracks and topples upon the process of aging as well as the vagaries of diasporic duplication.

The original venue for *Bowl Problems*, the Taipei Theater in New York, also frames its feminist aesthetics within a stormy transnational context in which culture (and the Chinese acrobat as cultural representative) becomes an instrument of political maneuvering. Formerly part of the Chinese Information and Cultural Center, itself a division of the Taipei Economic and Cultural Office (TECO) in New York, the Taipei Theater is a Taiwanese-funded organization, established in 1991, and designed to promote cultural exchange and friendship between the United States and the ROC in the *absence* of formal diplomatic relations.[6] The fallen women of Yu's acrobatic troupe thus mock not only an American audience's desire to see and be astounded by Chinese automated precision but also the entire apparatus whereby nations reinvent themselves and shore up their legitimacy by way of their national theaters.

In Fu Qifeng's *Chinese Acrobatics through the Ages*, the Beijing-based author quotes 1950s Premier Zhou Enlai's dictum: "Acrobatics should give people an aesthetic appreciation and a pleasant sensation. Neither deformity nor excessive stimulus should be used to attract the audience" (105). Fu follows this maxim with a list of the many acts that were banned upon the founding of New China: "Climbing a Mountain of Knives," "Dismantling a Human Body into Eight Pieces," "Swallowing a Sword," "Rolling a Board Studded with Nails," "Eating an Electric Bulb," "Dancing on Broken Pieces of Glass," "Swallowing Five Poisonous Creatures" (scorpion, viper, centipede, house lizard, and toad), and "A Snake Worms into Eyes, Ears, Nostrils and Mouth" (105). Intended to suggest the immiseration of itinerant acrobats in the late Qing dynasty (when the mainland was overrun by foreign imperialists), this list of banned acts prompts Zhou's revisions to acrobatic repertoire, which, in turn, bespeak the modernization of Chinese culture taking place in the second half of the twentieth century. In addition, this list of self-inflicted torture harkens back to the political economy of pain and suffering that Eric Hayot examines with respect to Westerners' astonishment at the Chinese capacity to undergo physical duress with no observable signs of discomfort.[7]

According to Hayot, Chinese pain and suffering—or, put another way, the more placid and calm repertoire by which nineteenth-century Chinese presented and managed bodily pain, as compared to the amplified grimaces and groans associated with Westerners—riveted European philosophers and Western photojournalists and doctors in the nineteenth and twentieth centuries. The missionary surgeon Peter Parker, who conducted *nonanesthetized* surgeries on Chinese patients in the 1830s through 1850s, records in his diary that Chinese children undergoing harelip repairs are "almost insensible to [the] pain," that a woman undergoing removal of a cancerous breast "scarcely utters a groan during the extirpation," and that the patient Leang Yen, slotted for arm amputation, "fully . . . contemn[s] the idea of pain . . . [and] at the moment of sawing bone [inquires] when that part of the process would take place.'"[8]

Besides affirming the socio-cultural relativity of what we think of as a verifiable human universal—bodily pain—Hayot's argument establishes personhood as emerging in a social and ethical economy of affective recognition that hinges upon alienable (and thereby exchangeable) affects—that is, energetic intensities and qualified styles of emoting. We can think of the money or species equivalent in this economy as care and sympathy, with the commodity being another's culturally specific "brand" of external or surfaceable indices of pain. Cultural

protocols establish a relationship between what one might call the descriptive "evidence" of pain—the visible or invisible wound—and the narrative "expression" of it, in which legitimate expressions earn the subject the right to have his or her pain recognized, tended to, sympathized with, and the like, and the illegitimate ones are written off as complaints or not recognized at all.[9]

Acrobatic entertainments, of course, suspend those protocols of legitimate recognition, with the audience left to marvel at the incredible discipline and virtuosity—exhibited as performed ease—when the flesh is contorted or punctured with knives and other sharp instruments. The Western attitude of amazement at Chinese endurance—i.e., appearance of equanimity and calm exterior while the body is being plied pain-fully—treats the Chinese as if they were all acrobats; in other words, it solidifies a repertoire and economy of the circus (and freak show), rather than a sentimental economy of moral witness as the proper one in which to regard Chinese embodied (but nonamplified) suffering.[10]

Fu's list of banned acrobatic acts also reveals the way in which Chi-nese national pride is aligned with a spectatorial position that is aes-thetically appreciative and pleased rather than excessively aroused (i.e., responsive to amplified anguish as in the American sentimental tradi-tion). The right relation between the nation and its civic performer—referring here to both the acrobat and the audience for whom she per-forms—is one of moderation and reciprocity. The performer ought not to do anything to overexcite the passions in her spectators (I will return to this idea of affective moderation in chapter 5). Breaching into overstimulation are those displays that capitalize on the body's orifices, its points of nonintegrity or disintegration—e.g., snake worming into eyes or human body dismantling into eight pieces. Such excessiveness is threatening to the nation precisely because of its implied emphasis on the vulnerability of the body politic—its capacity to disintegrate, to be punctured, or to merge to the point of perilous indistinction with another member nation or species-being, as in "Swallowing Five Poi-sonous Creatures." Spectacles of national disintegration must be seques-tered from view, a logic that also underwrites the anxiety toward having more than one China. In the same way that the excessive stimulus of seeing a body dismantled would render a citizenry overwrought by the spectacle of its nonintegrity (its being menaced by the challenge to its singularity), China imagines the ROC as, likewise, a renegade acrobatic act—an improper performance of the nation.

Burlesquing pre-Communist Chinese tradition and adopting an ironized stance toward Qing decadence, *Bowl Problems*, from one per-spective, remains in league with the People's Republic's call for mod-eration in entertainment as one hallmark of modernity. But because of its commission under the auspices of the Taiwanese TECO, the show also challenges Red China's singular claims of modernized succession to dynastic rule. Overlaying *Bowl Problems*, these international dramas, pivoting on national and gendered forms of performed virtuosity and performed suffering, contort the Asian female's multiply instrumental body into a kind of monstrous beast or pretzeled pose. In her more subtly comedic work on the topic of American dentistry, Yu delves further into the desire for highly polished bodies who are pressed into the service not of proving the nation's integrity against diasporic and duplicative dis-integration, as much as testifying to the biopolitical modes of managing life itself.

My Father's Teeth in Five Parts

Much of the humor of *My Father's Teeth* emerges from the juxtaposition of high and low—from the fact that it is a meticulously rehearsed, sumptuously produced performance devoted to crooked teeth. The dancer's movements on stage capitalize upon a series of inversions, as in the opening sequence in which Yu switches the bottom-top relation between chair and person—the chair sitting *atop* the performer. Such inversions are not only comical but also suggestive of Yu's overturning the primacy of corporeal embodiment (her fleshly dancing body) as it competes with the socio-technological apparatus crowding upon her. I refer, here, both metaphorically to the cultural codes of dentistry and the proper gendered life cycle that press upon the performing subject— here the solo dancer, Yu—and more literally to the audio-visual components of the production—e.g., loud sound effects of hammering and drilling, as well as massive slide projections of dental charts, extracted molars, and the quattrocento aesthetic "masterpiece," Leonardo Da Vinci's *Mona Lisa*.[11]

When I first began exploring *My Father's Teeth*, I was very much persuaded that a racial reading of this work was a matter of drawing out the way this dance contested cultural codes of "straightness and whiteness" enshrined in U.S. dental practices. Pursuing this racial reading, however, left unexplained certain aspects of the performance: its emphasis on the gendered life span and its kinesthetic evocation of two nonnormative figures of generativity, that of the hermaphrodite and that of the extractable and reimplantable stem cell. A facile tension infused my prior approach, situated as it was between the dueling propositions that

Fig. 2.3. Cheng-Chieh Yu performing *My Father's Teeth in My Mother's Mouth* (2001) at St. Mark's Church in New York. *Photo by Tom Brazil. Courtesy of Cheng-Chieh Yu.*

this dance was really about race—about U.S. social codes regarding cosmetic beauty hailing the immigrant—or that it was really about a more broadly construed biosociality and will to health that were not racially specific. What follows is an attempt to model another critical approach that speaks to that tension but doesn't become incapacitated by it. Here, I frame Yu's dance as one very much concerned with being biologically profiled but in ways not overtly calling forth an older "chromatic" typology of race (black, white, yellow, red, brown) and thereby changing the terms of "racial" determinants so that cultural comparisons of phenotype begin to hold less importance than the tracking of populations by way of their less outwardly visible lifestyle defects (nonoptimal nutrition, illness, pharmaceutical use, etc.). Such tracking, in turn, produces other categories of somatic difference (other kinds of biosocial groupings) that may or may not overlap with racial ones. Rather than trying to ignore the work's central fixation on biological reproduction and genetics in order to produce a racialized reading of this dance that is politically correct by not being biologically essentialist, I endeavor an

Asian Americanist approach to the same work that is attentive to the biological—that, in fact, places the biological at its core.

To begin, let me briefly outline the overall structure of *My Father's Teeth*, which falls roughly into five sections. Following the silent prologue (described in the opening paragraphs of this chapter) in which the dancer foreshadows the show's major movements—inversions, balancing, gravitational swoops or spills from high to low—and its props—dental instruments, metal chairs, and tin cans—Yu launches into a series of movements timed to a Laotian courtship duet, with male and female vocals alternating. In sync with the male voice, Yu performs, stage right, masculinity writ large, the eponymous "father" of her title enacted as a muscular stomping that settles into a deep horse stance, with Yu intermittently adjusting her pants and cupping the genitals. As the female singer retorts, Yu moves stage left, playing the coquette in stylized flourishes reminiscent of Balinese court dance, curtsying slowly onto a chair and making a big show of adjusting the bra straps. Overlaying the folk duet are the whirring sounds of a drill powering on and off. This section of the dance ends with Yu pushing a series of haphazardly overturned chairs into a tight cluster, a visual allegory of the straightening of her teeth.

Next follows a sequence evoking the tortures of early dentistry, with the dancer—to the sounds of sledgehammers chipping away at concrete—tilting back precariously on the hind legs of a chair placed downstage left, her face illuminated by a hot white spotlight. Her mouth is held wide in a grimace of distress, while her legs and arms flail. Mimed in these hinged and swinging body parts is the dental patient awaiting the tooth puller's forceps, but also the birthing mother in the throes of labor. When the chair slips backward, upending the performer's body, Yu magically lands on her hands, tumbling into a set of cartwheels that takes her to the fourth sequence, the one most overtly alluding to her career as a highly trained dancer *and* as an exotic spectacle.

In a reiteration of the amazing moves scandalously mocked in *Bowl Problems*, Yu balances upside down on a folding chair (fig. 2.4), and in this inverted position, grabs a can, rattles it, and rolls six molars onto the floor, then rolls her body off the chair, to strike her lucky number— a grand finale pose. Her furious open-mouthed smile plastered on her face (and held several beats too long) elicits an initial hearty laughter

Fig. 2.4. Part 4 of *My Father's Teeth in My Mother's Mouth*. The dancer's face eats the metal. Dental instruments in the left foreground. Conversation with Dr. Cutler plays in the background. *Photo by Tom Brazil. Courtesy of Cheng-Chieh Yu.*

from the audience that fades into embarassed coughs.[12] Before ending this sequence, Yu, right side up, remounts the chair, and through a prolonged abdominal crunch, holds her feet close to her face as she rotates slowly, her toes distorted into the shapes of "lotus blossoms" (fig. 2.5).[13] As she steps off the chair, her foot slips into an open tin can (ballet slipper), with Yu then walking in the hobbled, weight-in-the-heel fashion of ballerinas in toe shoes, as if to equate the French high art practice of crushing the feet *en pointe* with the American dental practice of bracing the teeth in metal bands, and both of these with the twenty-first-century-BC-up-through-Qing-dynasty Han[14] female practice of binding the feet (shaping the soma through deliberate stunting of growth—i.e., the deadening of tissue by the closing off of blood vessels). All three have, at some point in time, become aesthetic fetishes or popular entertainments for a Western audience.

In *My Father's Teeth*'s fifth and final section, the choreography combines the musical associations of part 2 (i.e., the courtship of father and mother ending in the straight line) with the signature move from part 4: the scattering of extracted teeth through the roll of the dice. To a reprise of the Laotian duet, Yu performs an elaborate game of shooting "dice" (teeth) from tin cans, but this time the "hand" that shoots is also the genitals. Having attached one tin can at her groin, Yu rises on one leg, the dangling dildo and/or vaginal vessel emitting a shower of white debris onto the floor, suggesting both the vagina dentata and seminal ejaculate (fig. 2.6). As the dancer throws and scoops, she rattles the cans on the floor, regathering these body parts back into the vessels. At one point, she raises the jangling can to her lips as if to drink and recapture those loose molars in her mouth. Posing in profile, one tin vessel between her legs and the other suctioned to her mouth, Yu strikes a figure both technologically optimized and bound or muted (fig. 2.7). She then places the cans on the floor, scatters teeth on that same surface, and backs away, turning upstage toward an illuminated slide of six loose molars atop a dental chart. Lights fade.

We might begin by framing *My Father's Teeth* as an autoethnographic performance of racial identity told in relation to and through technologies of movement (cf. Pratt).[15] The performance engages movement on several scales: there is the microphysical rearrangement and

Fig. 2.5. *My Father's Teeth in My Mother's Mouth.* Lotus blossoms. Still shot from videotape of performance at the Japanese American Culture and Community Center, Los Angeles. *Courtesy of Cheng-Chieh Yu.*

Fig. 2.6. Part 5 of *My Father's Teeth in My Mother's Mouth*.
Teeth shower down from can at groin. Still shot from video-
tape of performance at the Japanese American Culture and
Community Center, Los Angeles. *Courtesy of Cheng-Chieh Yu.*

replacement of teeth enabled by modern orthodontics as well as the
expansive movement of individuals across national borders facilitated
by air travel, with both of these mobilities kinesthetically conjured by
way of the dancer's movements on the stage. In the subtle movement of
teeth and the transport of whole bodies across the globe, technologies
of movement are thought to enhance individual embodiment, by way
of extending function: cosmetically improving the person's capacity to
take in the world, or temporally quickening and spatially expanding the
range of things to take in. This is the dream of technology (orthodontia, airplanes) as that which more-than-completes the subsistence body.
However, for the Asian immigrant coming to the United States, this
movement also means inhabiting a marked corporeality that is figured
as both biologically superhuman (with "amazing moves") and primitive,
as evidenced by crooked teeth. (The very problem of not having straight
teeth has a distinct national dimension, as Americans are known the
world over for their perfect dental alignments.) From one aspect, then,
Yu's dance alludes to the Asiatic who through her great capacity to suffer contortions—as in part 2's depiction of dental torture—embodies
not so much the preferred labor of Fordist capital but rather the vigilant
caretaker of the self's healthy and hygienic future, one maintained (or

Fig. 2.7. *My Father's Teeth in My Mother's Mouth*. Penultimate pose. Still shot from videotape of performance at the Japanese American Culture and Community Center, Los Angeles. *Courtesy of Cheng-Chieh Yu.*

risk mitigated) by proliferating medical-dental procedures: cleanings, polishings, pickings, flossings, periodontal and orthodontic interventions, and eventually prosthetic bridges, dentures, caps, and crowns. In this way, the choreographer updates and feminizes Hayot's analysis of the coolie body, the Asiatic who through her contortionist capacity to bear twisting and reshaping embodies the preferred laborer of post-Fordist flexible accumulation, the "whatever" identity that must constantly adjust, mutate, and transform again. Drawing upon her training as a modern dancer and martial artist,[16] Yu thus explores the convergence of virtuosic labor with (racialized and feminized) servile and cosmetic-assimilationist labor that keeps intact boundaries both around and within the nation.

Anatomical Theaters: Ethnological Showcase and Early Dentistry

As her conjuring of Chinese bound feet makes clear, Yu is also overtly concerned with the fetishizing spectatorship of Asian women's bodies. *My Father's Teeth* speaks to a history of Asian (women) put on display in the United States for the edification and amusement of whites.[17]

In 1834, P. T. Barnum's American Museum exhibited a "Chinese lady," Afong Moy, dressed in upper-class regalia and exhibited among fine Chinese furnishings. According to Robert Lee, the total effect of this living diorama was to perform "Chineseness" at various venues, including the Brooklyn Institute, the City Saloon in New York, and Peale's Philadelphia Museum.[18] In spite of these perambulations, Afong Moy, or Chineseness, always traveled in context—the Chinese lady's placement among exotic comestibles suggesting an organic and reassuring correspondence between people and the material goods they produce, the total portrait confirming an impeccable geopolitical order in which nations, persons, and culture affirm their congruency—all under one roof and monolithically saying the same thing (Gellner's *Nations and Nationalism*).[19]

Yu's dance theater, likewise, puts the Asian woman on display in America, but through a hyperbolic visualization of her oral interiority, and through an emphasis on her physical and psychic lability (that which predisposes her to easy assimilation to Western embodied norms). In *My Father's Teeth*, there is no longer the clear placement of the Chinese woman among Chinese things—the singular correspondence of person to culture and nation cannot be presumed. Put another way, this mode of combined clinical and ethnological entertainment does not confirm national boundaries between things and persons Chinese as distinct from things and persons American. As suggested in my discussion of *Bowl Problems*, the disarticulation of a person from cultural items indexed to his/her national (natal) identity is partly due to the nonsingularity of the national referent China, itself, fractured into the PRC, the ROC, as well as Hong Kong (pre-handover) and the sites of diasporic Chinese settlement across the globe.

While Barnum's exhibit pierced the privacy of the Chinese living room, the medical apparatus here probes the person, enlarging her points of entry but in a way not specific to race, or so it seems. The dental chart bespeaks a universal application of biopower's surveillance techniques, with all bodies—not just those marked by gender and race—mapped at the mouth. One of the inspirations for *My Father's Teeth* was the dancer's visit to her dentist, Bradley Cutler. A recording of their conversation overdubs part 4 of the dance (the section where Yu balances upside down on a chair), with Dr. Cutler's stressing the exactitude of the teeth's manifestation of "environmental insults," for instance, the effects of antibiotic intake, exposure to "high fever," and the damage due to inadequate protein in the diet: "You can look at teeth and see defects in certain places, and you can know at what stage of life the defect occurred. Because it's like the rings in a tree. You can follow the defect to different heights of the tooth," Cutler says.

Placing herself before a magnified dental chart projected onto the upstage wall (the way the dance begins and ends), Yu literalizes the way she both is positioned and positions herself in relation to this power-knowledge formation of simultaneous gross abstraction—where all bodies are made strange by visualization technologies—and excessive specification—where each body is encoded by the exactness of its hygienic prophylaxis and epigenetic exposures (i.e., the timing of food/nutrients important to metabolism and cellular growth).[20] Additionally, the tinkling of the dental instruments as Yu walks barefoot over them and the magnified sound effects of drilling and hammering—these become the auditory echo of a biopolitical governmentality that seems larger than oneself but that also, paradoxically, exercises its pastoral power not through grand spectacles of death (execution) but through smaller, incessant private surgeries that would enhance life. The effects of these governmental strategies of late modernity are, from one aspect, ambiguous with respect to their specific racialization of Asian Americans. This apparatus of biopower is not specific to what performance scholar Karen Shimakawa calls the "national abjection" of Asians but catches all subjects (or at least those with dental insurance) in its panoptic orders.

Moreover, while the dentistry that Dr. Cutler practices is decidedly late modern in its mode of governmentality—his recorded consultation exemplary of the biopolitical will to health practiced in the privacy of the doctor's office—*My Father's Teeth* also revives the performative history of medicine, with that precursor to modern dentistry—the "art of tooth-pulling"—very much a public affair: "Up to the nineteenth century tooth-pulling was for the great majority of Europeans a public event, performed in public, outdoors, attended by an audience; it was part sacrificial drama, part street or fairground entertainment, part judicial execution."[21] In its seventeenth-century incarnation, this early dental spectacle collectivized those gathered in a quasi-religious

Fig. 2.8. *My Father's Teeth in My Mother's Mouth.* Dental chart
looms in the background. *Courtesy of Cheng-Chieh Yu.*

ritual intended to uproot a sinful desire or sweet indulgence, somaticized in the worm of lust buried deep in the tooth. Yu's production harkens to this early modern theater by way of the dice play with extracted
molars, even as the overall dance is occasioned by her interface with
orthodontia—not the pulling of teeth but the regularization of their
ungapped arrangement.[22] The proleptic desire to intervene earlier and
earlier to prevent tooth decay and tooth pulling is exemplified not only
in orthodontia but also in the idea of manipulating the genetic codes
for skin, teeth, and hair, if one could (an anticipatory or proleptic desire
that will inform my discussion of Margaret Cho in chapter 3).

While artistic renderings of tooth drawing (such as those by Flemish,
Dutch, and French painters Theodore Rombouts [1597–1637], Jan Steen
[1626–1679], and Adolphe Eugene Gabriel Roehn [1780–1867]) figure
it as exemplary of the barbarism and charlatan practices of itinerant
"early dentists" from which we are happy to have progressed, less notice
has been paid to how the affective force of these live theaters reminded
the onlookers in a visceral fashion of their fleshly continuity with the
displayed body of the patient. These carnivalesque gatherings focused
on the flesh and teeth of the very folk attendees who awaited the professional services of itinerant apothecaries and dentists. In other words, a
communalism extended between the onlookers and the dental patient.

After the somatic and spiritual extraction (of the aching tooth), the operable embodied subject would be reintegrated into the fold. This is not to understate the lower-class markers of those who underwent public tooth pulling. Wealthier sorts (e.g., Queen Elizabeth I) had access to tooth pullers in their private chambers.[23] Nevertheless, according to David Kunzle, public dental rituals did evoke sympathy for the patients both as fellow persons whose traditional remedies and knowledge were being uprooted by historical changes (e.g., professionalization of the healing arts) and as persons whose lack of funds rendered them only the external, visible icons of conditions plaguing all classes (i.e., tooth decay and loss)—an early modern intimation of a less divided-up biosociality, if you will.

To a Taiwanese audience, Yu's evocation of public dentistry would also call to mind the hybrid spiritual and medical conversion practices of Canadian Presbyterian missionary George Leslie Mackay who migrated to Taiwan in 1871. Acting as an itinerant dentist and establisher of churches, hospitals, and educational institutions, Mackay later

Fig. 2.9. Protestant missionary and itinerant dentist, George Leslie Mackay, pulling teeth in Taiwan in the late nineteenth and early twentieth centuries. *Courtesy of Mackay Memorial Hospital, Taipei, Taiwan.*

published the missionary ethnography *From Far Formosa* (1896). He also married a Taiwanese aboriginal woman, with whom he had three children. It is estimated that Mackay pulled twenty-one thousand teeth while in Taiwan,[24] his doctoring part of his evangelical mission to tend to the body and spirit of the Taiwanese.[25]

With its protocol of spectatorial sympathy extended from the public witness (whether European carnival attendee or Formosan with a toothache) to the operable suffering body, the theater of public dentistry greatly contrasts that of the ethnological theater that put racial exotics and "freaks" on display in Europe and the Americas in the nineteenth and early twentieth centuries. World Fairs, while mingling Europeans and Anglo American settlers to the United States with Asian, African, indigenous, and other tropical subjects, also stressed the distance between the fair-going audience and the displayed (colored, foreign) body.[26] Even though not a stone's throw away from the Igorot men come to America as part of the Philippine Reservation at the 1904 Louisiana Purchase Exposition in St. Louis,[27] the white fair-going audience could not be affectively (sympathetically) farther away.[28] Late-nineteenth- and early-twentieth-century World's Fairs and sideshow amusements had their eyes trained on extraordinary somatic anomalies (e.g., giants, dwarves) and exotic specimens (e.g., foreigners), the point being not to "cure" these bodies of their difference (qua sufferance of imperial occupation and dependency) but *to demarcate* the invisible gawker, who "actively" sees but cannot be seen, from the freakish non-normate body, who seems not to see but only, passively and object-like, to be seen. The theatrical frame of ethnological showcases educated the audience in this way of seeing, inculcating a lesson in the legibility (somatic surface) of differences, rather than extending a worldview in which interiorized characteristics (whether faith based or physiological) are key to communal boundaries.

The exhibit of Afong Moy falls into the category of ethnological showcase. Its theatrical-pedagogic frame inculcated a lesson in the legibility of (cultural, national, behavioral) differences manifested on the exterior of the body. It is worth repeating that ethnological showcases teach the onlooker not strictly about the exotic specimens in their replica environments but also about how to "know" by seeing difference. While I here emphasize the continuity between the contexts of

Fig. 2. 10. White onlookers watch Igorot singers at the 1904 St. Louis World's Fair. *Photo by Jessie Tarbox Beals. Courtesy of the Missouri History Museum, St. Louis.*

reception characterizing dancer Yu's *My Father's Teeth* and the ethnological theater, it is also the case that as the choreographer of *My Father's Teeth*, Yu (Barnum-like) herself evokes ethnological theater in her use of a Laotian folk duet to accompany a heterosexual courtship dance, comprised of one part stomping primitive and one part courtly lady. Collectivization happens via these caricatured bodies but *not across and through them* (in empathetic identification with them). One can know these bodies—see their distinctiveness—but not ontologically feel their interrelatedness to the distanced and distancing "eye" one has become. In contrast to the alienation effects of ethnological showcases teaching the onlooker to "know" by seeing difference, the earlier tooth-pulling theaters were more *onto-epistemological*, emphasizing the seamlessness of watching suffering, being/becoming one who suffered, and knowing suffering as this "felt" porousness and changing embodied state.

What then do we make of Yu's bid to display for her audience not simply the final product of orthodontic success—an ungapped white smile—but the arduous and painful process of getting there? In the sections of her dance where she tilts back on a chair and mimes enduring the pangs of nonanesthetized dental work (fig. 2.8), is the aim to solicit sympathy from the spectator against the distanced seeing invited in the preceding more ethnological section—the dance choreographed to the Laotian duet? Speculative answers to these questions are further complicated by the economy of sympathetic witness between Westerners and the Chinese as previously outlined by both Hayot and Rey Chow.

To recapitulate, in his study of how Chinese pain riveted Westerners in the nineteenth and twentieth centuries, Hayot contours the way in which personhood emerges in a social and ethical economy of affective (sympathetic) recognition that hinges upon externalized styles of emoting. Hayot details the emergence of this political economy of compassion in a specific period in which the British hankering for tea and, more broadly speaking, the West's hunger for Chinese material goods (the luxurious objects such as displayed in the pavilions of the 1904 World's Fair) engendered trade deficits. The British, for their part, scrambled to find domestically produced fashions and commodities that the Chinese might want in exchange. The Chinese rejected these goods, "the Qianlong emperor famously [writing] 'We have never valued ingenious articles, nor do we have the slightest need of your country's manufactures'";[29] China demanded only silver as payment. However, as Hayot argues, what the Chinese could not reject because it was given as a gift was sympathy for Chinese suffering (one didn't need Chinese consent to give it). Contouring the "compensatory relationship between the economic and the sympathetic," Hayot writes, "the idea of sympathy itself . . . ought to be thought [of] in relation to the politics of international trade as a kind of affective and cultural surplus, as though compassion itself were a good whose excess in the British Isles would allow it to be sent, along with British silver, to the Far East."[30] If the British were not as successful as China in creating tradeable objects, what they had in great supply were these feelings of pity, empathy, and humane concern, feelings that were newly being constructed as "universal" (global) sentiments. With respect to contemporary American denouncements of human rights abuses in China, Rey Chow draws out how the United States, extending this British-European tradition of leveraging a comparative "greater compassion" for the suffering of others than demonstrated by the Chinese themselves, rhetorically conjures America's own noble sentiments (its desire to rescue abused, imprisoned, tortured, or "bound" women and minorities from abusive governments) as moral justification for its armed occupations, military and economic, across the globe.[31]

While part 3 of Yu's dance (the pantomime of duress at the clinic), to my mind, does induce empathetic witnessing of Yu's precarious embodiment as a clinical and female subject undergoing assimilationist (normalizing cosmetic) work, her dance literally cartwheels away from that affective bid for sympathy. My argument, here, is that we can only understand this oscillation toward and away from soliciting sympathetic witness by way of recognizing Yu's being situated in the double bind of the American sentimental economy. On the one hand, this sentimental protocol would humanize her (the exotic other) through acknowledging her appropriate externalized display of "suffering": her tense and precarious holding open of both mouth and legs as she tilts way back (part 3 of the dance). On the other hand, that sentimental economy only elevates her American audience's spectatorial compassion by condemning Chinese national character precisely as that which

Fig. 2.11. Part 3 of *My Father's Teeth in My Mother's Mouth.*
Awaiting the dental or obstetrical forceps. Still shot from videotape of performance at the Japanese American Culture and Community Center, Los Angeles. *Courtesy of Cheng-Chieh Yu.*

remains dispassionate not simply in the endurance of pain but in the witnessing of others' pain. To accept the gift of the West(erner)'s compassionate witness is to accept, simultaneously, the premise of the Chinese/Asiatic deficit in the same.

Interestingly, by way of part 5 of the choreography (the dance of dice and tin cans), Yu poses an alternative to this double bind. From part 4 of the dance, where Yu's body has been exhibited anomalously—contorted upside down on a chair as the dentist's voice runs down a clinical profile—Yu untwists her body and virtuostically enacts a detournement of the very diagnostic phrase "[her] father's teeth in [her] mother's mouth." She literally pours extracted molars into her buccal envelope, and not in a bid toward the audience's compassion. Rather, as I argue below, with her shaking, rolling/scattering, reading, and rescooping up of dice/teeth, Yu stages a kinesthetics of germinal disassembly and reassembly suggestive of an autoerotic generativity. It is to this part of the dance to which I now turn.

The Tale of Genetics

The felicitous and sexy phrase "My father's teeth in my mother's mouth" conjures an image of wolfish masculinity preying upon a damsel in distress that has inspired Yu's choreography more than once (her 2006 production *Hood Veil Shoes* overtly alludes to the Little Red Riding Hood fairytale). Even as it evokes a heterosexual oral consumption of the other—a too-aggressive kiss—the phrase turns out to be a quip by a dental hygienist describing Yu's teeth and their relation to her jaw. Dr. Cutler's voice plays in the background, while Yu inverts her body on a chair, explaining the hygienist's logic: "it's simple [Mendelian] genetics. . . . [Y]ou have a one in four chance to have [your mother's] pretty teeth [in your mother's jaw]." The hygienist's phrase comes to signal fatedness, a genetic heritability into which modern dentistry can intervene. Yu, I would argue, uses her chancing upon this salacious phrase as the occasion to think through not only the performative history of dentistry with its dynamic of sympathetic witness so distinct from that of ethnological theater, as outlined above, but sex, generativity, and the production of a surplus (still open-ended) life. Yu's kinesthetic riff on procreative sex begins in part 2 of her theatrical production, which I earlier described as accompanied by alternating male and female singers in a Laotian courtship song. In sync with the male voice, Yu performs stage right a wide-legged muscular stomping punctuated by a grasping of the groin. In sync with the female voice, Yu curtsies, elongates her fingers, and preens on the stage left. Yu oscillates at increasingly greater speeds between these two kinesthetic repertoires and two parts of the proscenium space, as the male and female singers alternate in call and response. As previously mentioned, the sequence culminates with Yu pushing the dozen or so folding chairs lying in pell-mell fashion across the masculine stage right and the feminine stage left into a tidy line. In this singular arrangement, we have the metaphoric merger of the divided stage space—the biological theater of heterosexual reproduction realized in a set of teeth.

Notably, the single-sexed organism (male *or* female) is not the somatic form testifying to courtship's success; it is rather a body part, and a peculiar one at that: compare for instance to the eyes—windows of the soul—or even to the feet—highly charged parts in the context of dance. Moreover, contributing to these mandibular growths as an odd site for the recognition of biological kinship is that they are not manifest at birth (they are not the points of exclamation affirming family resemblance—as in "she has her father's eyes"—or a prenatal genetic reference in negating paternity, as in blood type). And yet the actions performed in this sequence are faithful to the dental hygienist's inspirational phrase and its emphasis on biological reproduction as a vertical transmission from the parents, or what Melinda Cooper calls the "Weismannian paradigm of germinal transmission, in which the heritable essence of an organism is transmitted, through sexual recombination, from one generation to the next."[32] This emphasis on genes stresses the idea of somatic form as predetermined by heritable traits coded into biological matter itself.

As noted earlier, Yu follows this sequence with a pantomime of a patient tilted back under the glare of a surgical spotlight, subject to the dentist's drill or in the throes of labor (see figure 2.11). But the first move in this section is Yu's placing *two* chairs downstage left (on the distaff side), with the live dancer sitting and flailing in the farther one. The audience must look past the other vacant chair in order to watch Yu's own somatic labor. This empty chair is also tilted backward, one of its legs propped up on a tin can. In the doubling of her own chair in which she flails, and the vacant chair also hinged open (e.g., her mother's antecedent labor), the choreography dramatizes the dancer's agitation at the stage of life after courtship in which the expected biological activity for women is to reproduce. In other words, what is heritable are not only physiognomic characteristics coded in the genes but also social prescriptions on the shape of the life cycle—these too are heritable, passed down from one generation to the next.

This part 3 of the dance, however, does not end in another vertical notch in a tale of germinal transmission, but segues transversally across the stage (via a series of cartwheels) to the dance's fourth part, already discussed, wherein Yu balances upside down on a chair with the voice of Dr. Cutler overdubbing the scene. To reiterate, this movement from part 3 to part 4 of the choreography alludes to Yu's sideways movement—her choice of career as a dancer whose muscular, martial arts training (read: masculine kinesthetics) is both her signature style and a possible notation on her nonprocreative body, her coming under medical and theatrical scrutiny not for the contents of her womb but for her teeth, her smile, her calloused feet, and her contortionist abilities.

My Father's Teeth parodies the narrative of the gendered life span and its encoding of a valorized (hetero)reproductive mission, by first subtly mocking the desires for immortality undergirding biological procreation: what results in the dance of "my father" and "my mother" is a set of teeth—i.e., bony structures that do outlast the human organism's life span but that when loosed from the rest of the flesh heighten anxiety over decrepitude. Second, Yu's finale where she rolls dice/teeth repeatedly out of tin vessels—symbolizing an engagement with the aleatory—also performs a repetitive display of corporeal fragmentation: the dislodgement of teeth, the body part extracted, shook, and shot, in short, reassembled in another combination. This repertoire evokes biological disintegration as decrepitude, the repeated scattering of one's (mineral and protein) parts; however, in our contemporary moment, it also implies a technologically assisted generativity.[33] Yu's dicey somatic play figurally gestures toward a revised, noncopulative generative technique: the creativity of the soma diced, in both senses of the word—fragmented and recombined.

To recall my earlier description of Yu's penultimate moves, white debris (teeth) shower from a tin vessel attached to the dancer's groin, simultaneously suggesting seminal ejaculate and the vagina dentata (see figure 2.6). (The can through its placement, shape, and function suggests both the penis and the vagina.) Using another can (simulated vaginal vessel) to scoop up that germinal and dangerous matter, Yu then shakes up those corporeal fragments and reinserts them elsewhere on her body—in fact, *at the mouth*—instantiating one literal representation of Yu's full title, *My Father's Teeth in My Mother's Mouth*. These actions pantomime a kind of self-impregnation, a queer regeneration at the wrong sites of conventional germinal reproduction—a mocking up of a limit-testing form of life generated via the transversal reorganization of parts and an image of overabundant fecundity and intersexuality. This intersexed, almost self-fertilizing pose, struck for several beats, personifies the soma undifferentiated as to sex organs or hermaphroditically of both sexes. This body's generativity has been engineered—via biotechnological instruments (the tin cans)—to offer a plenitude of sexually transformable and (re)generative possibilities.

While I have used the terms "intersex" and "hermaphrodite" to describe the developed organism evoked by Yu's doubly dildonic silhouette (see figure 2.7), it is also the case that the fertile game playing (casting and recasting of dice) and generative amplitude of her choreography bespeak a vitality untethered to the telos of a singularly sexed (male or female) organism. I refer here to the pluripotent stem cell, its replicative capacities, and its property of becoming almost any type of cell.[34] Drawing out the fetish and also monstrosity of pluripotent stem cells with a limitless capacity to divide or grow, Melinda Cooper reviews some biological basics, noting that as a "cell differentiates, attains a specialized function, and contributes to the functional organization of the body," it also undergoes "a loss of potentiality; in taking on specific functions, cells sacrifice some of their embryonic plasticity; cell differentiation thus moves through a progressive, irreversible exhaustion of possibilities, to final cell senescence and death."[35] The cancerous cell (as in the HeLa mo cell line discussed in "Parts/Parturition"), interestingly, "avoids aging and death by refusing to differentiate,"[36] and such cells have been deemed pathological precisely because of this "manic, uninhibited overproduction of life . . . that reproduces itself *outside the proper ends of germinal, sexual reproduction and organic form.*"[37] Maintained at a stage of ample plasticity, the pluripotent stem cell comes to embody "*biological promise itself, in a state of nascent transformability.*"[38]

Simultaneously pathologically monstrous and "regenerative[ly] therapeutic,"[39] the undifferentiated or pluripotent cell's suspension in "a state of nascent transformability"[40] is an apposite description as well for the fertile, self-renewable, hermaphroditic figure Yu strikes as she pauses on the verge of some next directional movement, undetermined by a singular bearing. To be sure, I would not argue that the choreographer intends to make a literal reference to stem cell research. Rather, Yu's self-impregnating posturing remains of a piece with biotechnology's fetishization of the somatic stage when biological life is most plastic and bountiful (aka undetermined, anterior to aging into a complex organism differentiated into either male or female). Moreover, as bioengineering continues to develop, that pluripotency may become separable from the early somatic stage of embryonic potential, the fetish redirected toward the stem-ness of the adult.[41]

In my earlier interpretation of *Bowl Problems*, I noted that the extremes of itinerant Chinese acrobats of the late Qing dynasty who literally bent themselves backward were rejected by the dictum of moderation and social equilibrium voiced by Zhou Enlai. To recapitulate, Zhou cast acrobatic feats of extreme bodily duress (e.g., snake worming into eyes or dismantling a human body into eight pieces) as threatening to the singular national body of China and argued instead for a more harmonious and pleasing relation of spectacle to spectator, one that eschews agitating extremes. Assessing the current political, economic, and cultural moment from a Western perspective, Melinda Cooper, quoting an array of global leaders, scientists, and corporate financial speculators, argues that not equilibrium but "extremophilia"[42] marks the worldview of a good portion of the global elite in the first decade of the twenty-first century.[43] In other words, in our current moment, to resist stability (to recombine for the sake of recombining) may be the most conventional practice rather than the least. Even though *My Father's Teeth* choreographs the dancer's divergence from the female hetero-reproductive life course and defiance of the "biological clock," her final image also indulges in the fetish for endless biological potentiality, of generativity toward no final form.

If what is supposed to comprise the Asian (American) female is her relation to two patriarchies (Eastern and Western), two beauty myths, two narrations of national femininity, Yu suggests contrarily that the specificity of this Asian American body—like that of all bodies—lies in the teeth, or, more accurately, in the simultaneous generalized estrangements and hyperspecifications of bio-surveillance. The pleasure afforded by Yu's production is not the pleasure of seeing the immigrant Asian resist her bio-optimization but the pleasure afforded by the spectacle of a body caught up in the machinery of premodern biopower (the art of tooth pulling), palimpsestically overlaying late-nineteenth- and early-twentieth-century biopower (the ethnological showcase), blurring into post-Fordist, neoliberal biopower (Cutler's orthodontia and regulation of diet). Moreover, Yu's choreographed finale speculatively hints at the next (or already here) phase of biopower's techniques, where the body becomes estranged, reified, and aestheticized as it undergoes resectioning and recombination, or is reverse engineered into its component parts through a cultural impulse toward greater and greater plasticity.[44]

Conclusion

As rehearsed in the introduction by way of Lawence Cohen's work on kidney selling, one avatar of agency in contemporary biopolitics is that of becoming "operable." In the foregoing, I have emphasized Yu's dance as the occasion to contemplate the uneven distribution of operability as an avatar of agency. That is, while the perpetually "indebted" woman in Chennai performs her operability through undergoing tubal ligation prior to nephrectomy, Yu appears to avoid surgical "ex-corporation" (tooth pulling) via prophylactic orthodontics.[45] Yu's somatic flexibility is dictated by a modern clinical technique, namely, the arrangement of teeth in an optimally "normal" bite, the aim of which is to avoid future extractions (oral surgeries due to decaying teeth). However, such surgeries are never entirely avoided but only temporally deferred. Seen from this perspective, orthodontics does not exempt the "braced" individual from dental excisions, as much as postpones certain procedures (extractions) and necessitates the patient's longer-term enrollment in clinical tinkerings (bracing, drilling, fillings, canalization), not all named as "surgeries" even as their "open-wide" bodily postures, Yu reminds us, certainly look and feel like operations. As I interpret her choreography, Yu's virtuoso labor, as an Asian woman and master dancer of all three—Western balletic, Asian martial-acrobatic, and hybridized modern—traditions, becomes the analogue of tubal ligation, that through which the dancer bodily makes her case for her agency as a supple patient in biotechnical times. So, too, in playing with the diced soma—throwing, reading, and regathering body parts (teeth/ dice)—Yu attends to further operations that have become external to the aim of reproducing the organismal human body, that have repurposed the fragmentable body's bits and pieces for regenerative ends, or rather, endlessness.

As if prompted by the double bind of both being denied and being gifted the compassionate witness of her Western audience, the finale of Yu's choreography gestures toward an autoerotic and self-governed regeneration. In performing the Asian (American) woman suspended in a stage of nascent transformability, Yu poses in literal profile, that is, sideways of the copulatory narrative of hetero-reproduction as the means of becoming folded into "life." The production plays with the exoticized interest in Yu's oriental female body to dramatize the surreality and fetish of a life cycle, no longer journeying toward any end, but suspended on the incipit.

In Yu's playing with extracted molars and scattering them on the floor, *My Father's Teeth* does not militate against the body's general lack of integrity and the fragmentation of body parts as much as it explores the combined racial and gendered typing of her particular body: she is simultaneously geopolitically mapped via "Han Chineseness" and its hallucinated association with discipline and demureness; and mapped in a quasi-Mendelian fashion, by way of genetic combination of (maternally and paternally linked) trait differences. Yu's theater comedically dances her biology as acrobatically Asiatic and mapped at the mouth— a lucky combination allowing for critical experimentation as much as muscular turns.

3

Pussy Ballistics and Peristaltic Feminism

The protection of the right to elective abortion and to birth control methods beyond abstinence became synonymous in the United States with a *cause célèbre* of the liberal faction of the second-wave feminist movement. However, it also occasioned reflection on how for indigenous women, U.S. women of color, and women of the global South, reproductive justice did not equate with protecting women's choice to elective abortion but reoriented around a history of racist eugenics. As Dorothy Roberts put it in 1998, "white reproduction [is thought] to be a beneficial activity [bringing] personal joy and allow[ing] the nation to flourish. Black reproduction, on the other hand, is treated as a form of degeneracy."[1] Comprising the U.S. history of family planning and population policy have been violent forms of reproductive foreclosure such as coercive sterilization aimed at poor women, indigenous women, and black and Latina women, a history that has led Chicana feminists, for instance, to recontour feminist choice as the choice both to have an elective abortion and to give birth.[2] More recently, Jodi Kim has asserted in the case of Korean women that reproductive justice includes access to life conditions that allow these women to raise their offspring if they so choose, rather than compel them to offer their biological offspring up for adoption. Kim's argument focuses on reproductive justice in contexts of current or historical military occupation.[3] Affirming the heterogeneous, complex web of feminist stances on reproduction, Laura Briggs points to the rise of infertility rates in the global North (related to delayed childbearing as these women were entering the workforce)[4] as one factor in an amplified cross-racial and transnational demand in adoption. She points to the past three decades of transnational adoption as premised on the forsaking of impoverished (oftentimes single) birth mothers in the United States, Asia, and

Latin America who are also deemed insufficient custodians to raise another life.

It is in this context that Korean American stand-up comedienne, Margaret Cho, announces both her amazement while attending her friend's birthing of a newborn and her own reluctance to embark on a similar path:

> How powerful women are. . . . We bring forth life. I was so . . . amazed [witnessing] my [friend's delivery] because at that point, she was not just a woman, not just a mother. She was creation. She was life. She was god. . . .
>
> And, as I looked into her eyes [blows hard into the mike] . . . HER PUSSY EXPLODED!

Cho shatters the sanctity of birth, dramatizing it as a frantic dance by onlookers and medical personnel to return an exploded pussy to wholeness. Cho continues, "The nurse was running around collecting pieces of her pussy in a basket." She pantomimes collecting debris, then lunges low to grab a hard-to-reach nugget from under a stool. "*She's just panning for pussy,*" Cho says, casting her arms out in a winnowing motion. "They had to sew it back together." Pivoting from panning for treasure to perineal suturing, the comedienne mimes the surgical imperative to mend the wound as embroidery work, weaving her clasped forefinger and thumb in big figure eights. She then finishes off the knot by tearing the thread between her teeth! Cho enacts the labors of obstetrics and nursing as ones of fleshy proximity (mouth next to perineum) and cross-bodily confusion (the nurse plucks "pieces of pussy" out of her hair).

Though the birthing scene conventionally stars mother and infant, Cho's scene focuses on the female nurse. In theatrically blocking her racialized female body in the delivery room, Cho slips into yellowface, playing the second-string aide whose tasks, in fact, resemble types of labor Asian immigrants to the United States have historically performed—panning for gold and seamstress work. In adopting this Orientalist act, Cho emphasizes the racialized subject's relegation to the role not of national hero-mother but of nonsettling sojourner, working toward the nurture of privileged life, yet not biologically (genetically) commensurate with it. Yet, even though Cho points to the edifice of U.S. healthcare structurally supported by the immigrant labor of Asian nurses as key to the maintenance of the American national body's robust health (see Choy 2003), she hedges on whether challenging that structure translates to a defiant political praxis of birthing and raising her own Asian American child. Disgusted at the utter messiness of birth as pussy explosion, Cho loudly announces, "I'm not a breeder. I have no maternal instincts whatsoever. I am barren. I am bone dry. When I see children, I feel nothing. [Long pause] I ovulate sand." Cho's characterization of her reproductive body parts as desert-like and bereft of life grows beyond a mere personal significance, staging a debate as to whether, as a woman of color, her reproduction is regarded as degenerate or, as a U.S. citizen, her reproduction also implies an optimal to-be-protected life.

Successive comic bits in the comedienne's 2003 concert *Cho Revolution*, from which the above scene is drawn, riff on the pussy ballistics at the center of the above scene, drawing out how the undecidability of boundaries between bodies that can elicit disgust, for instance, when localized in the scene of parturition, can transform via the Asian woman's body into pornographic entertainment. The comedienne tells of a recent visit to a Bangkok nightclub district where doormen tout the live acts inside:

> "Pussy eat banana!"
> [Cho mimes a look of disbelief.] Nooo, thank you . . . not in the mood for dinner theater.
> [The barker continues.] "Pussy play ping pong!" [Cho hesitates, inching toward these promised entertainments]. . . .
> "Pussy . . . write letter!"

This "pussy" does not scatter into parts and splatter Cho's body but rather an incessant hawking of its capacities keeps it in contagious circulation.[5] As we shall see, with this second reference to the explosive (ping-pong–playing) pussy of the Thai sex worker, Cho initiates a leitmotif where she randomly barks out commercial "deals" and practical "tricks" that pussy will do for you: "Pussy change oil every 3,000 miles!" Cho and her audience are repeatedly terrorized by these pussy blasts across the length of her show. Put another way, the worry par-layed via the specifically Thai vagina takes the contours not of pussy literally exploding into fleshy fragments but of *vocal* explosions that spectacularly document that pussy's hyperanimate possibilities. What my chapter title calls "pussy ballistics" refers at once to (1) the parturi-tion characterizing the privileged and procreative good mother of the global North, (2) the contrastive gratuitous explosions from Asian sex workers' vaginas (e.g., of ping-pong balls) and the relationship of both of these to (3) the gut(teral) explosions from the mouth that sell Asian pussy and terrorize the audience with their surprise regurgitations.

In this chapter I develop how these pussy bombshells erupt strategi-cally across the concert and how Cho uses this stylistic repertoire to mount a critique of U.S. empire that focuses on the Asian sex worker as logistical support for the military troops of commodity capitalism. As she goes on to do in the segment partially described above, Cho allies these sex workers' identities with those of gays and lesbians serving in the U.S. armed forces: both are not only defined by muted or forbidden speech—e.g., as in Don't Ask, Don't Tell—but also support the privi-leged lives and cult of the heteronormative Mother and Child of whose thriving future they are not a part. Cho's stand-up might be said to work a sleight of hand, focusing on "lite" domestic issues of maternity, reproduction, cosmetic surgery, pop culture, diet fads, body image, bad boyfriends, and the like, all the while connecting these domestic issues to a U.S. expansionist history in Southeast Asia during the Cold War and building toward a performative citation of explosive suicides by West Asians in the post–Cold War era (diverting passenger airplanes into kamikaze weapons) as responses to a parallel expansion of (U.S.-backed) Israeli settlements in occupied Palestine.

In attending to this formal aspect of the concert's overall structure, I develop a theory of Cho's pulsing aesthetics as a valuable mode of pur-suing a femiqueer and racial studies critique. Inciting rhythmic waves of (commercial) terrorism that first register below the belt as belly-shaking laughter, the felt actions of the viscera intrude into the cognitive reg-isters where apparent rationality doesn't rule as much as (imperialist) disavowal and contradiction. To put it another way, Cho's lobbed pussy bombshells wash over Cho's audience like a peristaltic wave. Peristalsis, both a propulsive and a radial action that moves materials inward and

outward of a cavity or through a tube in a wave-like motion, characterizes the uterine-cervical tract; the walls of the esophagus, stomach,
and intestines; and the linings of the ureters, bladder, and testes/vas
deferens. It describes as well the process whereby nonhuman organisms
such as annelid worms locomote.[6] Though Cho herself never names the
underlying muscular agency of gut and uterus as peristaltic, she amply
enacts and vocally performs this kinesthetics as a motility produced by
an unconscious flesh-coordination shared across regions conventionally considered distinct zones of the body (e.g., the reproductive and
the digestive systems, the uterus and the esophagus). *Cho Revolution*,
I argue, tackles so-called consequential matters of war, empire, occupation, and militarism by way of imitating both the pyrotechnics of
high-tech armaments and the lowly contractions of the smooth muscles. Toward the conclusion of this chapter, I reflect on critical habits that implicitly prefer (or craft as more sophisticated) interpretive
frameworks modeled on the machinic and defensive rather than on the
organismal and connective (or amphimixed).

My last chapter extended theories of spectatorship by attending to the
contrastive affective dynamics of compassionate witnessing extended
to the "suffering" patient but withheld from the virtuoso and acrobatic
alien—the latter referring not only to the Asiatic female dancer but also
to a form, scale, and stage of biological life fetishized for its "innate"
plasticity (and thereby viewed as an exemplary entity for financial capitalization). In this chapter, I use Margaret Cho's concerts to introduce
the distributed bodily arenas—beyond mental cognition and the discerning eye—and the visceral ways through which Asian Americans
ruminate over their bodies and body parts as sites of governmentality
and norming, as well as living testaments to the organism's resilience
and unpredictability in expressing biopolitical agency.

Race and Reproduction

We can think of Cho as being pulled in different directions by a politics
of feminism that affirms not only *the burden* of maternity from which
grew second-wave feminist calls for birth control, rights to abortion,
and recognition of unpaid labor of domestic work but also—under
pressures of critique by women of color—a more broad-based notion

of *reproductive justice* acknowledging that indigenous women, Latinas, and black women have been compelled not toward maternity but toward coerced sterilization and vacated custodianship of their offspring through the circuits of transracial and transnational adoption (Briggs 2012; Riddell; J. Kim; Tajima-Peña). To recall the earlier point, Cho stresses her choice not to be "a breeder" with a series of hyperboles: "I am barren. I am bone dry. . . . I ovulate sand." While claiming an exaggerated infertility for comic effect, her earlier memoir, published in 2001, states, quite to the contrary, that after becoming pregnant in the 1990s, Cho electively terminated the pregnancy. One might construe the comedienne's recourse to biologized claims making—"I ovulate sand"—as a response to the resurgence in biopolitical techniques stressing not pregnant women's rights to adequate health care and financial support but fetal rights to an unsullied gestational environment. In this atmosphere, a woman's fertility equates not simply with a biological proficiency to ovulate and gestate to term but with the capacity to endure a formal and informal policing of one's bodily habits, intake, and lifestyle by society and the self.

In her account of being pregnant, published in her memoir, Cho emphasizes contradictions between "abortion [being] the only solution [I] considered" and fantasies about the "something in me [that] was alive" (147). In the midst of drug addiction and depression, she notes,

> there was no room in my life for me, much less someone I would have to raise from scratch. . . . [But] I don't understand why there isn't an easier, less traumatic alternative to first-trimester termination. Does the scarlet "A" we sew to our chest stand for "abortion"? I might be sad for my unborn, but I do not mourn that I could not have offered it much of a life at that point in mine. (147–48)

These comments ought to be considered in relation to the moral panics around "crack babies" and fetal alcohol syndrome in the late 1980s and 1990s that research shows were out of proportion to their actual confirmable incidence of harm. As Jean Reith Schroedel and Paul Peretz's study notes, "Between 1989 and 1991 . . . the *New York Times* devoted a total of 853.5 column inches to fetal abuse . . . by pregnant women's use of illegal drugs and/or drinking. During the same period there was not a single column inch dealing with adverse birth outcomes due to the physical abuse of women."[7] Hysteria around fetal alcohol syndrome had the effect of demonizing mothers and localizing responsibility for good and bad care to a very small enclosure—the mother's womb. Even though Cho proclaims in her stand-up to have "no maternal instincts whatsoever," she cannot avoid becoming entangled in reproductive futurism. Cho's abortion, in other words, attests to her having already been governed biopolitically. She chooses in accordance with healthy imperatives that cast her own maternal capacities as degenerate.

Cho's concert emerges at a historical moment of contradictions in the techniques of biopolitical racism. This biopolitics has been practiced, on the one hand, by way of limiting colored births in the United States through surgical sterilizations, which occurred as late as 1975 (see *Madrigal v. Quilligan*) and, on the other hand, by channeling and easing the entry of colored children into the United States via transnational adoption: "[A]fter the 1970s . . . the adoptable babies and children became disproportionately black, Latino, and Native, or came from overseas."[8] What at first appears a contradiction, however, can be reframed as a shift from a genetic to an epigenetic ground of affirming white supremacy, and even more specifically, to being raised but not necessarily birthed in an evangelical Christian nuclear family household as producing this ideal embodiment of white supremacy.[9]

In her political history of transracial and transnational adoption, Laura Briggs attends to an array of non-nuclear kinship systems— i.e., here synonymous with family and childrearing practices—across racial groups and nations that *de facto* acknowledged that, especially in conditions of duress, there is the need for multiple mothers and fathers beyond the heteronormative *two* of the nuclear family. The mid-twentieth century saw nontraditional (non-nuclear) parenting systems enacted in the extended family networks of Native American and African American families (as well as the "paper son" traditions of Asian immigrants).[10] In addition, the middlebrow British program temporarily to foster children fleeing Nazi encroachment (called Kindertransport) and the "moral adoption" of "Hiroshima orphans" by U.S. citizens after World War II[11] also enacted a networked type of parenting. Cho's 2001 written memoir and her book *I Have Chosen to Stay and Fight* note her own personal history of being raised nontraditionally, initially by her grandmother in Korea while her parents were in the United States, and when a teenager and adult by gay fathers whom she informally adopted when she was at odds with her biological father.

Tremendous political work needed to be done to demonize particular instances of these collective repertoires of raising children. While not romanticizing a prior time of overwhelming support for reproductive labor as a common social concern, Briggs cites

> "mother's pensions" in the 1920s . . . a concern for migrant mothers and children in the 1930s under the New Deal . . . [and] a White House conference on the family [during the Jimmy Carter administration of 1976 through 1980,] suggesting that government had a responsibility to help families because for the first time, a majority of mothers of young children were in the paid labor force.[12]

All of these were politically viable policies and proposals before a neoliberal shift (starting under Ronald Reagan) rendered them unthinkable.

In parallel fashion, temporary fostering of (foreign) children would give way to "the kind of exclusivity we call plenary adoption—where a new birth certificate is written for the child, creating the legal fiction that the birth parents never existed."[13] Briggs calls contemporary adoption

> above all the neoliberalization of child welfare. . . . As states abandon public services like subsidized health care and staple foods . . . they have placed impoverished children in privatized families, rather than provide state services to support them with their birth families. . . . That facilitators make a tremendous amount of money by turning the child into a quasi-commodity itself is a side benefit.[14]

Moreover, what was normed and disciplined through neoliberalization was unruly kinship structures not conforming on the surface[15] to the evangelical Christian family.

Against this background, Cho baldly voices contradictory sentiments. On the one hand, she will not become a mother through her own pregnancy—indeed, this gestationally based surveillance is something she can refuse—and, on the other hand, as a First World American subject, she can become a mother through adoption of some other Asian woman's child: "I suppose if I ever get the [maternal] urge I could adopt one of those kids from Cambodia . . . like Angelina Jolie. . . . Cause really, like who's gonna know." Through her reference to transnational adoption, Cho draws attention to how the capacity of wealthy women and men of the global North to delay childbearing and childrearing, all the while maintaining their option eventually to become parents, relies upon the outsourcing of gestational and nurturing labor to women from the global South, what Ann Anagnost dubs "just-in-time reproduction" (quoted by Vora 2012, 694). In our contemporary moment, Latin American, Asian, Eastern European, and African populations are envisioned as suppliers to U.S. couples of adoptable infants. Moreover, the transnational traffic in these adoptees born of women from the global South indexes a changing scene of eugenic legislation, as it were, one in which the surface phenotype and genetic "givens" of a soon-to-be-privileged (because optimizable) life figure as less significant as compared to being delivered into a normative kinship structure (heterosexual nuclear family, preferably male headed and middle-class to wealthy)—i.e., the "whatever" child's future "home" environment.[16] Whiteness, in other words, becomes figured not genetically but epigenetically—contoured through transnational adoption into evangelical heteronormative households anchored in monogamous marriage.

The assault on the idea that government has a legitimate, obligatory, and even moral duty to support the social welfare, through the financial and affective caretaking of mothers, children, pensionless widows, and the poor, dovetails with a shift in the prioritization of sectors of national spending. The shrinking of so-called domestic priorities (health, education, housing, welfare, care of the elderly) coincides with the ballooning or holding steady of "foreign," aka defense and security, priorities (military arms, high-tech weaponry, surveillance systems, information infrastructure—aka technologies for flexible, at-a-distance resource extraction and market penetration). Cho's concert reminds us of the thorough entanglement of these two "domestic" and "foreign" sites of empire's consequences, even as the comedienne makes us scratch our heads with her initial leap from Saddam Hussein and the war in Iraq to her friend's birthing room miracle. This interleaving of the foreign (military maneuvers) and the domestic (birthing and raising life, optimizing the body through consumption) is made manifest in the very delivery of Cho's standup, to which I now turn in more extended fashion.

We Interrupt This Program . . .

Transpiring between Cho's 1999 break-out concert, *I'm the One That I Want* (hereafter *IOIW*) and *Cho Revolution* (2003) are two events, one personal for Cho and the other "historical." By the latter I refer to the events of 9/11 and its immediate aftermath—the U.S. war in Afghanistan, the creation of the Department of Homeland Security, the anthrax scares, and the 2003 U.S. invasion of Iraq on concocted evidence of Iraqi president Saddam Hussein's intent to fabricate "weapons of mass destruction." All these become the pretext for zero tolerance for political dissent. By the former, I refer to the bodily changes and alteration in legal status Cho undergoes; she slims to a petite, narrow frame and she commits herself to a male partner in marriage. Given that she has staked her brand of comedy on an appeal both to fat politics and to a fan base of sexual and racial minorities, Cho's challenge is to relate this comedy to both the changed circumstances of her life and the changed global outlook of Americans in a post-9/11 world.

Upon seeing *Cho Revolution* live at the Wiltern, I characterized the show as beginning and ending with overt political commentary on the 2003 U.S. military invasion of Iraq, but in between filled with the mainstays of Cho's past acts—anecdotes on dating and bargaining for sex, the limited roles available to her as an actor, her struggle with her weight, and her relationship to her Korean family. However, this outline of her concert's structure relies on the identification of Cho's comic segments according to their topical content. When reassessed in terms of the concert's overall visceral impact, achieved through its stylized and interruptive rhythm, Cho's concert emerges as a performance consistently pursuing a critique of American empire. We might construe *Cho Revolution* as an elaborate staging of Cho's own multicultural liberal spiel—that is, her stand-up act—being stalked by spectacular exploding vaginas, a kind of mock-heroic dramatization of an Asian American critic intent on addressing political differences internal to the United

States' racial and sexual diversity, disrupted by suicide bombers—qua hijackers—the latter embodying radical dissent from finance capitalism's expansion across the globe.[17]

To make this argument, allow me to characterize in more detail the vaginal blasts with which Cho interrupts her main narrative. In a lengthy section of Cho Revolution that might well have been part of the 2001 concert I'm the One That I Want, the putative main focus regards the racial typecasting limiting Cho's choices as an actress (significantly, it is her incapacity to be cast in a period drama nostalgically glorifying British empire—i.e., a Merchant Ivory production—that provides the lead-in to this sequence). Cho claims that she frequently turns down the roles she is offered because she doesn't want to play an angry liquor store-owner, a geisha, a kung-fu artist, or a tragic heroine in the mold of Puccini's Cio-Cio San or Alain Blubil and Claude-Michel Schönberg's Miss Saigon:

> [The problem is] I don't think there were any role models [in popular culture] that I had when I was growing up. The only thing that [was like that and] was Asian was Hello Kitty. I don't want to model myself after Hello Kitty. She has no mouth.
> She cannot even say "hi" back to you after you say, "Hello Kitty!"
> She can't speak; she can't eat; she's just a pussy with a bow on it.
> [Pause]
> "Pussy Made by Sanrio!"

At this point in the concert, Cho has made references to her friend's exploding pussy (a racially unmarked American figure) and the Thai sex worker's pussy (a foreign figure), to which she now adds Hello Kitty or "pussy with a bow on it," a reference perhaps to the Asian immigrant as model minority[18]—a racial other beloved because lacking a mouth or dissident voice. Declaring her distaste for this "role model," Cho implies further that having a mouth—"talking trash"—remains central to her "revolutionary" Asian Americanist project. More importantly, with the tagline "Pussy Made by Sanrio!" voiced in the mock pidgin of the Bangkok tout, Cho tantalizes her audience with the possible echo effects of these verbal missiles. We have, on the one hand, the demure Asian figured as an adorable stuffed animal (commodity-as-companion) and, on the other, the pushy Asian pimp who not only loudly hawks Asian women and boys as sex companions but also reminds one of the shared psychic and moral economy of the furry and juicy skin trades.

Oddball advertisements, imitating and directly alluding to advertising copy, randomly blast through the remainder of Cho's comic repertoire—e.g., "Pussy come with ranch, thousand island, blue cheese, vinaigrette!"; "Pussy strong enough for a man but made for a woman"; "Pussy may contain nuts or particle of nuts"; "Pussy come with fruit on the bottom" (see table 3.1). Indeed, what if we looked at the concert from a perspective acknowledging that much of televisual programming is merely the vehicle for selling commercial slots to advertisers? Might it be that the familiarity of Cho's joke track filling the broad middle of this show—its retreading the ground of her previous performances—is more than deliberate? Could the main points of her political humor be carried not by the lengthy anecdotes (narrative set-ups) but by the jolting surrealism of her interruptive explosions?

Ostensibly, the pussy ballistics Cho vocalizes throughout her performance hail the addressee not as Althusser's subject of the law but as a subject of liberal freedom, specifically defined by the freedom to choose niche-market consumables. At the same time, the advertisements Cho mimics leverage and incite anxieties around the transgression of bodily (and occupational) boundaries—as can be seen in the parody of "strong enough for a man, but made for a woman," Procter and Gamble's campaign for Secret antiperspirant. First marketed to women in 1956 under a strategy that encouraged women to live life "fearlessly"—i.e., with "arms up"—the Secret campaign was revamped in 1969 by the Leo Burnett Company with the famous phrase coined by their African American summer intern, Carole Henny Williams.[19] If the original ad campaign for Secret wished to appeal directly to the new career women, the late sixties revision reassured a U.S. audience that binary gender was safely intact, even as styles of dress and affirmative hiring policies were aiming to lessen differences (qua inequalities). The deodorant industry bespeaks as well the marshaling of affects of anxiety in modern biopower toward a contemporary will to health that seeks not simply prophylactics against disease and sickness but an endless optimization of the soma.[20]

Table 3.1. Cho Revolution's *Scene Selection Titles Punctuated by Pussy Explosions*

Flashcards for the President	
Whose Is Oilier	
Taking It Off	
Monogamy Is Weird	
Pity Sex	
Double Dutch	
Explosion	Refers to the sewn-up perineum after childbirth as "Franken-pussy."
Not a Breeder	
Bangkok	Announces spectacular feats that "pussy" can do: "eat banana . . . play ping pong . . . write letter." Ends with "pussy free with purchase of one or more pussy of equal or greater value."
Immigrant Family	
Sticky Rice	
Ambitious Actor	
Hello Kitty	The joke turns on the sexualizing of this juvenile icon, a "pussy with a bow." The sequence concludes with the shout-out, "Pussy made by Sanrio."
Can't Tell You Apart	
North Korea and Chicken Salad	Punctuating the end of this sequence: "Pussy come with ranch, thousand island, blue cheese, vinaigrette."
Anna Nicole Smith	Transitioning from this to the next sequence is the line, "Pussy come with fruit on the bottom."
All Persimmon Diet	
Accident	
Fresh Cadaver	
The "F It" Diet	
Plastic Surgery	
Eye Work	Shouts out, "Pussy may contain nuts or particle of nuts."
Problem Dinner Guest	
Incredible Asian Hulk	
Chew Chow Ching Chong Lady	
SARS	
Expressing Love	Responds to a theological student's equation of homosexual love with fisting and then interrupts with, "Pussy change oil every 3,000 miles."
Gay Children	
Don't Ask Don't Tell	Ends with, "Pussy strong enough for a man but made for a woman."
Revolution Is Change	The last line of the show: "Pussy crack corn . . . [long pause] and I don't care."

By metaphorically outfitting her Asian "pussies" not with pretty bows but with ballistics, Cho both amplifies and deflates her own (reproductive) choices and the American audience's consumer choices. To recapitulate, the Reagan/Bush/Clinton-era mainstream feminist line on reproductive rights rallies around First World women's "choice" to opt out of maternity (to terminate pregnancy and liberate themselves from childcare). To put it crassly, agency is commensurate here with rational control over rather than chance-driven sufferance of pussy's biological (i.e., untimely, erotic, contagious, infertile) capacities. What terrorizes the First World subject is the loss of control, the suggestion of nonautonomy, or, put another way, linked (inter)dependence upon vital resources not one's own.

To put it in more historical terms, the biopolitical aim of securing the American way of life against the post–World War II "spread of communism" (and post-9/11 "recruitment of Muslims to global Jihad") rationalizes long-term troop deployment and intelligence collecting in the Far and Middle East(s). Prostitution zones, such as the Patpong district in Thailand, are an outgrowth of the *de facto* outsourcing of the sexual and affective labor that supports Allied (and U.S. empiric) military occupation. For instance, during the 1950s when the United States was assisting the French colonial effort to regain control of Vietnam, the CIA "moved into vacant offices in the Shell Oil Building of Patpong" and used a "second building on the south side of Patpong nearer the Silom end as a safe house. Today, it is a short-time hotel . . . which is still frequented by the retired CIA types who never left."[21] Because of an official ban on prostitution in 1960, the sex industry in Patpong occurs in alternative places of entertainment, "massage parlors, nightclubs, bars, coffee shops, tea houses, and barber shops,"[22] with the women working there referred to as "phi or ghosts."[23] In *Cho Revolution,* Cho alludes to the spectral quality of the Thai prostitute's bodily labor by never claiming to see first-hand this "pussy [playing] ping-pong" but only experiencing her/its loud advertisement. Rather than reverse this ghostliness, Cho renders the third-party brokering of the Asian sex worker part of the mechanism by which American consumers do not see or claim not to see that which they transact. Put another way, rather than simply condemning the performer for not bringing these workers into a fuller, more capacious representation, I would argue that her concert, here, emphasizes how consumerism works through spectrality.

In her final and most bizarre shout-out, "Pussy crack corn . . . [long pause] and I don't care," Cho makes a peculiar claim on behalf of the Thai sex worker. Alluding to a lyric from the mid-nineteenth-century minstrel song "Blue Tail Fly," Cho substitutes "pussy crack corn" for the original phrase "Jimmy (Gimme) crack corn." Told from the perspective of a plantation slave, "Blue Tail Fly" recounts how a white master has gotten a new horse and assigned his slave (the narrator) to shoo away the flies while the horse is being broken in. When the blue-tailed fly bites the horse's hindquarters, the master is thrown and dies.[24] The musical refrain "Jimmy crack corn, and I don't care" puts in rather subdued terms ("I don't care") the slave's glee at this turn of events.

Two theories on the meaning of "cracked corn" are worth mentioning. One is that it refers to corn whiskey, hence confirming the slave's intent to celebrate the master's demise. Another, perhaps more dubious, interpretation postulates that cracked corn refers to poor-quality feed reserved for livestock.[25] If the latter, the lyric alludes to the slave's thumbing his nose at the reduced food provisions as punishment for contributing to the master's death by not reducing the master's exposure to risk (a rearing horse). The minstrel performance's joyous expenditure of energy in spite of the meagerness of the sustenance offers a texture of inappropriate capacity that Cho then marshals into a new pattern of surprise explosions and recursive circulations in her guerilla shout-outs. That Cho turns to a besmirched source—a blackface minstrel song rather than a revolutionary manifesto—for the lyrics of this pussy missile goes toward her use of advertising jingles more generally. That is, the broadcast commercial has effectively penetrated the North American living room, making it a showplace for the U.S. market and the American lifestyle. Hitching a ride parasitically on the catchy phrasing of these commercials, Asian "pussies without mouths" land in those living rooms too. Through her punctuated lobbing of ping-pong-playing pussies, Cho intones to the American consumer that there is no escape, no quarantine from an ethical entanglement with sex work.

As argued by Jodi Kim, the aim of Cold War containment was not to prevent the spread of communism in the "nonaligned" nations but rather to maintain the uneven split between which aspects of industrial capitalism were "enjoyed'" by the Western metropolises as distinct from those aspects "enjoyed" by former colonies—aka those territories and populations that would remain sites of resource extraction, rather than being invested in their own sovereign industrial and agricultural production. Containment, in this view, accords with deterritorialized modes of empiric expansion channeled through corporate trade, IMF agreements, security pacts, installation of military bases, and even peace agreements. If containment as pursued by the War on Terror likewise aims to keep centers of privileged life separate from former colonial sites that are to act as dumping grounds for the stresses of capital accumulation and financial speculation, Cho's pussy ballistics trespass containment's boundaries.

The performer wrests commercial discourse out of its milieu (its utility within capitalism) and smuts it up with queer-of-color critique (Ferguson; Reddy), a major plank of which involves circulating too much information about the lasting legacies of slavery, indenture, and American militarized empire. The phrase "too much information" alludes to an earlier sketch where Cho admits being tagged as a "bad dinner guest" because she inevitably says something that prompts another guest to say, "Too much information! Don't go there." Declaring "I live there; I bought a house there," Cho relishes her self-nomination as "inappropriate" eater and speaker in polite company. Being "inappropriate" has less to do, however, with absolute excessiveness than with determinations that the amplitude of one's verbalizations remains outsize to the event being commented upon or infelicitous to the setting in which one comments. Indeed, this is the very crux of the challenge the comedienne faces in her 2003 concert. At a time when the only topic felt to warrant outrage is terrorism, how can Cho continue to make salient the "hurt" of homophobia and racism?

In a lengthy exposition near the conclusion of her concert, the comedienne directly addresses this issue by placing her usual political priorities side by side with ones circulating in the international media:

> I'm very worried about the troops but I'm also worried that my reproductive rights might be taken away from me. . . . I'm so sorry that there is so much starvation in Iraq . . . but I'm so sorry that there are young

girls here starving themselves to death so they can look like the actresses on TV. I am hurt all over for this awful war . . . but I am hurt because someone just got called a fag . . . dyke . . . pansy . . . sissy . . . bulldyke . . . chink . . . nigger . . . kike . . . wetback . . . injun . . . jap . . . bitch . . . whore . . . cunt . . . [with] that person . . . being attacked because of who they are.

The revolution that Cho endorses is one where, as she puts it, populations targeted because of "who they are" rise up and vocally fight back against hatred directed at an aspect of themselves they "cannot change." Indeed, Cho raises the official policy of "Don't Ask, Don't Tell" (effective from 1994 to 2011), requiring gay and lesbians in the U.S. armed forces not to acknowledge their sexuality publicly, as one means of bringing domestic matters (homophobia) and foreign matters (service in Iraq) together: "How dare they! How dare they ask you to die for your country, yet not allow you to be who you are." Then, Cho proclaims that racism and homophobia

are the exact same thing. When someone insults me and says I'm fat, ugly, or stupid or not funny, I can argue [with] that; but when someone says something about my race, I feel it, because that's who I am. . . . You can't change [your] sexuality and race[; they] are the essential parts of ourselves. . . . They are the you of you, they are the me of me.

Whether or not we find convincing the corollary to Cho's statement—that there are modifiable aspects of us open to attack precisely because these traits or behaviors *can be changed* (this supposition underlay dreadful psychological experiments performed on homosexuals in the postwar period [see Ha])—we can nonetheless comprehend the attempt, here, to analogize the trauma of experiencing racism to that of experiencing homophobia. The exposition, in other words, serves Cho's purposes if not exactly to equate both kinds of anguish to the grief of 9/11, then to question why massive troop mobilizations in Iraq (distinct from the search for Osama bin Laden) necessitate the pretense that these other sorrows do not exist.

Exposition only goes so far, however, for the felt texture of "living as a [racial] minority in America" that Cho wishes to convey is one of "dying of a thousand paper cuts." Instead of one big, unfunny, witless holler,[26] then, Cho in pulsing fashion delivers several smaller screams. Precisely through comic bits regarding "pussy explosions," Cho peristaltically moves her audience from one topic to the other, connecting arenas foreign and domestic, outside and inside, racial and seemingly nonracial, even as the convulsive action initiated by her jokes works through a repetitive pressing on the same spot.

Food and GI Matters

As we have seen, the reproduction of the privileged life of the unmarked child of the global North is constituted by the resourcing and perpetual indebtedness (neo-indenture) of the intimate labor of Asian (women) of the global South. Thai sex workers form part of the infrastructure of a militarily assisted market penetration. Troops on the ground use armed "persuasion'"—including handing out candy—to convince occupied populations of consumer democracy's stature as the most moral (as opposed to merely the most salient) political economy, precisely because—in biopolitical terms—consumerism channels the ever-expanding optimization of "life itself." Optimized living remains inseparable from both a "security" structure of military expansion (misnamed defense) and the formation of a well baby and thriving child (the first is justified in the name of protecting the second). At the same time, anxiety is instrumentalized such that this thriving child can never be protected or raised well enough.[27] On the one hand, this phantasmatic baby/child is an end product of artful, technological manipulation— e.g., from amniocentesis to intervene early in non-normative anomalies to prenatal vitamin supplements to ensure optimal cell formation. On the other hand, s/he figures as the innocent beginning, the *tabula rasa* of further indoctrination into a lifelong consumption of supplements to render her/his vitality more and better. Here, I highlight the paradoxical effects of biopower's will to health (will to optimization) that remains symbolized in both birthing the perfect child *and* the need for endless supplementation over the life course of any given person. Biopower's anatomopolitical regulation—the cordoning off or dissuasion from certain risky behaviors correlated to increased morbidity in potential parents and in the general populace (i.e., the social environment that also "parents" or teaches the child)—is done in the name of that same optimized but ever-lacking neonate.

The logic of biopower, however, works paradoxically to foreclose the future of that very neonate (or the neonate two to three generations down the line) who embodies *bios* or privileged, protected life. To wit, the efforts to optimize this neonate's great-grandmother's diet and behavior in the present (aka that future neonate's gestational provisioning grounds as well as, if they are poorly managed, grounds of genetic mutation) work to cocoon that neonate against risk, contingency, and accident. Anne-Lise François, looking at a parallel phenomenon of manipulating food stocks to ensure the future against hunger, argues that such a well-intentioned desire exhibits the urge to insure against (foreclose) risk or chance in the future.[28] This has the effect of denying autonomy to that (utopian) future one plans for, an autonomy that precisely lies in the accidents—detours and unplanned-for contingencies—of that future (child)'s time, *not ours.*

To recall the earlier point, Cho chooses not to be a "breeder," opting *out,* it would seem, from the futurism of endless optimization and lack. Yet others would still enroll her in the caretaking—the assuring of a secure environment—for this child, as dramatized by the conclusion to the first pussy-explosion sequence with which I opened this chapter. After remarking that her friend has turned out to be an excellent mother, the comedienne pantomimes that same friend thrusting her baby girl into Cho's arms despite the latter's gesticulating aversion. The sequence ends with Cho, finally resigned to taking the child in her arms, doing so and then gulping her down: "So I just ate her." By her swallowing whole this avatar of a future that must be proleptically stabilized in the now, it is as if Cho can only put an end to this "anticipatory" logic[29] by inhabiting or trading places with it. Rather than feeding the endless demand for optimization (the new and better life that will grow and thrive), Cho eats this non-nourishing item just to get rid of it. Her consumption affirms her ideological interpellation to empire's logic of market amplitude—but here not in the way we would imagine as optimal—and thereby perversely cleaves (to) its logic: consumption consumes the child's future. Put another way, that future child can never mature to a fruitful sufficiency, because the "present" has already enrolled his/her future in an endless aspirational devotion.

That reproduction encompasses breastfeeding, tactile stimuli, adequate caring touches, and so forth is remembered perversely in this episode of the adult gulping down the child rather than the infant gulping from the proverbial teat.[30] Significantly, across Cho's corpus, stories of food and eating repeatedly provide the *mise-en-scéne* in which Cho is surveilled both racially and misogynistically (see Lee 2004). The most obvious ways in which the comedienne presents herself as subject to an intense anatomopolitical regulation is through the demands from media networks. Cho recounts that after her screen test for a prime-time situation comedy, "All-American Girl,"[31] in which Cho would eventually star, the American Broadcasting Corporation (ABC), set to air the pilot, voiced concern over her size, hiring a personal trainer and dietician to resculpt her body because "clearly I couldn't be trusted to make my own fatty choices." The studio never expressly says that it is the Koreanness of her visage that strikes studio execs as uncomely, but carefully uses "deracializing racialist" euphemisms, to use Khiara Bridges's terminology[32]—i.e., concern over "the fullness of [Cho's] face"—that target her physiognomic non-normativity in a pastoral mode of concern. When she later notes that her canceled situation comedy has been replaced by a show starring a hefty white male comedian, namely, Drew Carey, "because he's so skinny," Cho pointedly underscores the gendered and racialized aspects of the meager food provisioning required as a condition of *her* twenty-first-century employment in the entertainment industry but not *his*.

As noted earlier, *Cho Revolution* continues Cho's focus on racial issues at table and her struggle with weight, but, oddly, after the performer's visage and figure have narrowed. In interviews, Cho attributes her new slenderness to her learning to belly dance and to her ceasing the hypersurveillance of her food intake.[33] Hollywood clinicians (e.g., trainer, dietician) treat Cho's facial fullness as a symbol of her deficient moral character in not refraining from overeating. From that narrow locus of Cho's person as the site of intervention, pathologies linked to eating and consumption are reproposed by Cho as material manifestations of circulating impersonal affects saturating the environment through promotions for tasty edibles ("Pussy come with ranch, thousand island, blue cheese, vinaigrette"; "Pussy come with fruit on the bottom"). Cho figures the tyranny of body image and eating disorders as very much an issue of hers—the possession of a "cured" or optimally slim figure changing nothing with respect to her political advocacy—and an issue of everyone else washed over by this promotional network.

Standing before her audience as a slim and petite Korean American beauty, Cho nonetheless stresses this transfiguration into monocultural optimal skinnyness as utterly contaminating. She recounts that, while on an all- persimmon diet driving her car in Los Angeles traffic, she finds herself compromised:

> I was driving in my car . . . about four o'clock in the afternoon . . . kind of rocking out "Holiday!" . . . [hums a few bars from the Madonna hit]
> . . . and I realized, I am going to SHIT RIGHT NOW!
> [mouth agape, horrified for close to a minute]
> [in a diminutive voice] And it caught me off guard. . .
> . . . because normally you have a good twenty minutes. There is this window of opportunity where you know to look for a Barnes and Noble or some kind of equivalent book-music superstore. We all take that for granted. But I did not have that luxury.

A ten-minute sequence ensues in which Cho speaks of bargaining with God, trying to release just a little, and then, as she flops her body to the ground, fists pounding the floor, screams, "AND IT ALL CAME OUT!!" She then verbally evokes the squishy warmth of the fecal matter turning cold, eliciting an audible groan from the audience.

Cho editorializes, "because I thought I was fat, ugly, because I believed those media images . . . and thought I was just gross. . . . I was now paying the price, by sitting in a pppwwhhhhoool, of my own shit." In this tidy moral, the comedienne suggests a straight chain of events: bad representations in the media upholding super-skinnyness leads to a woman wallowing in her own abjection. However, this sequence needs to be read in light of the earlier explosive riffs and later ones to follow. Instead of becoming a sanctified mother (with an exploding pussy as the proper feminine channel for extruding and gifting to society a part of her body), Cho spews gifts from her bottom orifices and makes her audience revel for a moment in those evacuations.

Cho undercuts her tidy moral that would localize the object of this lengthy sequence's critical lesson to solely *Cho's* consumption issues.

From her literal slide onto the stage floor, Cho metaphorically picks herself up (though she physically stays seated) by using talk and publicity as other channels of circulation that take over when she is physically immobilized in a pppwwhhhhoool of her own shit: "The only thing left to do at that point, was to call people," she says as she mimes the flipping open of her mobile device. " 'You better call me right back, because you are not going to believe what I just did. I'm in my car right now. I just shit my pants. And I'm coming over.' " Satellite technology provides the infrastructure of this cell phone circuitry. Empiric military residue, in short, "comes over" as fecal ooze, suggesting insecurity at the very core of a satellite-assisted will to total surveillance, even and especially when in the name of more and better control. Cho stresses the gargantuan efforts to contain, indeed, squeeze the life out of her Asian form, resulting in the contaminating return (the "coming over" en masse) of the designated "surplus populations" ("those not worth the costs of their own reproduction")[34] birthed from the hot wars and occupations of U.S. nonterritorial empire and market penetration ("we [Asian immigrants] are here because you were there").

Cho's pussy explosions are only figural fusing and fissioning forces. She does not spread shrapnel or radioactive fallout in her (virtual) bombings; but what is not strictly figural is the radiating contagion—the lateral, sideways spread of her explosions. Laughter—the rhythmic, gut-shaking plosive of "har har" punctuated by gulps of air to feed more frequent shaking—also moves the abdomen in waves that resemble reverse peristalsis (vomiting). As playwright Suzan-Lori Parks quips, "Laughter is very powerful—it's not a way of escaping anything but a way of arriving on the scene. Think about laughter and what happens to your body—it's almost the same thing that happens to you when you throw up" (1995, 15). To be sure, the laughter Cho provokes in her audience does not enact a literal reverse-peristaltic action; nevertheless, I call attention to the consilience between the visible belly-shaking kinetics of laughter and the invisible underbelly radial waves of peristalsis partly to follow her concert's own stress on the distributed agency and cognitions of the organs themselves—on zones of the body beyond the central command and control of the brain. Her audience, too, may want to let just a little out, but these hiccoughing intestinal waves have a rhythmic agency of their own, as anyone overcome by laughter knows firsthand. (And woe betide the concert goer with any pregnancy- or otherwise-induced "incontinence.") Through speaking about and also inciting bodily leakage, Cho reminds us of her and our repertoires of belly dancing. She puts our brains back into our guts (as tactile, muscular, respiratory knowledge) and then has us laugh alongside the something mechanical (the militarized, consumer product edifices) encrusted on our worm-like gastrointestinal materiality (that paper over our diapered pasts and diapered futures).[35] Perhaps dwelling in our shit—modeling ourselves more akin to worms and snails, babies and the aged, that is, in relation to an annelid (worm)[36] ecology where actants are more proximal rather than removed from their environment (the soil that houses and feeds worms is also comprised of their shed casings or excreted waste materials)—would have us understand better the consequences of militarism, of our culture devoted to death and dying as life's improvement and securitization.

In short, Cho doesn't extricate herself from the excrement but only circulates news of it by phone. Moreover, she suggests that it is perhaps the desire to be freed from the muck (from obligation and responsibility for costs incurred—for the toxins we produce—as part of the gain or palliatives we uncover) that underlies our insecurity in the first place. She amphimixes high-tech GI equipment, as in the satellite technology of star wars, with the everyday, trivial emissions of that other GI (the gastrointestines).

I borrow the term "amphimixis"[37] from Elizabeth Wilson's own borrowing of it from Sandor Ferenczi as a springboard to outline what she calls "gut feminism." In her highly suggestive account of the enteric nervous system and the distributed quality of visceral "thinking," Wilson speaks of the motive capacity or "psyche" of our biological parts distributed beyond the brain, claiming that "temper, like digestion, is one of the events to which enteric substrata are naturally (originally) inclined."[38] Recently confirmed by digestive disease specialist Kirsten Tillisch's medical research is the finding not only that signals from the brain affect the gastrointestinal tract but also that signals from the human intestine are sent to the brain.[39]

Key to Wilson's specific crediting of how the enteric nervous system and "gut" not only digest but also ruminate (think, register dissent) is the biological notion of amphimixes:

The rectum communicates its retentiveness to the bladder; the bladder communicates its liberality to the rectum. Without such inter-organ exchange, the bowel would become hopelessly constipated and the urinary tract incontinent. Amphimixis . . . is the very means by which these organs are able to function naturally at all. . . . Various organs of ingestion, expulsion, sensation and expression are borrowing from one another.[40]

While Wilson, here, associates "amphimixis" with the expressive borrowing of one organ system (bowel) from another (bladder), we can think of "amphimixis" as referring to a leakiness or continuum of cellular memory among what later become distinct organs. Wilson's concrete illustration of amphimixis in this latter ontogenetic aspect is the soft tissue at the back of the throat—the fauces. This antechamber or proto-pharyngeal area is the "'embryological source of several important structures in vertebrates . . . [T]he breathing apparatus (gill pouches of fish and lungs of land animals) arises in this area. . . . In humans, the pharynx is particularly important as an instrument of speech.'"[41] It is also the site of the gag reflex, the aperture where mouth is connected to esophagus, and the meeting place of mouth, nasal passages, and ears: "[T]he back of the throat is a local switch point between different organic capacities (ingestion, breathing, vocalizing, hearing, smelling) and different ontogenetic and phylogenetic impulses. . . . The fauces is a site where the communication between organs may readily become manifest."[42] Using this idea of amphimixis, we can contour Cho's lengthy and singular sequence on anal splatter—i.e., this gastro-enterological anecdote—on a bodily continuum with the earlier articulatory explosions on pussies and eating babies (the icon of the endless consumption to achieve optimized futural being).

Rather than the back of the throat, Cho speaks from the amphimixed entry points of the gastrointestinal and erotic-libidinal tracts,[43] places that we think of as inside us but that from the perspective of anatomy and cell biologist Michael Gershon are enclosed spaces that are nonetheless part of the outside world: "The space enclosed within the wall of the bowel, its lumen, is part of the outside world. The open tube that begins at the mouth ends at the anus. Paradoxical as it may seem, the gut is a tunnel that permits the exterior to run right through us."[44] Both this bio-physiological framing and the belly techniques of Cho's concert tactilely communicate the lie of containment, the amphimixis of laughing felt in her audience's guts (as intestinal/abdominal waves of radial flexing and release, as well as pulsating respiration and vocalization coassembled). The affective style that she parasitically imitates is both advertising style and explosion/surprise; but it's also the basic biological action of peristalsis (shitting, vomiting, swallowing, passing gas).

Through critical prose informed by a feminist-inflected neuroenterological science, Wilson propositionally tells us of the agency and intelligence in the cellular materials of the worm-like intestinal tract, whereas Cho in laboratory fashion performatively stimulates that GI knowledge felt in her audience's guts, rather than having it consumed cognitively primarily through their central nervous systems. Choreographing a politics pursued on the somatic or gut level, Cho's concert tactilely communicates the lie of containment, the amphimixis of knowing laughter ruminated over and sensed by the belly.

Conclusion: On Peristaltic Choreographies

In her efforts to broaden the terrain of reproductive issues to include the petrochemical industry, Michelle Murphy urges a broadened terrain of conceptualizing biological reproduction: "What counts as reproduction? Where does biological reproduction reside? . . . What is the place of industrial chemicals in reproduction?" My argument very much accords with the spirit of Murphy's questions even as it figures U.S. militarism (a specific armament to further petrochemical extraction and that which petrochemical extraction—combustion—supports) as a key infrastructure of the denied futurism evoked both in the Thai sex worker's "pussy" and in Cho's phrase "I ovulate sand." Foreclosed from the reproductive model of the heteronormative nuclear (male-headed) family, Cho's queer agency lies in her smutting up the living rooms of American households with the highly eroticized servicer of "rest and relaxation"—i.e., the Asian pussy providing gratification (gifts) without obligations (relational ties established by reciprocal care giving).[45] Cho uses her humor to emphasize not only the ubiquity of biopower's disciplinary apparatus, its making her own self—rather than some authority outside herself (e.g., a sovereign father)—the very instrument of bodily regulation but also her and others' excessive bodily intransigence to this clinical and empiric containment.

In terms of Cho's salience as a thinker and affective modulator of turn-of-the-twenty-first-century racialization, she doesn't offer any promise of justice achieved. Her concerts do not affirm that we could get to a place beyond race or beyond biopolitical contradictions. One response to this divestiture from a notion of "progress"—of the liberatory seduction of getting out of a relation of rule premised on militarism, violence, sex trafficking, racism, and the like—is to get stalled in what Rei Terada calls an "impasse" of radical anxiety (a play on the anxiety of leftist thinkers).[46] But there are sideways approaches to this recognition of the damaged feelings produced when confronting one's implication in violence or, put another way, the suspension of the dream of total divestiture from subjection by and subjecting of others to the delirious and mutating channels of capital.[47]

One sideways approach that proves an alternative to impasse is suggested in a turn to Asia and what Colleen Lye and others articulate as Mao Zedong thought. In her account of the Asian American sixties, Lye proposes that while traditional Marxism privileges the dialectical moment of contradiction's resolution or transcendence, Maoist thought emphasizes instead the ongoing ceaseless character of "contradiction" (*maodun*)[48] and construes those contradictions as multiple or multisited; and whereas in a Western, Aristotelian tradition contradiction "designates a condition, in which one of two contradictory entities can exist, but not both," in the polysemous Chinese idea of *maodun*, *maodun* (contradiction and dialectics) both can mean an impossibility (akin to the Western idea of contradiction) and can designate a "unity of opposites . . . [of] phenomena which seem anomalous and paradoxical, but which are, in any case, quite commonplace."[49] Bringing these insights to Cho's performances, we might construe her stand-up as working on a principle that values less cognitive resolution and more the dwelling in embodied contradictions. Rather than exposure leading to justice—all is right with the world as long as we expose what is wrong—Cho dwells in the inaugural moment of surprise, of antagonisms that can't be ironed out, e.g., the birth (of the other) entwined with the tissue morbidity of parts of the self. Reframing Asian Americanist critique in biopolitical terms, Cho's comedy instantiates a specific type of repetitive aesthetic—intensely vital *and* morbid—that formally imitates not forward progress but cyclic or helical stagings of opposite phenomena.[50] Instead there are only repeated convulsive discoveries of these iterative contradictory opposites; or put another way, no subsumption and no transcendence but only peristaltic waves that push (or connect us to) the world through both ends.

Let me finally reflect on my own framing of Cho's pussy explosions as imitations of the low-tech thanatic fissionings of suicide bombers, which high-tech U.S. drone bombings are aimed to "contain." To state the obvious, the $5.78 billion defense budget in 2013 devoted to such unmanned bomber-qua-containments (a Maoist unity containing contradictions, if there ever was one) materially figures such pyrotechnical weaponry as a high national priority.[51] From my place listening and laughing in 2003 to *Cho Revolution* performed live at the Wiltern Theater during the arc toward U.S. military occupation of Iraq, Cho's riffing on the low-tech methods of the terrorist, neo-kamikaze "Arab/ Muslim" appeared unquestionable—they, like she, parasitically convert humble technology (box cutters, pussies) into big weapons of explosive affect and effect. On a metalevel, my own recourse to the military metaphor of the exploding bomb to characterize Cho's bodily theater both emerges from the historical context of its initial delivery and participates in the critical fetish for machinic metaphors against the givenness of organic biology—as if describing organisms as combustible, hightech armaments makes them sexier, more evolved in time, high theory, and so forth.[52]

From the perspective of this essay's writing (on the downward arc of troop pull-out from Iraq) and through an STS-informed engagement with the historicity of biology itself, it appears equally the case that *Cho Revolution*'s explosive, rhythmic style adumbrates (reverse) peristaltic actions. Reverse peristalsis is commonly associated with the radial waves moving food from the stomach to the mouth, as in the vomiting up of half-digested matter. At the outset, I noted peristalsis characterizing the locomotion of worms as much as the mammalian gut. As dictated by Western epistemologies of linear progression, a conceptual framework stressing human composition within and through phylogenic forebears has an atavistic air (the mark of temporal backwardness). Human (critical) agency wants to get above the worm, that lowly creature moving laterally; but as I have argued elsewhere, stand-up is about the vertical made prone,[53] the inversions of such distinctions, or, in a more Maoist lexicon, the vertical (erect homo sapiens) contains contradictorily and complementarily the procumbent (undulating annelid).

"Gut feminism," in Wilson's inauguration of this school of thinking, negotiates as well with the highly valued findings of neuroscience, gastroenterology, and molecular endocrinology, coassembling them with the (devalued) feminist arena of psychosomatic feelings as knowledge, or put another way, a feminist acknowledgment of the body's (and feminist analytics') situated and distributed sensory perception. For Wilson, the distributed character of the human mind or psyche becomes most evident to the organism, especially under conditions of trauma: "after normal psychic structures have been violently destroyed by trauma," the organic substance of the body itself "begins to think."[54] The hierarchical divisions of consciousness and subconsciousness, high-tech and below-the-belt GI matters, and somatic organ systems devoted to producing more life qua surplus and those systems devoted to eliminating "waste" (also qua surplus)—all these show themselves as continuous, inseparable, cross-fused, or amphimixed. Similarly, with respect to my reading of Cho's critique of militarized market imperialism, amphimixis bespeaks the contamination between what we think of as clearly bounded toxic and diminished parts versus healthy/optimizing parts of the planetary ecology.

While Wilson highlights the prominence of "gut thinking" as an effect of trauma, I would dovetail her insights with that of another affect theorist, Raymond Williams, who claims that a historical period's "structures of feeling" (with cultural texts poised as particularly useful sites for data collection of such structures) index a nascent apprehension of some larger historical shift not quite articulable in the mainstream lexicons of that particular moment's hegemony. Both Wilson and Williams, in other words, make the case for our sensory perception and epistemological techniques not improving or getting better over time, but simply expanding in one domain (cognition, central nervous system, calculative, informational thinking, large-scale data crunching), while shrinking (or "auto-amputated" cf. McLuhan) in another—e.g., in our tactile, enteric, affective, distributed body parts and somato-sensory systems.

Yet we can still aspire, or, more aptly, "feel [and grope our way] backward" (Love) to the amphimixis of the past. Parallel to the cellular matter of amphimixis, Wilson argues, is the distinction between two kinds of methods or approaches, those that are marked by "an overriding concern with clearly demarcating causal primacy . . . as if determination is a singular, delimited event"[55]—which she shorthands as Boolean logic[56]—and a "more plastic model" attuned to "the amphimixed inclinations of the [biological] substrata involved."[57] Cho solicits her audience's amphimixed apprehension of containment's lie, even as we continue headstrong into the optimistic, anticipatory belief in endless optimization.

A Boolean version of this chapter would conclude here with the singular assessment of Cho's message, but one wonders whether a normative message can emerge from amphimixis or a peristaltic squeezing out of both ends. Isn't the point, rather, that an amphimixed message laughs, but in revision of the Medusa, not via plural heads but from the messy assemblage of bottom orifices—urethra, anus, vagina, and, yes, vomiting mouth—at the demand for a single message: the normative point or straight build-up to the end (see Margaret Cho's belly tattooed with image of Medusa at http://jezebel.com/5992256/in-a-room-full-of -naked-koreans-margaret-chos-body-is-an-unwelcome-sight). Instead, Cho's giggling peristaltic waves intensify and wane, in waves that overlap and fold, producing whirlpools that are the wider-environmental (spatial) and durational (temporal) point that mocks Anthropocene's sense of itself as progressing always into a more wealthy, ethical future simply because of the directionality of the arrow of historical time. The belly knows that it jiggles in all sorts of directions, a queer refusal of normative argumentation as political critique, but critical nonetheless.

4

Everybody's Novel Protist

Chimeracological Entanglements in Amitav Ghosh's Fiction

Amitav Ghosh's award-winning science fiction novel *The Calcutta Chromosome* (1995) speculates on the somatic transformations to biological life in an era where the world's waterways have become imperiled. Lauded for its "hypertextual" interweaving of speculative fiction, Bengali literature, and the history of medicine through which it challenges the West's monopoly on "scientific" knowledge (Chambers 2003; B. Ghosh; Schulze-Engler), this third in Ghosh's corpus of highly regarded novels articulates a vision of biological hosting and cross-species enmeshment that is central to critical discussions of the ethical and political stakes of race, postcolonial, and femiqueer studies. And yet, with their commitments to conflict and antagonism as consciousness-raising and revolutionary ideals, postcolonial and race studies often regard as suspect an ethics that endorses hospitality (alternately, caretaking) across conditions where parties refuse to or cannot recognize their reciprocity and interdependence.

Nonetheless, this chapter dwells at length on undocumented caretaking/hosting as a framework for comprehending Ghosh's postcolonial novel, despite the fact that parasitism and biological experimentation provide alternative lenses that are perhaps less inclined to understate, through the sentimentality of "care," the antagonism and conflict of self-other relations alluded to in Ghosh's book (whether colonizer-indigenous, parasite-host, scientific researcher–experimental medical subject, or baby sahib-amah). I will do so not only because political alignments with feminist studies warn against the taken-for-grantedness of caretaking work but also because this caretaking work remains under-documented as a key structural feature of Ghosh's narrative, despite its being in the literal foreground—in the frame story. Taking a cue from recent critical methods in endeavoring "surface" readings (one eschewing the paranoid modus operandi of hidden-shown),[1] we might reconsider the frame story of Ghosh's novel functioning not as an empty plane or window to be looked through (to enter the real field of engagement within the perimeter) but as an assemblage device in the mode of One Thousand and One Nights' Scheherazade and her crafty, seductive, and instructive struggle to stay alive and caretake her sisters in doing the same.

Ghosh's frame story takes place within the apartment of the protagonist Antar, an Egyptian immigrant living in New York City at the turn of the twenty-first century and working for an international conglomerate, the International Water Council, whose mission is to investigate "the depletion of the world's water supplies" (7). In practice, however, Antar has no sense of how his work, staring at electronic databases of items gathered from the council's shuttered offices, fits into the organization's mission. Once Antar's computer gets "tripped up" by an object recovered from a satellite office in Calcutta, Ghosh's novel launches into a time-bending narrative that, on the one hand, loops back to nineteenth-century colonial India—specifically, the laboratories of British researchers investigating the vectors of malarial transmission—and, on the other hand, elongates the narrative present into a stretched-out time of (electronic and biological) labor, in which the male information worker, the aforementioned Antar, with the aid of his supercomputer, reconstructs what has happened to a former employee, an oddball researcher named L. Murugan, who made Antar's acquaintance shortly before disappearing in August 1995. Obsessed with the biography of the Nobel Prize–winning scientist Ronald Ross (1857–1932), Murugan journeys to Calcutta, determined to prove that this colonial scientist's discovery of the Anopheles mosquito's role in the malarial infection of humans is not what it seems. According to Murugan, without Ross's knowing it, the Nobel Prize winner has been covertly aided by a set of dhooley bearers (dung scoopers) and dust sweepers under the sway of a mysterious woman named Mangala.

As one might infer from this summary, Ghosh's novel remains structurally and conceptually complex, complicated by its forwarding plots in three settings: New York City in the early twenty-first century (the

locale of the frame story); the mid-1990s, when Murugan travels to Calcutta; and British-occupied, colonial India of the late nineteenth to early
twentieth centuries. Across the narrative, however, these temporal distinctions fade, with Antar (in the 2000s) virtually connected to the two
other time periods by way of a simulated environment helmet or Sim
Visor. The novel's conclusion finds Antar's physical person in the narrative present also on the brink of a somatic transformation, a three-way
parasexual[2] "crossing-over" into a new life form (a recombinant entity
comprised of protoctist, vertebrate animal, and electronic-informational
substrates). The book, however, concludes before the reader can find
out if indeed Antar has crossed over, that is, if a new life form has been
birthed, so to speak, and what chimeric form it would take.

Drawing on a critical biopolitical studies framework, microbiologist accounts of the protist *Plasmodium* and a feminist and queer
reconsideration of reproductive labor and value production, this chapter argues for a reading of Ghosh's novel in both a historically specific
fashion—tied to the political projects of postcolonial feminism and
Asian Americanist critical studies—and a cosmological and ecological
one. I begin by characterizing Ghosh's novel as offering several alternatives to a "carved up" modern episteme that places Western science
in advance of other ancient beliefs and other (temporal and material)
ways of thinking and behaving.[3] I then turn to microbiology and considerations of hosts and parasites as they figure in both the novel and
the philosophy of ethics. Finally, I loop back to the terrain of reproduction, and draw out the structure of Ghosh's novel along the lines
of an elaborate babysitting narrative. Here, I argue that the sexual and
reproductive aspects of the novel—e.g., the emphasis on chromosomal
transfers, bodily changes induced by another species' multiplication
of offspring, and the work of postnatal care of the younger sibling—
remain critically neglected thus far because they have appeared almost
too obvious, hidden in plain sight, and deemed surface detail epiphe-
nomenal to the meaty postcolonial structures driving the narrative. My
point is not to dispute the importance of what prior postcolonial and
race studies critics have considered as primary,[4] namely, Ghosh's mapping of the uneven and violating relations between white imperialist
and colored denizens and emigrants from the global South, whose bodies serve as "risk bearing" labor for medical experimentation (Cooper

2012). With those important insights in the background of my critical tableau, I instead focus on questions driven by an ethical orientation toward the "hospitality" work of gestating the alien. In doing so, I urge an expanded postcolonial and Asian Americanist Studies project.

While nurturing work in the novel makes an explicit appearance around the secondary characters Tara and Urmila, the overlap between information work performed explicitly by the protagonist of the novel's frame story, Antar (who tends to a petulant supercomputer for the duration of the narrative present), and the embodied affective labor of caretaking and hosting work has been obscured by Antar's male embodiment. Though past critics have noted the bureaucratic alienation—e.g., surveillance by and servitude to a corporate system—characterizing the male information worker of the novel's frame story (which arguably feminizes him), the fuller work of analyzing the chiasmatic "crossing" of the "immaterial labors" (Hardt and Negri) of symbol manipulation and undocumented caretaking/hosting work has yet to be essayed. By doing so, this chapter also historicizes Ghosh's novel in a particular heady moment split between two concepts of reproduction: one in which global consortiums (both private and public) devoted themselves to genetics as the key to subsequent manipulation of organismal structures and another in which the importance of the "epigenetic" interrelations of nucleic materials and the (cyto)plasm in which they swim—i.e., the gestating, hosting environments whether on the scale of the cell, the womb, the geopolitical milieu, the planetary ecology, or the cosmos—was intimated.

Through the case study of Ghosh's novel, my argument advances the importance of an expanded notion of what counts as reproduction.[5] Michelle Murphy notes how pollutants from oil extraction industries in Chemical Valley (near the Great Lakes of the Michigan-Toronto border) have resulted in hermaphrodite changes in local fish as well as changed sex ratios in the Aamjiwnaang (Ojibwe) tribe whose reserves are surrounded by Chemical Valley ("Between 1999 to 2003, of the 100 children born in the community, only 35 were boys").[6] Even as they act as endocrine disrupters, these chemicals do not manifest their effects in the lifetime of the exposed organism but instead lie latent, only evident one or two generations down the line. Through the frameworks of "latency" and "reproductive infrastructures," Murphy urges the consideration of such seemingly indirect, because temporally lagging, factors as oil extraction, chemical pollutants, military occupations, contamination of or shrinking water supplies, as much as technologies of recombinant DNA and in vitro fertilization, as reproductive issues.

Murphy's examination of the "latent" effects of chemical exposure on birthrates continues the valuable work of enlarging what counts as reproduction, a project she notes as having begun with feminist and STS scholars—and one that Ghosh's novel productively enlarges. Beyond the mother-infant dyad, reproduction involves racializing dynamics in the health industry and U.S. housing, education, and welfare programs that operate from the presumption that white reproduction is precious and black and Latino/a reproduction are "degenerate" (Roberts 1998; Bridges 2011; Tajima-Peña); international geo-economic inequities that have led to a gestational surrogate industry in India (Vora 2009; Vora 2012; Thompson 2010); and—as my chapter on Margaret Cho suggests—military structures of occupation and R&R (rest and relaxation) servicing that help reproduce white families at the center of our current relations of biopolitical rule. I read Ghosh's novel as contributing to an expanded notion of reproduction not just because it behooves an Asian Americanist feminist project to do so (to show how the particular entrée of women, gender, and sex opens onto broader, if not the broadest of, questions) but also because biological, technological, and economic flows have already distributed reproduction to arenas beyond sperm, eggs, and family.

Dissectional Magic

The Calcutta Chromosome offers an alternative story to the one recounted by Scottish bacteriologist Sir Ronald Ross (1857–1932) in *Memoirs, with a Full Account of the Great Malaria Problem and Its Solution* (1923), regarding his discovery of the link between the *Anopheles* mosquito and *Plasmodium*, the parasite causing malaria. Within Ghosh's novel, an Indian expatriate named L. Murugan devotes himself to correcting the historiographical record that, according to him, effaces the central role played by untouchable Indian lab assistants qua janitorial staff in Ross's Nobel Prize–winning work. Along the way, Murugan proposes the Indian origins for the concept underlying recombinant DNA, and speculates on the far-reaching technological-spiritual experiments that these subaltern assistants conduct and at which they succeed.

Through the travails of Murugan—who journeys to Calcutta seeking further support for his Other Mind theory (more on this later), the book not only contours an alternative to Western science—an express "counterscientific" epistemology—but also dramatizes the resistance to and mockery of these counterhegemonic ideas by even those immigrant confreres who might be expected to be sympathetic. For instance, when Murugan speculates that a local Indian group in the late nineteenth century led by a mysterious woman named Mangala has succeeded, through the modification of the process whereby *Plasmodium* transports itself from host to host, in transferring human personalities across bodily substrates, thereby effectively instantiating "immortality," Antar laughs knowingly and mocks Murugan's explanation, comparing it to ancient beliefs in "Osiris, Horus and Amun-Ra" (107). It is through such overtly debated clashes between scientific method and its counter, namely, non-Western belief systems that Science remade into primitive superstitions, that Ghosh forwards his postcolonial treatment of epistemic authority. In short, Ghosh's novel critiques the way Western modernity denigrates Asian and African cosmologies in order to promote its culturally specific science as the most authorized way of knowing.

Punning on "tropic"—the equatorial zone as well as the adjectival form of "trope," a discursive figuration—Diane Nelson claims that storytelling—troping—can be thought of as a kind of technology, a colonial laboratory or "hot, fertile . . . space" in which one "[finds] things out," specifically about how tropical medicine has hypothesized and "produce[d] new ways of figuring the human."[7] Nelson considers as technological then both the gestating grounds of tropical colonial encounter where imperialist occupiers experiment on local indigenous bodies—"Mechanical and biological experiments are nothing new for colonized peoples: their sinews, hearts, minds, bodies, and germ lines repeatedly have been used in the service of alien invaders"[8]—and the very time-bending strategies of Ghosh's narrative that James Thrall neatly divides into three distinct chronologies. In the first time frame, New York City in a futuristic moment in the late 1990s–early 2000s, the protagonist Antar (an Egyptian immigrant information worker and colleague of Murugan) sits at his computer for the duration of two hours. This time frame flashes back to Antar's past in which he recalls his acquaintance with Murugan, an amateur historian of science who tends to lecture more than converse, and the many phone and email messages that Murugan sends to Antar and that the latter ignores as the ravings of an obsessed scholar. With the aid of his supercomputer and a Sim Visor, Antar eventually discovers Murugan in an Indian mad-house, but that discovery coincides with Antar's relapse into a malarial fever (he had contracted the disease in his youth). The three distinct chronologies among which the book alternates start occupying the same delirious plane of time-space (more on this in a moment).

The second time frame, Calcutta in August 1995, dramatizes Muru-gan's encounters with local denizens such as Urmila Roy, journal-ist for *Calcutta* magazine; Sonali Das, a celebrity actress and consort to the mysterious real estate mogul Ronen Haldar; Mrs. Aratounian, the Armenian proprietress of Dutton's Nursery and the person in whose apartment Murugan lodges; and a four-fingered (thumbless) teenager wearing a Pattaya Beach tourist t-shirt who follows Muru-gan around the city, and whose name is not revealed to Murugan but whose physical peculiarity suggests he is an iteration of the character Laakhan/Lutchman—a character interwoven in the novel's nineteenth-century plot. Much of the second time frame is devoted to conversa-tions between Murugan and residents like Urmila, in which Murugan explains his Other Mind theory, shorthand for Mangala's practice in opposition to Western science's privileging of positivist claim making or the empirical authority of observing repeatable events.

In the third time frame, late-nineteenth-century to early-twentieth-century laboratories in both the middle latitudes and the tropics, vari-ous British researchers are unaware that the actions of their colonial servants—Mangala and Laakhan/Lutchman—have been leading them toward key discoveries in the multiple morphologies of *Plasmodium* (particularly *P. falciparum*)—the species linked to fatal malaria. As Frank Schulze-Engler puts it, a "racist spirit of supremacy over the 'natives'" allows European scientists like Ross not only to conscript the indigenous as experimental medical subjects, akin to laboratory mice, but also to appropriate and disavow *as knowledge* the contributions made by indigenous sources.[9] According to Murugan, Mangala aids these Europeans not out of servile naïveté but because as a local healer of syphilitics, she requires proximity to cultures of malarial blood (deliberate infection with malaria acts as a prophylactic against syphilitic dementia). Her practice, in other words, capitalizes on a windfall characteristic that may have rendered the hosting of species of *Plasmodium* causing milder forms of malaria symbiotic (or selective for long-term survival) prior to the antibiotic treatment of the venereal disease.

Significantly, the narrative negotiates between two imperatives in recounting this temporally remote setting: dramatizing without comment the actions of Mangala's nineteenth-century followers and having Murugan in the later time frame recast these practices as affirmed by Western science. Explaining why Mangala's group operates through strategic silences that seem not to conform to standards of repeatable empirical evidence, Murugan posits their cleaving to a principle of radical uncertainty:

> [They refuse] all direct communication . . . because to communicate, to put ideas into language, would be to establish a claim to know—which is the first thing that [they] would dispute. . . . [Also] they believed that to know something is to change it [and the corollary that] one way of changing something—of effecting a mutation, let's say—is to attempt to know it, or aspects of it. (104–5)

Described here is what contemporary physics calls "the observer effect" (Thrall), with the operative principles of these late-1800s "counterscientists" corresponding in the 1990s to ideas in the scientific mainstream.

If imperialism places African and Asian beliefs—e.g., in Osiris, Horus, and Amun-Ra—in a past temporality that lags behind "the modern," Ghosh challenges such linear history in the very structure of his novel, offering three alternating time periods that meld, nest, and ultimately *coexist* on a single plane. During Murugan's August 1995 visit to Calcutta, for example, he falls asleep under a mosquito netting but then travels, whether by Lethe or through some other means, to the late-nineteenth-century laboratory of Ronald Ross:

> When he looked down at his body, lying flat on the bed, he could not tell whether he was waiting for them [the malarial mosquitoes] to show

themselves to him, or whether he was showing himself to them. . . .
Involuntarily he flexed his shoulders . . . waiting to discover where they
would touch him first, where he would first detect the tingling prick of
their bites. . . . They were standing around his bed in attitudes of concern,
like nurses and doctors' assistants, waiting for him to sink into anesthe-
tized oblivion. And now the bearded Englishman reappears, dressed in
his white coat . . . ; he reaches in, with a little butterfly net, pulls it out
and expertly traps an engorged mosquito in a test tube . . . puffs on his
cigar and [blows] into the test tube; the insect dies, the tiny buzzing creature that is carrying his blood inside it. (156–57)

"They" first refers to the malarial mosquitoes hovering outside the
mosquito netting under which Murugan lies in his rented Calcutta
rooms but then evolves into nineteenth-century colonial scientists sur-
rounding the research specimen, himself. When Murugan wakes, he
discovers traces of smashed glass—the broken test tube—near his feet,
suggesting not a dream but a transposition of late-nineteenth- and late-
twentieth-century time periods. In both eras, brown-skinned bodies
serve as experimental medical labor[10] (and gestational surrogates), the
only difference being the degree to which the medical research of each
period is *overtly* tied to a militarized project of colonial expansion.

Underscoring how "the big discoveries in malaria research were
primarily made by military scientists," cultural anthropologist Diane
Nelson recalls that "military campaigns [undergirding] colonial laboratories were waged against non-human actants as well as the 'restless
natives.' . . . 'Fever and dysentery are the "generals" that defend hot coun-
tries against our incursions and prevent us from replacing the aborigi-
nes that we have to make use of,' complained a French colonial official
in 1908."[11] Thus, a situational irony pervades the global environment of
the novel's frame story: antimalarial campaigns designed to eliminate
the watery breeding grounds of insects and parasitic microbes may have
been too effective, for as we are told in *The Calcutta Chromosome*'s narrative present (and, indeed, in our historical present), the world faces
a depletion of its potable water supplies.[12] The point to be registered is
that racialized military aims as much as, if not more than, any altruistic
desire to mitigate disease in natives propels the investigation of present-
day shrinking water supplies in Ghosh's fiction (and arguably in the real

world). Akin to STS scholar Michelle Murphy's claims with regard to the temporal bleeding of the current petrochemical extractive economy into unknown reproductive effects in future generations, the imperialist aims of conquering and dispossessing the Calcuttans in the novel feeds forward into the mutating reproductive milieu of late-nineteenth- and early-twenty-first-century New York City.

Both physically and metaphysically, the economic project underwriting imperialist expansion—the material extraction of mineral, botanical, fossil, and animal resources from far-flung lands and oceans—requires the conceptual wresting of human biologies from an embedded relation to the local environment. To be sure, not only human biologies but all biologies in modernity are displaced from the "tangled bank" of their natal ecosystems and made modular through a modern "scientific" classification system (Darwin). Biological organisms are translated into a discursive system that reaggregates them by way of their visible somatic features and functions, placing them into families or races (phyla) of structural resemblance, rather than by way of, for instance, the stories (*histoires*) told about them throughout time.[13] In such a system, the epidermal and (exo)skeletal boundaries of bodies come to matter more than in prior times (Barbara Duden's *Woman beneath the Skin*), paving the way for the Enlightenment notion of autonomous individuals disconnected both from the sheltering elements in which they breathe, swim, and move and from the preexisting social-semiotic order into which they were ushered. By crossing the supposedly distinct temporal periods of the novel and the distinct spatial boundaries between organism and milieu (the latter point to be developed in a later section), Ghosh precisely challenges the dissectional magic (called imperialist science) that allows for the treatment of long-term denizens as disentangle-able from living places, storied/mythic significance, ecology, and cosmos.

In the arena of medicine, Cindy Patton, drawing on Foucault's enunciation of biopower and biopolitics, points to the techniques of "the clinic" as exemplary of this wresting of the individual from a more embedded relation to the socio-natural environment: "The clinic [of the nineteenth century] is both a new 'carving up' of things and the principle of their verbalization in a form which we have been accustomed to recognizing as the language of a 'positive science.'"[14] As explained in chapter 1, epitomizing that new "carving up" were shifts in physicians' interactions with patients so that the key question "Where does it hurt?" displaced the more opened-ended query "What is the matter?" in the inauguration of doctoring and treatment. While one can imagine responses to the latter including references to imbalances of forces in the cosmos, to the divine, the kingdom, the village, and so forth, "Where does it hurt?" localizes the field of interest to the clinical subject's body. This new clinical gaze was decidedly noncosmological and pridefully so: its novelty, in other words, was staked on a proclaimed lack of an overarching theory and "its abandonment of systems."[15] Medical discourse was reorganized along lines of clinical empiricism, the idea that phenomena would surface as visible, observable evidence. The inheritance of such a carved-up system (clinical empiricism) goes hand in hand with the disdain for literary and cultural productions that, like Ghosh's novel, retain and resuscitate frameworks stressing the interconnectedness of organism and place/milieu, or the circling 'round—rather than mere linear progression—of biological events such as birth, growth, hosting, caretaking, aging, and decay—alternatively, the breaking down of complexly organized biological materials into simpler nutrients to sustain other (micro)organisms.

An alternative to modernist biopolitics, in other words, may also lie in a retrieved (latent) cosmological orientation—an enmeshed, entangled biospheric approach—in which the humans are not the only ones whose hurt we must mitigate.[16] In pursuing an interpretive method adequate to Ghosh's rejection of a "carved-up" epistemology that treats human bodies and the world in a disentangled and localized manner, we should consider the insights of the life sciences, in particular microbiology. As well, we might reconsider a mostly repudiated vein of feminist theory (one focused on the putative differences in the ego boundaries of girls and boys) for those aspects where it harmonizes with the insights of microbiology.[17]

The *Plasmodium* Parasite

Malaria (from the French for "bad air") is a catachrestically named syndrome characterized by lethargy, fever, delirium, and sometimes death in humans that manifests an "infection" by parasitic microorganisms or, put more precisely, the human host's becoming incapacitated by the reproductive robustness of the protist *Plasmodium*. ("Protista" refers to the kingdom of single-cell, nucleus-bearing organisms formerly called "Protozoa.") Malarial fevers correspond to the erythrocytic (or red blood cell) stage of *Plasmodium's* reproductive cycle as its merozoites multiply exponentially in the blood stream via schizogony (a kind of explosive mitotic division). To put it more starkly, though we think of malaria as a disease linked to morbidity and thus the antithesis of reproductive vitality, malaria is also *a sign of robust insect and protoctist reproduction.*[18]

Plasmodia are unicellular eukaryote (nucleus-bearing) organisms that predominantly live inside other cells, i.e., they are "intracellular."[19] However, when transiting from one milieu to another—e.g., from mosquito gut to vertebrate liver cells—*Plasmodia* take on an invasive form "specifically designed to find, recognize and enter a specific host cell."[20] These invasive morphologies, all characterized by an apical complex, are further distinguished into three types: sporozoite tailored to the liver cell, merozoite tailored to the red blood cell, and ookinete tailored to squeezing in-between mosquito gut epithelial cells (see figure 4.1).

This "polymorphism," according to parasite biologists Christophe Rogier and Marcel Hommel, comprises an "important survival strategy in *Plasmodium*," and it has a characterological corollary in Ghosh's novel—Mangala's research team, Murugan speculates, has found a way to transport themselves across different bodies (and thus different times).[21] Thus, if Mangala is the life form (akin to *Plasmodium*), the sporozoite, merozoite, and ookinete phases of her correspond to Urmila, Tara, and Mrs. Aratounian (the Armenian woman renting rooms to Murugan and the mentor of Urmila). Similarly, Laakhan is to *Plasmodium* as Ronen Haldar/Lutchman/Lucky are to these same three morphologies of the protoctist. To speak of this horizontal personality transfer perfected by Mangala's group as reincarnation or body jumping colors this technology with the aura of the fantastical or counterfactual. But through his evocation of the malaria "bug" (251), Ghosh makes legible the polymorphisms of his main characters through Western science, namely, microbiology, as he also emphasizes correspondences among scientific and spiritualist theologies. It is microbiology that connects sporozoite to merozoite to ookinete, seeing them not

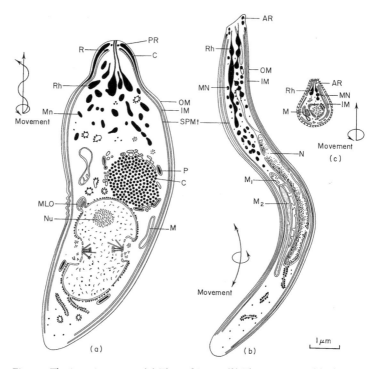

Fig. 4.1. The invasive stages. (*a*) The **ookinete**. (*b*) The **sprozoite**. (*c*) The erythrocytic **merozoite**. *Abbrevations*: AR, apical ring; C, collar; Cr, crystalloid; IM, inner pellicle membrance; M, mitochodrion; MLO, multilamellate organelle; Mn, microneme; N, nucleus; Nu, nucleolus; OM, outer pellicle membrane; P, pigment; PR, polar ring; R, electron dense ring; Rh, rhoptry; SB, spherical body; SPMt, subpellicular microtubules. *Courtesy of Elsevier Books.*

as separate, disconnected entities but rather as stages of a mutating nucleic and cytoplasmic choreography. In parallel fashion, by the end of Ghosh's novel, separate characters inhabiting different spaces and historical time periods—the dust sweeper, Mangala, of unknown origins, employed in Ronald Ross's malaria research lab in Calcutta c. 1898; the journalist Urmila Roy living in Calcutta c. 1995; and the Armenian hostel proprietor, Mrs. Aratounian, also living in Calcutta c. 1995—are implied as various phases of a single biological entity who in the narrative present appears as Tara, the undocumented nanny living in New York in the late twentieth to early twenty-first centuries.

Publicity shot for *Bowl Problems* (2004). *Photo by Peter Melville.*

My Father's Teeth in My Mother's Mouth. Lotus blossoms. Still shot from videotape of performance at the Japanese American Culture and Community Center, Los Angeles. *Courtesy of Cheng-Chieh Yu.*

Part 5 of *My Father's Teeth in My Mother's Mouth.* Teeth shower down from can at groin. Still shot from videotape of performance at the Japanese American Culture and Community Center, Los Angeles. *Courtesy of Cheng-Chieh Yu.*

My Father's Teeth in My Mother's Mouth. Dental chart looms in the background. *Courtesy of Cheng-Chieh Yu.*

Uyehara catches projected images of a post-9/11 "Vigil," from *Big Head* (2003). *Photo by Marcel Schaap.*

From Allan deSouza's *Rdctns* (2011). "Mango" (*left*) redacts Rousseau's *Amerindian with Gorilla* (1910). "Oriental Iris" (*right*) redacts Gaugin's *Women Bathing* (1892). *Courtesy of Allan deSouza.*

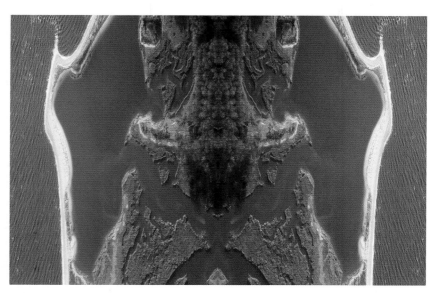

Allan deSouza's "Divine 3815" from (*I don't care what you say*) *Those Are Not Tourist Photos* (2006), Talwar Gallery. *Courtesy of Allan deSouza.*

The multiple embodiments of *Plasmodium* provide a template for comprehending human migration, colonialism, and encounters be-tween hosts—relatively "static" and large-scale bodies compared to the organisms inhabiting them—and guests—motile or traveling micro-ontologies. In one major tradition of the philosophy of ethics, hosting work turns on the alienness of, rather than the scalar contrast between, the guests and their hosts, with the limits of ethics contemplated via the hosts' capacity for unconditional hospitality—to protect one's guests from the violations proposed by others, even if that protection entails that the host's daughters be served up for sexual violation (Diprose; Derrida). Hosting—as I am using it here—raises the issues of the entanglement of the natal and the alien, and the unclear, involuted spa-tial boundaries that perplex us when thinking about the *Plasmodium*'s intracellular and intercellular invasive forms. That is, even *Plasmodium*'s "invasive" or transiting forms (figure 4.1), in which they shuttle from one cellular milieu to the next, remain "in bodies"—that is, bathed in the fluids of a host's tissues—an observation adding complexity to the firm border between the inside and outside of cellular bodies. *Plasmo-dium*'s life cycle reminds us that while from the microorganismal per-spective, there is indeed a milieu—e.g., the bloodstream of the verte-brate, the gut of the mosquito—seeming to be outside the invasive form of *Plasmodium* bodies (these are their infrastructures of reproduction, to use Murphy's terms), from the host species' perspective that outside is also embodied or "in body" (the cosmos becomes also an inside, so to speak).[22] The point to be registered regarding this changed perspec-tive is not that there is no outside the body, but rather that, through a transformed ethico-epistemological "touch and regard" for *Plasmo-dium* (Haraway 2008)—as opposed to an infectious-disease approach to malaria—we become attuned to the entangled web of interspecies dependencies.

In her work on *Companion Species*, Haraway uses the etymological root of "companion"—"*cum panis*" (with bread, eating well together)—to characterize the texture of human-canine relationality she at other times calls "touch and regard"—a mutual learning and caretaking that is intimately proximate ("touch") but still remains separable and at some distance ("regard," which involves esteemed "looking"—with sight, as opposed to touch, historicized as a distancing sense): "Messmates at table are companions. Comrades are political companions. A companion in literary contexts is a . . . handbook [to] help readers consume well."[23] For Haraway, a companion species orientation would make us less anxious toward symbiogenesis and "potent transfections" across species divides.[24] Ghosh's novel proposes such a potent transfection in vertebrates' existing reproductive integration into *Plasmodium's* life cycle and in the hypothesizing of humans' eventual reliance upon *Plasmodium* to reproduce themselves (the technique that Mangala's group refines). Yet the scalar disproportion of humans and *Plasmodium* makes mostly illegible their possible *cum panis* (eating with, instead of feeding upon) relationality. Instead of a companion relationality, then, we might speak of Ghosh's novel installing a "touch and regard" for the entangled web of interspecies dependencies—what I call a chimeracological embeddedness or onto-epistemology.

My neologism, "chimeracological," is formed through the merging of the terms "chimera," derived from ancient Greek "*Khimaira*," referring to a hybrid monster composed of several different animal parts,[25] and "ecological," a secular subset of the cosmological. Chimeras have become a humdrum reality of the laboratory, which we know by way of bioreactors—the modification of animals to produce human hormones—and the use of bioluminescence from fireflies and sea pansies introjected into mammalian tissues in medical imaging, for instance. My usage of the term refers not simply to these instrumental uses of animals in the medical and pharmaceutical industries of the late twentieth and early twenty-first centuries but to the more longstanding entanglements of species that are intuited by that ancient term but that biogeneticists have in the last forty-five years confirmed underlie complex organisms' thriving and evolution. Haraway stresses that "nothing makes itself in the biological world, but rather reciprocal induction within and between always-in-process critters ramifies through space and time on both large and small scales in cascades of inter- and intra-action. In embryology, [Scott] Gilbert calls this 'interspecies epigenesis.'"[26]

A feminist ecological project might associate the chimeracological with the females of the human species due to either their biological capacities of gestating alterity or their cultural histories of nurturing other life. The proposition of some variants of American feminism in

the late 1970s and early 1980s, that "women's relationally defined existence, bodily experience of boundary challenges, and . . . experience
[of] others and themselves along a continuum" derives materially from
women's gestational labor, needs only a slight modification to figure as
a standard bearer for the chimeracological: "[T]he child [aka uterine
guest or parasite] carried for nine months can be defined 'neither as me
or as not-me,' [with] inner and outer . . . not polar opposites but a continuum."[27] Accused of essentialism, this vein of feminism remains distinctly out of fashion; yet we might consider aspects of it anew given its
harmonizing with microbiologists' calling into question the virtue and
reality of species' and organismal autonomy (which is to say "the self
experienced as walled city . . . discontinuous with others").[28] Indeed,
one path of reenlivening this variant of feminism involves blending its
insights on the affective (psychic) dimensions of reproductive, hosting work with materialist analyses concerned with crediting as valuable (and life-enhancing) the embodied, metabolic, and affective labors
demanded of women from the global South that are often uncompensated in their contracts of gestational surrogacy and low-wage "intimate
labors" (Vora; Boris and Parranes). While a feminist object relations
approach (of the Nancy Chodorow variety) looks to women's reproductive labor as seeding a possible greater comfort with the lively continuum of interspecies epigenesis, the microbiologists' rejection of organismal autonomy (and prizing of entanglement and what Lynn Margulis
calls "endosymbiogenesis" as a condition of health, life, and existence)
sees that insight or comfort as a function of viewing the world at the
scale of the microbe. Splitting the difference, Ghosh produces in his
character Mangala, a dung scooper/service worker and a DIY micros-
copist, a person whose habituation to symbiogenetic risks and rewards
can be credited both to her situated knowledge as a colonized servant
and her scientific (self-)training.

   While we may hesitate to endorse the claims made by Chodorow
for an empathetic feminine disposition, whether historically or biologically patterned, attuned to hosting the alien, we can nonetheless
notice a queer excess or promiscuity in *Plasmodia*'s seeding grounds.
We might regard the *Plasmodium*'s reproductive technique as both
queer (nonheteronormative) and hyperbolically hetero—the latter
alluding not to object choice or the requirement of haploid "male" and

"female" gametocytes that subsequently fuse—but hetero in terms of the distributed epigenetic seeding grounds, as it were, of its multistaged schizogony: the multiple migration of the *Plasmodium* from intestinal wall of the mosquito to salivary glands of the same to the liver and the red blood cells of the vertebrate. The *Plasmodium's* morphologies and kinetic processes require hosting milieux comprised of other animal body parts akin to the polluted waterways Murphy dubs "infrastructures of reproduction."

By framing the novel as offering a portrait of queer reproduction—one that prompts a rethinking of normative heterosexual reproduction "between a man and a woman" as at the core of the future continuance of an elect species-being—my point is *not* that the narrative centers gay/lesbian desire. Rather, Ghosh's novel, read through a microbiologically informed lens, limns the entangled reproductive cycles of several species. Mangala's group in Ghosh's novel, in other words, treats not as pathological but as natural and even advantageous the being entangled in an Other's alter-reproductive habits (be the Other gay or "schizogonic"—a neologism drawn from the fissioning of protist sporozoites in the bloodstream of vertebrates). Here, I suggest a productive contagion between a microbiological-animal studies and femiqueer approach, especially in their shared political ethics toward reaffirming intimate entanglement with other social and biological life not as something to be feared (that which induces panic) but as part of the *vis medicatrix naturae* (Ed Cohen).

According to Ed Cohen, our current notions of biological "immunity" began as a political metaphor, i.e., the state of being dis-obliged from others, freed from responsibilities to the *munis* or community of belonging, and it is only in modernity that this political idea migrates into the spheres of science and medicine, described as an innate capacity of an organism's biology. These forgotten political origins are partly responsible for our construing as "natural" the idea of an atomistic cell (or individual) at war with each and every one. What this view of the defensive body forgets, according to Cohen, is a prior view of the *vis medicatrix naturae*, the healing power of nature: "According to this worldview, healing manifests the organism's natural elasticity: it incorporates the organism's most expansive relations to the world, embracing the forces that animate the cosmos as a whole."[29] Citing the microbiologist Lynn Margulis, Cohen's critical biopolitical studies approach suggests the need for a politics attuned to how

> organisms evolve not just by competition and "survival of the fittest" but also by cooperation and symbiosis. . . . [Margulis claims] that all nucleated cells represent the successful fusion of two or more bacterial lineages [aka chimeras]. . . . "The human body is an architectonic compilation of millions of agencies of chimerical cells. . . . We are all multiple beings. . . . The body is not one self but a fiction of a self built from a mass of interacting selves."[30]

Speaking to humans' cooperative entanglement with bacterial cultures, Heather Paxson coins the term "post-Pasteurian"[31] to refer to a (re)new(ed) regard for bacteria and other microorganisms as also symbiotic actors alongside humans, rather than "anthropocentric[ally] evaluat[ing] such agents" as carriers of disease.[32] To what extent can these compilations of chimerical cells, and an orientation toward the post-Pasteurian, offer a model of cross-species, cross-population intimacy that forms a queer[33] alternative to, not mere apology for, imperial-colonized relations?

Adventures in Babysitting

I want to bracket that question for now in order to turn to how Ghosh's novel dramatizes an onto-epistemological shift (crossing over) that hinges upon a maturation or learning that inverts the conventional liberal narrative equating growth with the leaving behind of obligations of descent and biological dependencies of nurture and care. Here I expressly draw on a feminist framework attentive to the immaterial (unacknowledged) labor of caretaking—a caretaking disavowed in the fetishizing of autonomy. It is the disillusionment with this carved-up world of autonomous individuality that prepares the subjects—the protagonists of Ghosh's novel as our readerly avatars—for crossing over into an onto-epistemological realization of collective and cross-species enmeshment.

As noted earlier, the narrative present of *The Calcutta Chromosome* spans the duration of a couple of hours with Antar confined to his apartment abutting the Holland Tunnel. In the opening chapters, the reader learns of Antar's increasing isolation. Orphaned as a child, widowed, nearing his retirement, and progeny-less (his wife, in fact, having died from complications in pregnancy), Antar spends his days logged onto a computer while situated in a building nearly empty of tenants, the units given over to storage. He is a bleak caricature of the atomistic individual.

While one might presume digital access would provide virtual travel to other worlds—as suggested by the inaugural animated icon of a rotating globe featured in the 1990s web browser Netscape Navigator—Ghosh's novel presents Antar as stifled by his occupational tethering to his AVA/IIe computer system. Formerly an employee in the accounting department of a small, independent public health constituency called Life Watch, the ripely middle-aged Antar has been absorbed into the behemoth IWC (International Water Council) and spends his days telecommuting, which is to say, stuck in his apartment, epitomizing in negative the unobliged individual. His energies go toward tricking the computer into thinking he is working—tending the inventory lists scrolling down on the computer screen—when he is actually sneaking a read from his electronic book (4). Antar has no sense of how his job, helping to compile enormous catalogues of items received from the IWC's various satellite offices (now closed), fits into the IWC's overall mission of investigating "the depletion of the world's water supplies" (7); he only "[stares] patiently at those endless inventories, wondering what it was all for" (5).

Rather than expanding his human agency, the computer both surpasses and displaces human mnemonic and calculative capacities (recall that Antar was formerly in the *accounting* department), but nonetheless demands the servitude of Antar as a kind of gratuitous tech support in case some odd debris crosses "the system's" path:

> [I]t was the chain [on the identity card for L. Murugan] that tripped the system. . . . Once it got started [on its routine inventories] it would keep them coming, hour after hour, an endless succession of documents and objects, stopping only when it stumbled on something it couldn't file: the most trivial things usually . . . a glass paperweight, of the kind that

rains snowflakes if you turn them upside down; another time it was a bottle of correcting fluid. Both times the machine went into a controlled frenzy, firing off questions, one after another. . . . Somewhere along the line [the AVA system] had been programmed to hunt out real-time information. (3–4)

The "machine" here is placed in tension with human sociality and significance—especially in an affective register (the kitsch nostalgia of the snowflake paperweight). Having a rendezvous with friends at a doughnut franchise located in New York City's Penn Station, Antar wishes to leave his apartment but cannot due to a late-breaking hiccough in the learning curve of the AVA/IIe, a learning dependent upon the human organism, despite Antar's attempt to make the machine autonomous— e.g., "routing [the AVA] to her own encyclopedias" but finding that for AVA, "that wasn't good enough" (4):

> Antar had met children who were like that: "why? what? when? where? how?" But children asked because they were curious; with *these AVA/ IIe systems* it was something else—something that he could only think of as a simulated urge for self-improvement. He'd been using *his Ava* for a couple of years now and he was still awed by *her* eagerness to better *herself*. . . . *She* wouldn't stop until Antar had told her everything he knew about whatever it was that *she was playing* with on her screen. (4; emphases added)

More so than his information stores, which surely could not compete with the capacity of a supercomputer, the AVA/IIe relies upon Antar's social attention or affective labor. Notice, too, the way the "system" designated by the brand and model AVA/IIe acquires a gendered organismal (chain of) identity across the course of this paragraph, being called "she" and "her," compared to a curious child, and familiarized by the sobriquet "Ava," which replaces "AVA/IIe." Discovered in these inaugural moments of the novel, then, are not merely the physical identity chain recovered in Calcutta that links Antar and the reader to Murugan's investigations into the history of malaria research but also the enmeshment of that story of malaria (the etiology of which bespeaks a three-way chain of Protista, arthropods, and humans), as it attaches to another tethered composite identity, that of Ava-Antar (and to a gendered syntax).

While other critics have remarked on Ava as symbol of bureaucratic and corporate surveillance (B. Ghosh; Shinn), we would do well to consider how a more domestic relation analogizes the Ava-Antar coupling: Ava appears as the intelligent, high-needs child of the imperial occupier to Antar's colored nanny. This relation is characterized by mixed combinations of age-related and racialized power inequities, with the imperialist's offspring not quite the boss of the nanny, but also not quite the nanny's underling.

When in a resentful moment Antar mutters under his breath that Ava is just a "dust-counter," her response renders him awed and speechless, as we might find ourselves in trying to light upon the exact term to name their relation: man-tool, colonized-imperialist, master-slave, parent-child—all of which are both precise in some respects and wanting in others:

> [Antar muttered under his breath in Arabic,] "That's what you are Ava, a Dust-Counter, *Addaad al-Turaab*." . . .
>
> Her "eye," a laser-guided surveillance camera, swiveled on him. . . . Then Ava began to spit out translations of the Arabic phrase, going through the world's languages in declining order of population: Mandarin, Spanish, English, Hindi, Arabic, Bengali. . . . It was funny at first, but when it got to the dialects of the Upper Amazon Antar couldn't bear it any longer. "Stop showing off," he shouted, . . . "*Iskuti*; shut up."
>
> But it was Ava who silenced him instead, serenely spitting the phrases back at him. Antar listened awestruck as "shut up" took on the foliage of the Upper Amazon. (7)

If, for heuristic purposes, we were to figure the social relation here in terms of the antagonism of master and slave (or some corollary dichotomy), we would quickly realize that paradigm's inadequacy. In this reading, Antar (the slave) verbally resists Ava's superior calculative mastery by framing her intelligence as serving trivial ends (dust counting), a judgment only confirmed when Antar names as superfluous ("stop showing off") Ava's super-fluency in the world's languages, which includes the hierarchical ordering of them according to a biopolitical calculus of population. At the same time, we can read the passage as one in which the human parental figure (Antar) admonishes the exuberant child (Ava), only to be astonished at the irrelevance of social regulation (e.g., norms of productivity) to this other life form's algorithmic logics that turn out to have a playful side.

The last three sentences of this passage, however, underscore what is really at hand: the intertwinement of Ava's will to "surveillance, identification and documentation"[34] and Antar's intimation of the limits of this hyperverbalization through the significatory capacities of silence. While Antar's directly executed command, "*Iskuti*," fails on the diegetic level of this encounter—with Ava favoring the capacity to code and recode the phrase rather than obey/execute it—the passage nevertheless underscores the key significance of silence "as 'shut up' [takes] on the foliage of the Upper Amazon." That is, the registering of the magnitude of Ava's superfluency is dependent upon Antar's *awestruck wordlessness*, even as Antar's silence cannot be qualitatively equated to any one positivistically delineated feeling—admiration, disgust, surprise, astonishment, exasperation, envy, tenderness, and so forth. The instrumental imperative to be silent is, simultaneously, rejected by the imperialist offspring (the computer) at the same time that the affective (aesthetic) import of silence *performed* by Antar is that which delivers for the reader the significance of the passage. In this way, this passage foreshadows the method of silence affirmed by Mangala and postcolonial counterscience against the value system of imperialist science favoring documentation as *the* mode of becoming a subject of (and becoming subjected to) knowledge.

The capacity of that which either is not or cannot be affirmatively coded also speaks to the value of undocumented phenomena, which returns us to the thread of my argument vis-à-vis the uneven power dynamics of caretaking structuring the exchanges between Antar and Ava. Undocumented caretaking work—as in caretaking that is not recognized as such—which I have metatextually claimed characterizes Antar's relation to Ava, characterizes another person in the novel's frame story. Introduced to Antar by a coterie of fellow immigrants who gather with Antar at the doughnut franchise, Tara, Antar's sole neighbor and the unpresuming "star" of the narrative ("*tara*" is Sanskrit for "star"), works as an undocumented babysitter:

> [She] had been brought into the country by a Kuwaiti diplomat and his family, to care for their children. The arrangement hadn't worked out so she'd found another babysitting job, in Greenwich Village. . . . [Antar] guessed that the change of jobs had made Tara's status illegal and that she needed to find a place [to reside] where she could pay cash without having to deal with a lot of questions. (18–19)

Tara and her friends successfully press Antar to allow Tara to squat in the vacant apartment next door to him (indeed, the whole building is vacant as management wishes to convert it from living space to storage—biological life displaced by durables, commodities, and archives of information). When she loses her job, Antar again lends assistance, hooking her into his computer network so that she can search for the selective babysitting jobs posted online. Evoking a digitized forum for the procuring of undocumented nannies, Ghosh's narrative highlights the racialized conditions of U.S. labor stratification in the late 1990s[35] that only extends the hierarchy of white masters and colored serving classes established under territorial colonialism.

Through informal immigrant communities like those gathered at the doughnut shop, migrants from the West's former colonies caretake each other, the newer immigrants like Tara assisted by the earlier, more established arrivals like Antar (a pecking order of pedagogical mentorship emerges, structured by years lived in the metropolitan West). Yet this hierarchy of caretakership is also inverted by the novel's end, when Antar discovers that Tara is the coalesced assemblage of several personalities who have appeared in the time frames set in the Calcuttas of the late nineteenth and late twentieth centuries: (parts of) Mrs. Aratounian and Mangala have been transported to Urmila Roy/Tara's morphology through a bioengineered technique modeled on *Plasmodium*'s polymorphism. Babysitting has provided Tara a most suitable cover story: her real interest has been to stage an intimate experiment—a cyborg, malarial connection—with Ava-Antar, the latter of whom contracted malaria as a child. Tara's ruse of babysitting work, then, is both a ruse—she takes no jobs with rich families in New York City—and not a ruse: she caretakes—helps gestate and births—a biotechnological chimera whose key component, Antar, is himself multiple—a wet vertebrate organism also comprised of (alternatively coexisting with) the intracellular malarial parasite *Plasmodium* and the informatics of the Ava/IIe network.

While the foregoing has mapped unobvious instances of caretaking in the novel (between babysitter Antar and the imperialist offspring Ava; between the undocumented nanny Tara and her unwitting charge, Antar), let me now turn to a more legible instance of domestic labor in Ghosh's narrative: Urmila Roy is expressly asked to subordinate her own career as a journalist, and that which provides her waged income, to act as a sororal caretaker to benefit her brother's potential athletic recruitment to a cricket club. Urmi's mother breathlessly tells her daughter of a call from a national team informing the family of their intention to visit and talk to her brother, Dinu, the next day. Dinu's first thought is of Urmila—according to their mother—and how she must prepare a fish so that the family might ask Ronen Halder, the team's owner, to stay for dinner. Exasperated, Urmila informs her mother that this request will conflict with her paid work—her press assignment to attend a morning speech by the national communications minister—because acting the host and cook requires her going to market at daybreak for the fresh catch. For Urmi's mother, a First Division cricket contract for Dinu means "money" and the possibility that Urmila can "give up this stupid job and stay at home. . . . Maybe we can even get you married before it's too late" (132). For Urmila, her newswoman's job—the household's current sole source of income outside her father's pension—*is* her service to the family: "[I]f I didn't have the job . . . how would we get by? . . . How would we feed the children?" (133), she asks, to which her mother counters, in contradiction to her earlier excitement at the prospect of more household income, "That's all you think about. . . . Money, money, money. . . . You have no place in your heart for our joys and sorrows. You should have seen how happy your brother was. . . .'" (133). Staged here explicitly is the conflict between material and so-called immaterial labor. That is, what is to be considered the core component of caretaking work: wage earning or emotional support? While Urmila's work for the family will produce a product—the cooked fish—the "immateriality" of labor, here, refers to the elusiveness by which certain forms of energy expenditure—caring, pedagogic, and metabolic forms of work—are credited as productive or wealth-producing.[36] Here, the novel would seem to chime in with feminist research on the invisibility and denigration of unwaged housekeeping—that which certainly enhances vitality but does not count in economic assessments of GNP. What the reproductive (or domestic) laborer produces is not simply an energetic equivalent (nutritional sustenance) that allows the waged worker "to return to work each day" but also the "rehumanizat[ion of] the worker as more than a commodity, 'creating the illusion that he is an individual with unique characteristics and a real personality'" (Vora 2012, quoting Leopoldini Fortunati, 689). However, in order to produce this humanistic view of the waged worker (a view irreducible to his material role as alienated labor in capitalist production), the housewife, mother, or sister must appeal to a value system outside of material wealth production, a value system in which her own labors (to rehumanize, which is to say, to concoct a human worth transcendent of materialist value) must necessarily go unrecognized.[37]

Significantly, Urmila capitulates to familial expectations and attempts to cook the dinner:

[By] seven fifteen in the morning [she is] grinding spices, perspiration dripping off her face onto her grease-spotted sari. She had already been up an hour: she had given her parents their breakfast; she had cleaned the kitchen; she had fed and bathed her nephew and niece; she had washed her younger brother's uniform for his afternoon football match. She would have to leave within the hour if she was to be on time for the press conference. . . . Urmila looked out the window, trying to estimate how long it would take her to run to Gariahat Bazaar and back [for the fish]. (171)

As it turns out, and despite her labor, the immaterial product—the well-being and happy face of the family performed by Urmila's hosting a dinner in her brother's honor—is not realized, because the wrapping of the fresh catch in very old newspaper spoils the fish, which sends Urmila on a hunt for restitution from the fishmonger.[38] In other words, Urmila's procuring and preparing of the fish—her exceptional sacrifice this day—only metonymically materializes in the narrative by way of the list of mundane activities she does *every morning* quoted above. It is perhaps this bodily habitus in caretaking and hosting others—placing priority on the care of others over care of the self or public recognition—that outfits her as the one who, according to Murugan, will be "chosen" (307) by Mangala-bibi for a grand experiment in cohosting an emergent biology-ecology.

The circumstance where caretaking labor is placed in rivalry with waged information work bespeaks not simply the reporter and daughter Urmila Roy's situation but Antar's too. However, in the latter case, Antar's information work—his patience tending to Ava as she "show[s] off" her acquired skills—is not that which liberates him from affective obligations, but is one and the same with them. It may be useful to recall here that Michael Hardt and Antonio Negri speak of the diagram of power in the late twentieth and early twenty-first centuries as post-industrial and informational-empiric with labor no longer conforming to the Fordist model of industrial commodity production analyzed by Marx. They attempt a better lexicon to bespeak the "immateriality" of some late-twentieth-century labor: service work, affect work, calculation and communications work.[39] With two characters, Urmila and Antar, who are thoroughly embedded in the affective work of, on the one hand, caretaking and, on the other hand, communications work (information processing/journalism), Ghosh's novel illustrates the continuum of these labors but also puts a finer point on Hardt and Negri's framework.

Why, for instance, does Antar resent being tethered to Ava—who requires the emotional work of constant attention (of sustained interest and regard)—more than he seems to resent his work as an accountant doing routine symbol manipulation for his former employer Life Watch? Similarly, why does Antar—who contracted malaria as a child—resent being at the beck and call of the supercomputer Ava when he merely accepts the service of his biomaterials (liver, blood cells) to *Plasmodia*'s growth—when he biologically gestates these parasites, so to speak? And while these parasites do take a physical toll (the malaria remains mostly dormant but, when active, generates bouts of feverish delirium), Antar issues no complaints regarding these somatic effects. If, as Hardt and Negri's schema suggests, the *immateriality* of the labor is key to understanding these differences in engendering resentment, the laboriousness of Antar's affective labor toward Ava rises in proportion to its immaterial "mystique"—the way it does not have a clear somatic sign of exertion or value production. In comparison, there is a material sign of the labor Antar performs for the *Plasmodium* albeit of a pathological sort: fever and delirium. These nonetheless physical manifestations (a writing on the body) show that Antar is laboring, as it were, producing potential signs of recognition in a moral economy where not merely work but visible, material products of that work are prized.[40]

Ghosh's novel, however, gives us another framework in which to comprehend the distinctiveness of the kinds of affective labor Antar and Urmila emotionally struggle to perform; this affective labor is distinguished less by its not producing material products or symptoms and more by its efficacy as labor working toward healthy bonding, the prizing of one's obligations to the *munis*. That view of communal obligation as healthy reverses the priority placed on autonomy and immunity prized in modern societies of the global North (rehearsed earlier by way of Cohen's *Body Worth Defending*).

Let me return, briefly, to how a gendered division of labor differently textures Antar's and Urmila's faith in a mystified autonomy that forms a (temporary) barrier to each one's recognition of his/her familial, communal, and chimeracological embeddedness. As noted earlier, Antar exemplifies the atomistic individual, with his desires to leave his apartment bespeaking, it would seem, desires for human sociality at the doughnut franchise. Yet, his social mingling at the shop exposes him to relatively little emotional or bodily risk (or so he thinks), for at the franchise, he consumes a sociality hosted by others: the owner of the shop prepares his tea "just the way [Antar likes it] . . . thick and syrupy, with a touch of mint" (15)—after which he plans to join Tara for a dinner *she* is preparing. Antar resents the affective obligation to Ava that preempts his cognitive and affective consumptions realized elsewhere (in his ebook, in his tea taking, in his dinner cooked by another). Antar exercises an avatar of autonomous choice in the realm of consumption. He must learn to choose or surrender to the caretakership of the nonhuman entity Ava—must exercise affective/biological hospitality against a proffered autonomy via economic and gustatory consumption—whereas for Urmila Roy, as we shall see, it is the autonomy of wage earning that she must pass up.

Dramatizing Urmila's readiness to be "chosen" for the hosting of Mangala's recombinatory experiment, Ghosh crafts a situation in which Urmila can choose an embeddedness in obligations to others—e.g., to Dinu and the family—against a countering degree of autonomy represented by her reporter's job. For Urmila, the prospect of autonomy through waged work, a prospect fragile and illusory from the start, is pitted against her gendered obligations to her family, obligations that supersede and take precedence over her "own" desires. Confirming her embeddedness in obligations to others only requires Urmila's "return," so to speak, to her gendered place in the family, whereas to become embedded in obligations to the *munis* requires of the orphaned Antar the taking on of what looks like a new risk—becoming the animal biology (zoon/*zoe*) whose flesh (cellular organization, metabolism, tissue systems) feeds the alien—in ways similar to the phase one (male) experimental medical subject described by Melinda Cooper whose imbibed dosages up and through the point of toxicity in pharmaceutical trials render him the "new" neoliberal sacrificial subject bearing risk for the collective.[41]

Despite Murugan's exposition informing the reader that Urmila has been chosen as the next host for Mangala/Mrs. Aratounian, in the dramatization of an affective sublime at such merging, it is Antar's male embodiment and Murugan's mosquito-exposed torso (in the aforementioned dream sequence) that provide the readerly avatars for staging the visceral violence and erotics of hospitality.[42] Ghosh uses the male body, supposed as less contradictorily inhabiting the illusory status of autonomous personhood, to make strange, unfamiliar, and more terrifying the porousness and mutations of cross-species assemblage—a parasexual form of generation.

By novel's end—which is to say, in the looping back to the *mise-en-scène* of the novel's opening, Antar's New York City apartment in the late 1990s–early 2000s—Antar's person provides the readerly avatar for a discovery felt as the bodily risk of self-obliteration—a distributed, centrifugalized feeling (to which I will return) synonymous with his coassembling with the *munis*. To intimately join the collective at the doughnut franchise, Antar (the reader's avatar) will become akin to an experimental medical subject, his body parts undergoing a possible schizogony—a centrifugal fissioning into fragments not unlike Margaret Cho's comic narration of the birthing mother's "exploding pussy" (see chapter 3). I say "possible" because the novel concludes at the moment of threshold.[43]

At the novel's finale, Antar has fallen into malarial delirium, corresponding to the human host's experience of the erythrocytic stage of *Plasmodium*'s schizogony in the human bloodstream. The feeling of this onto-epistemological shift is one of gothic haunting—the house is occupied by unknown others—and literalized in creepy coincidences such as Antar's hearing a beep he identifies as coming from his phone headset as he talks to Tara but also as ambient noise from the apartment next door, even though Tara claims she's at the park. The onset of fever coincides with Antar's donning his Sim Visor (he becomes an appendage of the AVA/IIe) that allows him to witness the identicalness of Urmila c. 1995 and Tara of the present. At the same time, Antar's offline body feels a heightened sense of tactile and aural claustrophobia, as the shadows—possessed of the voices and aspects of his acquaintances at the doughnut shop (who are the self-same members of Mangala's group)—come alive and crowd in: "[I]t was as though a crowd of people was in the room with him [murmuring] 'we're here, we're all with you . . . you're not alone; we'll help you across.' He sat back and sighed like he hadn't sighed in years" (311). Here, the narrative collapses the distance between organismal subject and the world: the environment and *munis* that Antar had imagined were at least forty blocks away at Penn Station now close in on him, as in a centripetal action. At the same time, the novel's concluding lines centrifugally distribute readerly cognition across Antar's peripheral body: "a cool soft touch under his shoulder" startles him, he feels a "[restraint on] his wrist . . . a voice in his ear, Tara's voice, whispering: 'Keep watching; we're here; we're all with you.' There were voices everywhere now, in his room, in his head, in his ears" (311).

By ending just here (before a portraiture of the new life to emerge— the assemblage of Antar/Ava/Tara/Urmila/Mangala/Lutchman/Ronen Haldar/Mrs. Aratounian, etc.), Ghosh effects the reader's dwelling in a processural distributed feeling of something like a fragmented body or, more precisely, a cytoplasmic, noncentralized proprioception: a "cool soft touch under his shoulder," a "[restraint on] his wrist," "a voice in his ear," a somatic awareness of senses unconfined to the brain. Here I want to suggest that while we can project beyond Ghosh's ending for the morphology that will contain the personalities preserved in the chromosomes of the historical persons who have horizontally transferred their nucleic essences, by doing so we will have missed the distributed sensations that actualize the novel's ending.

These centripetal- and centrifugal-izing actions of the novel's final moments, I argue, dynamically mimic (in a kinesthetic vein) two conceptualizations of reproduction historically significant in the era of the novel's composition and publication: one in which the centralized command and control of nucleic materials—sequences of genes—held the promise of organismal structure and development as a code book (Roof) and another resurgent idea in which environment (*munis*) or epigenetic influences were credited with coeval influence over the development and subsequent inheritance of traits (even allowing for so-called acquired traits).[44] Ghosh's novel, published in 1995, was itself gestated in a period of genetic euphoria, where cracking the human genome—aka "book of 'life'"—was rhetorically collapsed into a kind of *uber*-agency over vital processes (Roof). According to Eugene Thacker, key moments in multipurpose computing—1981, when IBM introduced personal computers, and 1984, when Apple introduced the Mac—mark an acceleration in coding literacy (and thereby coding metaphorics), even as the watershed dates typically cited in genomic histories rehearse (1) the Human Genome Project's official launch in 1990, with the project internationalized as the IHGSC (International Human Genome Sequencing Consortium) in the late 1990s and (2) J. Craig Venter's formation of the private competitor corporation Celera Genomics in 1998. Across the 1980s through 1990s, it was possible to think of the chromosome (biology collapsed into genes) as containing the key to an organism's subsequent development.[45] In the historical moment we now find ourselves in—whether we dub it "epigenetic," "interactionist," or "developmental systemic"—milieu, niche, environment, and contingent conditions—what used to be shorthanded as "nurture" but which Murphy dubs "infrastructures of reproduction"—have been granted an ascending importance as distributed, codetermining factors shaping vital materializations.

As the foregoing account of *The Calcutta Chromosome*'s frame story is meant to suggest, Antar's technical means of recovering missing pieces of the past—his AVA/IIe system—does not present a mere surface, beyond which lies the true story (the ongoing inequities of empire), but comprises the main drama in which a lesson regarding humanity's (and all of biological life's) chimeracological embeddedness unfolds: a lesson on the necessary labor of gifting one's attention and time toward some other entity's learning. Urmila's filial duty to her family, Antar's babysitting of Ava, Tara's undocumented looking after Ava-Antar, and Mrs. Aratounian's mentorship of Urmila in the basics of plant care[46]— all these forms of caretaking appear as gateways for later alliances figured as xeno-assemblages. In a preparatory manner, these *within-species* practices of nurture entrain a somatic cognizance of biological life as hardly autonomous but in its (cyber)entwinement and, down to its microscopic scale, a chimeracological choreography. Ambivalently for a racial justice project, then, Ghosh's dramatization of cross-species reproduction, alternatively parasexual coassemblage, features caretaking work as the novel's most salient figure of both (resented) contemporary indenture (racialized labor filling the jobs that the U.S. economy produces but that "only third world workers find attractive")[47] and that which endows an openness to a chimeracological onto-epistemology lost or suppressed in modernity.

Conclusion

To recall my earlier point, postcolonial and race studies have had an uneasy relationship with an ethics endorsing hospitality (alternately, caretaking) precisely because the latter can seem synonymous with an acquiescing to injustice and unevenness. In my urging of an expanded postcolonial and race studies project informed by theories of feminism, queerness, histories of bioscience, and companion species, one would not abandon justice and fairness (simplified between two historical antagonists) but would temper these goals with a healthy surrender to the complexity of contingent and arrayed obligations. If we are quite literate in the notion of history as a dialectical unfolding of antagonisms, how might we also entertain vital movement contoured as cascades of interdependent webs of enmeshed reproduction? The politics this yields—if we were to translate this into an identity politics—is one on behalf of the insect and unicellular organism as much as the racialized subject. To be sure, I am not arguing that Ghosh's novel requires or even endorses an identity politics now in the service of the-animal-as-centered-subject (Ghosh's novel, *The Hungry Tide*, in fact, questions the imperialist disregard for Dalits going hand in hand with the eco-preservation of the Bengal tiger). Instead, I distinguish a postcolonial and race studies project in an identity politics mode—illustrated by those critics fixated on the subaltern female counterscientist, Mangala, as a figure lost to history and thus in need of counterfactual (re)construction—from one in a more queer mode that regards Mangala, for instance, as part of a lesson on the necessary caretaking of a more broad-based chimeracological worldview.

The novel, in fact, plays with whether a human person is the ultimate reference for Mangala. That is, in the narrowest sense, Mangala refers in the novel to that distinctive female character contemporary to Ronald Ross, "found at Sealdah Station . . . dirt poor and . . . [with] hereditary syphilis" (245), uniquely gifted in microscopy, and who "chanced upon . . . the malaria [bug's] recombinatory powers" (249, 251–53). This Mangala is subaltern, expert, infectious, and parasitic—in the sense of (ab)using the labs of her British employers, which she is supposed to sweep rather than tamper with. As well, she is host/age to parasites: from her nativity, she's been entangled in a contagious, cross-species milieu—gestationally with the spirochete *Treponema pallidum* that causes syphilis and in adult life with the protist *Plasmodium*. At one point, Murugan describes Mangala as god-like: "the mind that sets things in motion" (249, 251–53). In this sense, Mangala stands for a principle of generativity less manthropomorphic and monotheistic (as in the Judeo-Christian tradition) and more interspecial, plural, and microorganismal. While "mangala" (when pronounced "mongola") corresponds to the Bengali word for "well-being, weal, welfare, good, benefit,"[48] textually "Mangala" also evokes the phonemic cousin term "*mancala*," itself a derivation from the Arabic word "*naqala*" ("to move"), but which Ghosh's readers might be more familiar with in its incarnations as various Egyptian, Syrian, and Lebanese "sowing games" in which the key principle is to distribute seeds or stones in a pattern of holes (centrifugalizing motion) and, intermediarily, to gather up seeds or stones that have (centripetally) collected in these pockets in order to redistribute them again. Counterposing the singular portrait of the Nobel Prize–winning British Man (Ronny Ross), helping to conquer disease and tame the tropics for the comfort of the pale races (i.e., the vital extension of their species-being), is not a subaltern brown-skinned woman, then, but more of a kinesthetic practice of careful sowing, a pedagogical repetition in assembling and reassembling seeds, of combining and recombining them not in stable fixed holes (empty vessels) but in changing, animate hosts.

In a political mode, we would want to proclaim as to whether viscerally learning one's integration with a multispecies ecology or, put another way, one's composition as multiple species of distributed intelligence, is ultimately resistant to capitalism or to racialized colonial processes of extraction. Is such a whole earth, ecological, even cosmological view of the connectedness of all things (alternatively, the human's diminishment as a particular species organization in a vast web of nature-cultures) incongruent with the perpetuation of exploitative violences? Ghosh's novel not only leaves that question open ended (by concluding the novel at the moment of Antar's and the reader's "crossing over" to this connected, chimeracological tactility) but also implies that underlying such a question is the yearning for the linear continuity of history—the future answering or resolving the past's unresolved losses/violence, or assessed in terms of the past's dialectics—that paradigm of movement qua temporal unfolding.

Key to the ethical affective work (movement) of *The Calcutta Chromosome* is its vertiginous effects, its kinetic involutions that approximate the sublime. As rehearsed by Donna Heiland citing Edmund Burke,

[S]ublime experience is terrifying experience that threatens to subsume individuals into something larger than themselves; it is experience in which boundaries blur and differences of all sort threaten to vanish: the difference between subject and object, between self and other, even between one time or place and another. An individual might finally be overwhelmed by that "something larger," or might avoid self-loss by instead internalizing and so mastering the idea of the infinite.[49]

The sublime, in other words, bespeaks the condition of discovering oneself a parasite, living on an animate host formerly mistaken for inert ground, with the "terror" and "self-loss" naming the scalar surrealism of realizing one's engulfment in a cosmos of which one is simultaneously apart (by way of a species distinction) and a part (vitally entangled).

By dwelling at length on the types of hosting work the novel explores and by figuring caretaking and hospitality/hosting on a continuum, I have attempted to call attention to an enlarged notion of reproduction and reproductive politics with which the novel is concerned, one that is not confined to sexual intercourse, embryogenesis, parturition, and neonatal care (nursing, etc.) but encompasses the entire life cycle of the organism and sometimes the life cycles of other species in generations backward and forward. As Michelle Murphy reminds us, the larger project of femiqueeer studies poses the question of how the presumption that reproduction is only a small temporal period beginning with fertilized gametes and ending with birth forecloses the analyses of wider, exo-maternal processes as also part of reproduction.

We might see this project of enlarging what counts as reproduction as sharing sympathies with an assemblagist, femiqueer politics, with the assemblagist—as I evoke it here—an effort to counter the clinical "carving up of things," to counter the manipulating of human-bodies-and-world primarily in a disentangled and localized manner. Ghosh's novel stylistically sows recursivity and complexity (as my many iterations of its criss-crossing plots have attempted to concretize), a complexity in which the exposure of the nonsolo nature of Nobel Prize–winning biological work as embedded in native knowledge and in complicated histories of British expansion resembles, on the one hand, the experiments of late-twentieth-century (postmodern) literary assemblage, but on the other, the ancient (Arab, Egyptian/African, Asian) game, *mancala*, of arranging and rearranging narrative and technological seeds. Ghosh's cast of characters features an (unknowable) figure whose name is a homophone for the sowing seed game—and whose very incarnation as an anthropomorphic character functions as a container metaphor. She is the mover, the principle we call God if we find security (legibility) in an anthropocentric contouring of the sublime ebbs and flows comprising ecosystems; and that which we call genetic codes—preformationist essence as sequences—if we find security in textuality (qua codes) as a substitute, compensatory God.

In giving us "Mangala"—a coded human mother figure of well-being—Ghosh merges the god-like and the textual and remains *expressively silent* in any exact reference to (*naqala*) "motion" itself, or choreography, as that which is generative (but not necessarily "just"—i.e., tending toward equilibrium). In her work on ontogenesis, Susan Oyama calls attention to the stubborn habit (in both the sciences and the humanities) of looking to singular causes—e.g., whether genes or environment—that preexist and thus have primary agency in the subsequent development of life forms:

> Organismic form . . . is not transmitted in genes any more than it is contained in the environment, and it cannot be partitioned. . . . Chromosomal form is an interactant in the choreography of ontogeny; the "information" it imparts or the form it influences in the emerging organism depends on what dance is being performed when, where, and with whom. The dance continues throughout the life cycle, and everything that occurs in that cycle . . . from the most typical feature to the most divergent, is constructed from these interactants.[50]

This choreographic or process-oriented emphasis that Ghosh's novel shares with Oyama opens the door for thinking more explicitly about how the language of kinesthetics and dance might help in construing, in an ethical mode, the nonsovereignty and nonautonomy of biological life processes and species-being (biopolitics and race). For now, we might think of this choreography and dance as pointing toward a race studies lexicon enabling an epistemological, meditative disposition especially attuned to not simply its own expendability and possible disappearance but its chimeracological entanglements that render its choreographies a part of some other entity's historical, lively continuance.

5

A Sideways Approach to Mental Disabilities

Incarceration, Kinesthetics, Affect, and Ethics

With head close-shaven, unafraid of speaking on sexually frank themes, Denise Uyehara emerged as a fresh talent in Asian American theater and the Los Angeles performance art scene of the 1990s. This artist launched her career at precisely the moment when "body art"[1] and queer performance were not only building critical audiences but also coming under increased scrutiny from the U.S. Congress (Hughes and Roman).[2] From 1993 to 1997, Uyehara performed with the multiracial feminist troupe, the Sacred Naked Nature Girls (SNNG), their nude performances a means of stripping away social masks.[3] At the same time, through residencies and commissions from museums, Uyehara mentored others in an array of practices through which to circulate memories. Her performances and installations have solicited audience involvement by way of writing and acting in relation to a specific prompt—e.g., "write about something you've lost" ("Lost and Found, I"), "form these bones in the shape of a childhood reminiscence" (*Senkotsu (Mis)Translation*), "return this object to the Lost and Found Department of the Sokos Department Store" ("Lost and Found, II").

Most of Uyehara's collaborative and solo works emerged from the rich environment of the Eighteenth Street Arts Complex in Santa Monica, commonly known as Highways, established in 1989 by Linda Frye Burnham and Tim Miller to nurture and showcase artists hailing from marginalized sexual and racial communities. The U.S. premiere of *Hello (Sex) Kitty*, the performer's signature work of the mid-1990s, took place there, as did the 1999 show, *Maps of City and Body*, a compilation of previous performances reshaped under the direction of Chay Yew. Across the past two decades, Uyehara has written and performed on a variety

of topics, much of it autobiographical, such as her grandmother's suicide by self-immolation, the internment of her great-grand-uncle during World War II, intraracial hate crimes in the United States, and the
difficulties of hooking up at lesbian bars.

With her propensity to launch her storytelling through anecdotal
and often eponymous reference to body parts or corporeal remains
(e.g., "Big Head," "Mapping the Body," and "Charcoal," the latter referring to the bodily remains of Uyehara's grandmother), Uyehara is both
an obvious and an odd choice with which to conclude a book examining the fragmentation of bodies as a primary vehicle through which
Asian American artists contemplate and critically theorize widespread
anxieties of being biological at the turn of the twenty-first century. She
is an odd choice in that no obvious bioscientific discoveries wend their
way into her work, nor does she mock the experience of being remade
into a carved-up body via late-twentieth-century encounters with clinical medicine (as in Yamanaka, Ishiguro, Cho, and Yu), nor does she
further a chimeracological view of the human organism's mergers with
information technology and microbiologies (as in Bear and Ghosh).
She is a productive choice in that much of Uyehara's corpus contemplates mentally disabled figures and the containments to which they are
subjected, in the name of the will to health. Overtly addressing disability, this artist's work nevertheless troubles any easy overlay between a
race studies and a disability studies approach to cultural productions.
Uyehara does not advocate on behalf of non-normate bodies or the differently abled as much as she contemplates and works through the relations of caring, misunderstanding, and irritation between those with
disabilities and their temporarily able-bodied intimates.[4]

Like Ghosh's novel, Uyehara's performances underscore the entanglement of biopolitically divided populations—here the able-minded
and differently abled. While Ghosh posits the caretaking of the young
as preparatory training for an embodied knowledge regarding humans'
hosting of and coassemblage with parasitic and commensal "alien"
microorganisms, Uyehara choreographs a local, highly contingent ethical "doing" in relation to the aged and mentally impaired. In contrast to
Ghosh's broad recognition of the chimeric fusions at the core of humanity, Uyehara's concerns are more traditionally (i.e., anthropocentrically)
humanist. Moreover, while the preceding chapters have scrutinized

artists concerned with the way in which, as Hardt and Negri propose, the prison is everywhere, this chapter's examination of Uyehara's performances tackles both formal and informal incarcerations—internment, concentration camps, indefinite detention, as well as clinical modes and practices in civil society that together produce the shut-in. Here the focus is on who gets segregated, left behind, and incarcerated, with these internments being gendered and disabled as much as racial.

Through an examination of two of Uyehara's works, one produced in 1999 and the other in 2003, this chapter reflects on central debates within performance studies and intersectional analyses of women of color, queers of color, and crips of color regarding the form and social obligations of memory. *Maps of City and Body* (1999) recalls salient moments in the formation of a queer Japanese American woman, while *Big Head* (2003) investigates American patriotism just a year after the United States' invasion of Afghanistan and a month shy of its invasion of Iraq. Both productions have recourse to neurological disorders— Alzheimer's and encephalitis, respectively—in their ruminations over how we choose to remember or forget "racial" violence, whether it takes the form of the World War II internment of Japanese Americans in the United States, the genocidal gassing of Jewish, queer, and disabled bodies in Europe during the Third Reich, or the indefinite detentions and extraordinary renditions of Muslims and Arabs worldwide in the first two decades of the twenty-first century.

One method of this chapter involves close scrutiny of contemporary biopower's anatomopolitics through a performance studies lens. Uyehara revisits the disciplining and ideological hailing of bodies by late-twentieth-century American choreographies called coming out/ getting "OUT" and acting patriotically (aka enlisting as a soldier in war). The artist reflects upon the retraining of these habits toward more ethical orientations, involving what affect theorist Teresa Brennan calls neuropsychological "entrainment" with regard to chemical or ectohormonal triggers.

In the first half of this chapter, I examine several of Uyehara's performances that feature mentally disabled characters, sequencing my presentation according to the increasing prominence of those characters. This sequencing is one befitting an identity-politics approach to the subject of disability. Across all of these works, dance and tango provide Uyehara a methodological alternative to the conventional "narrative" technique of penetrating mental anomaly, that is, presenting it as a problem of knowledge—a pathological unknown to be made narratologically meaningful and "cured" or rehabilitated (Mitchell and Snyder 2001). Uyehara's "Dream" of dance bespeaks an ethical orientation that reaches beyond rationality (moral universals) and mere sentiment (aimed at garnering sympathetic recognition from others) to focus also on conduct and techniques of the embodied self.

The second half of the chapter provides a counterpoint to the identity-politics approach to the subject of mental anomalousness. Taking a cue from Saba Mahmood's articulation of techniques of the self as not simply the vehicle of power's subjection but also the practical conduct wherein "a subject transforms herself in order to achieve a particular state of being, happiness, or truth,"[5] I draw out the extent to which Uyehara's performances *enact* a critical alternative to the dominant biopolitical grid of eugenics pursued as and through abjection of the mentally defective, a bio-logic driven by "modern" and late-capitalist imperatives prizing ability, autonomy, and proleptic speed (getting there first). In theorizing Uyehara's valuing of a "time-slip" (elaborated in my conclusion), I turn to strains of ethical philosophy and affect theory that value meditative conduct over and above the primacy of self-determination, when the latter becomes synonymous with imposing one's will on and against one's surroundings.

Tangoing with the Mentally Disabled

> We sit around a large circle of tables facing each other. A woman is presenting her manuscript for critique, but a floral wallpaper pattern in brilliant lime-green, yellow, and orange has been printed over the text. The flowers hide the words, but I can still follow the story. . . . Turning a few pages, I see one that's filled by a bright red wooden door frame. Small photographs line the top and bottom of the page. People are getting frustrated. *How can we critique this?* they ask. . . . *We can't even understand it!* (*Maps of City and Body*, 19)

The collection of playscripts that includes *Maps of City and Body* and *Big Head* begins with this "Dream" of an anomalous text that frustrates its would-be "knowers." Uyehara's dream-self enters this fray by proposing that "someone [make] up a dance in response," in other words, surrender to the media plurality of the work by responding in kind, through another cross-platform action, namely, dance. In Uyehara's dancing proposition, we have a mimetic recognition that the piece has "moved" its audience, despite its resistance to semantic parsing. We can take this "Dream" as a guide to the aims, intentions, and technique of the performance artist. Across her shows, dance is figured as sensual, physical conduct involving the whole body, rather than merely the textually structured mind. It is a subset of kinesthetic practices more generally (sporting, walking, eating, typing, dressing, laboring, orgasming) that contour identity as much as, if not more than, genetic endowment or biopolitical profiling according to belonging in a gendered, racialized, or sexually reproductive aggregate.

In the retrospective show *Maps,* the performance artist uses dance to orchestrate her audience's relational ties to several nonheroic, nonautonomous, mentally ill persons. Significantly, her dancing stories do not achieve an expressive interiority for these subjects nor do they leave them entirely opaque. A particular style of dance, tango—famous for its contrapuntal alternating between tension and intimacy (Savigliano)— provides an apt metaphor for the texture of feeling with which the performer approaches mental anomaly. The potential of tango as a heuristic framework for contextualizing Uyehara's work derives from its duality as an absent presence in Uyehara's 1999 retrospective show, *Maps.*[6] Tango dancers acted as key collaborators in rehearsals and earlier staged versions. However, in the 1999 retrospective staged in Santa Monica (and archived in the volume of playscripts), the only overt reference to tango occurs in the show's final sequence when Uyehara slips on her deceased grandmother's tango shoes.

I begin my examination of *Maps,* then, by looking at the sequence on learning how to swim in which tango dancers, no longer prominently featured, nonetheless linger in the story structure. Particular choreographic gestures and symbols (the sharp intake of air upon surfacing, the trope of a BIG EYE that emerges from the watery depths) unite "Swimming's"[7] fragmented assemblage of childhood recollections. The sequence begins with Uyehara—in the persona of her mother— announcing that swimming lessons are to commence in the living room: "'If you can learn to draw [by sitting and watching] 'Sketch the World' on PBS, then you can learn to swim in the same [living] room' [she said]. . . . We bent at the waist and churned the air like slowly moving eggbeaters" (80).[8] Imitating a freestyle stroke, the performer stretches and pulls, before drifting to other memories of pleasurable and suffocating kinesthetics.

The sequence then brings in the young Denise's swimming partner, Elle, a friend in her apartment complex, who acts the sororal caretaker to a mentally retarded sibling. From Elle, Denise learns to play the out-of-water game "Bad Man and Little Girl":

> Elle told me to choose a crayon. . . .
>
>   I chose Bronze. She told me to put the crayon on her spot. [Gasp]
>
>   [Uyehara mimes the motions of breast-stroking as if surfacing for air timed to the "Gasps" indicated in the stage directions.]
>
>   Then we switched places, so she could be the Bad Man.
>
>   She said, *Spread your legs.* [Gasp]
>
>   *You are mine.* [Gasp]
>
>   *Don't tell anyone.* [Gasp]
>
>   *Don't make a sound.* [Gasp]
>
>   In the next room, I could hear her retarded brother watching *Dragnet* turned up loud. (80–81)

The performer lets the disturbing character of this pedophilic role-play hang in the air, neither condemning nor approving this pantomimed predatory relation. As noted by Kathryn Bond Stockton, the sexualization of the child is always also the queering of the child, because normative childhood is presumed to be asexual and "innocent."[9] In the kinesthetic queering of her younger self, erotically pleasurable choreographies—such as exploration of the genitals and swimming—become filtered through shame-inducing affects—with adult filters, let's call it the Law (*Dragnet*), ambiently structuring how these young girls learn to move.

The "Gasps" of the stage directions (accompanied by the arm movements) link Elle's touching game to swimming. The sensual exuberance of these tactile kinesthetics—of slipperiness and floating aloft—become tinged with anxieties of varying biological and social origins. On the biological front, learning to swim involves not only ticklish feelings of wet immersion but also panicked sensations of suffocating and drowning. It is a choreography innately wedded to entwined feelings of pleasure and panic. In parallel fashion, Elle introduces Denise to another choreography of genital touching socially filtered through the braidedness of pleasure and anxiety.

Extending this braidedness, "Swimming" figures Denise's mother as offering both helpful and harmful lessons: she teaches her daughter how not to drown but also "how to fear" by conjuring the specter of a "BIG EYE" (of some lagoon creature) that lurks in the apartment pool and comes out at night (84). That double-edged quality to maternal caretaking, likewise, characterizes the relation of Elle toward her mentally disabled brother. After eating candy until they are sick, Elle and Denise confront Elle's brother, the latter discovered in the kitchen drinking chocolate syrup straight from the can. Elle prohibits her brother a chocolatey aphrodisiac similar to her own partaken indulgence:

> "No!" she said. "That's bad for you!"
> "Yes!" he said.
> "No!"
> "Yes!"
> "No!"
> "Yes, yes, yes!"
> I had never seen Elle look so tired. She looked at me.

Across this back and forth of "No/Yes," Uyehara mimes a hugging close of a treasured object and its being tugged away, a lunging tango with an invisible partner. The sequence ends with neither party winning; rather, both parties break into laughter.

In this image of sibling caretakership, Elle (French for a generic "she") guards over (embodies the "big eye") *and* affectionately attends to her disabled brother. First acting as the disciplinarian of his body so as to inculcate healthy dietary norms and prevent excess (nonproductive) sensual enjoyment, Elle transforms into someone doing a delightful dance with her brother, a tango of push and pull. Through a sideways step accompanied by copious amounts of laughter, Elle shifts to an encounter defined neither by ruling over nor by being overruled—an encounter, however, not devoid of tension and irritation. In the end, Elle laughs with her brother and his whole can of chocolate sauce, as does Denise, the change in registers being the only conclusion to this layered narrative of entwined disability and capacity (in swimming, sexual exploration, and familial caretaking).

In part because he is a secondary character—Elle and the mother being primary—Elle's brother's "retardation" escapes figuration as the central anomaly that must be figured out. In their landmark study, *Narrative Prosthesis*, David Mitchell and Sharon Snyder extrapolate from Michel deCerteau's claim vis-à-vis travel literature that all narrative can be seen as a "search for the strange" (53). Bringing this insight to what they see as a preponderance, rather than a paucity, of narratives featuring disabled characters (from Oedipus onward), they claim that "literary narratives begin a process of explanatory compensation, where perceived 'aberrancies' can be rescued from ignorance, neglect, or misunderstandings for their readerships" (69). Deviance, they argue,

> serves as the . . . common denominator of all narrative. . . . Whereas a sociality might reject, isolate, institutionalize, reprimand, or obliterate [the] liability of [blindness, a peg leg, or a mental impairment], narrative embraces the opportunity that such a "lack" provides—in fact, wills it into existence—as the impetus that calls a story into being. Such a paradox underscores the ironic promise of disability to all narrative. (55)

Narratives, in this sense, lean on disability, even as they propose themselves—their functionality—as akin to medical prostheses: they "resolve or correct . . . 'prostheticize'—a deviance marked as improper to social context" (53). According to these critics, literature and the dramatic arts use disability to narrate inexhaustibly, and sometimes along very conventional lines, the obliterating of difference via salvation from disabled life ("cure") or the disabled character's dying ("kill").

Responding to these same circumstances, Lennard Davis identifies narrative (particularly in the form of the novel) as part of the bourgeoisification of disability.[10] I call upon these thinkers as useful interlocuters in understanding Uyehara's location of disabled figures at the generative core of her work and, more importantly, for interpreting the dance she incorporates in her performances as an alternative and supplement

to her narrative storytelling. "Swimming" includes caretaking of a disabled sibling as one of its many embodied practicums through which
a subject comes to be and through which a microethics of the flesh—
what Akilah Oliver calls the acquisition of "flesh memory" (see note
3)—occurs. In doing so, Uyehara suggests that caretaking the invalid/
in-valid might be a corporeal task that must be learned and continually practiced.

Another sequence, "Blue Marks," uses dance as a framework to
think through how certain styles of movement express an ethical relation both to place and to the mentally anomalous other. "Blue Marks"
focuses on the Uyeharas' new neighbors after the family's move to
Orange County. The sequence begins with the young Denise learning
how to boogie on her front lawn to disco beats from the Bees Gees and
ABBA, while being mesmerized by the teenage "Bad Girl" living across
the street. Celia Abrams—the "bad girl"—greets the Harley Davidson
crew come to pick her up by "caress[ing] their purring feline machines"
and strutting around "like she [is] the Queen of Hearts."[11] Mexican by
birth, Celia rebels against her adoptive parents by rejecting their Jewish
identity and proclaiming herself a "Chicana" (90).

At first, Uyehara depicts Celia as an inspiration for her own teenage
self, hungry for other young women-of-color role models who coura-
geously express their defiant sexual energies despite being stuck in con-
servative Orange County. Celia's success at leaving her childhood "cul-
de-sac" on the back of a Harley enacts a sexual liberation, a "GET[TING]
OUT" (87) later expressly speculated as Celia's coming out "as a fierce
and sexy dyke" (91). This "heroism of departure" is later copied by the
performer herself: "I escaped to L.A. to cut out some space for myself
in the world. I had to GET OUT of Orange County" (90). While alluding to the valorized act of coming out of the closet, the emphasis on
needing to "GET OUT" also corresponds to modern realist theatrical
conventions of "geopatholog[y]," where identity and agency emerge via
"a heroic overcoming of the [painful] power of place."[12] Celia's escape
from the fixity of her parental home—her striving toward autonomy
and liberation—reiterates this dramatic geopathology, with not simply
her parents or the heteronormative family embodying the geopathological, but specifically Mrs. Abrams.

Uyehara then orchestrates the emergence of this latter figure from

Fig. 5.1. Denise Uyehara performing "Blue Marks" in *Maps of City and Body* (1999). *Photo by Craig Schwartz.*

peripheral to mainstage character. In "Blue Marks," Mrs. Abrams begins as only the dull grey background rendering more vibrant Celia's swaggering and charismatic (as well as racialized) "color." Holding her arms out wide in an upside down "U," the performer impersonates the slow shuffle of Mrs. Abrams, and describes her as "a large figure draped in a housecoat, grey hair up in a bun." Celia's adoptive mother enters the scene pleading with her daughter "to stay," but her request comes "too late [for] Celia was already jamming keys and money into her pockets, her navel pointed like a radar toward freedom" (*Maps*, 89). Later, we learn that Mrs. Abrams is abandoned by her husband, who elopes with "a girlfriend half his age" (90–91).

The depiction of Mrs. Abrams, however, takes a dramatic turn when the performer tells of glimpsing blue tattoos on the older woman's wrists: "They were blue like varicose veins, but in small digits like alphabet soup" (90). Saying these lines, Uyehara uncaps a thick marker and draws a curving line, starting at one end of an arm, squiggling up her clavicle, then down the other arm (see figure 5.1). She continues looping this blue line across her pale skin as she finishes relating the encounter:

> I knew they had something to do with the camps—not the same camps my parents were in, but a different kind from the same war. I had seen these people in my World Book Encyclopedia. They were long, thin bean people dressed in striped pajamas whose faces met the camera. When Mrs. Abrams saw me looking, she turned her wrists away, so I knew it wasn't something to discuss. (90)

The choreography turns from the hill-shaped Mrs. Abrams—the geopathological background to Celia's outward growth—toward the inscriptive act of marking the elder woman. By drawing swerving lines up and down her own arms, the performer mobilizes these identity markings—or, more precisely, marks meant to strip one of personhood. In doing so, she highlights the paradoxical kinesthetics of inscription— here line drawing. It is a movement process usually forgotten in the focus on the end product: a word, a sentence, a picture, a narrative meaning.

Line making—or contour drawing—simultaneously creates a negative space of blankness: the shapes of everything outside the darkened marks of intentional highlighting, as in the unfocalized background of white paper, childhood home/mother, or dehumanized flesh. Uyehara thus mobilizes the blue marks in myriad ways. Though the performer eventually caps the marker—arrests the drawing movement—these blue lines continue to move, literally, as Uyehara's arms gesture and swoop while finishing the sequence. She also mobilizes marks/marking by playing upon their nonsingular effects of simultaneously bringing a shape into the foreground and erasing or rendering blank the skin behind or besides that shape.

The activity of drawing, of bleeding and blurring the lines of Mrs. Abrams onto other bodies, works as a metaphor both for Uyehara's approach to her dramatized subjects and for my approach to her dramatization. That is, in her initial narration of seeing the tattooed serial number, the performer anchors those tattoos' meaning to the World Book—Mrs. Abrams is a Jewish survivor of the Nazi death camps. But like Mrs. Abrams, who "turns her wrists away," Uyehara herself turns from that singular interpretation. These blue tracings ultimately emphasize multiple corporeal markings that sequester the twice-over abandoned Mrs. Abrams. After succumbing to Alzheimer's disease, she is placed in a nursing facility ostensibly for her own health. Mrs. Abrams's restricted circumstances, due both to misogynistic social disdain for aged women and a clinical eye toward the mentally ill, fall under a more pastoral regulation of subjects, in contrast to an overt necropolitical atrocity (the Nazi gas chambers).[13] Because of this, they may not seem to warrant remembering as crimes against humanity. If we are to remember these widespread and yet invisible confinements, we do so because they piggy-back on what has been more habitually remembered as morally repugnant. Here, my interpretation of Uyehara's work bears on which woundings circulate as significant to World Book history and which seem ordinary or habitual.

Weighing in precisely on this point, philosopher Avishai Margalit ponders the criterion and means by which we feel compelled to care about the distresses of a broad swath of humanity or a more select group defined by links of kinship, shared belief, and geographic proximity. Noting that "most people . . . carry on by not caring for most other people" (33), Margalit concerns himself with the question of how memory (the attention to others in the past, or the past attention we've paid to others) promotes and grounds our obligations and protectiveness toward these same people and populations in the present and future. Arguing that caring is a "scare commodity" (34), Margalit elaborates that

> a diffused good will does not amount to that unselfish heed to the particular needs and interests of others that caring requires. . . . Caring does not necessarily require liking. What we find hard is the *attention* that is implied by caring. . . . We pay attention not only to our friends but also to our foes. Still, only our friends command our concern for their well-being. We need morality to overcome our natural indifference to others. Indeed, we need morality not so much to counter evil as to counter indifference. (33; italics in original)

For Margalit, morality (as opposed to ethics) is our relation to a generalized humanity, and in this sense, his discussion harmonizes with

Foucault's characterization of morals as referring to "sets of norms, rules, values and injunctions" with universal applicability. Ethics, in contrast, "[is] always local and particular, pertaining to a specific set of procedures, techniques, and discourses through which highly specific ethical-moral subjects come to be formed."[14] Saba Mahmood continues, "Foucault's use of Aristotelian ethics is not geared toward asserting its universal validity" but points instead to "practices, techniques, and discourses through which a subject transforms herself in order to achieve a particular state of being, happiness, or truth."[15] I will later return to caring practiced through such local techniques.

As focalized attention "toward others" that makes demands upon us, caring is bound to our memories;[16] and indeed, Margalit uses the inability to *not* remember certain emotionally thick memories (as compared to the fleeting caring that one feels, e.g., after reading once about an atrocity far away but never encountered again) as confirming this point. Though he ultimately proclaims it as impossible, Margalit's overall project considers the hypothetical existence of "moral" memory, which he defines as a caring obligation and sustained attention to those we regard as remote and strange (those to whom we have "thin," indifferent relations)—as counterpoised to "an ethics of memory" with which we ritually reaffirm near and dear "thick" relations:

> Thick relations are grounded in attributes such as parent, friend, lover, fellow-countryman. Thick relations are anchored in a shared past or moored in a shared memory. Thin relations, on the other hand, are backed by the attribute of being human. Thin relations rely also on *some aspects of being human, such as being a woman or being sick.* Thick relations are in general our relations to the near and dear. Thin relations are in general our relations to the stranger and the remote. (7; emphasis added)

The seeming naturalness of "the ethics of memory"—for instance, exemplified by the obligation of those with Jewish relatives, neighbors, friends, lovers, or fellow countrymen to remember the atrocity of the Third Reich's genocide of Jews—contrasts moral memory: our remembering what has happened to those considered remote or to whom we relate by virtue of shared membership in the same species-being of *homo sapiens*. Put another way, what makes moral memory a conundrum, for Margalit, is not the specific content of that memory—he tells us that moral memory ought to attend to "striking examples of radical evil and crimes against humanity, such as enslavement, deportations of civilian populations, and mass exterminations" (78)—but the way in which lasting memory has a way of turning the dispassionate or "thin" goodwill toward other humans into thickly described specific relations "to me," as if transforming that anonymous fellow human into an extended member of one's family.[17]

Most curious in the foregoing assertion, as indicated by my italics, is Margalit's both evoking and canceling out femaleness and sickness (aka disability) as personal attributes—i.e., onto-epistemological filters or standpoints—that might channel memories in a particular way and thereby create corresponding communities of ethical (near and dear) memory analogous to those Margalit designates as "natural" ones, namely, "families, clans, tribes, religious communities, and nations" (69). Yet, Margalit never returns to this nugget on illness and femaleness as exemplary of human types of distress that do *not* seem to make a special claim on our or "my" particular caring (they only claim our goodwill or sympathy as they comprise a slice of the general distress of humanity).

Perhaps because Margalit's distinction between ethics and morals so much turns on spatial distance,[18] we might surmise that to the extent that heteronormativity distributes women throughout communities and to the extent that sickness and disability are likewise distributed across geopolitical entities, these particular attributes cannot function as significant boundary markers separating relations of the near and dear (that which ethics governs) from those of the distant and remote (that encompassing the ground of morality). Writing in 1949, Simone de Beauvoir made a similar point with respect to the specific case of women's anemic consciousness of themselves as an oppressed class, especially in comparison to the decolonizing Indochinese (aka Vietnamese nationalists) and the Negroes in Haiti, both of whom had a sense of themselves as a distinct group with a common history and shared future interests. Partly in response to de Beauvoir's observation, second-wave feminism forged women-based collective identities that were to compete against the relational, mnemonic, and obligatory (emotional) thickness of relations solidified by marriage, by shared places of residence and work, or by biological and adoptive kinship (identities segueing into tribal notions of race and nation).[19]

Taking the above as context, I argue that Uyehara's performances, akin to the other cultural productions examined through the Asian Americanist critical biopolitical lens modeled in this book, struggle to exceed what Margalit calls an ethics of memory and practice a moral memory—one directed at populations, species-beings, and cellular scales of life considered remote and strange. While not restricting his examples to Asian American contexts, as in his previous monograph (*Asian/American*, 1999), David Palumbo-Liu's *Deliverance of Others* (2012), in a similar vein, argues that the *sine qua non* of modern litera-ture is its delivering others to the self in ways that make those others both relatable—not a threatening otherness that would overwhelm the self—but also strange enough to be interesting. Contrasting literature as a specific type of "delivery system" that, like advertising, manipu-lates affect but to ethical ends (189), Palumbo-Liu claims for literature a leveraging of neither a strictly rational calculus nor a strictly enflamed turbulence of emotions but something in between called "imagina-tion."[20] Thus, while Margalit focuses on the limits to an ethics of car-ing as a function of the remoteness of "the other" in a community's live memory, Palumbo-Liu concerns himself more with the promise of a particular mnemonic repertoire—that of modern literature—to keep that mnemonic, ethical connection alive in the face of numerous competing bids for our attention in the crush of data streams, images, memes, tweets, and the like characterizing late capitalist informa-tion society.

Like Margalit, Uyehara's performance appears less sanguine on the possibility of moral memory. The conclusion to "Blue Marks" implies that overcoming most people's indifference (aka limits of caring atten-tion) requires inhabiting an adoptive or neighborly proximity to the dehumanized other, a relationality once or twice removed rather than seven times removed (six degrees of separation being a shorthand now for a global network encompassing all humans). Speculating that Celia returns to Orange County to visit her mentally impaired mother, Uyehara says, "'Hey mom. It's me, Celia. I'm your daughter? [pause] Those blue marks. . . . It's because you're Jewish, and somebody wanted to erase you.'"[21] The performer's artistic impersonation or "adoption" of the role of surrogate daughter to Mrs. Abrams preconditions her caretaking of the latter's memory. The counterfactual scenario hinges on Mrs. Abrams's mental deterioration. She can no longer act the mnemonic steward of her own history, much less others', thereby making Mrs. Abrams an outcast to any interdependent, reciprocal ideal of a community of emotionally thick ethical ties. Medical anthropologist Janelle Taylor eloquently depicts the friendlessness and social death that is visited upon those with Alzheimer's or related dementia (ADRD). Noting the "ethical judgment" that befalls those who fail to recognize others in a society where reciprocal attention and caring underlie our communal bonds, Taylor recalls a prior friend of her ADRD-afflicted mother who, upon being told of the deteriorating cognitive function of Taylor's mother, remarked that she hadn't received a Christmas card from Taylor's mother in years and "still sound[ed] quite indignant" over the fact (as if to explain why this friend hadn't visited her mother in all that time).[22] Mrs. Abrams, like Taylor's mother, becomes the *zoe* of a socio-ethical community of *bios*—the latter, here, referring to mnemonically robust forms of life with the capacity for ethical, because mutual, recognition.

Celia notably narrativizes the marks on Mrs. Abrams's arms in a singular way, linked to her racial and religious identity as a Jew. However, I would like to emphasize what immediately follows that narrative. Uyehara returns to the moving possibilities in relating to mental anomaly through dance. Squeaking out a final bar of ABBA's "Dancing Queen," the performer slowly raises her arms, visibly criss-crossed with blue lines, above her head: "See that girl, watch that scene . . . the dancing queen." With its ambiguous reference to "the girl" to see and watch, the performer conjures both the celebrated "scene" of sexual liberation as and through disco dance and the backward glance toward those still lost to confinement and slow social death. In essence, we are still on the lawn of Denise's childhood home—the progress of this tale not to be measured in the distance traveled (the independence from home) but in the connections and contour (drawings) made.

Here, I call attention to Uyehara's queer act of looking backward, drawing on Heather Love's formulation. Preoccupied by the closeted or indeterminately homosexual figures of the past, and, more significantly, the tendency of post-Stonewall gays and lesbians to dismiss these pre-cursor figures as self-hating queers, Love rehabilitates the "backward" and melancholic feelings of shame and loss instantiated by remem-bering these figures as an interventionary drag on the forward march of modernity:

> The idea of modernity—with its suggestions of progress, rationality, and technological advance—is intimately bound up with backwardness. If modernization in the late nineteenth and early twentieth century aimed to move humanity forward, it did so in part by perfecting techniques for mapping and disciplining subjects considered to be lagging behind—and so seriously comprised the ability of those others ever to catch up. Not only sexual and gender deviants but also women, colonized people, the nonwhite, the disabled, the poor and criminals were marked as infe-rior by means of the allegation of backwardness.[23]

By impersonating Celia—or, more precisely, returning to the story's opening of wanting to and partly succeeding in impersonating Celia—Uyehara transforms that avatar of the forwarding-looking lesbian, with "navel pointing like a radar toward freedom," into an agent who looks backward, who returns but cannot fix her mother's isolation—this "crip" well of loneliness.

The sinuous visibility Uyehara grants to the blue marks raised above her head in this final sequence stands in stark contrast to Mrs. Abrams's own desire (quoted earlier) to keep those scars discreetly tucked away. Besides the scaling up of the blue marks as a mode of outing the sacrifice of Mrs. Abrams (she is the erased/blank figure in the cherishing of more mobility, amplified life, and healthy species-being), we might also think of this final mobilization—a slow-mo raising of the arms—as an outing of the performance artist, herself, and not in the way we might initially think. The tale outs a widely held fetish of departure and expansive-ness (expansionism) as progress, with its flip-side disdain for the more contained, sustainable lifestyles dubbed "subsistence," "handicapped," "retarded," or "backward." Lest I be misinterpreted, I am not saying that Uyehara endorses the closet and the prison, but rather that she registers her own ambivalence with scripts of liberation as reduced to departure and outing—demurring on the certainty of those narratives.

As in "Swimming," which ends in a tango between Elle and her brother, "Blue Marks" ends its emotional contemplation of a mentally disabled person with a dance move: a disco arm pump slowed to the point that we can see it as movement in place (rather than a movement that flees from or conquers over space). What does it mean to move in place? Or put another way, what prevents us from conducting ourselves in accord with an environment where Alzheimer's and cognitive variability are givens, where sustained synchronization with these ways of being doesn't require a curing or killing (a transforming of the disabled "them") but, instead, a changing of our own sped-up devotions to improving, willing, and surplus-productive modes of conduct?

When Uyehara turns to her grandmother's story, her closest kin relation with mental illness, we do find a deeper engagement and identification with this elderly woman's psyche and less of an unsettled choreographic ending. As in her focus on Mrs. Abrams, the sequence "Charcoal" raises the question of whose histories get left behind in the U.S. exceptionalist narrative of itself as the national embodiment of health, wealth, and tolerance for racial and sexual minorities. With tango shoes sheathing her feet, Uyehara lyrically alights on her grandmother's "leaving"—"[She] leaves things around the house. She leaves the light on in the bathroom . . . a peach on the windowsill. She leaves herself" (117); and later, "She leaves her teeth. An egg, half a cabbage, 3 Bartlett pears in the refrigerator. She leaves . . . she leaves . . . she leaves" (121). The performer refrains from framing her grandmother's suicide as an irrational act, even as it must always be considered so, under the dictates of the imperative to live.[24]

This tale of suicide by self-immolation, perversely titled "Charcoal," alternates between the performer's reenacting her grandmother's motions on the morning she killed herself and editorializing on the meaning of this act, offering both the clinical language (she commits suicide by self-immolation after her "physical and mental health [starts getting] bad" [*Maps*, 122]), as well as a gendered framing of the act by prior literary and dramatic narrations: "We think of them as weak, women suicides. . . . Hamlet's girlfriend strewing daisies on the glassy water. If she had been my grandfather, then we would've said, 'Well, I guess he just knew it was time to go'" (*Maps*, 117–18). Following this reflection on how different textual authorities, from the mental health assessment to the theatrical canon, dictate the meanings imputed to her grandmother's final actions, Uyehara abruptly stages those very movements:

> It was an average Wednesday morning and [my grandmother] got up, got dressed . . . [and] drove around the corner to an empty lot, next to Wendy's House of Hamburgers. Wendy's *Charbroiled* House of Hamburgers. And she locked herself inside [the car] and she thought "The sky is blue and the sky is blue. And the windshield is so clear. And the dirt is brown. And the canister is red."
>
> Gasoline along the dash and it trickles down her forehead. A pungent perfume that lifts her skin up, it lifts her skin up, and the sky is blue, the sky is blue—a match. . . . [Uyehara strikes her hand in the air and then swoops her arms in a reverse breaststroke.]
>
> The smoke swirls like Santa's beard and she breathes in, and goes under. [Big inhalation as Uyehara leans back] (*Maps*, 1999)

In order to stave off the reduction of the grandmother's actions to the remnants—the ashes (of meaning) left after the fire (figure 5.2)—this performed sequence vividly describes the object world of the grandmother's self-immolation rather than interiorizing her state of mind. The simplicity of visual impressions—blue sky, clear windshield, red canister—tonally matches the sparse sensations that gasoline and match induce—wetness trickling down her forehead, the lifting of the skin, and the "go[ing] under." The performance figures the action, here, not so much as "suicide" but as a series of tangible sensations and physical moves. The reverse breaststroking of the arms is both literally mute and multiply articulate, suggestive of the path of smoke swirling around the body and recalling the kinesthetic memory of "Swimming." In short, Uyehara performs her grandmother's suicide as a kind of dance—as a kinesthetic event.

Within the context of her retrospective show with its emphasis on a range of bodily mobilities, from traveling, scavenging, and orgasming to getting out/coming out, "Charcoal" exemplifies the dual impulses, on the one hand, to approach this act as a series of motions akin to swimming or dancing and, on the other hand, to find a more coherent meaning for the suicide. From a dance methodology, the grandmother's

Fig. 5.2. Publicity shot for "Charcoal" treating Uyehara's grandmother's suicide. *Photo by Chuck Stallard.*

suicide becomes an exploration of the body's physicality—not simply its physics, as in contact improvisation, but its chemical conversion into carbon and its sensual capacities when on the verge of expiration. From a semantic, narrativized, and historicized view, the grandmother's suicide must mean, must have significance as the last act of an entire life lived in national—that is, racialized, gendered, and heteronormative— context. Here, Uyehara's repeating of the location of her grandmother's suicide imputes a deliberateness to the actions: she sets herself aflame at a destination famous for cooking meat. The perverse rationality of the setting calls into question funerary rites that make cultural claims for the distinctness of human remains (*bios*) from cattle or animal remains (*zoe*) even after both specimens expire (i.e., what doesn't cease with their deaths is their being folded into those qualified categories of privileged or bare life).

As if to provide the historical meaning of her grandmother's suicide in national context, "Charcoal" stages Denise visited by an apparition. Showing the scarred places on her wrists, this ghost of her grandmother declares, "Denise-girl, there's nothing worse than killing yourself except failing to kill yourself. This time I make sure" (*Maps*, 122). She then hums the melody to "Wakare No Isochidori"—the "Hawaii send-off song to all the Nisei soldiers," mentioning that her husband, Jerry, sang it "all the way to Europe [where he was to be stationed] . . . scared, maybe he wouldn't come back" and now she "want[s] to go. . . .You bury me next to my dear Jerry" (*Maps*, 122). Uyehara renders her grandmother's suicide comprehensible through sentimentality, linking it to a romantic return to her deceased spouse. Punctuating her own departure with the farewell song to Nisei soldiers, the ghost musically suggests that her suicidal leave taking compares advantageously to Jerry's patriotic act of going to war. In other words, she is a soldier whose only tactic is suicide. Sentimentally, then, Uyehara performatively renders her grandmother's suicide comprehensible by linking it both to a romantic return to her husband and to the trauma of a state-sponsored persecution based on race. She makes an incendiary act familiar by domesticating it, framing it both within a family romance as well as within a narrative of domestic racism, namely, the imprisonment and dispossession of Japanese Americans during World War II.

As part of this race-based segregation and confinement, Japanese Americans were given loyalty questionnaires. Two infamous questions— "Are you willing to serve in the armed forces of the United States on combat duty, wherever ordered?" and "Will you swear unqualified allegiance to the United States of America and faithfully defend the United States from any and all attack by foreign or domestic forces, and forswear any form of allegiance to the Japanese Emperor or any other foreign government, power, or organization?"—expressly made combat service in the armed forces the proof of loyalty to the United States, a mode of conduct only open to men during this historical period. In this highly charged context of racially contoured, gendered modes of living a *de facto* conditional citizenship, Uyehara dramatizes her grandmother's regard for the "good citizen bees" that attempt to rescue her from the burning car she has put to flame: "First there is one bee, then two bees, then a whole group of good citizen bees, and they're coming toward her pointing, they bring their good-bee citizen fire engines . . . and the bee people are saying, 'There's a fire, get her out, there's a fire, get her out.' . . ." (*Maps* 1999). Tongue in cheek, Uyehara notes the heroic concern of these citizens—their buzzing distraction. If to be a good citizen is to be law-abiding (even when the law is effectively unjust), the grandmother—in her act of suicide—breaks the law and laughs at those who conform to what we construe as normative citizenship, or normative soldiering.

As a fire rages, so does the suicide against the notion of good citizenship, if this entails rescuing a Japanese American woman from a burning car but doing nothing when her family was shuffled off to concentration camps. To be a good citizen remains a structural impossibility for those against whom normative citizenship is defined—the indigenous, the (colored) immigrant, the poor, the disabled, and the queer. Acts designed to combat this structural impossibility—like Jerry's service in the armed forces—risk one's "[not] coming back." The grandmother's suicide, rather than risking her death to combat the foreclosure of citizenship, assures her death and performs the outrageousness of her condition.

Before going further along these lines, allow me to halt this renarrativization of Uyehara's reperformance of her grandmother's leaving (a narrativization stressing the historical context of Japanese American internment) and return to the earlier point that the incipit to "Charcoal" remains the grandmother's anomalous act and the poorness of interpretive penetrations of its meaning ("a weak woman's suicide" on the model of Shakespeare's Ophelia's). In fleshing out the historical contexts evoked through "Charcoal's" musical component, that which speaks to the grandmother's racialized injuries as a former Japanese American internee, I don't mean to suggest its *definitive* meaning—to wield the authority to interpret her actions presumed as signs of mental disability as really her mode of interrogating normative practices of "good citizenship."

The artist conveys as well that the suicide does not have *a* meaning—as an enactment that must be conjured via the body's sensations and movements. Here, I return to the alternative methodology of broaching the grandmother's self-immolation kinesthetically, as a set of dance-like motions (pouring oil, lighting match, going under), which Uyehara's storytelling and my own interpretations of that storytelling seem compelled to renarrativize. In the context of a book about Asian American cultural production, my own narrativization of this piece (however I would want it otherwise) inevitably closes down its inexplicable remainders (the in-valid excesses) of the actions, which highlights my next point regarding Uyehara as both a storyteller and a dancer. The dance she performs tangoes with her own and her audience's renarrativizations, even as what might be most important to the artist is the process—the dancing on the stage—rather than the product. The product, here, is the fully formed (and closed) semantic meaning of the dance according to frameworks of female dependence, racial injury, disability studies, or a combination of these—that which will resolve the anomalousness of the grandmother's dancing actions.[25]

What then is the contribution of these performances to disability studies? Uyehara's performative storytelling with regard to the cognitively non-normate reaches out to those construed as impaired by neurological disorders, but respects an inherent constraint regarding the extent of the interpretive authority of the temporarily able-brained with respect to cognitive-mnemonic anomaly. One question immediately begged by the endeavor to forge a caring relation to the mentally disabled is, "Does relating and obliging oneself to those considered neurologically 'remote and strange' automatically require a lessening of the opaqueness of non-normate ways of thinking characteristic of these disabled subjects?"

Mitchell and Snyder contend that disability studies ought not to be imagined simply as the "search for a more 'positive' story of disability, as it has often been formulated, *but rather* [*as*] *a thoroughgoing challenge to the undergirding authorization to interpret that disability invites.* There is a politics at stake in the fact that disability inaugurates an explanatory need that the unmarked body eludes by virtue of its physical anonymity."[26] In offering caring kinesthetic attention to those with mental disability, Uyehara leaves Elle's brother and Mrs. Abrams—figures from whom she is once removed—neither antipathetic nor expressively interiorized; rather, they pose for their other-minded relations the question of how to caretake and connect with them.

The foregoing has emphasized the artist's investment in dance as a wedge to break apart narrativizations guided by the penetrative authority to know and expose (lay open to view). Turning to Uyehara's post-9/11 production *Big Head*, I focus on the performer's employing similar oral storytelling and dance techniques but not so much to conduct an ethical mode of caring for, relating to, and remembering those with impairments of brain function. Rather, in *Big Head*, Uyehara metaphorically likens much of American behavior from October 2001 to February 2003 (aka the show's premiere) to a mindless devotion to a militarized ideology of aggressive expansion dubbed "defense" and "security." While Uyehara's premillennial work uses dance to draw out the limits of adjusting particular identities (the alterity of the mentally ill and the backward-looking "queer" child) toward an ableist orientation of fast-paced futurity and productivity, her postmillennial work, in contrast, uses choreography to emphasize how an aggressive, militaristic, and expansionist kinesthetics, far from being delegated or *particularized* to a sector of armed professionals such as the police and armed forces, seeps across the civilian landscape—ritualistically affirmed in the everyday actions of Americans.

Big Head, however, doesn't entirely abandon Uyehara's preoccupation with debilitating mental illness. In her script notes, Uyehara reveals that the "Big Head" of the show's title refers to the encephalitic's condition, even as no overt references to this medical terminology surface in the actual performance. *Big Head* implies the transfer of psychic and somatic dysfunction to the atmosphere of anxious "insecurity" and the socially engrained proleptic alert toward potential woundings in the future.

With *Big Head* (2003) and *Senkotsu (Mis)Translation* (2009), Uyehara performatively responds to the lengthy effects of U.S. military involvement and occupation of West Asia and East Asia (Okinawa). The 2003 show has much in common with contemporary "docutheater" (Kondo 2000), exemplified by the work of Anna Deavere Smith, where an alternate form of witnessing occurs by way of performers' bringing to stage the verbatim accounts of local subjects shortly after a crisis event, one often involving the scapegoating of members of a religious, sexual, or racial minority group (Anna Deavere Smith's *Fires in the Mirror* and *Twilight, Los Angeles*; Moises Kaufman's *Laramie Project* around

Matthew Shepherd's killing; also *Black Watch* by the National Theater of Scotland).

As in Smith's theater, which relies upon the words of interviewees reflecting on a crisis event (the 1991 Crown Heights riots in *Fires in the Mirror* and the 1992 Los Angeles riots in *Twilight, Los Angeles*), preproduction for *Big Head* involved interviews with local Arab, Muslim, and Japanese American subjects shortly after 9/11, with Uyehara performing verbatim the text of at least one of these interviews in the show (more often she incorporates these interviews into the performance via recorded voice-overs). In other works in her performance *oeuvre*, however, Uyehara has been less willing to don the speech inflections and verbal tics of the members of other races. To draw the comparison another way, while Smith's solo work relies heavily upon the importance of words—of listening to and being able to speak across the gap of racial difference (of the linguistic inflections across bodies of phenotypal variation)—Uyehara's work remains consistently indebted to the kinesthetic or movement dimension of theater as a mode of achieving a bridge across historically distinct experiences of racialized trauma.

~~Take~~ Recite Five Times a Day: *Big Head*'s Dancing with Anatomopolitics

Premiering at Highways Performance Space in February 2003—a month prior to the U.S. invasion of Iraq and over a year after the U.S. invasion of Afghanistan—*Big Head* concerns itself with both the need to connect pressing political events of the day with the past and the ethical responsibility as well as difficulty of being responsible as a U.S. citizen for acts committed by the state. Among the major impetuses for this production were the airplane attacks on New York's Twin Towers and the Pentagon on September 11, 2001, the high-alert aftermath of these events, which included the profiling of Arab/Muslim-looking individuals as potential "terrorists," and the coalitions developing between Japanese and Arab Americans around the mass and illegal imprisonment by the United States of a racial group without due process.[27] In her performance notes, Uyehara states, "[S]ince . . . the Fall of 2001, our government has imprisoned over 2000 people, mostly non-citizens. . . . Many have been secretly deported. . . . They were simply 'disappeared'"

(65–66). *Big Head* attempts to make such disappearances tangible, imparting to the audience an ethical obligation to be bodily witnesses and purveyors of a collective memory focused on how the U.S. state disregards its constitutional principles and "forgets" its scapegoating of racial groups.

In her dance with the security state, Uyehara choreographs vigilance as affirming obligations to those deemed alien and strange, precisely through remembering the shared pietistic rituals of poetic, repetitive devotions (practiced five times a day) in both the Muslim and Christian monastic traditions. The performance recovers and rechoreographs ethical conduct in these pietistic quotidian flesh memories as a stark alternative to the somatic entrainment evident in post-9/11 hate crimes directed at brown-skinned and turbaned American immigrants. Below I focus on how *Big Head* takes the audience through a set of choreographies we associate, on the one hand, with a formal realm of citizenly duty—jury trial (witnessing) and national fidelity (pledging)—and, on the other hand, with informal, grassroots, intimate obligation and friendship (safekeeping a letter, practicing kindness). Indeed, the structure of the show moves from anecdotal storytelling—a combination of oral narrative and movement in the mode of her 1990s work—toward more imagistic vignettes, capsules of emotions that haven't been made into meaningful (historicized) sense, that inchoately circulate still unprocessed and in-process.

Big Head opens with a recollection of the holiday devoted to the nation's birth, the Fourth of July. Uyehara tells of burning her hand on a sparkler when she was five, the same night that a fire, coincidentally, ravaged another family's apartment in their building. Telling of her physical wound, Uyehara spreads her right palm wide, arm raised to shoulder height—a gesture reminiscent of one who gives testimony at a jury trial and which, in modified form, is repeated throughout the performance (22).

In the context of U.S. legal procedure, truthful testimony depends as much upon a bodily ritual—raising one's right hand and placing one's left on a sacred text (the Bible)—as upon any extra-performative, extra-discursive content. Uyehara's gestus underscores scenarios of truth: how "truth" is produced, in what forms, through what corporeal mechanics, conventional tropes, gestures, and movements.

Fig. 5.3. *Big Head* (2003). Uyehara tells of a Fourth of July when her hand was burned by a sparkler. *Photo by Pete Lee.*

The tale of the two fires is also a tale of two kinds of witnessing, one directly in the body, and the other indirectly via several levels of mediation. After grasping the hot end of the sparkler, the young Denise feels "hot-cold pain [shoot] through my palm, up my arm, then, strangely, up into my armpit" (22). In contrast, because the burning apartment is "on the other side of the complex," Denise's family does not have to evacuate, and thus she doesn't "actually see the fire" (22). Still, she remembers it clearly because "my father filmed the entire event on our family's super-8 camera: Giant flames licking at a two-story building. Trucks, ladders, water. Firemen pushing *us* back" (22; italics added). While acknowledging not having been at the conflagration, Uyehara's account converts the film footage into a tangible memory—"firemen pushing us back"—as if she had been directly pressured by another's touch. In this way, Uyehara plays with ideas of communal memory and collective witnessing, as both of these are linked to the performance of citizenship.

Importantly, the scenario of truth privileged in court would strike as hearsay this vicarious memory of the fire at both a physical and a social remove from the performer's community of "near and dear" relations, to recall Margalit's ethics of memory. The law, in other words, restricts truth to a curtailed autobiographical testimony of one's direct experience. Thus, even while the subject under the law raises her right hand—that is, in a volitional, muscular movement—this corporeal act of volition mystifies the much narrower parameters of what style of recollected memory makes good testimony (for instance, one establishing injury and linear causality to some responsible party).

This July Fourth recollection ends with a visit to the burned shell of the now vacant apartment. When Denise and her siblings go to view the remnants, they delightfully assign flavors to the "melted, bubbled, blistered" wall of what appear to be "Ice Cream Bricks": "Ice cream! Ice cream! Chocolate, strawberry, peach, vanilla . . . butterscotch ice cream! Look what the fire made! Ice cream mixed with fire" (24). That this ice cream acts as the trace of a dispossession—a family's loss of home—is irrelevant to the pre-adolescent children, caught up as they are in the fun and frolic of the summer holiday. The giddiness of the American national holiday—of ice cream!—becomes part of what Uyehara would have us notice: the automatic, mindless ways in which the repetition of national festivities obscures the view of dispossession, for instance, of indigenous peoples, coincident with the birth of the United States. This beginning sequence, in condensed fashion, turns a remembrance of the Fourth of July into a tale of getting burned by patriotic paraphernalia, and somehow not noticing the full ramifications of another's parallel or prior wounding.

Additionally, toward the conclusion of *Big Head*, Uyehara returns to this opening anecdote and calls into question the privilege of being a direct witness to a trauma. When she speaks to her sister about "that Fourth of July . . . when I burned my hand on a sparkler, and that fire raged in the apartment complex," her sister responds, "You didn't burn your hand on a sparkler. *I* did. That happened to *me*" (51). While one might be tempted to interpret this scenario as evidence of the unreliability of the narrator/performer, I think it is more important to see the anecdote as interrogating the epistemological privilege of direct witness and singular truths; and correlatively, suggesting that having an indirect knowledge of a violation—be it of bodily injury, dispossession, imprisonment, or the more subtle injuries of racial discrimination in civil society—necessitates the kind of response that would be provoked if one had been touched "first hand" by the traumatic event. As in her earlier work, Uyehara traffics in invalid memories—recollection robustly backed neither by patriotic sanction nor protocols of clear (nondigressive) witness in trial testimony.

From its opening Fourth of July story, *Big Head* proceeds with pieces indebted to the techniques of Augusto Boal's "theater of the oppressed," one in which Uyehara teaches her audience to salute the Stars and Stripes according to the Pledge's original staging, and another in which she pantomimes a driver of an SUV, flags attached to her head.[28] In this latter sequence, she grips her fingers around an imaginary steering wheel, thrusts her middle finger in the air, and then pantomimes the full-scale crashing of this flag-waving sports utility vehicle (seemingly ubiquitous on southern Californian freeways after 9/11) as it careens out of control. Silently signifying in the mode of Boal's Image Theater on the American love affair with driving big cars, this sequence connects an automotive addiction to speed and force with U.S. military aggression abroad and anti-Arab, anti-Muslim violence domestically, as both masquerade as American patriotism.

Exploiting the "twice-behaved behavior" that is performance (Schechner), Uyehara reflects back the theatricality of everyday life, the automotive and, arguably, automatic reliance on props such as the Stars and Stripes to affirm love of country and unswerving support for one's heads of state. One's head, in fact, sprouts that highly charged symbol of the state, with Uyehara visualizing the occupation of even this real estate—the minds of the American people—by the government's party line. The sequence also returns to the romance with driving as icon of freedom and self-determination explored in *Maps* that, here, ends in a traumatic accident—in the possible injury of innocent bystanders.[29]

In another sequence involving toy flags, Uyehara leads her audience in the varying postures constituting the Pledge of Allegiance across time. Originally, the salute to the flag involved an extension of the arm aloft, palm raised upward, as if trying to venerate it in a gesture of "behold!" During World War II, this posture (described by the performer as too much resembling the Nazi "Sieg Heil" salute) was altered to the now familiar hand over the heart, as the wording of the pledge also changed with the addition of the phrase, "under God." In having her audience switch between these two postures and recitations, she requires them to be *mindful against* the roteness of the (post–World War II) Pledge as they've incorporated it into their arms and tongues. In these dueling salutes to the flag, audience members variously perform patriotism in a way that violates the singularity of the normative ceremony, *even as* this enlisting of the audience's incorporated memory also means that they drift back to their habitually entrained postures and words. By staging this alternative practice of mobile patriotism, no longer the automatic veneration of the flag but a mutable, responsive form of embodied citizenship, Uyehara both challenges mindlessness and affirms it, or, to put it another way, affirms the persistence of corporeal mnemonics or what Janelle Taylor calls "procedural memory" as rival to conscious will.

Big Head's choreographies, as noted earlier, differ from Uyehara's earlier use of dance as an alternative (nonpenetrative) mode of relating to anomalous persons. In this postmillennial performance, Uyehara reenacts small actions—like pushing foot to gas pedal and pledging—that most of her audience themselves have probably repeated mindlessly. She allows other voices to ghost and interweave with these seemingly harmless automated actions, tingeing them with traumatizing inferences. In this way she scrutinizes bodily repertoires—and the repetition that renders them halfway between mindful and mindless, volitional and autonomic—as the site of ethical intervention.

In the interests of brevity, I restrict my remaining discussion of *Big Head* to three additional sequences through which Uyehara theorizes affective vigilance. The title of the first of these, "Vigil," refers to a candlelight gathering among Japanese, Muslim, and Arab American groups in the United States in the immediate aftermath of 9/11, held at the Japanese American National Museum in Los Angeles. Film footage of that gathering shot by John Esaki is projected into the theater. Accompanying this choreography is a musical sound track threaded with voice-overs from Americans of Japanese, Middle Eastern, and North African heritage. One voice-over—Shady Hakim's—tells of the murder of a close family friend, an Egyptian Coptic Christian grocer and close friend of Hakim's uncle, who is mistaken for a Muslim.

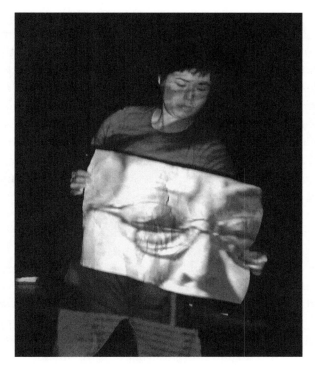

Fig. 5.4. Uyehara catches projected images of a post-9/11
"Vigil," from *Big Head* (2003). *Photo by Marcel Schaap.*

Other voice-overs in this sequence, however, have no dramatic violence to recount. Instead, local, ordinary citizens question the government's monopoly on defining proper national feeling, sonically assembling a counterpublic watchful of the repetitive militaristic alerts (e.g.,
code orange or red) characteristic of the U.S. response toward trauma
and loss. Rather than the punitive, immoral strategies, such as torture,
indefinite detention, and top-heavy state action, of the $43.2 billion–
budgeted[30] Department of Homeland Security (other top-heavy actions
include the passing of the U.S. PATRIOT Act and the high-tech apparatus and bureaucracy of the TSA), this audible counterpublic voices a
grassroots activism as simple and radical as talking to one's neighbor[31]
or sending "a continual flow of letters out into the world" (32).

The dance ends with Uyehara's folding into a series of smaller
squares the paper upon which she has "caught" (temporarily archived)

the projected images of this live vigil. After the house lights come up, Uyehara offers this paper envelope to a random audience member and asks, "Could you do me a favor [and] keep this for me until the end of the war?" (44). The words echo those of Japanese Americans during World War II. Allotted a single suitcase of belongings to accompany them to concentration camps, Japanese Americans prior to their departure asked neighbors and friends to care for their possessions. The request deliberately plays with the ambiguous referent for "the war." Is it World War II, the current war on terror, the current war in Afghanistan, the future war in Iraq, the future wars in which the United States will surely engage?

The performance enjoins not just the singular performer on stage but also the sunk-down-in-her-seat bystander to enact vigilance non-militaristically. It kinesthetically transmits a positive entanglement with alien others by way of choreography—a hand raised palm up and open rather than balled into a fist, a reaching out to support or safe-keep for the other rather than a foot to the pedal to drive away. While these actions somatically rehearse the flesh in life-affirming qualities of answerability to the stranger, the types of alternative actions the performer frames as vigilant are those that even progressive movements invested in liberal autonomous agency associate too often with an in-valid quiescence—not marching but gathering, not revolutionary uprising (and rock throwing) but letter writing,[32] not vigilante revenge but safekeeping and dancing.

Big Head enacts a contradictory affective work that both amplifies the intensity of aggressive, frustrating, mournful, shaming emotions and wills the body's conduct in choreographic delay, lag, and incongruence with an active immediacy that would project those emotions outward as punching fist—a purging of negative affect onto another. Her show alternates between rehearsing actions of those who have rechanneled their injuries into aggressive-defensive road rage and those who have acted vigilantly not to do so but whose internal action in processing and transforming negative affect into something else can appear as inaction—as dramatically boring and illegible. In the sequence "Hate Crime," Uyehara launches a choreographic debate over the seemingly inefficacious but still necessary investment of this artist (and other like-disciplined citizens) in aesthetic-cultural practices of singing, dancing, and molding clay as ritualistic, meditative processes that do political work by quieting the externalized affects of aggression and "hate."

Beginning with Uyehara standing on the unlit stage, a recorded newscast fills the darkened space with details of an October 21, 2001, hate crime. A group of young adults of East Asian descent have brutally beaten a South Asian man and his family as they exited an Orange County karaoke lounge. (The violence happening just outside a venue where people gather to sing communally—to chorus together—is not insignificant.)[33] The perpetrators have mistaken their targets for Middle Easterners. As Uyehara stands against the back wall, a filmed image of a clay figure appears next to her, grossly magnified.[34] The performer's live body on stage both overlays and starkly contrasts this reddish-brown clay body: the roughly hewn figure lacks the finer phenotypal markers used to taxonomize races—e.g., nose width, eye shape, hair texture—even as its nonwhite hue of indeterminate brown or grey tones[35] evokes the "colored" designation assigned to Asian Americans. Precisely because of its crude indexing of racial specificity, this clay figure enables Uyehara to call attention to the imprecision of biometrically and phenotypally based aggregations, an imprecision underlying both a key rallying cry for pan-ethnic Asian American community ("remember Vincent Chin!") and, ironically, the October 21, 2001, beating that promises to fracture that same pan-ethnic coalition.

In 1982, at the height of U.S. automakers' anxiety over Japan's growing dominance in that industry, two autoworkers recently laid off in Detroit beat and killed Vincent Chin, a Chinese American whom his assailants mistook for a Japanese. Symbolic of the way in which anti-Asian racism spreads indiscriminately to all Asian-looking bodies, the call to "remember Vincent Chin!" emphasized the importance of a pan-ethnic, pan-Asian response to racism directed at any single Asian national group. Chin's case mobilized the formation of pan-Asian coalitions in the 1980s, in contrast to strategies of "ethnic disidentification" prevalent around World War II (see Wei; Yamamoto).[36]

Documentary film extended the relevance of the Chin case to a subsequent generation of college students who would learn the importance of pan-Asian identification through these films. Bookending the decades before and after the millennial turn are Renee Tajima-Peña's Academy Award–nominated "Who Killed Vincent Chin?" (1989) and

Curtis Chin and Tony Lam's "Vincent Who?" (2009), both of which frame Chin's homicide as part of a wider history of the United States' devaluing of Asian lives. The light sentencing of Chin's killers, Ronald Ebens and Michael Nitz, to probation and a small fine in 1983 epitomized, for Asian American activists, the state's furthering—rather than redressing—of racially motivated crimes.

Highly allegorical and abstract, Uyehara's own videographic response to the October 21, 2001, intra-Asian hate crime contrasts markedly with this prior documentary tradition. Never intended as a stand-alone piece, Uyehara's video renders cinema a part of her "danc[ing] response"[37]—i.e., functionally dependent upon the kinesthetic bodily rituals of the live show (which includes squeezing, tearing, poking, and punching clay).[38] Using inexpensive tools—a video camera mounted on a tripod and a mound of clay sitting atop her kitchen table—Uyehara moved a bilateral human shape as she successively deformed it: "Creating a clay man and then tearing him apart was a quietly horrific process. How does the body respond to blows? What happens to my fist if I hit a person? What does it take to hate a body?" (*Maps*, 67). In the resulting video, the clay figure's limbs twist, and its stomach absorbs (thumb) indentations, but the human hand enacting the abuse is absent from the recorded video (see http://vimeo.com/8755970). While the documentaries devoted to Vincent Chin were by no means mainstream or profit oriented, their relative polish stands in stark contrast to the low production values of Uyehara's claymation video. Yet, the rough end result of Uyehara's video making (linked to its kitchen-table construction along the lines of Jerzi Grotowski's Poor Theater)[39] serves the performer's purpose. Live performance will not be overpowered or displaced by this film archive but instead remain crucially partnered with it. The continuous, never-finished repertoire of interacting with corporeal materiality (with the clay of our bodies) forms the key message and medium of this sequence in both its preparatory stages (of Claymation production) and its "finished" stage debut.

As it unfolds in the theater, "Hate Crime" resembles a modified shadow puppetry. The performer's bodily silhouette tangoes with the shadows (preserved cinematically) of the tortured clay man, as Uyehara moves "inside and outside the image, sometimes attacking it, sometimes being attacked by it" (50). Comprising a choreographic refrain, Uyehara repeatedly caresses her own cheek, cups her hand around the projected clay figure, slowly stabs into the head of it, and twists her fists rapidly in front of her abdomen as if pulling out her entrails. Transmitted to the audience via this highly mediated and modified shadow puppetry is an inchoate swirl of passions, sensitivities, and anxious vulnerabilities that might be projected outward (onto some innocent bystander) or inward, into the churning guts. In a mood quite contrastive to the interpersonal exchange of a token of trust and connection between one performer and one audience member as in "Vigil's" conclusion, "Hate Crime" summons the audience's affective involvement, by stirring up a chaotic atmosphere—aggressive energies rather than calming ones— with Uyehara leaving open-ended the "actions" spawned by that stirring up of affect.

This movement practice places the audience in the moment of affect's transmission—a moment where the negative emotion lies unprocessed between what the polymath scholar Teresa Brennan calls a "masculine" response of projecting negative and depleting affects outward or a "feminine" response that turns that negativity inward, symptomized as depression and anxiety. Noting that both the "masculine" and the "feminine" modes can be performed by either men or women, Brennan speaks of affects as circulating energetics (to my mind, in a yang-yin sense). Her gendered terms make a political and historical point as well: she differentiates the habituated, somaticized modes connected to historical divisions of labor wherein the masculine party—and she extends this to colonizers—direct negative emotions outward via aggression toward others, whereas the feminine party—and she extends this to the colonized and poor—serve as receptacles of that emotional dumping. Using diverse sources—from biochemistry, neurology, theology, crowd theory, clinical practice, and psychoanalysis—Brennan takes aim at the "foundational fantasy" that we are self-contained individuals and pursues the longstanding (ancient) understanding of a "social wellspring" from which affects flow and in which our bodies are bathed. "Affects" name the circulating vital energies carried by hormones, pheromones, and other airborne neurochemicals. In this portrait, humans are nodal points for the transfer, projection, reception, and transformation—"the interpreter[s] rather than the originator[s]" of depleting and enhancing energies among and between us.[40]

Fig. 5.5. From Edina Lekovic's monologue in *Big Head* (2003). *Photo by Pete Lee.*

Brennan's observation on the gendered modes of channeling affect takes me to the final sequence of *Big Head* through which Uyehara choreographs a kinesthetic vigilance. Based on an interview with a young Muslim woman, Edina Lekovic, this monologue stages the persistence of a racial incident that its bearer can "never forget," not for its grave violence but for its lack of easy qualities through which to articulate injury.[41] Lekovic, a former editor-in-chief of UCLA's *Daily Bruin*, tells of starting "at the [newspaper in] my freshman year" and then becoming "outwardly Muslim . . . my sophomore year," an exploration of identity that was not "that big of an issue" since "people already knew me" (35). Throughout this recitation, the performer rubs a large piece of paper across her arms and head, as if to suggest her being wrapped up in the reporter's life, but also conjuring, in at least one reviewer's mind, the veil.[42]

The incident that "hurt so much" leading Lekovic to "never forget [it]" involves a Japanese American staff member challenging her qualifications when she interviews for the position of editor-in-chief: "[W]hat effect does your being Muslim have on the job that you will do?" the young man asks (35). As she recounts the staff member's challenge, Uyehara grasps hard the edges of the paper and whips her arms into an "x" across her chest, an audio-visual heart seizure as the paper crunches and ruinously twists. Lekovic tells of being "extremely offended" but handling the incident as "politely and courteously as possible." During the remaining recitation of memory, the actress slowly uncrumples and smoothes out the paper, the crackling sounds competing with the calm politeness of Lekovic's words:

> I said, "Beyond the fact that I'm going to be praying five times a day, which will take a few minutes here and there, and that I'm a moral person who believes in ethics, which will benefit the newspaper—beyond that, I don't think this has anything to do with anyone else." I was upset with myself that I let it upset me. . . .
>
> [It was one] of those experiences that hurt so much when it happened. Because I'd felt I'd made so much progress, and that people who knew me knew who I was, and that they wouldn't sink to that level. (37–38)

Strikingly, the recollected words never get to why this incident "hurt so much," but the kinesthetic practice through which Uyehara performs this piece underscores what the incident *feels like*. Timing her twist-whipping of the paper to the Japanese American man's query, she visualizes a thrombosis. The unique sound of paper snapping as it's pulled taut conveys, despite the normal tone of Lekovic's words, the surging shame at being racially profiled.

Despite the effort to smooth out the paper, the still-visible crumple marks upon it bear witness to the enduring qualities of being a recipient of racial profiling. Here, *Big Head* harkens back to the words of dramaturge Tamadhur Al-Aqeel that expressly compare the bereavement of racism with the national grief of 9/11:

> Will there ever be closure for the September 11ᵗʰ attacks? Probably not. But one thing's for sure: there is no closure for being the target of racism. It's like how I felt when I watched the towers fall. It was just as shocking and horrifying to watch the 50ᵗʰ time as it was the first. Being the target of racism is like that. It's shocking and painful and somehow

incomprehensible the first time, and every time after that. I'm always waiting and wondering: who out there with the careless or intentional remark or action, will send my pain and anger crashing through me? It could be anyone.[43]

Racism's lingering effects refuse to stay confined to a slice of time and melancholically linger, with the objective correlative to Al-Aqeel's claim performed in Uyehara's repetition of this paper-crunching pulse. Over-dubbing a later sequence, "Edina's Song," this rhythmic crunching and uncrunching of paper scales up the body's microkinetics—the autonomic pulses that circulate upsetting feelings that one, despite knowing better or wanting to forget, is helpless to avoid (e.g., Lekovic's "I was upset with myself that I let it upset me").

If racial scapegoating is a particular variety of negative emotional dumping committed by "masculine" colonizing parties (of any sex, race, or belief system), *Big Head* attempts to circulate that feeling of being a recipient of such emotional dumping within her audience and to prompt a responsive conduct designed not so much to eliminate it through passing it on to someone else as to figure out what to do with its continual circulation. Lekovic's response—both its emphasis on five-times-daily conduct that would somatically entrain a body (politic) toward politeness and courtesy (civility), and her normal rather than escalating tone—provides one kind of figuring out of what to do, one literally imbued with Brennan's definition of "kindness."[44]

Performative ritual functions as the vascular conduit of this ethical repertoire. While "being Muslim" can mean being a veiled woman for the visually objectifying Western onlooker, being Muslim for Lekovic means "praying five times a day" and being a moral person who believes in "ethics." This ethics, in other words, hinges not on geographic proximity (near and dear) but rather on liturgical kinesthetics. Emphasizing the potential of somatic choreography to intervene in militaristic and punitive notions of hasty revenge as justice, *Big Head* endorses a five-times-daily conduct of pietistic recitation as crucial to an ethical, moral, and affective conduct. The heroine(ism) of this type of action lies in its inward churn—its five-times-(or more)-daily "handling" of quotidian encounters with others' aggression—an ethics practiced as mundane, hardly noticeable conduct, rather than an ethics accomplished by way of a singular sentimental story, rhetorical hail, testimony at trial, critical exposure, or burst of qualitative empathetic induction. While this emphasis on ethical conduct harkens back to the anatomopolitical scale of embodied practices—the "how-to" of nonmilitaristic doing (discussed in chapter 1)—it also remains wary of the codified "protocol" as a certificate and script of ethical righteousness. "Five times a day," in other words, recognizes ethical conduct as always unfinished, in process, and ritualistically realized contingently and situationally in daily rounds.

Because Lekovic is a well-educated, First World "veiled" female subject (both familiar and unfamiliar to normative U.S. womanhood), the Highways audience's empathetic embrace of her woundedness and piety may not go toward a moral memory that reaches beyond near and dear to embrace the distant and strange (Margalit and Palumbo-Liu's global others). But in terms of theorizing and proposing how Asian Americanist cultural productions perform an alternative ethics, Lekovic's monologue and Uyehara's staging of it are crucial. The monologue juxtaposes masculine heroic forms of agency—the fire of revolutionary action (marching, expansive mobility, liberatory GETTING OUT)—and those no-less-heroic efforts of emotional management (the panicked pulse that will not be released as a verbal flame directed at another) that are belittled as reparative and quiescent (tools of the "still" oppressed).

Big Head dwells upon and performatively conjures affective transmission in its pantomime of autonomic responses—the way the chest seizes or heart races in a moment of anxiety, or the way a deep injury to the viscera prompts swelling to immobilize the area of trauma. In Lekovic's monologue, Uyehara focuses less on the total body's choreography (the arcs of departure, return, and even disco dancing, accomplished by gross motor skills) and more on the pulse and beat of the circulatory system. Through her pulsing sound effect (which is achieved through a rough handling of paper but which also imitates the dance of muscles—pumping action—internal to everybody in her live audience), Uyehara rhythmically transmits to the audience awareness of the body's hard-wired kinesthetics on the most autonomic (vs. automated) level. We could narrativize that echoing of the heartbeat in at least two ways. First, given that some corporeal movements are indeed mindless and necessarily so, we have no way to really change the aggressive (fight and flight) habits that are instinctive to animal life (*zoe*) to which humans belong despite pretensions of their separateness; in other words, we're doomed to war and militarism and only secure ourselves from these deathly imperatives to the extent we can maintain hypervigilance against others (even our fellow citizens and kin). Second, we are all creatures with hearts, with blood pulses, of animate life, and that kinship morally requires a calm answer, or attempt at connection, despite a panicked heart telling us to do otherwise (to punch rather than caress). I would propose that what separates these two universalisms is not pessimism versus optimism but the behavioral habitus toward immunity, on the one hand, and entangled obligation, on the other.

Autonomic responses—the microkinetics controlled by the sympathetic and parasympathetic nervous systems—would seem not to be under volitional control. (The enteric nervous system, discussed at length in chapter 3, is also part of the autonomic nervous system.) But it is precisely through this arena of emotional, affective, hormonal, and endocrinological bodily choreography—their epigenetic interactionist evolution and their (rhythmic) contagion across bodies—that Uyehara makes her point.

As mentioned above, for Brennan, affects are social: they are in the air, not saliently bounded by the individual organism but leaking into the atmosphere (or space between skin surfaces) as mood, smell, airborne pheromones, and the like (Sara Ahmed's theory of circulating emotions and their "stickiness" harmonizes with Brennan's ideas).[45] Moreover, procedural memory—how to do and how to act—in response to a discomforting stimulus such as negative affect are also social and entrained. Toxicity inheres not simply in individual anger but in a whole system of warrior celebration—the thanatic-aggressive-carceral-segregating-isolating effects of which, ironically, antidepressants in synthesized pill form are to pharmacologically manage. We might regard Uyehara's postmillennial show, *Big Head*, as offering an epigenetic portrait of disability's (mental illness, amputation's) structuring affective conditions—namely, the industrialized, militarized, hyperproductive environment of modernity—with disability not ending at the skin of the stigmatized person. Rather, disability emerges in an entangled, epigenetic, affective milieu of racialized permanent war, the military-prison complex, that generates both mental illness—specific conditions such as post-traumatic stress disorder (PTSD), concrete events like the grandmother's self-immolation, and culturally/populationally pervasive actions like the "masculine" (colonizing) projection of aggression outward.

Brennan dwells on the ideological resistance to the exploration of the environment—its saturation by "exogenous androgens" from one stressed party—having an effect on the production of neurochemicals—"glucocorticoids . . . and elevated levels of testosterone"—in another or, put another way, in the recursive production of "mania . . . in the environment" (84). She links this resistance to a "paradigmatic shift" that would regard the human being and her/his "brain response system (cortical as well as hypothalamic)" as "an interpreter rather than originator" of "feelings, affects, [and] attentive energy," to the resistance to an epigenetic view that acknowledges from fetal formation forward that the "chemosignals that affect us encompass more than our endogenous productions [but] come from others and the environment" (87, 92). Put more baldly and *avant le lettre* of current discourses on vibrant matter and feminist new materialisms, Brennan states, "[T]he notion that the sense of self is different from that which is outside it (because that which is outside is unconscious, passive, and material) is clearly untenable":

> Natural matter is active in certain natural cycles; it is only passive to the extent that it does not have free will, meaning that it does not implement any design or intention other than the one maintaining its place in the scheme of things. Active matter is passive in that it is not individual; its intentional activity does not place it at odds with its surroundings. Only humans have intentions at odds with the scheme of things. . . . Only the subject of free will differentiates itself from its environment by activity that is at odds with that environment. (93)

This theory of affects, in other words, destabilizes both the immunitary paradigm of biopolitics (healthiness imagined as the defended-fortress body [Ed Cohen]) and the vaunted humanist subject of modernity that has defined its "subjectivity" by degrees of "intervention in [and] an imposition on," rather than harmony in accord with, "[his/her] surroundings" (93). It explains as well the difficulty with which modern subjects of the West recognize meditative and calming responses to violent impulses as quiescent, passive, and thing-like rather than as an intentionally kind (kindred-making, kindred-supposing) activity.

On the one hand, the political aims of *Big Head* appear to invest in the audience's capacity to combat mindless aggressive behaviors (in response to fear/threat), that is, to invest in the idea that with better memory, or a more robust sense of history (e.g., that scapegoating of innocents has happened before and shouldn't happen again), we can act differently. But, on the other hand, it also stages the proliferation of aggressive beatings and verbal challenges enacted by minorities— East Asian and Japanese Americans in particular—who themselves have been subject to racialized scapegoating and thus who viscerally "know" first-hand that history. Knowledge, in other words, provides little immunity to this contagion of violence, with Uyehara specifically emphasizing Asian Americans' "susceptibility" to "xenophobic rage" (67). Here, Uyehara's performance harmonizes with the skepticism voiced by Sedgwick (and discussed in foregoing chapters) in the faith in exposure (hidden-shown) as critical agency.

Performatively, then, *Big Head* effectively leaves the audience with a pulsing of heightened affect[46]—of transmitted feelings of being attacked that are not resolved by the show, a blood-rushing flush to the cheeks that stands as the bodily fire that we have to figure out what to do with "this time" and "next time"—in express echo of James Baldwin's *Fire Next Time* (1963). The title of Baldwin's classic text itself alludes to the biblical story of the great flood, symbol of a "cosmic vengeance" that attests to human intuition that the sustained violation of a people will reap consequences (e.g., a great flood or, next time, a great fire). Referring specifically to atrocities committed by the white Christian world upon Jews in the Holocaust and upon American blacks, Baldwin specifically states that the vengeance in repayment for such sustained violence committed in the name of racial and religious superiority "does not really depend on, and cannot really be executed by, any person or organization, and [it] cannot be prevented by any police force or army [for it is a] historical vengeance, a cosmic vengeance, based on the law that we recognize when we say, 'Whatever goes up must come down'" (119–20). After 9/11, the term "blow-back" was used to refer to the same idea, but here evoking the specific ways in which American policies in the Middle East (e.g., support of the Israeli state's aggressive policies toward Palestine) sow discontent to the point of (suicide-bomber) explosion.

Importantly, Baldwin suggests that the theologians and fundamentalists (whether of Christian, Muslim, or Jewish faiths) share a philosophy that sanctifies the destruction of the other and that disallows the coexistence of these faiths. He calls upon a relatively enlightened camp of "conscious" persons—both black and white—"who must, like lovers, insist on, or create, the consciousness of the others. . . . [If we] do not falter in our duty now, we may be able, handful that we are, to end the racial nightmare . . . and change the history of the world" (119–20). Like Baldwin, Uyehara predicts another fire, another conflagration or war. Moreover, Baldwin's emphasis on "conscious" persons (if we take that to mean the rational Enlightenment subject) as the "we" who might intervene to prevent this cosmic burning of the world, initially appears reiterated by Uyehara. However, as we shall see, the performance artist's *oeuvre* remains less sanguine regarding a rational or "conscious" cure for this fire.

In *Big Head*'s final minutes, the performer recalls the disappointment of her great-uncle Masamori Kojima—imprisoned in an Arkansas concentration camp—that many Americans decided not to register as horrific the mass dispossession and rounding-up of Japanese Americans during World War II:

> "Many turned against us, or even worse, they pretended *they did not see.* . . ." And since that time, I have not been the same. [Here, Uyehara resumes her own voice.] No I didn't actually see it . . . but I remember it clearly: Giant flames licking at a two-story building. . . . "Was it arson?" "A stray firework." . . . "Dad says a man fell asleep in bed while smoking." "Ice cream! Ice cream! . . . Look what the fire made." . . .
>
> I was one—one of many—who filmed the fire on the Fourth of July. *We with our heads made big*, filled with voices from the past and the voices of now. It was a small, poor, imperfect thing that I did—to remember. Maybe I even got the facts wrong. . . . Or did I? What will we do, in the fire this time? (57–58; italics in first paragraph in original; italics in second paragraph added)

Recalling those who "pretended *they did not see*," the artist describes a pretense of innocence (of non-knowledge) that Lauren Berlant dubs "infantile citizenship" and that Ruth Ozeki terms the "faux-dumb," not a real ignorance, but the pretense of ignorance that offers an alibi for inaction. In advocating big heads of, let's say, mind*ful* patriotism, Uyehara's performance would seem to endorse the rational subject grounded in knowing who acts ethically and morally in accordance with all that he knows (all that he has been made conscious of). But, as the recollection of her own infatuation with the Fourth of July consumer treat of "ice cream!" also suggests, the faux-dumb condition of knowing about, for example, Native American dispossession (or, as in the Ozeki novel, the horrors of cattle feedlot practices) but continuing to settle and consume in contradiction to that knowledge characterizes not merely the outright hypocrite but also the average, majority citizen for whom knowledge is insufficient prophylaxis to ensure ethical conduct. Here, my argument is informed again by Sedgwick's questioning of new historicism's exposure of ideology (or hidden agendas) as the modus operandi of politically progressive cultural criticism—as if exposing an injustice were a hop, skip, and jump away from undoing that injustice. Here, Uyehara's emphasis on choreography speaks to a mode of entraining the "normate" mentally rational subject who does not translate what s/he already "knows"—that to which s/he has been multiply "exposed"—into a corporeal practice.

The published script of the show notes that the "Big Head" of the show's title refers to the encephalitic's condition, even as, within the scenario of the black box theater, the reference to brain disease is absent. What do we make of this buried reference to encephalitis, especially in light of the performer's other engagements with those clinically diagnosed as mental impaired? As I've suggested, the title "Big Head" can easily be mistaken for an endorsement of an enlarged, expansive mind, and we might see this soliciting of error as purposeful. The show's title is catachrestic, a deliberately "poor" textuality that misnames the show's emphasis on the limits of cognition and interpretive hermeneutics. Here, bigness does not correspond to better or most important. With the brain too big—that is, inflamed and swollen with aggressive affects—the need for conduct to be distributed across the body's wider members(ship) or, put another way, slowed by muscular-affective rituals that can counter or entrain a rhythmic alternative to that of "fight or flight," becomes all the more urgent.

Encephalitis—a swollen head—attains a polysemy in relation to this show's imitating the choreographies, both conventional and unconventional, of American patriotism. On the one hand, big heads might refer to the flag-festooned drivers of gas-guzzling SUVs—the bigness referring to U.S. expansionist imperatives to open markets—that is, to enlist the world's population as flexible labor for corporate manufacturers and to poach native resources as raw materials for proliferating consumables. By calling diseased such ableist, nationally iconic movements that colonize the body to a mindlessly expansionist style, Uyehara could be construed as dissing disability (reducing it to metaphor) in order to make a critique of American empire. Here, the healthy Americans (healthy because they are forgetful?)—rather than the now-aged survivor of the death camps—have become the ones with something like nationalist-induced dementia.

But perhaps we might read Uyehara's title as a choreographic metaphor, too. Encephalitis (which, interestingly, can prompt dementia and other mental disorders of memory) also refers to an autonomic and inward response to trauma that involves a swelling—the cellular activity around a viral infection, for instance. In response to receiving "a masculine party's" aggression, emotional dumping, or systemic necropolitical blows, the injured person's somatic micro-kinetics might be entrained to an inward-turned swelling as distinct from a repeated outward projection of negative emotion in aggressive acts that offer release but at others' expense. To be sure, neither the inward nor the outward represents a model of health. And in her economy of emotions, Brennan focuses on how the unhealthiness of this system proceeds from a mystified foundational fiction of bodies as self-contained rather than as linked through shared environment (with affects part of that environment). She proposes a horizontal line of affective transmission that she calls "the line of the heart" (and that she counterposes to the "vertical line" of history): affects are not "only inherited. They also flow from this one to that one, here and now, via olfaction and the circulation of blood" (75). Taking the social view, Uyehara invokes a head "made big" by autonomic inward swelling—aka encephalitis—and in that moment of affective trauma, relying on the body's habitual entrainment (which, importantly, can be a meditative entrainment—perhaps this is what Baldwin meant by being "conscious"). Or as Janelle Taylor remarks with regard to the progress of cognitive impairments such as dementia, "procedural memory (knowing *how to* do such-and-such) often persists much longer than propositional memory (knowing *that* such-and-such). People who are no longer able to speak coherently may often still take part in, and enjoy, activities such as walking, dancing, or singing that rely on embodied procedural memory."[47] Procedural memory as the capacity to care—to caress, laugh, and verbally commune or tango (despite loss of the capacity to identify names, places, times)—are conductive kindnesses that Taylor exquisitely outlines as within her propositionally forgetful mother's continued somatic rituals qua "flesh" competence.

The positive acts that *Big Head* models—distinct from the pantomimes of aggressive behaviors that the performance mocks—are those of "keeping this for me until the end of the war" and praying five times a day. The performance does not guarantee the end to or cessation of fire "next time"—it only choreographs "poor," lacking, in-valid actions (even by estimations of leftists) that we must engage in nonetheless. The performer leaves her audience with the open-ended question of "doing"—the iterative conduct to allay or channel the militaristic storm of late-industrial empiric biopolitics into a five-times-daily practice of vigilance and care.

Conclusion: On Temporal Lag

> People with ADRD [Alzheimer's disease and related dementia] lose the ability to comprehend chronological time systems that orient and unite so much of global culture. . . . People with ADRD become "disabled," then, because they cannot negotiate memory in the ways that come to be seen as necessary components of selfhood. People with ADRD are an extreme example of a self that is relational, formed through interaction with others. (Basting 203)

My specific interest in Uyehara arises from the challenge she poses to the implicit investment in rational cognition—the head, knowledge, consciousness—as primary loci of adjudicating and performing ethical action. Rather than simply using storytelling to expose lost histories that her audience is urged to remember better, Uyehara peppers her stories with figures who cannot remember—whose neurological or psychic disorders render "rationally" perfect recall of history impossible. She turns to dance, somatic entrainment, and meditative choreographies as possible responsive actions, or ethical modes of relating to those with conventionally conceived mental impairments. This movement practice remains in tension with continuous attempts to narrativize (epistemologically penetrate) an anomalous way of thinking-feeling. With tango as her movement idiom, the artist embraces being both *with* and *against*: *with* hopes for relief for vulnerable nonelect populations seeking a remedy with respect to the social injuries, containments, and homicides inflicted on them; and, at the same time, *against* the imperative for a healthier body politic, especially when health is conceived along the lines of an immunitary biopolitics (e.g., my health against your contagion) exemplified in plans to surgically strike against the disease of "terrorism" supposedly housed in brown-skinned bodies but bespeaking an affective atmosphere against which one paradoxically fights by fomenting more (so-called counter-) terror.

Uyehara's earlier work tangoes with neurological non-normative figures in a way that is not altogether atypical—trying to work out the impulse to cure/save them, not quite knowing how to do so, but tinkering with ways to break bread, drink chocolate syrup, and laugh beside and in accompaniment with them. Her later work's seeming turn away from actually existing mentally disabled people, even as the title of her 2003 show obliquely refers to encephalitis, could be construed as a universalizing move with regard to illness and somatic and psychic anomaly, but in this universalism, Uyehara's project *accords* with contemporary processural reframings of disability studies. Emphasizing the inherent instability of the category of "people with disabilities," Lennard Davis notes that this category exists as the "largest physical minority in our country"[48] and that its demography is especially unstable due to disabilities being acquired and subject to "cure."[49] Disability, rather than a minority identity, is one toward which we are all heading, acknowledged in the modifiers "temporarily able-bodied" or "temporarily able-brained." Optimal mental and physical capacity that characterizes the eugenic elect (*bios*) remains an extraordinary and unstable embodiment—the statistical "top" quartile in a bell curve flipped up at the midway point, so that the curve's normal downward arc appears a further ascension upwards (see figure 1 of Davis 1995, 34). Living individuals and aggregates only move toward optimal "ability" by simultaneously disavowing or shoving aside the *zoe* of our alienable, incapacitated body parts (or parts of the body politic) and our non-"immortal" aging scales of the self. Counterintuitively then (and in revision to prior articulations of *bios* and *zoe*), the mortal human organism who arcs through growth, aging, disability, and cellular mutation—this life course lived in delimited time-space (e.g., with factories, unsafe cars, and ectohormones of militarism) or what Didier Fassin (quoted in chapter 1) dubs life lived through "a body (not only through cells)"[50]—becomes at some point the nonoptimal *zoe* to be discarded in preference for the disaggregated human revised as "technologies of living matter" (Landecker 2010) whose vitalities or technological uses are extended and made semi-autonomous *in vitro* or *in vivo* (in another biology or another human to which they have been transplanted) (see my introduction). This is the tango of biopolitics in the current regime of bioscience and biovalues (Cooper 2008; Waldby and Mitchell). I return to this point in the conclusion to the next chapter.

In framing the Asian American performance artist Denise Uyehara in relation to disability, this chapter has itself methodologically tangoed with an identity-politics approach to the subject of mental anomalousness. While the first half of this chapter scrutinizes the portraits of "actual disabled persons" that figure in Uyehara's storytelling, the second half addresses how Uyehara uses kinesthetics to dance with and against what I call the figural disease of proleptic desire.[51]

Uyehara's performances positively value a rhythmic lag akin to a "time slip" (borrowed from Ann Basting's work on people with Alzheimer's or related dementia and quoted in the epigraph)[52]—a break or slide away from the dominant, "masculine" ways of linking negative affective stimulus and expressive action outward (e.g., hostile verbalization or punching fists). In the medicalized diagnosis of memory impairment, a torsion in chronological processing lies at the core of one theory of age-related disability where slipping in and out of normative time is, simultaneously, a mental disease—destructive of individual functionality (and the myth of autonomy)—and enhancing to an ethical affirmation of relationality. In Brennan's account of the sociality of affects, time-slip or lag—the conductive resistance to passing on the electrical current of aggression (and other negative affects)—is valued positively as the key to a "feminine party's" kindness that can also, in medicalized terms, be dubbed an illness, e.g., depression and anxiety.

Asynchronous timing, but in a rhythm quite opposite to that of lag and slowness, likewise, underpins the affective disposition of both what Eve Sedgwick defines as scholarly paranoia and the mechanisms of euphoric speculative capital (both of these are characterized by a proleptic rhythm). Speculative capital and paranoia prize anticipatory or proleptic speed—a getting there before everyone else and the maximization of value in this leading beat. The vigilance that Uyehara endorses, I argue, importantly differs from a paranoid vigilance that prizes anticipating and thereby undoing surprises that inevitably figure as bad surprises (Sedgwick). Instead of an anticipatory super speed—as in proleptic rhythms that are ahead of, rather than at the same time or belatedly arrived—as the ethical-epistemological pulse to which we must pace ourselves, Uyehara's performances meditate on the value of conduct in lag, a slowed-down, deliberative gift of attention or, put more in a performance lexicon, a twice-behaved (or quintuple-behaved) behavior. To be mentally slow is to unfold (neuro-muscularly) in ways that do not hit the "benchmarks" of normate development, with Uyehara proposing the positive ethical value of this retardation, choreographically and affectively.

Uyehara remains uncertain of the universal reach of her dancing efforts, and *this* as much as her specific gestures of caretaking—tangoing, discoing, caressing, staying with rather than departing from—models an alternative ethics—a fragmented, localized ethics, one in bits and pieces of practical, contingent, highly contextual conduct, distributed across people's bodies in ways not guaranteed by a top-down appeal to reason or obedience or rationality (or even pheromonal-affective transmissional fixing). It is a struggle uncertain of its ends, needing rehearsing everyday. In slow-mo, Uyehara dances an open-ended, sensual proposition, rather than narratively answering the final question, as to whether we are still discomforted by this discoordination and its implied slower pacing or whether we can caretake this "dismodernist"[53] ethics and practice affective kindness in such elongated, nonspeedy rituals.

6

Allotropic Conclusions

Propositions on Race and the Exquisite Corpse

Throughout this book, I have been stressing that literary studies of race would benefit from a more robust engagement with the altered scales of differentiating biologies that have come into dominance by way of biotechnical innovations. When we speak of races—for example, Blumenbach's influential quintuple chromatic schema—we refer to the differentiation of humans (*homo sapiens*) into subdivided populations distinguished, for the most part, phenotypically. At the turn of the twenty-first century, an epidermal notion of race rubs against and in tension with other modes of aggregating populations, for instance, according to (1) often microscopically coded (genomic) markers of disease propensity as well as attempts to document unfolding behavioral-environmental-dietary (epigenetic) regulation of such propensities; (2) a biomodification regime of primary class or economic stratification in which wealthier sectors of society supplement and extend their optimized bodily transformations, while poor and perpetually debt-ridden sectors of society become bioavailable to service this sector's amplified transformations; and (3) scalar perspectives that begin with nonhuman biologies such as those of bacteria and protoctist parasites that potentially promote a less defensive, less immunitary response to our entanglement with alien species and bring consideration to how the organized assemblages called "human" have coevolved and helped comigrate other nonanimal bare life (plants, fungi).[1] Critical studies of race have begun to explore the implications of the newer techniques for aggregating populations on the governance of, and niche advertising to, those populations (Fullwiley; Duster; Bolnick, et al.; Bliss; Tallbear, *Native DNA*; D. Roberts 2012; Wailoo, et al). More research along the lines of Karen Cardozo and Banu Subramaniam's on "invited invasive" species needs to be done regarding transformed notions of kinship and nonterrorized modes of facing bio-ecological entanglement with strangers and alien species as a consequence of the revised aggregates proposed by phylogenetics.

Like these scholars concerned with the impact of genomic science and clinical practices on determinations of the biological species who will form the (emerging) racial other (Gilroy; Duster; K. Bridges 2012; Bliss), I was prompted to ask, at the outset of this project, whether and to what extent the new "hatreds" provoked by microscopic scales of differentiating biologies would simply supersede those tied to a chromatic racial schema, with populations become distinguished by way of their mode of reproduction (Ishiguro's *Never Let Me Go*) or scale of organismal organization (Bear's *Blood Music*) rather than their "color"—with other "postracial" markers of difference including rate of metabolism and ease of enrollment in laboratory experiments—or whether these emergent demarcations of populations would be made legible by way of recourse to epidermal racial taxonomies.[2] In the various literary works and performances examined in this book, the chromatic schema of the five races brushes up against the nonisomeric categories of *bios/ zoe*. Arguably, theories of biopower supplant the chromatic schema of the five races as heuristic devices: these governmental techniques stratify populations at the turn of the twenty-first century precisely due to their greater simplicity and thereby clarity. Biopower operates along a binary—*bios* (the protected, "ethical life of the free citizen" or a biographical form that narrates this life [Scheper-Hughes 2004, 156; Jerng]) and *zoe* (bare, animal, unmourned life, or the unnarrated "lived" life cycle and possibly the kinesthetic choreography of cellular processes)— a dichotomy more facile than a fivefold-or-more array of distinctions.

As noted in my introduction, the salience of placing Asian American cultural texts and Asian Americanist cultural study in relation to the question of the biological lies in the peculiarities of the Asian Americanist critical field's articulation of its weakness as an immanent discursive formation and its overreliance on the biological. Rather than contesting that Asian Americans have no common language, history, and so forth, to call their own (as argued by Frank Chin in the 1970s), I am saying that precisely because of these noncommonalities, the question of biology looms larger, making the anxiousness of biological embodiment in Asian Americanist contexts a ripe arena of study and opening up the question of what being biological (bioavailable, biosupplementable, clinically carved up, etc.) means for race, postcolonial, gender, queer, and disability studies more generally. Racial figurations, as I demonstrate in *Blood Music*'s "a billion Chinese," play a role in making comprehensible the multiply operating, often conflicting scales of biology, or, put another way, in designating as fearfully alien and difficult these scales of biology that are "unknown even as they are lived" inside and as "us." Relatedly, in my consideration of humans' cohosting of the protist *Plasmodium*, I argued that discussions in the philosophy of ethics regarding the stranger are relevant to analyzing racial encounters. The strangeness of the biologies in question in that chapter (4), however, is not due to their coming from another geopolitical locale (i.e., their "arrivant" status [Jodi Byrd]) but to their remaining "autonomous" microbiota (self-organizing systems) that reside intimately within the self, symbiotically and parasitically. A further argument, pursued by way of my analysis of Taiwanese American choreographer Cheng-Chieh Yu, addresses the plasticity of the dancer corresponding on the whole-organism level to something akin to the nascent transformability of the stem cell. I imply that racializing techniques are used to segregate, abject, and fetishize other scales of (our and others') biologies, and in this implication Bear's lexicon—cited above—speaks as evidence. Though this nascent transformability of the stem cell performed as a so-called Asiatic capacity remains fetishized, this does not mean that it is not also, at the same time, hated.

In pursuing these plural scales of the supreme or primitive biology that must be either killed off directly—or, counterintuitively, eradicated through assimilation/inclusion—I outline the way in which the struggle between European settler races and colored immigrant and indigenous races bespeaks a struggle between distinct onto-epistemological systems of knowing, inhabiting, and caretaking other human and nonhuman actants. Whiteness—embodied in Ghosh's novel, for instance, by the military scientist Ronald Ross during British territorial imperialism—stands not simply for a blind and arrogant empiric ethnocentrism but for a bumbling and narrow anthropocentrism that remains antiscientific, as well as anti-indigenous, in its underestimation of the agencies and intelligences acting from "below"—the microbes and janitorial staff, both deemed primitive forms of life.

The new (epi-)genomic age within and to which these artists I've examined are speaking has produced significant revisions to older models of racialization and racism. In the six sections below, I offer "propositions" that grow out of the way in which familiar theories of race, beyond the chromatic, biological schema (already outlined in chapter 1), take on new forms when cross-pollinated with ascendant biopolitical regimes. These familiar theories are (1) the labor theory of race, (2) the necropolitical theory of race, (3) the psychic life of racial projection, (4) racial minoritization as it relates to *zoe*/"bare life," (5) racial critique forwarded through aesthetic forms, and (6) the worry and hope over racial distinction overridden by commonality of species. The propositions, which I include as well in text boxes, are hypotheses and invitations for further dialogue and discussion rather than established theories as of yet. I conclude with a brief foray into the styling of this project on the surrealist figure of the exquisite corpse.

The Labor Theory of Race

In commonplace usage, racism refers to the dehumanization of populations for the purposes of enslavement, other forms of labor alienation such as indenture, the stripping of political protections, the imperialist seizing—and seeing—of territories occupied by such populations as merely empty land (Pratt), and the general brutal treatment, including extermination, of those slotted into "inferior" racial categories (there is the "inferiority" of the savage qua primitive as well as the inferiority of the decadent—populations deemed overripe, as it were, in their civilizational trajectory). As proposed in my introduction, at the turn of the twenty-first century, racism takes the form, too, of the procurement, from poor, politically unprotected populations of the global South, of impoverished persons' biological organs and metabolic products. My chapter on Margaret Cho details the comedienne's scrutiny of racialization manifested as segmented, stratified allotments of reproductive labor: white reproduction remains cherished while black reproduction is treated as degenerate (D. Roberts 1998). Racialization, as my analysis of Cho's concert draws out, is thoroughly entangled with putative "self-determined" choice, with Cho speaking "whiteness"—a reproductive capacity and self-regulation posed in opposition to the foreclosure of parenthood to those assessed as at risk, e.g., because of poverty, war, uprooting from homeland, sexual abuse, and subsequent depressed, anxious behaviors—when she (1) adjudges her pregnant self incapable of taking care of a child she might have birthed; *and* (2) when she notes that she can "always adopt" an Asian child. Here the biological product procured under the logic of a racialized biopolitics is not an organ but the whole child.

Dehumanization comes to light here in the form of the internalization of certain colored and queer promiscuous behaviors as dysgenic, accompanied by the psychic and somatic labor of disciplining the self to conform to the eugenic viewpoint—seeking abortion while young and drug-addicted, and considering oneself eligible to adopt when normatively corrected into married heterosexuality. Cho's memoir and concerts put flesh on the way in which eugenics shifted across the twentieth century from an endeavor (prior to World War II) overtly bent on population control—the elimination of "poor stock" figured as immigrants, darker-skinned people, the indigenous, the diseased, and other biological "defects," including those with mental disabilities (see chapter 5)—to one focused on cultivating healthy and effective repro-sexuality, thereby inciting categories of sexual perversity, the demonizing of homosexuals and liberated women. In other words, part of the shift to "positive eugenics" was toward a more process-oriented approach that endeavored to channel styles of gene-swapping and enculturation—or protocols for the raising of the child—that would be endorsed as normative, productive, and healthy.

In *Immigrant Acts*, Lisa Lowe offers a definition of racialized-immigrant labor that turns on capital's need for a population who, by lacking political protections, becomes willing to take on the types of poorly remunerated jobs that politically protected American citizens do not wish to do.[3] Informal and unorganized laborers are especially vulnerable to tactics that deny that they are doing valuable "work," rather than simply doing "what comes naturally" to these laborers' bodies.

My work highlights forms of racialized labor that occur outside the realm of formal waged work. Racialization, in chapter 2, is approached less as a classification system of population aggregates—though these are certainly the background of World Fairs' ethnological showcases—and more as a cosmetic and embodied process of binding and bracing that demands a somatic plasticity and acrobatic flexibility from the immigrant to get her to line up with straight whiteness. Here, the specular economy of minoritized racialization works through a dynamic of denied sympathetic witness wherein the suffering endured by the racial or ethnological other neither solicits the audience's identificatory compassion nor is credited as a type of value-producing labor.

Relatedly, anatomopolitics as a form of governmentality, of corporeal management, functions as well to ratchet up the demand for unwaged embodied labors that were heretofore termed reproductive and immaterial labor, and at the same time figure this labor as its own reward, justifying its poor-paying or nonremunerated status.[4] Grasping this invisible labor, at the dawn of the twenty-first century, may be not simply a matter of listing the occupations that fall under the category of "feminized" work requiring intense affective regulation, accomplished by nurses, hostesses, tour guides qua docile native informants, entertainment workers, health coaches, food service workers, sex workers, and so forth. It may also require attending to the pace and proleptic speed-up of such work.

> **PROPOSITION I:** Racialized labor bespeaks not only the types of clandestine low-wage labor "that only third world workers find attractive" (Lowe 21) but also proleptic aspirational labor whereby colonized and immigrant populations attempt to render their bodies "healthy" and normative, so as to be included in the biopolitical elect rather than the "surplus populations" from which capital has disinvested as "unprofitable."

To extend the insights of Vincanne Adams, Michelle Murphy, and Adele Clark, the biomedical arena through which the tropical indigenous colonials are experimented on and through which the immigrant is normed to dominant codes of health remains saturated with affects of anticipation—"the palpable sense that things could be (all) right if only we anticipate them properly" (259). Being made healthier, or made epidemiologically safer for cohabitation with urban privileged subjects of the West/Global North is a form of often unwaged work at which populations differentially labor at differentially frenzied paces. Future research needs to develop finer articulations of how exactly epidermal races align or not with labor populations that, on the one hand, are enrolled in risk-bearing medical experimental labor and, on the other hand, enrolled in aspirational, anticipatory capitalization of the eugenic and dysgenic parts of themselves.

The Necropolitical Theory of Race

Still operative at the turn of the twenty-first century is the extracting of value and, indeed, of biological materials from populations construed as biologically distinct species-beings that are assumed not to suffer or feel pain in the same way as the valued humans of the global North or Western metropole do (witness the Body Worlds exhibits, or the kidney donors from Chennai interviewed by Lawrence Cohen). More provocatively, this book asks, "Does racism also refer to the fierce germ-phobic attitude toward viral and bacterial contamination that rides along on certain human bodies—call them Asiatic—or, more precisely, the bacteria and other microorganisms with which those human biologies more frequently cohabit and that Asians themselves target for extermination?" The potential responses to this question turn on how historically bounded one wants to designate or speculate the longevity of raciology's reach. To make this more concrete, let me borrow from Vijay Prashad's periodization and definition of race specifically tied to the Atlantic slave trade. Only a particular *combination* of *biological rationales*—of innate, self-evident bodily differences—and a historically specific mode of *enslavement* and *slaughter*—for Prashad, at least, remains the hallmark of racism.

According to Prashad, enslavement alone is not evidence of racism at work, for ancient civilizations enslaved "their own to enjoy the free labor slavery provided":[5]

> In China, as in most of the world, prisoners of war became the property of their captors. . . . The Chinese, like the Arabs, Indians, Africans, and Europeans, enslaved their own to enjoy the free labor slavery provided. . . . [H]owever . . . although there was trade in humans in the premodern Indian Ocean perimeter, it was not a trade that necessarily dehumanized

a biologically or even regionally delimited set of people, however brutal the treatment meted out to them.[6]

The biological discourse, in which "fear" of the outsider, now figured as a separate species-being, is newly embedded, stands as the key feature distinguishing modern racism from ancient ethnocentricism and xenophobia. Prashad observes that though ancient records show a fear of outsiders, "it would be inaccurate to reduce this ethnocentrism or xenophobia, to racism, mainly because there was little sense that the difference was predicated on the body (biological determinism) and that those who are biologically inferior can be put to work in the service of their biological betters."[7] If at the core of modern-day racism is a notion that a biological inferior can be put to work by a biological better, then how does that idea of incorporating biological inferiors into one's enslaving mode of production—or biopolitics practiced through economic inclusion, albeit as exploited "surplus" labor—square with that other signal "moral . . . rupture" that Paul Gilroy, for instance, nominates as the epitome of racism—wholesale extermination of "inferior" races as in the German Third Reich's decimation

> **PROPOSITION II: Race operates as a mode of class-labor exploitation (incorporative parasitic biopolitics), but racism as it engenders moral repugnance refers to genocidal obliteration (necropolitics), including the keeping of half-alive dehumanized others as bioemporiums and as scientific/clinical resources for the biopolitical elect.**

of Jews, homosexuals, and the disabled,[8] to which we might add the genocide of indigenous tribes as foundational to the establishment of the U.S. nation-state?[9] Put another way, this time taking into account that slavery did indeed occur prior to the biologism of raciology, we might observe that as language and literacy in a common book were challenged by biological or epidermal taxonomies as primary vehicles for differentiating populations or tribes, enslavement took on a specific biopolitical/necropolitical character on a continuum with what later became known as negative eugenics—total war against the further breeding of inferior species. Enslavement and segregation of *biological* inferiors qua other races was not only about taking advantage of the free labor slavery provided and, in the case of Native Americans, taking advantage of New World terrain as private property "liberated" by the death and removal of First Nation peoples but also about the necropolitical urge and moral good to punish and decimate these distinct species-beings, distinct from "us," so as to ensure the flourishing of "us."

While the Atlantic slave trade, especially in U.S. historical memory, serves as a synecdoche for racism, it is not the extraction of wealth from unfree labor that primarily acts as the connector for that synecdoche. It is rather the brutal dehumanization—the animal-ification of black bodies as mere chattel, as livestock packed in the hulls of transatlantic "middle passage" ships, whipped like beasts of burden in plantation fields, and anatomically dissected after death by their doctor-owners[10]—that serves as the ligament coloring the Atlantic slave trade with a moral repugnance intimately wedded to the post-humanist horizons of biological science. By this, I refer to the displacement of the idea of *human agency*—and the survival of humans as opposed to, let's say, the ongoing creativity of bacteria, protoctists, algae, or fungi—as primary drivers of historical and planetary changes. Or as microbiologist Lynn Margulis pointedly puts it, "No evidence exists that [humans] are 'chosen,' the unique species for which all others were made. Nor are we the most important one because we are so numerous, powerful, and dangerous. Our tenacious illusion of special dispensation belies our true status as upright mammalian weeds."[11]

At the turn of the twenty-first century, the Atlantic slave trade and the World War II Holocaust still epitomize the horror of epidermal racism, down to the Star of David armbands and serial number tattoos—the latter melancholically rechoreographed by Uyehara (chapter 5)—designed to make difference reside on the surface of bodies. As the foregoing chapters suggest, puzzling out more "pastoral" forms of contemporary evolving racism may involve documenting microscopic markers of biological difference as well as processional differences in modes of biological reproduction and cross-indexing those with an epidermal schema of anatomical difference.

Importantly, "pastoral" refers to the tonal qualities of governmentality *directed toward the human individual as whole organism* who then decides—exercises his/her choice—whether or not to wage war against her/his own body parts (witness the preemptive radical mastectomies of women holding the BRCA1 gene on behalf of an anticipated greater health benefit for the women themselves).[12] Once again, the pastoral shepherding of life is wedded to the murderous and necro-regulatory (to coin a new term), with the term "pastoral" being catechrestic or, more specifically, narrowly characterizing the texture of power at the populational or professional-interpersonal levels—the king to his subjects, the doctor to her patient—precisely because the diffusely effective channels of a more brutal, endo-organismal power have become "capillary."

The Psychic Life/Function of Race

My work delves into the affective work accomplished by projecting intimations of historical change—dehumanizations consequent upon being enrolled as the most risk-bearing subjects of the next phase of modernity—onto an Asiatic biology in particular. This affective work helps contain in the figure of a supposedly biologically distinct population—a sub- and/or superhuman species-being—the suffering of modernity—that is, the material and metaphysical displacement of humanity, at least in its current specs. In the case of the Asiatic, this separate race iconically evokes both hypermutability—as in assimilation to displacing conditions requiring incredible flexibility as danced, for example, by Cheng-Chieh Yu—and the phantasmatic containment of the negative effects of this hypermutability in this alien population aggregate. Here, the Asiatic is doubly instrumental, as a life form considered so alien that it is contained, and as so adept at change and assimilation that, as Tina Chen argues, impersonation is considered her/his very form of agency.

As both Colleen Lye and Eric Hayot historicize, late-nineteenth- and early-twentieth-century American white "nativist" labor allayed and displaced its anxieties over the incipient form of life in modernity due to industrialization's speed-ups and poor working conditions by concocting the "Asiatic"—a part-reviled, part-envied superhuman figure with the capacity of "indifference" to suffering. One might expect that racial fear—manifest as defensive, murderous rage toward the alien other—arises especially at times of high anxiety over not having the vital capacity to withstand the next phase of technological upheaval (for example, the industrial revolution, green revolution,[13] information revolution, petro-fracking revolution). Racial minoritization names the abject condition of part-self merged with part-other—the present self who is me now, and the alien other being who I was or will eventually become. To become marked as racially other is to become flung forcibly into the past and/or future, to be denied coevalness, as Johannes Fabian puts it, and to inhabit a chronotope demarcated as nonsynchronous or, put another way, as "in time with but also in antagonism to" the present modernity.[14]

To recapitulate, when looking at how race operates as a modality of extracting labor or service for the accumulation of either imperial lucre or commodity capitalism, or simply for gratuitous expenditure more generally,[15] it is important to note the feelings of tenderness that are consequently shut down in the instrumental regard for the racial other as primarily a worker-servant or competitor for scarce resources. We often turn to literary forms for a thick (and usually verbally adept) description of how it feels to be subject to the colorline, to be epidermally profiled, displaced from home,[16] and denied companion relationality.

My implicit argument across this book is that the desire for an adequate interiorized view of the immigrant psyche is in keeping with an older tradition of Asian Americanist critique that "returns to humanistic wholeness" the partial, reduced, and thereby presumed negative image of Asians. In my method of examining the artists featured in this book, I reject this necessity. In short, the ethical challenge presented to the (former) imperialist subject who eschews the racism upon which the expansion of imperial whiteness is founded is to act the host to (and have tender feelings for) even those unfamiliar others who remain opaque, unknowable, and, thus, still affectively alien or strange (see chapters 4 and 5).[17]

The affective work mediated by racial others is incredibly flexible, at once bespeaking satisfaction that the racial other is biologically inferior and destined for servitude, anxieties toward the racial other as advanced and unfeeling and destined for future dominance, and antipathy that the racial other seems incapable of copassionate empathy with "us," thus relieving "us" of the duty to be compassionately responsive toward them. The effort to quarantine to the racial other the sufferings of what Hayot (2007) calls modernity, others call neoliberal risk culture (Rose; Beck; Cooper), and still others refer to as a deterritorializing empiric logic (Hardt and Negri; Byrd; J. Kim) results in the dis-obligation to caretake—by which one acknowledges entangled intimacy with—those whose affective labor crucially constitutes one's (false) sense of autonomy. This affective work has been carried as the burden of the feminine parties of every race, as suggested by Teresa Brennan, or has been thought of as the work of feminine parties regardless of whether women or men carry it out (see chapter 5).

Biopolitical and STS critics contour the amplification of affects of anxiety in information, neoliberal, and finance capitalism and how such affects devolve to the individual and his/her family members to manage by way of risk calculations (Rose 2001). Using the term "living in prognosis," Sarah Lochlann Jain names specifically an affective disposition that is particular to post–breast cancer diagnosis but that I broaden to refer to a more generalized, turn-of-the-twenty-first-century apprehension of not having mitigated enough one's statistical propensity toward a pathology. That is, one gambles on one's future closeness to past averages (of symptomology) derived from aggregates of profiled individuals who varyingly resemble one's individuality (genome and epigenome) and, therefore, risk of disease—or more specifically, risk of a certain tempo to the unfolding stages of a disease.

This book argues for the value of analytical treatments on racial projection and racial dynamics to such scholars of "living in prognosis" and more generally to biopolitical critics concerned with the instrumentalization of affects of anxiety regarding being last year's model or not behaving with the optimal proleptic speed to withstand a risk-related obsolescence at forty-five years, the latter exemplary, at the turn of the twenty-first century, of a life cut short by disease. In the past, fear of this obsolescence—what Scott Bukatman calls "terminal identity"—took shape through the projection of rage/hatred onto the future body (for instance, one racialized as Asiatic) seemingly already habituated to these new risks or, put slightly differently, the embodiment already habituated toward a somatic repertoire of cutting out—exiling and killing off—behaviors (meat eating) and parts of the self that were formerly definitive of one's humanness or mammalian warmth (the breasts)[18] but that now are framed as possible contributors to a speedier termination. Instead of intimations of "terminal identity" being predominantly projected as outrage toward racial others whose diminished lives represent both a degraded, lesser-evolved humanity and next year's biological model, we now see ourselves in a situation where everyone is *in the race*, so to speak, the race to become proleptically defensive against the future's risks—that is, where racism, a repertoire of necro-regulation and killing off, always intimately coupled with the optimization of one's privileged wellness, becomes directed at behaviors, diets, and environmental niches of risk exposure: race transmogrifies into these epigenomic factors or, rather, racism transmogrifies into a war against these epigenomic factors (Mansfield).

> **PROPOSITION III: One meaning of "postrace" is that we now see ourselves in a situation where everyone is in the race, so to speak, the psychic and material race to ward off anxiety by becoming proleptically defensive against the future's risks. Racism transmogrifies into a war against epigenomic factors.**

This is not to understate the simultaneity and overlap with racialization and racism qua an interaction between humanist wholes of population aggregates—as in the instance when the optimization of wellness for a person from the global North involves the taking or leasing of organs (of metabolic labor, ontogenetic labor, gestational labor) from the person of color, the indigenous subject, and the person of lower-rung caste.

Racial Justice and the Incongruency with *Zoe*-Egalitarianism

Sometimes when we speak about race studies, we are speaking about what kind of social justice struggle or ethical practice we feel best addresses the unjust situation we confront. To recapitulate the earlier point, minority racialization is a name we also give to those who denounce U.S. empire, the legacy of Jim Crow, the continuing fomenting of anti-immigration sentiment, and the continuing violence of settler colonialism. "Social justice" has become an umbrella term for those invested in decolonizing movements that critique the military-prison-industrial complex, the continued salience of colorism and eroticized violence against women in various quarters globally, and the ever more flexible ways in which greed (now in the modality of capitalist accumulation) expands, mutates, and adjusts to attempts to slow the priority of expanding surplus wealth (localized as the property of a narrow segment of beneficiaries) above all else.

Throughout this book, and most explicitly in my treatment of *The Calcutta Chromosome*, I pursue the question of whether a social justice orientation associated with race studies and Asian Americanist approaches can coexist with a post-Pasteurian bio-ecological outlook that regards the intimate entanglement with other social and biological life not as something to be feared but as part of the *vis medicatrix naturae* (Ed Cohen). While race studies scholars committed to social justice understandably might regard an attentiveness to the rights of the animal or to the collective agency of microbiotic assemblages going under the name "human" as a fanciful detour away from the deaths of persons of color, humans suffering under extant settler colonialism, and humans incarcerated and blithely killed the world over *because of their racial alienness*, my point is not that such commitment to social justice is less urgent simply because it is conventional in race studies. Rather, my point is that race studies may benefit from the same forces that social justice practices challenge. Those forces operate through the fetishizing and continuing materialization of immunity—the disobliging of privileged sectors (whether nominated *bios*, the white property-possessing liberal subject, the colonial settler, or *homo sapiens*) from the collective, the *munis*, and the entangled bank of human and nonhuman lives. Immunity both allows for and puts "positive" valence—for the good, for better health—to regarding sectors of world populations as discardable; their biological encroachment must be murderously defended against. Such a view depends upon the "immune" subject's mystified property—bounded self-possession—in his/herself and in an array of planetary materials that in actuality remain, biologically speaking, habitats for countless others.

In short, this book queries, "To what scale of community will the ethical project of race studies find itself answerable?" Here we might turn to the example of posthuman ethical philosopher Rosi Braidotti, who argues for an enlarged scale of ethical community—a community of nonhuman animals—but only after rehearsing her own intellectual genealogy in the radical antihumanism of the 1970s coming from quarters postcolonial (Said), antiracist (Gilroy), feminist (Braidotti 2013, 26–27), and ecological (48–49). Braidotti promotes a "*zoe*-egalitarianism," with *zoe* referring to "the dynamic, self-organizing structure of life itself" (60): "[*Zoe*-egalitarianism] is a materialist, secular, grounded and unsentimental response to the opportunistic transspecies commodification of Life that is the logic of advanced capitalism" (60).[19] Imaginative and creative power nourished in the arts and arts fields remains crucial to the "affirmative" project of Braidotti's "*zoe*-egalitarianism" that distinguishes it from the "negative and reactive grounds" of legal theorists and political philosophers who emphasize precarity and "shared vulnerability" (190).[20] Her invocation of "obligations" and ethical agency mark her project of "*zoe*-egalitarianism" as one that attempts to reaffirm local horizons of ethical "bind[ing]" (80) answerable to specific geopolitical communities and, at the same time, one that is conducted with a diminished importance of self and in ways that coordinate with the networks of all five biological domains of life: monera, protoctists, fungi, plants, and animals.

> **PROPOSITION IV: Critical race theory and those interested in pursuing social justice would benefit from construing racism as operating through the fetishizing and continuing materialization of immunity—the disobliging of privileged sectors (whether nominated bios or the whiteness of the property-possessing liberal subject) from the collective, the munis, and the entangled bank of human and non-human lives.**

Early twenty-first-century actors are more used to racial justice practiced in the register of bringing into visibility those from below, that is, the expertise of indigenous, subaltern (silent) populations whose knowledge remains unrecognized because of its nonconformity to protocols of Western "science." This notion of social justice can be complementary to rather than simply eroded by a chimeracological orientation toward interdependencies and an ethical surrender to our own parasitic entanglements—that we parasite others and others parasite us.

But I would also caution that a philosophy and ethics of *zoe*-egalitarianism, while seeming a more expansive scale of community that race studies might entertain once it reflects more critically on its entrenched humanism, can also contribute to the misapprehension that our current historical moment is marked primarily by abhorrence and denigration of *zoe* (bare life). Indeed, feminist STS and critical race scholars such as Melinda Cooper and Khiara Bridges clarify that the U.S. political, judicial, and economic spheres at the turn of the twenty-first century might be said to be characterized by a *zoe* fetishism, with the bareness or undeveloped vitality of *zoe* part of its unexpended potentiality, its promissary appeal.[21] As anthropologist and legal scholar Bridges (2012) points out, social activism and legislative acts protecting embryos and stem cells—*those* embodiments of *zoe*—coexist side by side with racism and hatred of adult and teenage racial minorities as in the incarceration and killing of African Americans as throwaway "bare life" (another manifestation of *zoe*). Bridges precisely queries the paradoxical, heterogeneous field of *zoe*, asking if it can name both the bare vitality of cells and the unmournable African American (male) life course lived in all its historical particulars.[22] In short, the exclusion of the racial minority from protected life—*bios*—is an exclusion that is not equivalent to that racial minority's defaulting in binary fashion to the status of *zoe*—a state of nascently transformable biological matter, the latter fetishized precisely because it has not yet lived a historical life course. We might think of *zoe* being split, then, into at least two subcategories: that of the bare vitality of cells whose bareness implies open-ended plasticity and that of the foreclosed, already instrumentalized vitality of biologies whose ends are ushered in too soon and with moral, sentimental indifference. The avoidance of the latter ontological state and socio-political status is a primary driver of biopolitical agency. In other words, comprising the substance of racism is the wholesale relegation of the metabolic materials (first sense of *zoe*) of certain population aggregates (second sense of *zoe*) into resources for elect populations—those able to avoid temporarily and partially their own total collapse into instrumentalized vitality.[23]

The Role of Aesthetics, Humor, and Ethics in Relation to Racial Justice

As noted above, literary forms have been regarded as the repository for the qualitative recording of the unresolved feelings of subjects consistently denied compassion. Counterfactual narrative and poetic texts as well as performance repertoires also comprise a speculative register where quasi-unintelligible structures of feeling emerge as to aspirational subjectivities that half strive toward optimization and half defend against living in prognosis. In the Asian Americanist context, Anne Cheng, David Eng, and erin Ninh have explored the literary archive of racializing and "tiger parenting" traumas for their melancholic articulations. Several of the artists whose work I examine have recourse to comic and parodic registers in their responsive commentaries on the flexible demands put upon them as racialized and feminized affective laborers. Especially in chapter 3 on Margaret Cho, I draw out how the comedienne's incautious glee in the line "pussy crack corn, and I don't care" amplifies, repeats, and deflates, through the structure of the joke, a faith in the "erect" and "wise" human who reigns dominant over the plants, worms, and "ping-pong-playing" pussies—i.e., the abjected parts of the human rendered punningly akin to a feline species-being.

Before continuing on the special province of humor and comedy as aesthetic tactics in a larger choreography of ethical praxis, let me first address how criticism invested in the genres of literature, art, performance, music, and other aesthetic cultural productions have made arguments on behalf of the work that these aesthetic genres perform. Most influential (indeed still hegemonic) in an Asian Americanist context is Lisa Lowe's argument that when the courts or congressional action guaranteeing equal treatment to all citizens—in short, the political arena—fail to address inequalities amplified in the economic arena (and structurally intrinsic to capitalism), these contradictions erupt in culture:

> Where the political terrain can neither resolve nor suppress inequality, it erupts in culture. Because culture is the contemporary repository of memory, or history, it is through culture, rather than government, that alternative forms of subjectivity, collectivity, and public life are imagined. This is not to argue that cultural struggle can ever be the exclusive site for practice; it is rather to argue that if the state suppresses dissent by governing subjects through rights, citizenship, and political representation, it is only through culture that we conceive and enact new subjects and practices in antagonism to the regulatory locus of the citizen-subject, by way of culture that we can question those modes of government.[24]

For Lowe and her students, culture acts as both a realm for dissenting to the efficacy of the political arena and a laboratory, as it were, for alternatives to these political inefficacies to be imagined.

Speaking to the field of early American literature, Waichee Dimock casts a similar problematic in slightly different terms. Her concerns are twofold: (1) as a comparativist, she acknowledges that distinct languages are not fully translatable to each other; there remains a residue of meaning that exceeds full conversion into another linguistic code; (2) as a scholar of early American literature, her interest in narrative depictions of the law and justice—iconically depicted as scales that balance—leads her to scrutinize the idealized notion of penalty or apology—materialized as some portion of wealth (the danegeld)—paying for or balancing the commission of an injury (e.g. death, genocide, dispossession). In their lengthy excesses beyond a pithy and adequate equation (danegeld = dead member of the family), literary narratives acknowledge in their supplementary work this pipe dream of full adequation. Though not specifically evoking aesthetics, Lowe's arena of cultural production and Dimock's domain of literary narrative can be thought of as belletristic registers toward which we turn precisely because of the inadequacies of the law, the polity, and the socioeconomic order of the U.S. nation-state. It is a mistake, in other words, to regard this turn to literature and the arts as a retreat from the more valuable and sincere work of policymaking; indeed, theorists of governmentality (following Foucault) have framed the earnestness of reformers of public policy as blind to their own unwitting extension of modes of subjection. My point is not to adjudge the aesthetic over and against the policy-minded or vice versa, but rather simply to point to the supplemental relation of each to the other. Indeed, in the Asian Americanist literary critical tradition, there has been a much more merged notion of aesthetics' capacity to engage in "necessary" work for the community (S. Wong).[25]

Above, I noted that the Asiatic is doubly instrumental to the affective life of society, in her role as a life form considered both so alien as to be considered intrinsically apart or separate and so adept at change and assimilation as to embody impersonation as her very form of agency. I now want to relate that dual instrumentality to the subject of aesthetics and art, which presents a specific mode of deflecting the dehumanization of being turned into a racial object or tool. Here, I draw on Joseph Jonghyun Jeon's expansion of Bill Brown's distinction between objects (defined by their instrumentality) and things (defined by their misuse value, as when a knife is used as a screwdriver).[26] Jeon tackles the problem of how to regard Asian American poets and artists who, in responding to social and historical objectification of Asians, themselves use objectification tactics—such as sculptural works that call attention to their compositional materials (to the artwork as tactile object) rather than those that primarily portray in a mimetic, realist mode an Asian personality of psychic depth. What is the relation, in other words, of aesthetic objectification to social and historical objectification? Is it a mere mirroring, or does the former work as a torqued or sublimated deflection of the latter?

To probe this question, let us first rehearse the Frankfurt School of aesthetic theory where taking instrumental objects out of their conventional use and making them valuable (aesthetic) in their arrested functionality—i.e., displacement from functionality to, let's say, capitalist and empiric codes of exploitable labor, raw materials, and commodity exchange—is the high ideological function of art. Even if not a disciple of the Frankfurt School, one might still abide by the modernist notion that defamiliarizing an object by tearing it from context, qua conventional uses, constitutes the very act of aestheticizing it. For instance, Sianne Ngai cites a long tradition of defining aesthetic objects as ones in which we (briefly) set aside our direct, instrumental pleasures in them to also make them into beautiful, or affectively endowed, objects of our concern.[27] The aesthetic regard and framing of the object—rather than any intrinsic quality to the art object itself—establishes it as aesthetic. Moreover, by wresting the object from its instrumental and subordinate use, art and aesthetics elevate the thing not into a mere object but into something that is beautiful. In opposing the functionalism of how objects and persons conventionally circulate as commodities or alienated labor power in capitalism, an artistic frame—an *aesthetic objectification* rather than an economic subordinating one—may deflect the dehumanizations of economic objectification, thereby tending toward a rehumanization[28] of persons made into objects by racist modes.

Put in more psychic terms, rather than processing as strictly a reifying trauma her coerced objectification into strangeness, the Asian

American artist's investing in the critical, "beautiful" capacity of this same alienness choreographs a calculated transformation of her prior *instrumental objectification*, the latter a register by which normative subjects announce their socio-ethical dis-obligation from her. Described here is the dynamic of "sublimation" of which I will have more to say in a moment. At the same time, art objects are thought to be "inhuman"[29] in the sense that they reify or make static what are living processes of constant change. In sum, art objects teeter in these valences of dehumanizing potential—they instantiate an objectifying fixity—and rehumanizing potential—they endow the aesthetic "thing" with a cherishing regard.

Nevertheless, invested in art's ennobling functions through its potential to rehumanize, this account of aesthetics is also thoroughly wedded to an anthropocentric worldview. What then of comedic art forms that deflate rather than ennoble? How can these art forms do work vis-à-vis comprehending or deflecting racialization? The philosopher Simon Critchley provides one avenue of addressing how humor and comedy function differently from a "heroic" mode of aesthetic rendition; felicitously, Critchley's work also returns us to the question of what scale of community race studies can be imagined to find itself answerable.[30]

Uncurtailed by the boundaries of institutional religious or national communities that delimit one's ethical responsibilities to the demands only of this select "near and dear" community, the ethical subject potentially faces a limitless set of responsibilities. In *Infinitely Demanding*, Critchley delineates an account of a livable and secular ethical subjectivity, an ethical subject who survives rather than martyrs herself, an ethical subject who does not renounce ethics despite the limitless responsibilities to be answerable to others. Claiming a "motivational deficit in morality" as the signal feature of secular modernity (8), Critchley characterizes active and passive nihilists as engaged, whether consciously or not, in "a metaphysical and theological critique of secular democracy" (5–8). Less interested in forging a more persuasive mode of moral enrollment (to be instrumentalized by various causes), Critchley instead seeks to outline "a model of ethical subjectivity with some normative force that might both describe and deepen the activity of those living, breathing moral selves" (10).

The ethical subject is faced with either turning away randomly from some ethical demands rather than others or confronting the contradiction that to live ethically means *both* acknowledging ethical calls to action in excess of one's ability to meet all of them *and at the same time* recognizing that, however sincere that attempt to recognize limitless ethical calls to action, a recourse to "masochistically persecuting the self with responsibility"—or "chronically overloading" to meet all those demands—is not the answer (10–11). That is, masochistically overloading only makes the ethical self a pathological impossibility. Divided against itself or at least fragmented over the desire for an idealized self that could fulfill every demand and an actual self that cannot (i.e., a self defined by "finitude"), this ethical "dividual"[31] experiences the pangs of "conscience," or an "ethics of discomfort, a hyperbolic ethics based on the internalization of an unfulfillable ethical demand. Such a conscience is not, as Luther puts it, the work of God in the heart of man, but rather the work of ourselves upon ourselves" (11).[32]

For my purposes, it is Critchley's contrasting the tragic-heroic and humorous-antiheroic modes of conveying and coming to grips with this ethical idealism and human limitation that is most insightful. Persecuting oneself for failing to live up to limitless ethical demands oddly maintains an idealized, "heroic" notion of the self (epitomized in Oedipus's blinding himself after he commits the crimes of killing his father and coupling with his mother, a visceral self-punishment that affirms his lack of compassion for his "finitude" or fated limits). Using the notion of sublimation or "passion transformed," Critchley proposes aesthetics as a form of sublimation.[33] Paraphrasing Jacques Lacan, Critchley speaks of sublimation occurring through a redirection toward beauty:

[C]reative artistic activity . . . produces beauty and the function of the beautiful is to realize the human being's relation to [the real, the realm of the ethical, the realm of finitude]. . . . In sublimation, we are momentarily lifted from the utilitarian world of calculations, the world of our familiar concerns, and allowed a relation to the [realm of finitude] that does not crush or destroy us. (72–73)

Death is the name that Lacan gives to the realm of finitude and the real; but that death, as I have explored it, is the death of the autonomous humanist organism in her Imaginary personhood replete with "immunity" as well as independent agency to meet infinite demands.

The discerning reader will have noted that my initial question—"To what scale of community will race studies find itself ethically answerable?"—has been invaginated into another implicit question: If no limit is set on ethical obligation, how do the humorous and comedic become all that much more important to a sublimated maintenance of ethical subjectivity that mitigates masochistic persecution of the self and provides friction against the cynical disinvestment from ethics altogether? My foregoing readings have drawn out the humorous, poetic, and choreographically creative forces amply displayed by the Asian American performers and artists I examine. In particular, I would argue that their humor, an area still underexplored in Asian Americanist literary critique, also partakes of an affirmative post-"paranoid" (Sedgwick) affective disposition of making visceral and felt a posthuman ethics— an ethics askew from a solely anthropocentric racial critique in our contemporary race-postrace moment.

To modify the earlier point, we often equate social justice with denouncements of the intersectional, or, to use another lexicon, the polygenetic effects of oppressions by other humans, as if human conduct is more reprehensible than that of nonhuman animals or bacteria when they are parasitic, sexual, and openly trophic. In the next step of proposing "what is to be done," advocates of social justice often implicitly turn to "heroic" humans and their autonomous willful agency as also the presumed foremost agents of imagining and materializing a better world. According to Critchley, "[H]umour is a more minimal, less heroic form of sublimation [than the turn toward the beautiful]. . . . Humour recalls us to the modesty and limitedness of the human condition, a limitedness that calls not for tragic-heroic affirmation but comic acknowledgement, not Promethean authenticity but laughable inauthenticity" (78–79, 81–82).

To make this concrete, let us turn again to Margaret Cho, whose peristaltic deflation of biopolitical governmentality and the endless aspirational desires for optimal health I examined in depth. Cho speaks of being a bad dinner guest because she refuses the politeness that acts as if racism has not been an immensely profitable mode of operation for white Americans.[34] In her visceral style, however, Cho rejects anything more than humor's double vision on every act of "erect" bearing—ideal (re)productivity and socially acceptable dinner behavior—trailed by a falling flat into a "pppwwhhhhoool of shit." Even as she continues to be outraged on behalf of those who consistently do not receive social justice, her comedy, I argue, does not in an earnest tenor implement justice. Instead, Cho peristaltically opts for promiscuous networking of bottom connections rather than assimilating into proper motherhood of the servile or dominating species (becoming the sex worker or fertile womb of future citizens). I leave it open ended as to whether readers will adjudge this comedy as cleaving to a wishy-washy amorality of humor or whether, as I have suggested, they will laugh alongside Cho's comedic commitment to undoing progressivist visions of modernity.

> **PROPOSITION V: Aesthetics and art valuably allow for a comedic, antiheroic mode of deflecting the dehumanization of being turned into a racial object. This deflection can take the form also of a posthuman, chimeracological orientation. If a critical biopolitical studies framework is to offer an adequate account of responses to contemporary relations of rule, it must also attend to the kinds of affect generated by (the affective quality of) those cultural responses.**

Also taking an antiheroic tack, though one not registered as humor, Denise Uyehara likewise ruminates over the contours of ethical practice, and, as I read her, forges an implicit critique of so much political-ethical theorizing based on better cognition (less forgetting). Uyehara, the least concerned with race per se of the artists and writers I treat, if we take race to mean epidermal, biological rationalizations of slavery and indenture, nonetheless focuses on events that are less debatable as legible instances of racial aggregation through confinement: internment and concentration camps. Here the focus is on who gets segregated, left behind, or incarcerated, with these internments being gendered and disabled as much as racial. Uyehara's emphasis is also on intraracial hostilities and friction among Asian Americans and among people of color; there's a *mea culpa*—a working through people of color's own nonimmunity to racist hatred and an attempt at liturgical virtue rather than simply rational knowing and cognitive mnemonics as the basis of ethical practice.[35] In Uyehara's kinesthetic emphasis on embodiment and the quieting of anxious, aggressive feelings as a gift to the social whole, we have one alternative to the visual documentations of racial taxonomy. The containment of anxiety still happens, but it is not done primarily through the projection of fear and aggression onto a chromatically selected aggregate. Instead, the containment of anxiety happens by way of corporeal practices that need rehearsing every day. In this book's attending to an array of tactics and aesthetic modes employed by Asian American writers and artists—from the humorous to the sublime, from the choreographic to the propositionally verbalized—my work has also suggested that in making the case for how art forms and aesthetic practices intervene and respond to biopolitics, we need to pay more scrupulous attention to the specific platforms and modalities of the cultural production in question, to not only their semiology and affective tone but also their phatic dimensions and entrainment of kinesthetic-ocular repertoires.

Fetishes of Convertibility

Post-humanist attitudes toward our present human morphologies not emerging the species-being of the future involve intimations of monist materialist equivalence as in the idea that humans, like all biological organisms, are made up of proteins, chemical elements, and atoms—the creative soup from which all life has sprung and to which all life returns. This post-humanist *sang-froid* regarding the nonuniqueness, nonintegrity, and decomposable-recomposable-modular (aka technological) qualities of living matter resonates with a capitalist *zeitgeist* or, put another way, an underlying belief in an abstract system of underlying exchangeability of, if not complete equivalence then translatability to, a common (microbial or chemical) specie(s)—whether money, information/communication, organic elements and compounds, atomic particles, or vibrant matter—that will act as a good enough mediator of exchange.

The idea of race as intimately wedded to the condition of slippage into monetary equivalence has been addressed in Victor Bascara's *Model Minority Imperialism* (13–17). Bascara examines select cultural texts for their depiction of the way money's mobility and circulation, in short, its sociality and connectivity, "displace people as the center of the universe" (65). Here, money is a figure of omni-convertibility—each person/thing can be disentangled from its unique particularities and made exchangeable via a money worth or value that makes x (angora hat knitted by grandma) quantitatively equivalent to y, precisely by abstracting from, or seeing as inconsequential to their value, these commodities' congealment of rich networks of human and nonhuman relations. Bascara tracks the rise of this mode of equivalence—and a market- and finance-based logic—as at the core of American empire: literary works at the turn of the twentieth century and at the turn of the twenty-first century mull over a "world [that] has come to be understood as a space for the circulation of money, and people just facilitate the process" (Bascara 65).

Money's abstraction into quantitative value,[36] justice as the dream of perfect adequation (Dimock), and molecular thinking are all characterized by both the desire for and anxiety over mass exchangeability qua unselective (completely democratic) intimacy—stickiness toward the furthest circles of social interactants as much as toward the "nearest and most dear." The worry and hope is that money will forge or allow relationships beyond natal and kin/affinal circles (So); the worry and hope is that a loss—a severing of a human relation of dignity or freedom, a wrongful criminalization, a dispossession of homeland, et cetera—really could be remedied by some form of monetary equivalent (Dimock); the worry and hope is that our biological matter will not simply cease or lose its best use and form with our mortal lives but restir as tools for extending other species' lives and other ways of living not yet imagined (Ghosh 2001; Braidotti 2013; Margulis).

While money's power to take the place of feudal, dynastic, and familial bonds of obligation appears revolutionary in systems where such bonds of obligation remain robust, artists like Amitav Ghosh and Denise Uyehara perform and write amidst social conditions in which the longing is for repertoires that might counter the atomistic individual's eventual stage of orphaned abandonment, segregated in midlife or old age in the loneliness of work and/or clinical institutionalization. Uyehara turns to flesh modes of memory as ways of making less important the waning of cognitive intellection and the diminishment of propositional knowledge of past acts of oftentimes brutal dis-obligation; this cognitive, propositional memory—while tremendously important—is not enough to inoculate our collectives from repeating such acts in the future. While Ghosh's corporeal memory refers less to autonomic neuro-muscular systems (and their seemingly uncontrollable pulsing effects) and more to cellular and subcellular scales of somatic memory, Ghosh refrains from framing such kinesthetics as ethical actants. The dance of the chromosomes in Ghosh's novel—evoked in the term "crossing over"—alludes to the lateral exchanges of DNA, across and via a chimeracological network, resulting in genetically new recombinant offspring. The reproduction of identicalness—the clonal morphology attesting to a robust conservation of somatic form derived from genetic sameness—is interrupted not only by sexual crossings-over but also by contingent historical-environmental factors affecting, epigenomically, the translation of DNA into the protein materials eventuating in somatic form. We can think of these recourses to distinct varieties of a processional flesh memory—kinesthetic, genomic, and transcriptional/translational (via mRNA synthesis)—presenting a hope in the soma precisely because money systems have melted all that is (socially, affinally) ethically obligatory and reciprocally solid into air.

To be a racial other is to be denied full personhood, which is to say, lacking in self-possession, autonomy, and rights vis-à-vis a sovereign state, or, put in more literary terms, denied the position at the center of the story of even qualified agency—the main character as opposed to "the many" of background or minor importance (Woloch). Indeed, the less delineated or more minor the character is, the more interchangeable with others in the background he becomes. Personhood, in this articulation, means characterization to a degree rendering the historical/narratological form of that individual life intrinsically valuable to the extent that his/her convertibility to a minor, background figure in this or another story—but significantly not convertibility to a major figure of another story—is tinged with loss. Anthropocentric sentimentalism, alternatively tragic and blind hubris, undergirds this notion of personhood; and like Oedipus, "persons" follow out their life courses under the sway of this sentimental and hubristic worldview, even if prophetically told otherwise.

The situation of the minoritized, not-quite-person—what society knows as the "infrahuman" racial other (Gilroy's *Postcolonial Melancholia*)—remains a key contemporary way in which a less sentimental concession to posthuman convertibility pierces through this humanistic veil or hubristic insistence on the specialness of the human person in the biological-ecological schema. In other words, while "sentimental" here means inspiring enough compassion to generate feelings of empathetic loss and grievability, "less sentimental" means conceding with either indifference and equanimity or angry fear this posthuman convertibility because it has been spatially projected onto another population (a race separate from one's own).

Race is a modality of recognizing and disavowing the contagious status of fungibility; and whiteness bespeaks the extremes of disavowing, projecting, and, indeed, materializing the contagious status of exchangeability as someone else's—another race's—problem. Race as a modality of dealing with such a contagious status of fungibility and commodification may appear too indistinct from class, or, more specifically, impoverishment and indentureship or enslavement. But this is precisely my point. Minority racialization as a condition of slippage into commodified, monetary, or energetic equivalence overlaps with the condition of other societal dependents, such as children, wards, slaves/servants, and women/daughters in patriarchal society. That overlap brings out anxieties that there is nothing inherent in one (dark-skinned) body that affixes race to that abject body and not to one's own (light-skinned) body. Here, we return to what may keep a traditional taxonomy and an epidermal notion of race affectively alive.

> **PROPOSITION VI: Race names a containment strategy making recourse to the authority of biological classification systems in order to disavow the biological similarities and significant same groupings across the animal kingdom and all biological life. Destabilizations of biological classification and amplification of somatic plasticity, counterintuitively, promote the psychic-affective cleaving to older, so-called defunct taxonomies that seem to provide, if not scientific advanced explanation, at least a familiar mooring.**

The force and utility of a quintuple chromatic schema of races that derives its function from the purported legibility of bodily surfaces provides a visual reassurance that the way one looks will serve as identifier of who will be on which side of the divide between bioavailable—chattel *and* carer—

and biosupplementable—new superhuman model *and* perpetual, aspirant life form. Race, in this aspect, names a containment strategy having recourse to the authority of biological classification systems in order to disavow the biological similarities and significant same groupings across the animal kingdom. In this respect, racism's rhetorical and affective reliance on scientifically debunked, but still residually circulating and thus socially live, raciology makes intelligible anthropocentricism's affective reliance on great-chain-of-being thinking. The latter, while also debunked, remains arguably more acceptably "alive" in the unapologetic ways human populations cling to their anthropocentrism, as in the elevated importance credited to human and mammalian over, let's say, microbial survival. As Lynn Margulis argues, a good deal of resistance to acknowledging the chimerical fusions comprising the planet derives from the unconscious threat posed by the unorthodox idea of bacteria (monera) and then protoctists as the evolutionary forebears of all life. (This is only a threat to the anthropocentric mindset that disavows this view of a networked, endosymbiogenetic relationality.) Here, zoon or animalist vainglory acts as the impediment to the perception that cellular organelles, with their own "non-nuclear" DNA, very much resemble and behave like free-standing existent bacteria. Observing just this, Margulis speculates that both the nucleated cells of multicellular beings and the first protist (eukaryote) organisms[37] originated as bacteria that had fused: "Our culture ignores the hard-won fact that [bacterial] 'agents' [of disease], these 'germs,' also germinated all life. Our ancestors, the germs, were bacteria."[38] As a hangover from Pasteur, humans tend to view protoctists and bacteria that dwell within them as germs or parasites (see my chapter 4) and not as endosymbionts as well as crucial partners in producing planetary atmospheres and conditions habitable simultaneously to all five kingdoms of life.

One of the key components of Margulis's SET phylogeny (SET = serial endosymbiosis theory)[39] is the recognition of not simply equivalence, as in we are all evolved from protoctists so we are all the same—reducible to some combination of carbon, oxygen, hydrogen, nitrogen, sulfur, and phosophorus—but of serial endosymbiosis: "a theory of coming together, of merging of cells of different histories and abilities."[40] Margulis doesn't deny that evolutionary branching or differentiation occurs, but she also insists, with phylogenetics to back her up, that the folding over and together of branches symbiotically also leads to new species. Here the point is quite subtle: branching graphically confirms movement outward into distinction, while endosymbiosis emphasizes that speciation occurs as well through interdependence, cohabitation, parasitic and symbiotic relationalities (of incomplete eating) that have happened across deep time.

The tendency to overlay a "progressive" or "advancing" tag on phenomena that have appeared more recently on a linear temporal schema colors both racial taxonomy and evolutionary classification with a perfidiousness based on species-arrogance and species-segregation. To recapitulate, Margulis challenges the idea of "'higher' beings" and "'lower' animals," claiming that "[w]e *Homo sapiens* . . . and our primate relations are not special, just recent. . . . Human similarities to other life-forms are far more striking than the differences. Our deep connections, over vast geological periods, should inspire awe, not repulsion."[41] If "whiteness" as I describe it above bespeaks the extremes of disavowing, projecting, and indeed materializing the contagious status of fungible exchangeability as someone else's—another race's qua species-being's—problem, to what extent can we say that "whiteness" also bespeaks phobic disdain toward microbes? Here, my aim is to provoke discussion as to whether one can act white[42] toward people of color but not act white toward microbes; and vice versa, whether one can act white toward microbes, but not act white toward people of color. Here, my aim is to extend subjectlessness analysis—initiated in Asian Americanist contexts (Chuh)—to whiteness studies, that is, to stress the non-identificatory ways of fleshing out how whiteness often contradictorily or inconsistently operates. In other words, while I've taken the occasion and instances of Asian American cultural productions and critical theory to explore questions of race, the method I employ is very much ripe for exploration vis-à-vis the aesthetic corpi of other (including unmarked) populations.

Sideways to Exquisiteness

In contrast to coherently modeled classical representations of the body premised on a homogeneous monolithic and hence centripetal system, the surrealist body [of the exquisite corpse] is essentially centrifugal, the proliferation of parts threatening the closed unity of the whole body. (Adamowicz 172)

The surrealist technique of the exquisite corpse both defies and relies upon a commonsensical coherence seeming to reside in the body and artistic portraiture. As detailed by art historian Elza Adamowicz,

> Renaissance drawing manuals presented rows of body-parts—eyes, noses, feet—from which the art student would choose in order to draw the human figure in stages, assembling it piece by piece on to the basic skeletal and muscular armature of the body, masking the process in order to create a harmonious configuration. This structuring principle is clearly parodied in the technique of the *cadavre exquis*. (167)

That is, a small group of artists such as Yves Tanguy, Joan Miró, and Man Ray would fold a paper into three to four parts, each one drawing in their section (between the fold lines) part of a composite body, but with the constraint of only seeing a small fragment (at the fold) of a single partner-artist's work—that fragment serving as an incipit to the next artist's imaginative extension. Flouting the Renaissance artist's primary aim of *masking* the assemblagist work underlying the appearance of harmony and coherence, the technique of the *cadavre exquis* produces what Adamowicz calls a "marvelousness [that is a function of its] dissociative metonymies" (83).

Because of the way it both cites and transgresses the ideology of coherence, the exquisite corpse serves as an apt metaphor for the compositional endeavor I have essayed in the foregoing pages. That is, topically (or content-wise), this book has been about race in relation to cultural production, gender, queerness, labor, governmentality, and Science and Technology Studies, scrutinized with an eye toward traditional humanistic concerns with ethics, agency, affect, sociality, and obligation. Stylistically, this book has also *primarily* been about how to engage viscerally with written literature and live performances reflecting on race and biopolitics within the bounds of a textual, long prose form—the critical monograph. The book's structure and mode of inquiry—part argument, part illustration, part deconstruction of its own argument, part tinkering and reassembling of those same parts into the previous argumentative coherence but, now, with a missense mutation—have constituted its message as well (i.e., have acted as pedagogical agents). In these ways, this book has broken bread intellectually with a number of feminist and STS schools of thinking, most prominently those called "assemblage theory" (Puar; Mackenzie), "companion species studies" (Haraway 2008; Mel Chen), "new materialisms" (of nonhuman agency) (Callon; Felski 2011; Love; Coole and Frost), and "sideways growth" and "non-Boolean structures" (Stockton; Wilson 2004; Sedgwick) and pushed them into alchemical proximity (and reaction) with social justice agendas of race studies, feminist modifications to the labor theory of value, and critiques of empire.

As Adamowicz clarifies, the technique of the *cadavre exquis* does not abandon the rules of bodily portraiture but is instead structured through the centripetal-centrifugal tension between

> a rule and a transgression, the essential characteristic of surrealist games . . . : the basic rules governing the articulation of the body are followed (head + shoulders + arms . . .), while the standard lexicon of the body is partly replaced by random elements which flout the rules of anatomical coherence. . . . By this subversion . . . the surrealists replace the mimetic model by a semiotic model, to produce a hybrid body, or the other of the body. (80)[43]

At this point in my book's unfolding, the rule of articulation requires a summative conclusion, but what I have delivered is a series of propositions that are also provocations for more discussion. In doing this, my aim has been to invite others to engage with the complexity of approaches to race that I know the hinged moment of race-postrace deserves and that the various artists working at the turn of the twenty-first century I feature here also understand and convey.

This movement not toward definiteness and closure refers to what others have called a "sideways" strategy. For Kathryn Bond Stockton, "sideways" queerly alludes to "the back-and-forth connections and extensions that are not reproductive" or vertically emplotted toward "height and forward time."[44] While we might think of such sideways directionality as an evasion (as in why not get to the singular point, why aren't you simply answering *the* question?), Stockton suggests that it is the rectilinear verticality we expect of growth, and I would add argumentation, that might be the impoverished and narrow method:

> [G]rowth is a matter of extension, vigor, and volume as well as verticality. And "growing sideways" would likely be an extremely apt phrase for what recent cognitive science recognizes as the brain's growth (throughout a person's lifetime) through the brain's capacity to make neural networks through connection and extension. Hence, "growing up" may be a short-sighted, limited rendering of human growth, one that oddly would imply an end to growth when full stature (or reproduction) is achieved.[45]

Sideways, in other words, points to a myriad array of positions, orientations, directionalities, and motile vibrations (or affective quales) exceeding forward growth (in an organism, an argument, a story of progress, an earnest referential use of language, an anecdotal set-up to a joke) *or* its rectilinear opposite (backward travel or arrest/stop). Sideways may be the invitation to "think some more," to coassemble Asian Americanist criticism and cultural productions puzzled by this hinged moment of race-postrace with nonconsilient but also sympatico thinkers in posthuman, feminist STS, and ecological studies. It can also mean a discomfort with the definitive one or two points and a more arrayed (e.g., quintupled) structure as style, a looking to another expressive, narratological, performative, graphic media for further inspiration and further provocation.

Eve Sedgwick uses the term "analog" to speak of this sideways or "besides" inflexion to whatever current relation of rule and its countering critical force (usually as paranoid strong theory) reigns dominant. Sedgwick introduces the term "analog," as opposed to the digital, to describe the array of relational values characterizing the affect schema of psychologist Silvan Tomkins, who theorizes at least eight affects differentiated by rates of neural firing, rather than focusing, as in more conventional criticism, on a single emotion, or, at most, two— that emotion plus its opposite.[46] Dubbing his an "analog" mode that attends to "finitely many (n > 2) values," Sedgwick also sets up a broad critique of the reliance on a binaristic or "digital" method that survives the structuralist moment.[47]

Speaking of this "many valued" model as harder to grasp and, in this sense, a weak rather than strong theory, Sedgwick both propositionally states the necessity for such an arrayed approach, even as her own formidable theoretical tendencies mean slipping back into a familiar order of two—the digital and the analog—perhaps as confirmation that we can only acknowledge the paucity of our binary models of theorizing, which, because of their binary clarity, are considered "strong," whereas a more arrayed qualitative accounting looks too much like description, in short, too much like what novelists, other storytellers, and arch essayists do. That is, while Sedgwick and cowriter Adam Frank concretely cite Sylvan Tompkins as an analog thinker (and provide graphical illustration of his "arrayed" approach to affect), it is in Sedgwick's more famous essay on paranoia that, to my mind, she herself delivers *in analog style* her point about the never-adequate quality of political remedies:

A disturbingly large amount of theory seems explicitly to undertake the proliferation of only one affect, or maybe two, of whatever kind— whether ecstasy, sublimity, self-shattering, *jouissance*, suspicion, abjection, knowingness, horror, grim satisfaction, or righteous indignation. It's like the old joke: "Comes the revolution, Comrade, everyone gets to eat roast beef every day." "But Comrade, I don't like roast beef." "Comes the revolution, Comrade, you'll like roast beef." Comes the revolution, Comrade, you'll be tickled pink by those deconstructive jokes; you'll faint from ennui every minute you're not smashing the state apparatus; you'll definitely want hot sex twenty to thirty times a day. You'll be mournful *and* militant. You'll never want to tell Deleuze and Guattari, "Not tonight, dears, I have a headache."[48]

In the setup to this long quotation, Sedgwick notes that the counter to paranoia's "strong theory" might be another strong theory:

A strong theory (i.e., a wide-ranging and reductive one) that has not mainly organized around anticipating, identifying, and warding off the negative affect of humiliation would resemble paranoia in some respects but differ from it in others. . . . [That is,] it can also be reifying and, indeed, coercive to have only one, totalizing model of positive affect always in the same featured position.[49]

Sedgwick is hesitant to pose *the* singular contestatory affective disposition that would counter biopolitical violences (the affirmative and celebratory, e.g., as articulated by Braidotti's term, "creativity") but instead moves sideways, through humorous references to several negative critiques offered by theorists of her day, but peppering their possible recommendations for an ethical alternative to paranoia (defensive warding off of govermentality, linguistic violence, racist or homophobic projections) with several moody flavors and feelings.

Sideways, in other words, recognizes that as much as we'd like the problems we confront to conform to a simple causal logic and thereby clearly to delineate aggressors and victims, our social-justice and biological systems do not quite operate in these mechanistically predictable ways. Sideways can seem a capitulation away from seeking justice (the singular blame-agent), but it is reparative in its distributed, complex strings of many distributed agencies and contingencies. Sideways (toward systems of greater complexity), in other words, here is used to contour an Asian Americanist method that realizes the inadequacy of the liberatory end qua seeking of autonomy—a singular agency that can enact justice rather than a coordinated, distributed set of actions that enact compromised symbiotic-parasitic acts at the same time.

Finally, to return to the exquisite corpse as a sideways structure, I would recall Adamowicz's assertion that the rule of compositional articulation, to continue a drawing using the springboard of a partial, deliberately obscured view of another's prior rendering,

> reinforces the relationship of contiguity with the other parts of the body . . . establishing metonymical relations. . . . [However,] where traditional metonymy draws its signifiers from the same semantic field . . . the lexicon of the surrealist body flouts the rules of anatomical coherence, producing a hybrid body. The limbs of the exquisite corpse remain spare parts, scarcely interlocking; their disparate character is irreducible and they remain ultimately allotropic. (82)

The allotropic is the turn toward another system of metaphor or figuration and is produced by certain critics, call them poetic critics—not strictly critics of poetry but critics with a poetic, creative deliberateness of style in designing the arrayed form of their scholarship. Does sideways mean a sublimation of the salient and continuing ethical concern with the violences of race and settler colonialism deflected into a concern with humanity's persistent anthropocentrism? My hope is that this is not the case. In bringing these concerns with epistemology and politics together with aesthetic forms and biological scales, the hope is to provoke a new symbiont species of inquiry and for others to do the same.

Tail Piece

Tail end of our tale for there must be an end
Is that Venus, Black Goddess, was
shameless, she sinned or else
Completely unknowing of r godfearin ways
she stood
Totally naked in her iron cage.
—Suzan-Lori Parks, 1996, 18

Stem cells . . . are biological plastics and we are in fact at
the dawn of an era of biological plastics where we are in the
process of trying to learn how to take this biological material that can become any cell type in the adult and can also
replenish itself, so we don't need to mine it, we can grow
them in the lab, we have to feed them (they eat), but they'll
grow to large quantities.
—Lawrence Goldstein, 2012

What does it mean to be "totally naked" at the turn of the twenty-first
century? What is total nakedness in an era in which synthetic body parts
(cultured tissues) grow in glass "cages," anatomically revealed at the
point of "birth" and in perpetuity without ever having to be deskinned?
Is clothing and skin a kind of protection, so that the unclothed—the
naked Venus Hottentot of Suzan-Lori Parks's play (based on the historical figure of the San woman Saartjie Bartmann displayed for ethnological amusement in nineteenth-century London)—is akin to *zoe* and the
clothed akin to *bios*? What happens when we try to clothe ourselves in
naked tissues, when the seduction of that nakedness does not bespeak
a wanting to become animal and caged but precisely the opposite, to

figure out sustainable ways of building in accordance with "more life" rather than killing existent life?

To address these questions, let me introduce a prototype architectural project that, at first glance, appears to pursue formally and stylistically similar "bottom connections" as does Margaret Cho in her stand-up comedy. In 2008, the conceptual art and design collective, Terreform ONE (Open Network Ecology) completed a prototype and building plan for *In Vitro Meat Habitat* (2008), a structure composed of pig bladder cells grown *in vitro*. In collaboration with Harvard molecular and cell biologist, Oliver Medvedik, Terreform ONE's lead spokesperson, Mitchell Joachim, grew tissue culture in the lab, placing the material on a scaffold to take on a shape, and then allowed the resulting structure to cure (turn into leather). The finished prototype of the habitat resembled, not surprisingly, a multiperforated football (see http://www .terreform.org/projects_habitat_meat.html). Nevertheless, to stress the architectural integrity of these cellular building materials, Joachim drew a cross-section of its walls, highlighting not the plywood and sheetrock of "the typical stud wall construction [but] fatty cells for insulation, cilia for wind loads, and lots of sphincter muscles for windows and doors . . . for letting the air out" (Joachim).[1] While the prototype was constructed with porcine rather than human bladder cells, we still might imagine Terreform ONE's efforts as akin to Cho's practice of reconnecting symbols of our upright mammalian civilization—whether book-music superstores or other monumental edifices—with the worm-like viscera from which, in Joachim's hands, they become literally composed.

Admittedly delivered with the intent more of making a media splash than of addressing an existing urban problem, *In Vitro Meat Habitat* reflects the canniness of a provocateur aesthetic masquerading as an ecological architectural proposal. One might not just raise a skeptical eyebrow but also laugh alongside Joachim as he claims that *In Vitro Meat Habitat* has been comprised of "victimless materials"[2] because "no sentient creature [was] harmed" in the engineering of the tissues from "an extracellular matrix of pig." Yet, given the myriad projects that Terreform ONE has developed and profiled on their website that are saturated with "green" tropology (some of which have won design awards), one wonders whether the fetish for synthetic biology as the exemplary resilient and recyclable material for building a better future is all tongue-in-cheek.

Indeed, a lecture Joachim delivered at Cooper Union in April 2012 on various Terreform ONE projects is replete with architectural jargon spliced with metabolic organicism. On his visionary theory of urbanism, Joachim notes that whereas at the center of old (and existent) cities stand either "historical grand cathedrals" or "downtowns" with skyscrapers of commerce as their monuments, Terreform ONE's urbanism imagines the center of the city to be "the network [itself], the infrastructure" being "multinucleic," its central "spectacle" comprised of the very "things that keep us breathing, *the lungs, the arteries*" (Joachim; my emphasis). Describing designs to "green the suburbs" by modifying arbor-sculpturist Mark Primrack's pleaching technique (the training of trees to grow into odd shapes as envisioned in Fab Tree Hab and Willow Balls), Joachim talks of "grafting inosculate matter into one continuous vascular system" to train the "geometry of plants." His combination of organic, topological, and specialized biomedical language is designed to be "sexier" one supposes than pleaching glossed as the bracing, binding, and pruning of the plant, using orthodontic—see chapter 2—or even bonsai arborist metaphors. Especially enamored at the prospect of learning to design in a way that would adjust to cellular biology's Hox genes[3]—glossed by Joachim as those that tell us what "the geometry of base tissues and the growth of cells want to be"—he seems not to want to admit that a good deal of interventionary labor goes into the marshaling of cells into, as Lawrence Goldstein puts it,[4] biological plastics. In ways oddly reminiscent of *Blood Music*'s vision of streaming intelligent white blood cells that through their modular and mobile networks can assemble into any shape, even the shape of an entire city, Terreform ONE aspires to assemble architectures from organic parts seemingly magically grown into human accommodations. By speaking of animal biology on the scales of the cell and macromolecule (in honoring cellular intention and ethical obligation to Hox genes), Joachim's lab (and its DIY mantra) ignores the entanglement of such cells in the labor of their growing: that they have to be generated on a "cell culture platform"[5] and sustained through the regular infusion of a serum- or chemically based "feeding medium";[6] and that an entire multi-million-dollar apparatus involving labs at Harvard, UC–San Diego, and the like coordinates the labor of numerous graduate students and postdoctoral fellows[7] acting as gestational-nutritive surrogates who replace the pig, as in the prototype of *In Vitro Meat Habitat*, otherwise growing this bladder before tissue engineering's replacement of the porcine body by glass. Is this infrastructure entirely "victimless"?

Whether in jest or not, Joachim weds Terreform ONE's architectural uses of synthetic biology to an old dream that would benevolently and pastorally pave over the ruins of past violent empires—their cathedrals, skyscrapers, pyramids, banks—by creating a new and renewable ("sustainable" qua autonomous and ecological) city on the hill. That is, imagining biological tissues (of pig's bladder) grown *in vitro* as a building material of the future is part of an architectural vision that would ostensibly avoid the type of ecological and historical violence accompanying past territorial imperialism—e.g., deforestation, monocultural agrarian development, and the conscripting of human (indigenous) slave and (immigrant) indentured labor. In direct contrast then to the implicated, guilty, and shameful slide into the muck that Margaret Cho emphasizes in her performance of the visceral and peristaltic as means of reconnecting empire's "positive" surpluses to its "negative" waste, the efforts

Fig. 7.1. Allan deSouza's *Terrain 8* (1999–2000), also known as *Terrain* (*"There is no here"*) after the accompanying text: "There is no here; it has been erased, trodden over by the down trodden, / their feet carrying them ever further, to greater, more beguiling promises." Compositional materials include earwax and eyelashes. *Courtesy of Allan deSouza.*

Fig. 7.2. Allan deSouza's *Terrain* (*"How to tell a story"*) with accompanying text: "How to tell a story before it is spoken, / before it descends from the convolutions of the mind onto the slippery slopes of the tongue" (1999–2000). Compositional materials include eyelashes, chocolate, and salt. *Courtesy of Allan deSouza.*

of the futurist urbaneers of Terreform ONE, especially in their claim to "victimless" sources, present a depthless account of sustainability.

The term "bio-designer" would normally not characterize Allan de-Souza, but let us do so in order to put his work in conversation with the flashier urban planning designs of Terreform ONE. DeSouza is preoccupied with the tricks of the eye not only that visual artists capitalize upon and, in meta-artistic fashion, now draw our attention to (as in the second look at a *trompe l'oeil*) but also that undergird imperialism's putative beneficial renovations (its modernizations and civilizing projects). Also working with body parts, but in an undeniably low-tech way, the Kenya-born artist of Goan descent, Allan deSouza, has worked variously with his blood, semen, ear wax, beard shavings, and nail clippings, composing miniature assemblages that he then photographs and blows up into *trompe l'oeil* landscapes, silhouettes, and C-prints of paintings. For instance, his "Terrains" series features a set of austere, unpeopled landscapes, devoid of everything but the hardiest botanical life. Yet, materially, the topographical features (grass, rocks, shrubs) of these synthesized landscapes have been molded from abject body parts—ear wax, eyelashes, and fingernail clippings—as well as a luxurious foodstuff, chocolate, a highly resonant commodity linked to African slave labor.

As in his "Threshold" series of oddly empty airport terminals, de-Souza plays with the unsettling dynamics of seeing spaces as unpeopled, places that are expected to be full of people (as in airports), or, depending upon one's indigenous or settler vision, desert spaces that are (not so) uninhabitable and empty. The works render noninnocuous what Mary Louise Pratt calls the "imperial eyes" through which moral justifications for territorial occupations rely: this way of seeing refers to a scientific trick-lens that converts areas inhabited by indigenous peoples into empty expanses, though also replete with wild flora and fauna awaiting imperial cataloguing and cultivation.

Several of deSouza's works also address the painterly and digital

Fig. 7.3. From Allan DeSouza's *Rdctns* (2011). "Mango" redacts Rousseau's *Amerindian with Gorilla* (1910). *Courtesy of Allan deSouza.*

Fig. 7.4. From Allan DeSouza's *Rdctns* (2011). "Oriental
Iris" redacts Gaugin's *Women Bathing* (1892). *Courtesy of
Allan deSouza.*

toolbox of visual artists, from Renaissance perspective to *trompe l'oeil*
to Adobe photoshop to Benjamin Moore color swatches, comprising
the evolution of art and design practices. In his 2011 "Rdctns" (Fowler
Museum), deSouza digitally manipulated famous post-Impressionist
paintings by Paul Gauguin and Henri Rousseau, color-matching a
background hue (at the vanishing point of perspectival visuality) using
the Virtual Fan Deck of Benjamin Moore. Using digital technology, the
artist "repainted" the tropical and jungle scenes favored by these French
painters by bringing variations on the background hue to the foreground or surface. The figures and lineaments, created by the original
paintings' stark relief between foreground and background hues, seem

to recede, the sharp contrast of the tropics (its distinction from civilization) "redacted" or whited out—hard to see—though still intact as a
ghostly presence.

According to deSouza, the names used by Benjamin Moore for its
contemporary color palette (e.g., Mango, Oriental Iris) still evoke "fantasies of escape from dull, workaday routines to sensual paradises in
faraway places, suggest[ing] the degree to which certain aspects of
late-nineteenth-century attitudes toward remote peoples and places . . .
still linger in contemporary Euro-American culture"—that is, in house
paint. Here, deSouza draws his audience's attention to the way suburban
habitats of the global North are awash with the nostalgia for empire,
a nostalgia that is not opposed to but continuous with the desire for,
and belief in, victimless materials. In this way, the artist also challenges
the realm of aesthetics and interior design as autonomous from that
of geopolitics.

While not quite considered an artistic technique as much as a military one, the adoption of the bird's eye view (the perception from the
airplane or satellite) also comes under deSouza's scrutiny. The challenge
of rendering aerial views defamiliarizingly fresh and startling so as to
deliver aesthetic punch constitutes an incipit to the series of photos and
encounters in the exhibit "(*i don't care what you say*) *Those Are Not Tourist Photos*" (Talwar Gallery, New York, 2006). Commuting at the time
from his residence in Los Angeles to the art institute where he teaches
in San Francisco, deSouza would take the window seat and snap photographs with his lens pressed against the thick pane he carefully wiped of
smudges. Using computer manipulation of the resulting photos to effect
bilateral symmetry (using mirror images of the photographed landscape, cloud formation, or aquatic body, that connected along a middle
vertical axis), deSouza crafted art works that—especially in the context
of his entire corpus—played on the imperialist gaze that either erases
natives from the landscapes (sees them only as part of the fauna) or
only sees the human "divine" self as the rightful possessor of these ecologies dubbed empty frontier, tropics, or jungle. The photos selected for
exhibit, e.g., "Divine 1881," "Divine 2944," "Divine 3815," "Divine 3838,"
deliberately conjure anthropomorphic contours in several instances
and the sublimity of vast, repetitive, nonhuman patterns ("Divine 1849,"
"Divine 1573," "Divine 4157"). A shot of a city or mountain range from

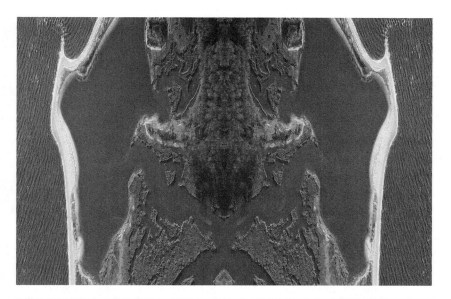

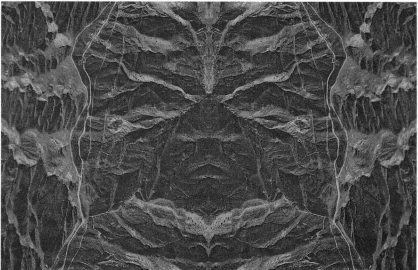

Figs. 7.5 and 7.6. Allan deSouza's "Divine 3815" and "Divine 2894" from (*I don't care what you say*) *Those Are Not Tourist Photos* (2006), Talwar Gallery. *Courtesy of Allan deSouza.*

the air becomes duplicated to emphasize the bilateral symmetry of many biological forms. Landscapes are also already persons, teeming with biomes, human and nonhuman. The aerial view is one that telescopes out to the point where human organisms are as small as bacteria (a perspectival switch at the heart of the chimeracological ethos mapped in Amitav Ghosh's novel) and yet also that which man anthropocentrically sees everywhere.

The title of the exhibit derives, however, from an encounter on one of the said commuter flights providing the raw material for deSouza's work, during which a fellow passenger, an African American man in his row, disbelieved deSouza's reply of convenience to the query about his taking photos in the first place: "I don't care what you say . . . those are not tourist photos." The post-9/11 context of profiling Arab- and Muslim-looking men on airplanes and the phenotype of deSouza (who is of South Asian/Goan descent) provides the context for the exclamation and adds a further layer of meaning to deSouza's artistic reflections on visual technologies and ways of seeing as they overlap with both the occlusion from the visual field and the targeting of racial bodies in both "wild," exterior and urban, interior spaces—an imperial (and Orientalist) vision that enables the project of colonial occupation, resource extraction, and xenophobia. That deSouza's own racial profiling should take place by the trained eye of a fellow person of color provides situational irony to the artwork as social archive. Through these works, deSouza variously unravels how seeing and designing our habitats—as in cladding spaces with color, envisioning the animacy or not in one's surroundings, imparting to the environment (where one sits) moods rich with anxiety or nostalgia or humanist triumph—are never politically neutral acts but thoroughly intertwined with histories of Orientalism and empire.

As the foregoing readings of Terreform ONE and deSouza's works suggests, the skin and cladding (clothing and built enclosure)[8] that render entities with an extra, desirable capacity to act "as if" modern—that is, disobliged, impersonal, and unbiological—are ones, paradoxically, that appear *more naked*, in the sense of approximating literal organs without epidermal sheaths, and in the metaphorical sense of shedding the skin of descent obligations, gendered distinctions, embeddedness in familial and kin statuses, and memory of interdependency on one's environment and social milieu. The dream of such stripping and dislocating from a social and physical suspension—what this book refers to as *zoe*-fetishism—can be countered precisely by re-entangling biology (liveness/living) with its historical and material interdependencies and violences—the making of victims and victors. It is through frameworks emphasizing co-enmeshment that our new terrains of material design, and our speculated new infrastructures and economies can do something other than breathe and pulse in the same empiric ways. In postcolonial novelist Amitav Ghosh's futuristic fiction, we see the current landscapes of the world imagined as imperiled (with shrinking water supplies) and the human body also perspectivally remade into a landscape or habitat for other parasitic microbiologies. Rather than seeking out a victimless position, Ghosh's novel, Uyehara's performances, and deSouza's mirrorings of "trick" perspectives, all emphasize the impossibility of any living biologies disentangling themselves from host-parasite relations. A contextual ethics that insists on entanglement (rather than abstraction) and the sublime vision of seeing too much relationality in any one event, object, dance, design, performance, quip, reprint, or artistic process of making culture may prove a worthy, if inelegant (because excessive) mode of cognitive-affective interaction.

Perversely mucking up the bid to closure offered in this book's "Conclusion"—realized even as a rumination on the openness, surreality, and allotropic character of the exquisite corpse—I stop here with the raw "tail end of our tale." While scholarly books are not necessarily bodies, this tail piece might be considered a supernumerary and unsightly appendage, its Asian Americanist effort to engage yet more instances of tissue culture and bio-design not heeding the regulatory signaling that would choreograph finitude fourteen pages prior. To draw a botanical analogy, this tail functions like the passion fruit vine growing outside the kitchen window that has tendrilled the branches of my neighbor's lemon tree, refusing to stay within proper bounds of settlement. Its trailing tale treating landscape, habitats, and bared skin (aka skinlessness) entwines around an archive proximal to the performative and literary archive focalized in the main chapters of this book.

However, looked at another way, this tail piece only declines to further a "trick" perspective induced by the semblance of being (and having) finished. The form of this trailing tail, in short, is its own tale.

Trailing tales in academic monographs—codas, acknowledgments, and epilogues rather than neat conclusions—have become common, maybe even normative, in cultural and literary criticism (to what extent that is true of feminist STS would make for another discussion). What might be less common is the second-order reflection on the ideological function of these dangling forms.

From a nonhuman perspective, tails are versatile appendages used to latch onto other environments, to sense the surrounds, to touch and connect with. The tales that I have been draw to, whether danced, narrated, joked, visually designed, or developed *in vitro* or *in vivo*, are open and hybrid entities, invitations for further assemblages. Even as tails/ tales can function to extend, invite, or host other experimental questions that cross the typical protocols of aesthetic-literary and scientific-biological research design, tails themselves can also become stuffed trophies pinned to a wall (exhibit A of what not to wag in the open). To use developmental metaphors from biology, this tail piece witnesses an undoing, an apoptosis of the tissue webbing that has developed thus far, a frayed "end" (or fraying of ends) that also comprises the choreography of somatic and onto-epistemological becomings.

Can an epilogue mark a becoming rather than an ending? Or, put differently, what sort of trailing tale would conserve, by framing in more explicit fashion, the processional unfolding and distributed actions that the substance of the book (the form of the scholarly monograph required for "advancement through the ranks") credits to the single author? As one sort of propositional answer, I would first acknowledge the insights from a coterie of feminist peers whose friendship and perspicuity have sustained all the distributed parts involved in negotiating parenthood, associate professor duties, and book writing simultaneously. Through immense kindness and shrewdness in matters of life and profession, P. Gabrielle Foreman, Alex Juhasz, Laura Hyun Yi Kang, Eve Oishi (who first apprised me of the exquisite corpse), and Cynthia Young have been crucial supports over the ten years of this book's steady growth and oftentimes unexpected turns. More recently, Chris Chism, Elizabeth DeLoughrey, Helen Deutsch, Yogita Goyal, Gil Hochberg, Francoise Lionnet, Kathleen McHugh, and Shu-mei Shih have in their genius and "rude" conviviality made the endeavor of revising and completing the foregoing pages a pleasure. Ongoing conversations with

Lowell Gallagher, Hannah Landecker, Deboleena Roy, Banu Subramaniam, Lisa Cartwright, Victor Bascara, Allison Carruth, and many others, that have grown out of the Life (Un)Ltd research group at UCLA have been crucial to this work, as has been the generosity of artists Cheng-Chieh Yu, Denise Uyehara, and Allan deSouza. I have benefited from the inspirational work of Anne Cheng, whose scholarly inquiry at the hinge of comparative race studies, performance, legal studies, architecture, and aesthetics is breathtaking. Karen Shimakawa assembled a marvelous group of critics and performing artists at the UC Humanities Research Institute in 2002, and I thank her for introducing me to Cheng-Chieh Yu and for her sophisticated forging of Asian Americanist performance theory. Her work and that of Performance Studies and femiqueer critics Jose Muñoz and Ann Pellegrini have been models for my own. Colleen Lye provided me with excellent and expeditious feedback and has pushed the field of Asian Americanist literary studies forward through her intellectual generosity. Many institutions have offered me invitations to co-assemble this work at various stages of this book's development with contributions from their gathered audiences. At UCLA, the Center for the Study of Women, English Department, Asian American Studies Center, Americanist Research Colloquium, and Institute for Society and Genetics, have provided various forums; the Center for the Study of Women, Dean of Humanities, Center for Asian American Studies, and Senate Council on Research have all provided generous material support for my research. Other institutions where rigorous engagement strengthened this book's arguments include the Graduate Center at CUNY, the American Studies Program at Indiana, the Post-45 Collective assembled at the California Institute of Technology, the English Department at the University of Southern California, Pin-chia Feng's seminar at National Chiao Tung University, and the Asian/American Studies working group co-organized by Guy Beauregard at National Taiwan University.

An earlier version of chapter 1 appears as "Biopolitics," copyright 2014, in the *Routledge Companion to Asian American and Pacific Islander Literature,* edited by Rachel C. Lee, reproduced by permission of Taylor and Francis Group, LLC, a division of Informa plc. Parts of chapter 3 appear in *GLQ: A Journal of Lesbian and Gay Studies* 20.4 (Fall 2014), with permission to reprint kindly granted by Duke University

258 << TAIL PIECE

Press. I owe a debt of gratitude to excellent graduate research assistance from Sharon Tran, as well as from current and former students Olga Desyatnik, Joan Lubin, Erin Suzuki, Anna Ward, and Grace Yeh, and to Idea Architects maven, Cecelia Cancellero for developmental editing. It has been a delight to work with Eric Zinner and his team at NYU Press; an additional thanks to Eric for providing the subtitle of this book. My admiration goes to my sister, Rebecca Lee, for her ongoing living with the effects of breast cancer and its allopathic treatment. The best kind of caretaking and creative tangoing have been my luck to improvise with poet and spouse Gabriel Spera. His extra doses of patience, compassion, and caretaking were necessitated by three little birds, Paloma, Raven, and Phoebe, whose arrival nine and seven years ago made this book's emergence slower *and* much, much better.

Surveyed in this book have been Asian American artists whose ruminations on their multiscalar, plastic, and racialized biologies theorize a contingent ethics dubious of both their own claims to innocence and the exemplarity of their actions as a model for others also pursuing, in hubristic and earnest ways, the aims of social justice. Neither moral righteousness nor ethical certainty remains a characteristic feature of the artists covered in this book, nor do these qualities define my own critical pronouncements. This dubious ending will undoubtedly annoy many readers longing for the normative and ethical final word. But in a sublimated turn from the expository to something akin to a performative speech act, the experiment here is not to enumerate propositionally but to play out through form an unfolding interpretive practice, a contingent and impermanent ethics of doing and undoing. Perhaps rather than a tail piece, then, what I (ex)tend here is a pseudopodia—the form or body part that names in arrest what is always an ongoing process of changing tack and tactics—not simply stretchings forward but also swirlings, foldings, radial movements, gestures of protuberance and retraction. An interactionist unfinal word best suits the spirit of what I am after here—an invitation to tango and entangle others in the ensemble choreography enacted by artists and critics and their support networks, all those trailing, tailing, and retelling of somatic, affective, and kinesthetic particulars.

NOTES

NOTES TO THE INTRODUCTION

1. On the anatomical blazon, see Vickers, "Members Only."

2. In Asian Americanist scholarship, a round of criticism has been aimed at those forms of racial critique that cast writing as a form of liberation. Skeptical of writing as the exemplar of agency and liberation, Laura Hyun Yi Kang's *Compositional Subjects*, for instance, links writing to documentation, surveillance, and specification (i.e., governmentality) following Foucault. In a similar vein, Kandice Chuh has argued for what she calls a "subjectless" Asian Americanist critique, one not motivated by the aim of bringing Asian Americans into better, that is "fuller," representational presence, but that deconstructs the way American liberalism is structured upon that very promise. Another position, emphasizing dialectical analysis, positions the cultural text (writing, discourse) as the site of registering the contradictions in liberal modernity and thereby a site in which to discover imaginative alternatives to its political economy (Lisa Lowe's *Immigrant Acts*). Even though Yamanaka's poem ends on an affirmation of "love," it refuses to offer the voice of its subject (the subaltern doesn't speak). The poem, in other words, doesn't pose literary writing strictly as either liberation or extension of governmentality but rather as something like suspended agency.

3. I propose that Fiona Ma's approach to Body Worlds falls more easily under conventional notions of Asian Americanist critique not because the exhibit is materially composed of real biological corpses on display (whereas in Yamanaka's poetry, materiality is ink on paper) but because the modality of action—returning the torn part to its supposed original wholeness—is conventional and expected in Asian Americanist critique.

4. The wording quoted in the epigraph was reported by Sewell Chan in the *New York Times* ("'Bodies' Show Must Put Up Warnings"). As of March 24, 2011, Premier Entertainment's website FAQ features this disclaimer: "The full body specimens are persons who lived in China and died from natural causes. After the bodies were unclaimed at death, pursuant to Chinese law, they were ultimately delivered to a medical school for education and research. Where known, information about the identities, medical histories and causes of death is kept strictly confidential."

5. "Science Museum of Minnesota to Welcome New *Body Worlds* and *The Cycle of Life* Exhibition." As of April 2014, Gunther von Hagen's official Body Worlds website lists total attendance of "more than 38 million visitors" ("Unparalleled Success").

6. Barboza, "China Turns Out Mummified Bodies for Displays."

7. Lifsher, "Dissecting Source of Cadavers."

8. As I draw out in my section on biomaterial labor and tissue culturing, where torn, extracted cells or organs circulate in tissue economies, one mode of scandalizing (tripping up) that circulation is by way of personifications that take the form of deep listening to the subaltern woman with a nephrectomy scar (L. Cohen 1999) or comparing the "labor" of

cells not to a chemical reaction emanating from a test tube but to the labor of Marx's alienated worker.

9. Summing up the fragmented quality of Asian Americanist critical practices, Eric Hayot parses the field's centerlessness thusly: "'[C]risis' is the form in which Asian American Studies finds its identity." He furthermore finds this particular ethnic brand of "crisis" an epiphenomenon of poststructuralism: that "Asian American studies has come to think of itself in such formal terms—as a crisis, a catachresis, as the subject of a barred joining . . . or as a fiction—makes sense when one considers that those forms are the same ones that poststructuralism has trained scholars in the humanities to discover, privilege, address. . . ." ("The Asian Turns," 908).

10. See also T. Chen's *Double Agency* as well as D. Kim's *Writing Manhood in Black and Yellow* on the cross-racial comparative approach as an extension of Frank Chin's foundational enunciation of Asian Americans' nonessence.

11. The introductory essay of this special issue meets this pluriform "crisis" by strategies of periodizing (into three temporal phases) and identifying at least five dominant strains in Asian Americanist literary criticism in the "current, post 1995 phase": "critiques of Asian American identity; the effects of the dynamics of transnationalism, globalization, and nationalism on Asian American works; gender and sexuality studies; the analysis of genre and form; and meta-critical texts" (Lim et al., v). Among the gaps identified are the paucity of work on "S. Asian American and Southeast Asian Americans, and Asian Pacific Islander literature, as well as on queer literary studies, genre-specific studies, and aesthetic investigations" (v).

12. Lye, "In Dialogue with Asian American Studies," 3–4.

13. Citing Lye in their "Call for Papers" for a 2010 Asian American special issue of *Modern Fiction Studies*, Stephen Hong Sohn, Paul Lai, and Donald C. Goellnicht put it more bluntly: "If existing rubrics of Asian American literature problematically collect texts under the eye of biology, what other ways might Asian Americanists approach, categorize, and consider their objects of study?"

14. The qualities "immanent" to texts rather than derived from "external" consideration of sociological or historicist utility is the rubric through which Sue Im Lee argues for an aesthetic framing of Asian American literature.

15. In terms of contextualizing the longstanding suspicion of biological rationales in cultural studies of race and gender, one has only to recall that comparative anatomy and the equation of colored bodies with primitive sexuality and infectious disease were used to justify, in the late nineteenth and early twentieth centuries, colonial policies in the Philippines and Asian exclusion legislation in the United States, as well as the quarantine and invasive inspection of Asian settlements on American shores (upon which I elaborate further in chapter 1). Subsequent humanist scholarship dislodged the notion of race as biological essence, emphasizing instead its social construction and historical variability. However, the historical exigency of responding to biological racism has also disabled antiracist critics from engaging other facets and implications of biological research that do not confirm eighteenth-century taxonomies of race and species but throw them into question.

16. The exceptions here would be the work of Karen Cardozo and Banu Subramaniam proposing Asian/America as a multispecies "natureculture" (2013), Nayan Shah's *Contagious Divides* (2001), Mel Chen's *Animacies* (2012), and the recent (2012) special issue of *Amerasia Journal* 39, no. 1, devoted to "The State of Illness and Disability in Asian America," edited by Jennifer Ho and Jim Lee.

17. Hardt and Negri make a similar assessment, though they too neglect to think through the possibility of biology's fluidity: "[M]odern anti-racism positions itself against the notion of biological essentialism [and operates] on the belief that social constructivism will free us from the straitjacket of biological determinism. . . . With the passage of Empire, however,

biological differences have been replaced by sociological and cultural signifiers as the key representation of racial hatred and fear" (*Empire*, 191). They then quote Balibar's argument that "while we are accustomed to thinking that nature and biology are fixed and immutable but that culture is plastic and fluid," from the perspective of "imperial racist theory . . . there are rigid limits to the flexibility and compatibility of cultures. Differences between cultures . . . are, in the final analysis, insurmountable [and] it is futile and even dangerous . . . to allow cultures to mix . . . Serbs and Croats, Hutus and Tutsis, African Americans and Korean Americans" (192).

18. Eugene Thacker makes this point as well in his insistence that biotech is both immaterial and material: he calls it a "hegemonic understanding" now that when assessing biological "life itself" there is no "hard distinction between the natural and the artificial, the biological and the informatic" (*The Global Genome*, xvi–xvii); and that the key tension within biotech is not between natural and artificial but rather between "biology and political economy" (xix).

19. Across my chapters, I specify that these reflections on Asian Americanness are disembodied from the scale of the autonomous organism—from skin boundaries of thinking subjects and humans—and that precisely the biological tales of transplantation and tissue culture shed light upon these scalar shifts—as well as theorize their conceptual implications for thinking about ethics, relationality, and (bio)politics.

20. On form and aesthetics see Davis and Lee; Park; Christopher Lee; Timothy Yu; and Jeon. On the ideological homogeneity of Asian Americanist criticism, see Viet Nguyen's *Race and Resistance*. On the Asian immigrant's abject structural position vis-à-vis the economy, see Lisa Lowe's classic and highly influential articulation in *Immigrant Acts* as well as Karen Shimakawa's *National Abjection*; and in terms of affective quale, Eng and Kanzanjian and A. Cheng have most notably explored melancholia as a dominant mode of the racial subject's textual processing of loss or endless grief in, respectively, *Loss: The Politics of Mourning* and *The Melancholy of Race*.

21. The biologists whose work I cite (e.g., Margulis, Roughgarden, Roy, Subramaniam), are those whose approaches and insights, to my mind, represent the most capacious and the most consilient with a critical race studies and femiqueer project. There are undoubtedly still "mechanistic" and reductionist strains of bioscientific scholarship that I do not address in this book. My main inspiration in forwarding what might be construed as a rather generous depiction of biology has been the effort to forge a transdisciplinary "cosmopolitical" ecology as outlined by Deboleena Roy in her own attempts to bridge neuroscience and gender studies research.

22. See L. Davis, "From Culture to Biocultures."

23. Hayot, "Chinese Bodies, Chinese Futures," 102–3. Hayot's specific historicization of the coolie's symbolry serves his critical analysis of an 1890 dystopic futuristic novel by Arthur Vinton, *Looking Further Backward*, in which the narrative proceeds as a historical lecture delivered in the year 2023 by a Professor Won Lung Li (a "Chinese" point of view) explaining how it came to be that America and France have become conquered territories of a wider China (119–20).

24. Ibid.

25. Haraway, "A Manifesto for Cyborgs," 96.

26. If Nature versus Culture bespeaks the false divide structuring modernity (Bruno Latour's *We Have Never Been Modern*), Donna Haraway and the schools of STS thinking she's spawned explore "nature-culture." See *Simians, Cyborgs, and Women* and *Modest_Witness@ Second_Millenium.FemaleMan©_Meets_OncoMouse‾*.

27. Hayot, "Chinese Bodies, Chinese Futures," 123. Hayot imputes deanthromorphization to Colleen Lye's historical materialist account in *America's Asia* of Orientalism in American naturalism, for instance, where she argues that Asian Americanist significance pertains not

simply when a coolie is depicted in a narrative but when the specter of an Asian market for American wheat is evoked in Frank Norris's *Octopus*.

28. Ibid. But why or how are these latter concepts inhuman ones? Does "inhuman" here mean emphasizing the surplus value of biologies rather than the uniqueness of human consciousness or soul? And would inhuman concepts of the body include the view of the body as interspecial on the molecular level, as an ecological assemblage because, as Donna Haraway puts it, 90 percent of the cells of her body are "filled with the genomes of bacteria, fungi, protists, and such," with human genomes found in "only about 10 percent of the cells [occupying] the mundane space I call my body" (Haraway 2008, 3).

29. Susan Squier notes that the first successful attempt to grow (nonhuman) tissue outside the body occurred "[in 1907 when] Ross G. Harrison . . . published his discovery that amphibian nerve fiber could be made to live and grow in nutrient outside the body" (Squier, "Life and Death at Strangeways," 28). Another prominent pioneer was Alexis Carrel at the Rockefeller Institute in New York City, who "achieved worldwide publicity for his accomplishment in keeping tissues from a chicken heart beating in vitro for over a decade" (28).

30. Landecker, *Culturing Life*, 108.

31. Landecker, "Immortality, in Vitro," 127–28.

32. Ibid., 58.

33. Ibid., 65.

34. Ibid., 68.

35. As Wald points out, to have noticed the wrong in Lacks's being biopsied and treated in a segregated hospital ward should not be contingent on her having had cells with a special utility to science. Moreover, the cultural narratives around cell lines such as HeLa that evoke futures filled with bioslavery—Wald asserts—demonize science as the cause of such violence rather than addressing how civil society and the state's lasting commitment to inequality (as in Jim Crow) extends racial violence from the past into the present.

36. Landecker, "Immortality, in Vitro," 54.

37. According to Wald, such conflation of cell lines with persons assists in producing cultural narratives that evoke "bioslavery" and that can have the effect of obviating discussion of present injustices by conjuring dystopian futures: "[F]ear of a dystopic science fictional future thereby displaces what should be a debate about a health care system in which the right to health extends differentially to the impoverished and the imprisoned, to women, children, and nonwhites, and to an expanding number of categories that reflect the increasing gap between the 1% and the 99%" (Wald 2012, 200–202). While Wald focuses on how futuristic journalese (by Alvin Toffler) diverts attention from repairing inequities in the here and now, she also implicitly poses as a question whether the only way to intervene in structural racism is by way of stories that have persons and anthropomorphized characters at their core.

38. Landecker, "Immortality, in Vitro," 69.

39. As usefully summarized by Eugene Thacker, Marx's notion of species being refers to a biology (aka the biological dimension of production) that is always already a part of a political economy: "Marx . . . refuses any 'state of nature' narrative that would presuppose a primordial species being prior to estranged labor in society. . . . 'Production by an isolated individual outside society is as much an absurdity as is the development of language without individuals living together and talking to each other'" (*The Global Genome*, 35, quoting *Grundrisse*, 84). For Marx, "the 'human' is understood here to be fully social and historical. . . . There is no life activity outside of society . . . and life activity . . . is divided among various 'means of life,' . . . productive or unproductive activity, necessary or excess activity" (36).

40. Landecker, "Immortality, in Vitro," 64.

41. "Scandal" is from the Greek for "trap" or "stumbling block."

42. An example of a bioreactor is a goat that has been modified to produce human insulin in its milk; exemplary of a model organism is Oncomouse, which, as its name suggests, is genetically manipulated and bred for its cancerous tumors in order to facilitate cancer research.

43. By crafting "biomaterial labor" (Thacker 5) as an alternative term to Hardt and Negri's immaterial labor, which refers to human persons laboring in the communications, calculation, and entertainment/affect business (Hardt and Negri's *Empire*, 289–94), Thacker highlights the ironies whereby human labor on the scale of the organism is dissolved into "immateriality" whereas human-derived labor on the scale of the molecule, protein, etc., as well as mammalian and microbial labor is credited with a material embodiment—a biology, however estranged. Moreover, alienation has a biological connotation as much as an economic or political-economic one. The body abjects or alienates parts of itself all the time (feces, hair, nails), and this alienation is part of its vital processes.

44. H. Hartmann, "The Unhappy Marriage," 99.

45. See Waldby and Mitchell on *Moore v. UC Regents* (1990). Dr. Golde, treating Moore for hairy-cell leukemia, recommended the removal of Moore's spleen. Moore's lawyers established, however, that, before he surgically removed said spleen in 1976, Golde knew that "Moore's diseased cells produced unusually large amounts of lymphokines," rendering a subsequent cell line derived from the splenectomy commercially attractive. The California Supreme Court, however, ruled that Moore had no property right to his cells (Waldby and Mitchell, *Tissue Economies*, 88–89).

46. Another motivating aim of STS is to show the social as part of the "natural" all the way down.

47. L. Cohen in "The Other Kidney" writes of the luxury franchise the Apollo hospital chain, a five-star hotel that doubles as a hospital, often allowing persons fleeing from the law to disappear into an illness (16–17).

48. In her work on kidney selling, Nancy Scheper-Hughes (whose primary field site is Brazil) casts contemporary organ (kidney) trafficking as the delaying of mortality for privileged recipients from the First World/Global North, a delay made possible by rendering anonymous—"social and semiotic zero[s]" ("Commodity Fetishism," 55)—the forms of life, and the narratives of sacrifice, particular to organ donors, most often the urban poor and peasants. In fact, their "losses" are not construed as such. Rather, organ recipients rationalize as a huge remuneration (e.g., five thousand dollars, a "fortune" by donors' standards) the money traded for their body parts (Scheper-Hughes, "Last Commodity"). Besides emphasizing the two sets of unequal actors in biological exchange, Scheper-Hughes addresses the spread of new cannibal tastes for and false scarcities in organs, so that in the "new biosociality," one is either a client of it or a vendor to it (L. Cohen, "Where It Hurts," quoting Scheper-Hughes 147). Melinda Cooper, however, critiques the approach of Scheper-Hughes and Wacquant in *Commodifying Bodies* because, as she argues, what's new about tissue economies in our current neoliberal era is less their commodification of bodies than their engendering speculative promise from promise via the pluripotent stem cell. See Cooper, *Life as Surplus*.

49. Brodwin, *Biotechnolgy and Culture*, 10.

50. Ibid., 15.

51. Cohen, "Where It Hurts," 141.

52. Ibid., 148.

53. Ibid.

54. Ibid., 139–40.

55. As outlined in the 2013 issue of *The Scholar and the Feminist*, Life (Un)Ltd alludes to the way in which the promissory horizons of the biotech/health industries rely on and produce speculative and real desires for an amplified or limitless life. By dropping the parenthetical, the moniker Life U̶n̶Ltd also points to the curtailed futures of those bearing

uncompensated and unrecognized losses that simultaneously arise in relation to this pursuit (by some) of an unlimited life and an unlimited wealth. Referring to the limited liability company, the appended "Ltd" symbolizes the legally created means, in the United States, of enlarging the agency (qua decision-making power) of capital. Incorporation as a limited liability company (LLC) in Delaware as of 2013 allows for a minority of share-holding investors (holding 33.4 percent of total shares) to have effective decision-making control over the entities, and yet, still to enjoy limited liability from negative consequences following from those decisions because protected by LLC status (R. Lee 2013). LLCs enlarge their profit-making capacity precisely through disobliging themselves from full exposure (answerability) to social others negatively affected by their actions.

56. Cohen, "The Other Kidney," 25. This ambitious article thinks through the relation of medi-cal metaphors to imaginings of human connectedness (e.g., family, nation). Cohen closely reads a set of Hindi films from the 1970s to the 1990s wherein transfusion (of blood) across caste recodes new national families, comparing them to films from the 1980s onward wherein transplantation serves to buttress patriarchal familial order. He reveals the origins of the essay in a comment by several male acquaintances that they were thinking of selling a kidney to pay for their sister's wedding. He notes the way that this fantasy about filial, male agency is both caught up in an order of debt (24) and imagines the "sacrificial gift" of a kidney as "an avatar of agency"—akin to a second castration that attempts to "salvage his [the male son's] future as a trafficker" (25).

57. Lowe and Lloyd, *The Politics of Culture*, 15.

58. Tina Chen uses the term "secret agency" specifically in relation to literary depictions of Asian Americans, while "suspended agency" is a direct quote from Ngai.

59. Hardt and Negri, *Empire*, 58.

60. Wilson, "Gut Feminism," 75.

61. Citing clinical trials indicating antidepressants' efficacy in decreasing binging and vomit-ing, Wilson argues that fluoxetine hydrochloride (Prozac)

> does not just act centrally (on, say, the serotonin pathways in the hypothalamus, which are though to administer eating) and cognitively (to reorient infelicitous thinking); it also acts peripherally on the gut itself. Most of the body's serotonin (about ninety-five percent) is to be found in the complex neural networks that innervate the gut. . . . The stomach and attendant viscera . . . [are] being soothed. (ibid., 85)

In short, mood or "temper, like digestion, is one of the events to which enteric substrata are naturally (originally) inclined" (85).

62. Ibid., 84.

63. Wilson's concrete example of "amphimixis" in biological substrates is the soft tissue at the back of the throat known as the fauces (see also chapter 3's lengthier discussion of amphimixis). Taking into account amphimixed parts implies a more plastic, networked approach to the interrelation between "head and gut . . . appetite and mood; among disgust and antiperistalsis and the esophagus; among anger and hunger and loneliness and the stomach" (85).

64. I call this methodological approach "transversal" rather than "transplanted," in that the intent is to mobilize across jarring juxtapositions counterintuitive connections that illu-minate something we would otherwise not have thought or have been open to thinking. While a good deal of wrenching of things from their usual milieu is thereby committed in this modality, I aim to perform *within and for* Asian Americanist literary criticism an inter-rogatory tactic that, as mentioned previously, neither ignores nor becomes overwhelmed by the anxiety over these diverted fragments, that can relish the affects circulating—the ballistic force—of these tactile cuts, tears from context, and plastic transformations rather than seeking their return to their supposed originating milieus.

65. Borrowing from Sandor Ferenczi, Wilson uses the term "amphimixis" to refer to the shared

ontogenetic cellular matter that then differentiates across embryonic development into different organs and tissues. Sites of suture or vestibular passage between distinct organ systems are sites where the prior amphimixis are remembered or more evident.

66. Breton, *Manifestoes of Surrealism*, 181.

67. Ibid., 180, 182.

68. Ibid., 178–79.

69. Chow, *The Protestant Eth(n)ic*, 7.

70. Ibid., 7, 9.

71. Hardt and Negri, *Empire*, 188; see also 187–90 and "Withering of Civil Society."

72. In "The Other Kidney," L. Cohen expands upon and contests the "commonplace" that after tissue-typing in the arena of transplantation surgeries, new sites of sameness and difference were materialized:

> [T]he new recognition and its molecular specificity contributed to shifting the ground of self-other discrimination away from the individual body, dissolving the apparent solidity of both the citizen-patient of bourgeois revolution and his or her corporeal extension, the family. . . . Dispersed inward to cell membranes and outward to the population to be screened, the site of recognition no longer privileged bodily boundaries—skin or kin—as envelopes or guarantors of life. This move helped constitute late 20th century immunology, in Donna Haraway's framing, as one of the signal posthumanist sciences of the body (1991). (9–10)

73. Symbiogenesis refers to the formation of new species by organisms' acquisition of entire genomes: "Long-term stable symbiosis that leads to evolutionary change is called 'symbiogenesis.' These mergers, longer-term biological fusions beginning as symbiosis, are the engine of species evolution" (Margulis and Sagan 2008, loc. 336). "Endosymbiosis" is the term Margulis uses in her earlier publication, *Symbiotic Planet* (1998), to refer to the formation of nucleated cells—and the first species (i.e., microbial single-celled organisms, aka protists)—from precisely this process of symbiogenesis. Endosymbiosis also refers to the formation of cellular organelles—mitochondria, plastids—from such fusions.

74. Nicholson, "Interpreting Gender."

75. Norma Alarcón, "The Theoretical Subject(s) of *This Bridge Called My Back*," 360.

76. Shohat, *Talking Visions*, 24.

77. Ibid.

78. In their specific outline of "bioethics and biopolitics," Coole and Frost argue that a treatment of biomatter and bodies as continuous with "physical, environmental [and] technologically refrabricated matter" and as "a visceral protagonist within political encounters" were "marginalized by fashionable constructive approaches and *identity politics*. Of course, the latter have had a good deal to say about the body and its imbrication in relationships of power, but we are not convinced that they pay sufficient attention to the material efficacy of bodies or *have the theoretical resources to do so*" (19; italics mine). Given that identity politics is often a code word for "race" studies, the question arises as to why "new materialisms" have crafted their "newness" on a disjunctive relation to work in race and ethnic studies (characterized as having a lack of theoretical resources) rather than drawing upon that work as a tremendous resource for furthering the new materialisms project.

79. Laqueur, *Making Sex*; Dreger, *Hermaphrodites*; Fausto-Sterling, "The Five Sexes"; Halberstam, *Female Masculinity*.

80. Thompson, *Making Parents*, 146.

81. Hird, "Digesting Difference," 224.

82. Laura Hyun Yi Kang, 27.

83. Lye, *America's Asia*, 51.

84. Where Lye focused on American (read European white) literary figurations of this Asiatic racial form, I suggest here that within Asian American literary texts themselves, we find

instances of racially indeterminate characters' leveraging their own bodily materials—both autologous (self-same) and nonidentical to the "self" in their cellular scale and chemical character—as the biological forms and processes taking an "Asiatic racial form" that can suffer with indifference.

NOTES TO CHAPTER 1

1. Biotechnology also molds Ozeki's protagonists in their perception of both their microbiological processes and their situated, organismal place within a wider ecology. After Akiko is brutally raped by her husband and is recovering in a hospital, she sees through her mind's eye something happening inside her—the fusion of gametes, the cleavages of cells to form the blastula, and its burrowing into the wall of the uterus—in short, the cellular processes of embyrogenesis occurring two days after the rape (305–6). Similarly, Jane, examining an x-ray of her internal organs, notices her uterus's resemblance to a calf's head bashed on one side. Both women's reproductive futures are embedded in a macro-ecology comprised of high-tech science, urban Japanese and urban American consumer culture, industrial feedlot practices, and gendered divisions of labor (of procuring and cooking food and reproducing the population). In addition, at the scale of microbiology, chemical pollutants (synthesized hormones, endocrine disrupters, antibiotics) and radioactive infrastructures flout national boundaries and East-West dichotomies. In other words, the scene of reproduction—formerly iconic of nation-building (women as the wombs of the nation)—has gone simultaneously microscopic and planetary.
2. Esposito, *Bios*, 15. Giorgio Agamben famously challenges Foucault's premise of biopower's modernity, figuring as ancient and enduring the biopolitical distinction of life into privileged *bios* (the citizen's worthy and protected life) and mere or animal *zoe* (bare life).
3. Foucault *Discipline and Punish*, 3–69; Foucault, *History of Sexuality,* 1:144.
4. Ibid., 136. In subsequent lectures (*Society Must Be Defended*), Foucault abjured that "sovereignty's old right—to take life or let live—was *replaced*," arguing instead that it came to be "*complemented* by a new right which does not erase the old right but which does penetrate it, permeate it" (Eposito 40; italics Esposito's).
5. Ibid., 144. As Lennard Davis makes clear, biopower does not simply document the norm (privileging the apex of the bell curve) but also differentiates outliers into the bottom and top quartiles. Documentation segues into intervention so that normalization becomes riven by (eugenic) aspirations to reshape the population toward culturally specific top-quartile variations (*Enforcing Normalcy*).
6. Ibid., 134, 136.
7. See Adams, Erwin, and Le, "Governing through Blood," 169.
8. Rose, "The Politics of Life Itself," 9. In advanced liberal societies, the state tries "to free itself of some of the responsibilities that it acquired across the twentieth century for securing individuals against the consequences of illness and accident. . . . Every citizen must now become an active partner in the drive for health, accepting their responsibility for securing their own well-being" (6).
9. Ibid., 9.
10. Stern, *Eugenic Nation*, loc. 320–32.
11. Ibid.
12. C. Kim, "Objects, Methods, and Interpretations," 200.
13. These techniques included antiplague or sanitary fires and insular quarantine—the displacing of the diseased/leprous to segregated, remote "colonies."
14. C. Kim, "Objects, Methods, and Interpretations," 212.
15. Chow, *The Protestant Eth(n)ic*, 7.
16. Rose, "The Politics of Life Itself," 1.
17. Adams, Erwin, and Le, "Governing through Blood," 169.

18. Murphy limns this feminist movement less by its ideological genealogy and more through its "protocols"—the "*procedural script[s] that strategically [assemble] technologies, exchange, epistemologies, subjects, and so on.* Put simply, a protocol establishes 'how to' do something" (25; italics Murphy's). Women's health groups in the 1970s and the practices they popularized (e.g., gynecological self-exam, use of the menstrual extractor) exemplify, for her, a "protocol feminism" premised on an ethos of participatory science and self-help. While the Asian American performers and artists I examine in this book dwell upon and attest to the "seizing" and resiting of clinical practices in the home, they depict in much more ambiguous fashion whether the seizing of these tools and techniques—e.g., taking a needle to cut and bleed the self until feeling numb (as portrayed by Yamanaka and discussed in the introduction) or magnifying mouth and throat anatomy to teach the "speech impeded" how to exercise unnoticed muscles of the soft palate (as portrayed by Chang-Rae Lee)—endow their users with greater control over their bodies.

19. E. Cohen, *A Body Worth Defending*, 218, 226; R. Lee, *Orientals*, 38–39, 44, 71; M. Chen, *Animacies*, 110. On the nineteenth-century comparison of the Chinese to insects, see also Hayot, *The Hypothetical Mandarin*, 142.

20. See Zhan, "Civet Cats, Fried Grasshoppers."

21. Emily Martin, 270–71.

22. Ibid., 269. For a poetic exploration of microchimerism as a current medical/scientific discourse that is anticipated by Ojibwe epistemologies, see Heid Erdrich's *Cell Traffic*, 8–16.

23. Jerng, "Giving Form to Life," 369–93.

24. In related fashion, Yoon Sun Lee's argument with respect to the underlying ethos of Asian American literature as conforming to the tenets of Lukacsian realism, by striving to re-embed or find new typological patterns in incoherent fragments of otherwise inexplicable trauma, can be seen as another interpretive framework to comprehend aesthetically and formally Asian American literary responses to *zoe*-fication. Rather than focusing on realism as a texture of narration tied to a prose style resembling empirical reportage, Y. S. Lee argues that the signal characteristic of Lukacsian realism is its aspirational investment in an underlying unified material system to which fragments and instances of life might be re-embedded. She further argues that the realism of Asian American novels "derives not from positivism but from interconnections that lead from wholes to parts and back again" (418).

25. Mutations in the CDH1 or the "cadherin 1, type 1, E-cadherin (epithelial)" gene are associated with gastric, breast, colorectal, thyroid, and ovarian cancers.

26. Gilroy, *Against Race*, 35–36.

27. Ibid., 37.

28. See Blumenbach, *On the Natural Varieties of Mankind*. Vijay Prashad writes that "most scholars agree that the idea of race can be traced to the late 1600s and the conventional marker is Francois Bernier's "Nouvell division de la terre par les different especes ou races qui'l habitant" ("A New Division of the Earth by the Different Species or Races Which Inhabit It") (1684) (*Everybody Was Kung Fu Fighting*, 16–17). While using physiognomic markers such as facial type, cranial profile, and texture, amount and color of hair for his four "especes," Bernier downplayed the significance of skin color in his first grouping, which contained European, North African, Middle Eastern, South Asian, and Native American all in the same racial category. Bernier dismissed skin-color differences evident in Egyptians, Indians, and Native Americans, saying that while Egyptians and Indians are dark, "this colouring is merely accidental for them, and results merely from the fact that they are exposed to the Sun" ("A New Division of the Earth," 247–48). Bernier's other three groupings in his four-fold schema were comprised of (1) East Asian, Southeast Asian, and Central Asian, (2) sub-Saharan African, and (3) Lapp race (those in the region of contemporary Norway and Finland).

29. See Cuvier, *The Animal Kingdom*, 50. Compare to Linneaus's alternative terminology of the

Asiaticus, in his 1767 five-fold racial schema in *Systema Naturae*: (I) the *Americanus*, (II) the *Asiaticus*, (III) the *Africanus*, (IV) the *Europeanus*, and (V) the *Monstrosus*.

30. Foucault, by contrast, emphasizes that the science of life itself (modern biology)—where the most salient distinction is between "organic and inorganic"—is disjunctive with the taxonomy of the classical period (Aristotle through Linnaeus): "[T]he conditions for a modern biology are established when life 'assumes its autonomy in relation to the concepts of classification' and retreats from the order of visible relations into the physiology and metabolic depths of the organism" (Cooper, *Life as Surplus*, 6, quoting *Order of Things*).

31. Gilroy, *Against Race*, 22. See also Gilroy, *Postcolonial Melancholia*, 38 and 6–7.

32. Omi reviews the salience of racial classification in biological and medical contexts (i.e., biological notions of race) for activists opposing Ward Connerly's Proposition 54 (the Racial Privacy Initiative that would amend the California Constitution to ban racial data collection). Some of these activists were interested in racial data collection to fight against occupational stratification along racial lines, but they made recourse to biological notions of race to do so—suggesting, in other words, that marshaling biological evidence (affirming populational qua racial distinctions) does not automatically do work to solidify racial stratification (Omi, "'Slippin' into Darkness,'" 343–58).

33. Roberts 2012, 2 (Kindle Cloud Reader).

34. On the continuing salience of phenotypal race in forensic genetics and the marketing of race-specific drugs, see Duster, "The Molecular Reinscription of Race." Examining how molecular notions of identity and kinship affect indigeneity, Kim Tallbear notes that genetic tests marketed to Native Americans, while promising to affirm scientifically tribal memberships, often work in conflict and competition with indigenous people's own genealogical practices, nullifying tribal enrollment in various cases (Tallbear 2013).

35. Epidermal is catachrestic but so is physiognomic, the latter referring to facial features. Francois Bernier, who is credited with the innovation of "giving a physico-biological notion of race foundationalist status in the classification of the human species" (Stuurman, "Francois Bernier," 2), notably disregarded skin color in his categorization of his first racial type (unnamed but basically the category of "us"), which included Egyptians, Indians, Native Americans, and most Europeans all in the same species.

36. Stuurman, "Francois Bernier," 2. Stuurman notes that "most sixteenth and seventeenth-century anthropological and travel literature ordered the inhabitants of the known world in terms of religion, morals, customs, language, and politics, and made only accidental use of physical, 'racial' criteria" (2).

37. Prashad, *Everybody Was Kung Fu Fighting*, 3–4.

38. Foucault, *Order of Things*, 128–38.

39. Carolus von Linné (Linneaus) is credited with greatly advancing this systematic classification system through his introduction of binomial nomenclature applied to flora and fauna in the 1730s and then revised across the eighteenth century. "Biology" gained currency as a term in the early nineteenth century, specifically to denote the study of "human beings from a morphological, physiological, and psychological perspective" as suggested by German anatomist Karl Friedrich Burdach in 1800. Among the first to use the word "biology" were also Jean-Baptiste de Lamarck (1744–1829) in 1802, and Gottfried Reinhold Treviranus (1776–1837) in his *Biologie, oder Philosophie der lebenden Natur*, 1802–22 (Richards, 16). Foucault, famously, announces biology's inauguration not with Burdach but with Cuvier (1769–1832) and his shifting natural history's order of the visible (of taxonomic groupings by external resemblance of beings, or "the identifiable") to the order of life correlated by similarity of function, the "utilizable" (with the major functions of life being respiration, digestion, circulation, locomotion) (Foucault, *Order of Things*, 264).

40. Margulis, *Symbiotic Planet*, loc. 75–80.

41. The perceived resemblances stubbornly unrecognized by her scientific colleagues for so

long were those occurring not across races (across an intraspecies mythic divide) nor even across species (among all primates or all animals) but across "kingdoms" (among plant, animal, fungi, and protoctists—all eukaryotic, or having nucleated cells).

42. Margulis, *Symbiotic Planet*, loc. 80–85.

43. There is a parallel, in other words, between those who argue that one can recognize racial differences (i.e., observe morphological types and create lists of these) with the problem only being *in ranking those differences*, and Margulis's endorsement of the categories animal, plant, fungi, protoctist, and bacteria as different taxon groups (even if they are all derived from fused bacteria) alongside her denouncement of the great-chain-of-being thinking that overlays and ranks those differences (with bacteria at the bottom).

44. As reviewed by Michael Omi, biological research is far from consensus on whether race is "biologically meaningless" (Omi 247). While Cavalli-Sforza is well known for emphasizing genetic evidence as pointing to the spurious grounding of race, population geneticists such as Neil Risch argue that genetic evidence correlates to differences in five ancestral groups linked to geographic regions (sub-Saharan Africa, the Indo-European region, including the Middle East, Asia (including Siberia and the Philippines), the Pacific Islands, and the (indigenous) Americas.

45. Following Tomo Hattori's careful argument regarding Ishiguro's relevance to Asian Americanist literary criticism, despite his British natality and residence, we might consider Ishiguro a transatlantic Asian Americanist. Mark Jerng also has examined *Never Let Me Go* in a biopolitical register attentive to literary form, arguing that the intimate address of Kath H.'s first-person narration rhetorically claims fellow recognition from the human reader, a solicitation into the status of metatextual *bios*, that to which the book's audience presumably belongs, even as the *bios* of the novel's internal world eludes the students/clones.

46. In somatic cell nuclear transfer, the nucleus of an unfertilized egg (oocyte) is removed and DNA from the organism to be cloned is injected into this a-nucleated oocyte followed by an electric shock to stimulate cell division.

47. Race becomes epigenetically biologized through consumption advisories targeted to "atypical" consumers—i.e., "those who eat a lot of fish, especially in contaminated areas . . . primarily Native Americans and people of color, often poor, both rural and urban. . . . [Advisories imply that] it is these atypical people of color who have to change—including people for whom subsistence fishing is a central part of their livelihood strategy and/or cultural identity" (Mansfield 366). In this way, advisories "pass responsibility for pollution onto disadvantaged communities while letting polluters off the hook" (366), and more to the point, have the effect of casting "atypical" consumers of fish—including pregnant women of color—as forewarned and therefore responsible for possible harmful consequences to their fetuses from methylmercury exposure (which causes "cell death [and] affects cell division and neuronal stem cell differentiation" [357]). A woman of color's so-called "abnormal," racialized diet is written on her child's brain. Suddenly, racial differences in intelligence—long one of the key axes of racialization—become real" (368).

48. Kath H. describes how Madame—the normate woman from the outside who takes their artwork for the Gallery—freezes in fear and revulsion when a group of the students "'swarm out' all around her" (34). As the narrator Kath puts it, Madame "was afraid of us in the same way someone might be afraid of spiders. We hadn't been ready for that. It had never occurred to us to wonder how *we* would feel, being seen like that, being spiders" (35).

49. Shimakawa, *National Abjection*, 8.

50. Ibid., 13.

51. Chow, *The Protestant Eth(n)ic*, 7, 9.

52. Foucault, *Birth of the Clinic*.

53. Patton, "Introduction: Foucault after Neoliberalism," xvi–xvii.

54. Ibid., xvii.

55. This endorsement of a planetary commons performs a critique of Western notions of land as property and harmonizes with indigenous nationhood, which Andrea Smith delineates as "based not on control of territory or land but on relationship with and responsibility for land. . . . 'Earth is mother and she nurtures us all. . . . It is the human race that is dependent on the earth and not vice versa. . . . The Aboriginal request to have our sovereignty respected is really a request to be responsible'" (Smith 62, quoting Patricia Monture-Angus).

56. On the level of form, Ozeki's novel ostensibly surfs the fragmenting, disembedding currents of modernism/postmodernism, employing and switching across discursive formats such as Heian-era Japanese diary (Pillow Book), faxes, television treatments, documentary interludes, sociological surveys, and novelistic prose. Taking up the question of "what formal properties are needed to make truth attractive, persuasive, and affective," David Palumbo-Liu characterizes Ozeki's form as modernist, by which he means not the cleaving to an ontology of isolation but effectively delivering "others" to the reader in a way that makes one care about them (and as opposed not to realism but to the discourse of advertising) (*The Deliverance of Others*, 174; see also Palumbo-Liu, "Rational and Irrational Choices"). As much as we may want the external characteristics of a form to mirror their underlying ideology (toward centrifugal disassemblage, or centripetal reassemblage), the relation of form and style to realism and modernism as ideologies (in Y. S. Lee's senses) may not be that of consilience. One can have a work composed in a very fragmented, mulit-informatic prose style that nonetheless affirms connectedness in the end (as does Ozeki's *My Year of Meats*) and a very uniform and coherent narratological prose voice that ideologically confirms a postmodern meaninglessness and isolation (Tom Perrotta's *The Leftovers*).

NOTES TO CHAPTER 2

1. *My Father's Teeth in My Mother's Mouth* was performed as part of the Los Angeles Women's Theatre Festival, at Los Angeles Theater Company, March 30, 2003. Yu's first finished production of the show premiered at Dancespace at St. Mark's Church in New York City in February 2001. It was also performed at the Japan American Theater, Los Angeles, in 2001, the Thelma Hill Performing Arts Center, Long Island University, Brooklyn, New York, also in 2001, and at the Huayi Chinese Festival of Arts, Esplanade Theatre on the Bay, Singapore, in 2004. I thank C. C. Yu for making available a recording of the show, taped at a performance at the Japanese American Theater in Los Angeles, June 9, 2001.

2. Roach, *Cities of the Dead*, 27.

3. My description of "Bowl Problems" is based on the performance at the "New Original Works (NOW) Festival" at the REDCAT/Disney Hall, July 22, 2004, in Los Angeles, featuring dancers Yu, Ting-Ting Chang, Marianne Kim, and Mandy Wu.

4. Z. Wang 69.

5. Personal conversation July 22, 2004.

6. The mission statement of TECO (Taipei Economic and Cultural Office) prior to 2002 noted that

> after President Nixon began to normalize US relations with the Chinese communists and visited the Chinese mainland in 1972, US policy towards the ROC underwent major changes. On January 1, 1979, the United States switched diplomatic recognition from the ROC to the People's Republic of China (PRC). Nevertheless, given the long friendship between the peoples of the United States and the ROC, the two countries have maintained unofficial commercial, cultural, and other substantive relations. On March 29, 1979, the US Congress enacted the Taiwan Relations Act (TRA), [which] enables both countries to set up offices in each other's territory to handle substantive relations between the two sides.

TECO is such an office in the United States: "Following the termination of diplomatic relations, these offices perform most of the functions of the former ROC embassy and consulates general" (at http://www.taipei.org/who.htm). That iteration of the website is no longer active and links instead to a Taiwan embassy website.

7. Hayot's title, *The Hypothetical Mandarin,* refers to a recurring question in continental moral philosophy in which a speaker is asked a variation on this question: whether he would choose to save a close intimate if it meant a Mandarin in China—or indeed the entire Chinese empire—would be destroyed.

8. Report of the Medical Missionary Society for 1844, 4, quoted by Hayot, *Hypothetical Mandarin,* 120.

9. Hayot, *Hypothetical Mandarin,* 122.

10. Two economies brush up against each other, one in which the visible spectacle of human embodied suffering and pain induces empathy and moral witness with respect to shared vulnerability, and the other in which that same visible spectacle evokes surprise at the fortitude of the magnificent, athletic (or affective) prowess of the disciplined subject.

11. The Renaissance portrait is placed in an ironic relation to the dental chart's purportedly precise (and timeless) imaging of decaying teeth, for it disallows that open orality from (re)view—the Mona Lisa's lips are closed. Extreme magnification of the Mona Lisa's smile reveals the cracked and aging oils of the painting, bringing attention to the decay—or mutability over time—in the mode of representation, itself, rather than merely in the object represented. The plaque of temporality thus adheres not, as one might expect, to the object represented (the teeth) but to the technologies of early modern portraiture and late-modern surveillance, themselves. The bodily habitus that is "recorded" by way of either imaging technique proceeds from the differences not merely between the brute biological materials of the quattrocento versus those of the American twenty-first century but between the technologies themselves—the modes and ideologies of perception, personhood, and group belonging (i.e., population) regnant at the time.

12. In ways complementary to *Bowl Problems* replacing wonderment over the amazing qualities seeming to inhere in racial bodies with the audience's self-consciousness over the spectatorial relation, here Yu arrests the easy consumption of the immigrant entertainer's shiny aspect that offers a specious consent to the role of being consumed. I allude, here, to the way in which, as Sadiya Hartmann in the context of new world slavery notes, the commodification of dark-skinned people included the demand to appear happy and content so as to fetch a better price. Hartmann speaks of the requirement that slaves "step it up lively" at the auction block, for what their prospective buyers were fetching included the "dissimulat[ion of] the extreme [racial] violence of the institution" (23). In such coerced "fun and frolic" (37), racial abjection is "transubstant[iated]" into racial contentment, this fantasy of the slave's "enjoyment [becoming] ways for [slaveowners] to organize [their] own enjoyment" (23, 25).

13. Lotus blossoms poetically refer to Chinese bound feet. See Wang's *Aching for Beauty.* Wang notes that the bound foot resembles that of ungulates such as the deer and other cloven animals, e.g., the fox, and that the half-animal or chimeric qualities of the bound woman's appearance is key to her erotic allure (11–13). From a physiological perspective, the process of binding the feet results in necrosis of the foot flesh and thereby a "strong and odorous" deathly smell: "It is a smell of the living flesh being discontinued by a deadly bondage, smell of life and death, of dirt and purity fermenting and brewing in exuberance within a tightly compressed space. Men are ether totally repulsed by or addicted to this odor" (24). Interestingly, Yu's curling her toes and spreading them to resemble cloven feet also make them iconic of the roots of extracted teeth.

14. Wang notes that "footbinding began among the court and royal families roughly around the

eleventh century, spread gradually to the commoners, flourished in the Ming dynasty, and reach its peak in the Qing. . . . Footbinding was basically a practice among Han women. . . . Most of the minority ethnicities did not have this custom" (34).

15. To quote Mary Louise Pratt, "If ethnographic texts are a means by which Europeans represent to themselves their (usually subjugated) others, autoethnographic texts are those the others construct in response to or in dialogue with those metropolitan representations. . . ." (Pratt 7).

16. Earlier in her career, Yu danced with Taiwan's nationally renowned Cloud Gate Dance Theater, which incorporates martial arts exercises into their training routine.

17. Laura Hyun Yi Kang remarks on Afong Moy as one of the earliest (performative) representations of Asian/American women, juxtaposing the way this subject is made intelligible through this medium versus through legislative (i.e., restrictive immigration) acts.

18. Robert Lee, Orientals, 30.

19. According to Eric Fretz, Barnum's nonwhite exotics would adopt a stage presence corresponding to stereotypical roles—"Native Americans would whoop and chant, 'savage' blacks would grunt, and Asians would affect a demure and sedate demeanor" ("P.T. Barnum's Theatrical Selfhood," 101–2). Yu hardly remains sedate or demure in her performance, hunched onto chairs in postures of both cramped pain and virtuostic tension. My Father's Teeth, in short, puts the Asian woman on display in America as an icon not strictly of fixed ethnological difference but of somatic flexibility and a high pain threshold.

20. As Becky Mansfield cogently states, emerging scientific understandings of the body no longer see the body as "genetically determined, but as 'epigenetically' influenced" ("Race and the New Epigenetic Biopolitics," 353), with "epigenetics" referring to the factors (sometimes environmental) that regulate the expression of genes. Asking "What happens to race if biology is no longer something predetermined but is quite plastic?" Mansfield, looking specifically at public health advisories on fish consumption (and methylmercury exposure), finds that an "epigenetic understanding of life does not eliminate but rather transforms notions of biological race and can intensify racialization" (353).

21. Kunzle, "The Art of Pulling Teeth," 32. See also James Wynbrandt's Excruciating History of Dentistry: Toothsome Tales & Oral Oddities from Babylon to Braces (New York: St Martin's, 1998).

22. In this evolution from pulling teeth—tearing out the offender by the root—to dental interventions to save the teeth—as in caps and crowns, root canals, peridontal intervention, and orthodontia—we see an allegory of the shift in biopower that Foucault famously mapped as the transition (in the eighteenth century) from the power to kill (faire mourir) to the power to make live/thrive (faire vivre) (History of Sexuality vols. 1 and 2).

23. Kunzle, "The Art of Pulling Teeth," 33.

24. Huang and Gao, "Mackay the Unforgettable."

25. Unlike the tooth extractors of Europe, who were regarded as charlatans, Mackay remains a celebrated figure in Northern Taiwan where a statue in his honor stands in the Northern Taiwanese city of Tamsui.

26. As part of the spoils of empire, these late-nineteenth- to early-twentieth-century fairground displays of foreign peoples in simulated native settings participated in and furthered a transnational/transcultural worldview, guided by imperialist science's mode of cataloguing and categorizing flora, fauna, and artifacts from newly acquired or commercially "opened" territories. These World Fairs, of which Igorot, Visayan, Chinese, Japanese, and Irish villages were all a part, supported secularizing ideologies of global consumption, expansion, and technological invention as signs of progress. As a now familiar critique would have it, in their construction of technological prowess as the "measurement of man's" civilizational achievements (Michael Adas), these Fairs required the ethnological display of the primitive as a baseline against which American technological advances could be measured. Ethnology as it

currently morphs into biometrics and population genetics produces racial, geopolitical, and haplotype differences not strictly to rank nations and cultures so much as to multiply markets in different pharmacological futures for "whatever" identities united in the common pursuit of more life.

27. Christopher Vaughan stresses that the visitors flocked to the Igorot village not because they were the most primitive types on the Philippine Reservation—they were more popular than the "nomadic Negritos," for instance—but because of the prurient interest in their taboo-violating codes of dress, gendered habits, and diet ("[c]igar-smoking women, tattooed members of both sexes, dances celebrating the cooking of dogs" ["Ogling Igorots," 222]).

28. See Jessie Tarbox Beals's photo titled "Igorotte Song" at http://collections.mohistory.org/photo/PHO:34126.

29. Quoted by Hayot in *Hypothetical Mandarin*, 89.

30. Ibid., 93, 90.

31. See chapter 1 of Chow's *Protestant Eth(n)ic*.

32. Cooper, *Life as Surplus*, 32.

33. The technology of recombinant DNA has been instrumental to the production of life-extending biological materials. In 1972–1973, Herbert Boyer, Stanley Cohen, and Paul Berg developed methods to transfer sections of DNA from one organism to another and from one species to another—a process that has come to be known as recombinant DNA. Cohen's research focused on "plasmids—the nonchromosomal, circular units of DNA found in, and sometimes exchanged by, bacteria"—with this exchange known as horizontal gene transfer ("Genetics and Genomics Timeline: 1973"). Herbert Boyer's work was on restriction enzymes that could "cleave . . . DNA fragments," and Paul Berg's work was on both restriction enzymes (the scissors) and DNA ligases "that forge covalent bonds . . . a kind of chemical soldering that could restore DNA after a foreign gene was spliced into it" ("Genetics and Genomics Timeline: 1972"). Cohen and Boyer together used their methods to introduce genes from a toad into *e. coli* bacteria, genes that were evident from generation to generation. Recombinant DNA technology is used now to bioengineer insulin, by way of inserting the piece of human DNA (isolated genetic sequence) coding for insulin production into a bacterial host, the object of which is to have the bacteria express the insulin protein (i.e., manufacture it in greater quantities because of the rapid pace at which bacteria divide).

34. Pluripotent stem cells—e.g., embryonic stem, fetal stem, and iPS (induced pluripotent stem) cells engineered from adult stem cells—are characterized by slightly more development (specialization) than the "totipotent" zygote, the latter formed at the moment of fusion between male and female gametes in sexual reproduction and with the capacity to divide and mature into *any* specialized cell (hence totipotent). To transdifferentiate bespeaks the capacity to "[develop] into cell types seen in organs or tissues other than those expected from the [adult stem] cells' predicted lineage (i.e., brain stem cells that differentiate into blood cells or blood-forming cells that differentiate into cardiac muscle cells, and so forth)" ("Stem Cell Basics," http://stemcells.nih.gov/info/basics/pages/basics4.aspx).

35. Cooper, *Life as Surplus*, 137.

36. Ibid., 138.

37. Ibid.; italics added.

38. Ibid., 140; italics in original.

39. Ibid., 139.

40. Ibid., 140.

41. From http://stemcells.nih.gov/info/basics/pages/basics4.aspx:

    [I]t is now possible to reprogram adult somatic cells to become like embryonic stem cells (induced pluripotent stem cells, iPSCs) through the introduction of embryonic genes. Thus, a source of cells can be generated that are specific to the donor, thereby increasing the chance of compatibility if such cells were to be used for tissue regeneration. However, like embryonic stem cells, determination of the methods by which iPSCs can be completely and reproducibly committed to appropriate cell lineages is still under investigation.

42. Cooper, *Life as Surplus*, 47.

43. Cooper analyzes Bush-era environmental and energy policies that looked to a bio-based economy to regenerate waste and, as a result, was "in fact utterly dependent on the continuous expansion of waste production" (*Life as Surplus*, 49). She links this logic to the environmental scientific work of Paul Hawken, Amory Lovins, and L. Hunter Lovins's *Natural Capitalism* (1999) in which the "ability of life to self-regenerate—to transform 'detritus into new life' would be mobilized as a means of overcoming the waste-products of industrial production" (46) thus "transforming even industrial waste into a source of surplus value" (47). She notes that government policy papers in both the Bush and Clinton/Gore eras echoed this logic and placed "special emphasis on . . . using extremophiles for toxic-waste remediation"; extremophiles are "microbes that tolerate and even flourish under extreme geochemical and physical conditions" (47).

44. My thinking here is informed by Rey Chow's observation that to be automated is not only to be "subjected to social exploitation whose origins are beyond one's individual grasp" but also to become a "spectacle whose 'aesthetic' power increases with one's increasing awkwardness and helplessness" (*Writing Diaspora*, 61).

45. Cohen 2013, 318.

NOTES TO CHAPTER 3

1. Roberts, *Killing the Black Body*, 9.

2. As Alexandra Minna Stern puts it, "If surgical operations and marriage laws would protect the nation from the feebleminded and defective from within, then tight immigration laws would do the same from without" (*Eugenic Nation*, loc. 266–67). Stern notes that "California performed twenty thousand sterilizations, one-third of the total performed in the country . . . and . . . the impact of restrictive immigration laws designed to shield America from polluting 'germ plasm' reverberated with great intensity along the Mexican border" (loc. 350–51). See also Stern, "Sterilized."

3. Kim, *Ends of Empire*.

4. Briggs, "Foreign and Domestic," 50–51.

5. Emphasizing her travel to Asia at a time where Severe Acute Respiratory Syndrome (SARS) was the new global contagion, the comedienne allows her audience to see how this pussy travels, how the conflation of Asian women not with idealized maternity but with a commodified "hypersexuality" (Shimizu) contaminates Cho's own publicized body and performance practice.

6. "Peristaltic activity" and "peristaltic wave" are used in the scientific and medical literature to describe the uterine contractions that move material from the cervix into the uterine cavity and sometimes into the peritoneal cavity as in endometriosis (Leyendecker et al. 2004). Additionally, peristaltic waves were recorded moving from "the corpus uteri toward the cervix" and observed as "spontaneous" (occurring with calcium chloride but without estrogen perfusion or oxytocin) in an experiment with nonpregnant pigs (Müller et al. 2006). It is unclear from the literature whether the contractions of the uterus during birth constitute peristaltic activity or, technically, "reverse peristalsis." Reverse peristalsis, when occurring in the GI tract, results in vomiting. In other words, the nomination of the action as peristalsis or some alternative term ("uterine contraction") seems still to remain a function of the organ group engaged in the action. See also Philip Aaronson, "Smooth Muscle."

7. Jean Reith Schroedel and Paul Peretz, "A Gender Analysis of Policy Formation: The Case of

Fetal Absue," *Journal of Health Politics, Policy, and Law* 19, no. 2 (1994): 335–60, quoted in Briggs 2010, 54.

8. Briggs, *Somebody's Children*, 6.

9. Cathy Ceniza Choy also stresses the role of evangelical Christians (like Harry Holt of the Holt Adoption Program) in her study of transnational adoption of mixed-raced Asian children to the United States, though she notes that mixed-race children were placed in U.S. white and black families ("Race at the Center" and *Global Families*).

10. The Moynihan report's portrait of the damage produced by African American women's non-nuclear, nonpatriarchal raising of their biological offspring has been elegantly rebutted by Hortense Spillers. Rod Ferguson and Nayan Shah make clear that racialization and queering occur through the scrutiny of household formations—e.g., living in or being raised in boarding houses, single-mother-headed households, and so forth become marks of nonheteronormative nonwhiteness, just as any singular "genetic" claiming of colored and/or gay/lesbian/transgender status does.

11. Because bars on Asian immigration in 1949 prevented "actual" adoption, moral adoption entailed the financing of the cost of caretaking a Japanese child in Japan (Briggs, *Somebody's Children*, 138–39).

12. Ibid., 52–62.

13. Ibid., 130.

14. Ibid., 58.

15. The neoliberal portrait of familial or maternal self-sufficiency forgets the assistance of elder progeny and hired help to caretake young children.

16. Michael Hardt's "Withering of Civil Society" elucidates the capitalization of "whatever" identities in late capitalism.

17. During the run of *Notorious C.H.O.* the comedienne was made quite aware of how the aftermath of 9/11 could hijack her concerts. *Notorious* responds to the 1992 L.A. Riots and the much-touted enmity between blacks and Koreans by overtly crafting this show as an homage to African American stand-up comedian Richard Pryor, an experiment in how close a "Korean American fag hag shit talking" woman can cleave to his *outré* style and structure of delivery. For this tour, Cho wore a loose flannel shirt familiar as the uniform of hip-hop artists. However, on the scheduled tour date of Sept. 12, 2001, in Cho's hometown of Los Angeles, the concert fell flat with Cho performing the entire show in a sequined Stars and Stripes Wonder Woman outfit. The effect was a derailment of her politically sharp insights, with Cho unable (one day after 9/11) to costume herself in black swagger—i.e., to inhabit her critical alliance with blacks, as disenfranchised subjects alienated by the U.S. body politic.

18. Critics of the model minority myth object to its historical function to argue against the necessity of redistributive justice—i.e., that racial inequality, most evident in the enslavement of African Americans, Jim Crow segregation, and the continued post-civil-rights-era dispossession of blacks, needs affirmative material measures to undo decades of harm. Pointing to a minority race that has "succeeded" (e.g., the Jew or Asian American) functions not primarily to praise those "successful" minorities but to justify a status quo of doing nothing and thus continuing to let racialized violences fester.

19. "All about Secret," http://www.secret.com/deodorant-history.aspx. Secret's ad campaign is recognized as one of the most successful branding narratives, for while the ingredients in Secret are identical to those in Sure, they form entirely different products as argued by this Killian whitepaper, http://www.killianbranding.com/whitepapers/lessons-from-armpits.

20. Rose, "The Politics of Life Itself," 17–18.

21. Steinfatt, *Working at the Bar*, 199.

22. Manderson, "Public Sex Performances," 456.

23. Steinfatt, *Working at the Bar*, 300.

24. The song details how the master tells the slave to protect his skittish new horse from the bite of the blue-tailed fly; the slave doesn't overtly revolt, only sings of "one day [when the massa] rode aroun' / de farm, / De flies so numerous dey did swarm; / One chance to bite 'im on the thigh, / De Debble take dat blue tail fly / De poney run, he jump an 'pitch, / An' tumble masse in de ditch; / He died, an' de jury wonder'd why / De verdic was de blue tail fly."

25. Cecil Adams asserts that "cracked corn" refers to corn whiskey, while Pete Seeger surmises that "cracked corn" refers to poor-quality feed usually reserved for livestock that the slave is given as punishment for failing to keep the blue-tailed fly from biting the master's horse (C. Adams).

26. In another joke, Cho tells precisely of hollering at a woman's bumper sticker in such an unfunny way. The bumper sticker reads, "This car was made with American tools, not chopsticks."

27. Laura Briggs notes that starting with the Reagan administration,

    Narratives about protecting vulnerable children vastly expanded the private sphere at this time of rising labor force participation. Rather than taking the increase in middle-class children's unsupervised time to be normative, these narratives invoked guilt and fear. They insisted that it actually required more work than previously to raise children, more time, thought, and concern. The 1980s expansion of the private was at once an attack on feminism and the incursion of neoliberalism, replacing belief in public services with private, familial labor ("Foreign and Domestic," 55).

28. François, "O Happy Living Things."

29. Vincanne Adams, Michelle Murphy, and Adele Clark speak of the biomedical arena as saturated with an affect of "anticipation":

    Anticipation is not just betting on the future; it is a moral [injunction] in which the future sets the conditions of possibility for action in the present, in which the future is inhabited in the present.... This process entails a forced passage through affect, in the sense that the anticipatory regime cannot generate its outcomes without arousing a 'sense' of the simultaneous uncertainty *and* inevitability of the future, usually manifest as entanglements of fear and hope. (249)

    Dictated by the logic of optimization, this anticipatory ethos leads to a phenomenological state comparable to "abduction": "a felt wresting of the present into alien futures. It is not neutral [and] can present as the colonizing [and] coercing . . . of affective orientations in the name of the future . . . a form of kidnapping, where life in the present is held hostage to the potential violence of the future" (255).

30. As Landecker has pointed out, biologists studying metabolism have determined that it is not simply what mothers eat while pregnant that have "epigenetic" effects on the gestating neonate, but that generationally, environment (qua what and how much one eats or doesn't eat at what stage of the life cycle) transforms the genetic and phenotypal expression two generations down. In other words, monitoring what one consumes, while possibly intervening to optimize one's own body in the temporal duration of one's own individual life cycle, has effects on the life cycles of progeny two generations into the future. Not for nothing, then, do the monitoring of consumption (what one eats) and the monitoring of pregnancy come together as particularly intense sites of political investment.

31. Aired for one season (1994–1995) on ABC, "All-American Girl" was the first prime-time situation comedy to feature an all Asian American cast.

32. In her 2011 study of an urban New York City hospital servicing low-income clients (going by the pseudonym Alpha Hospital), Khiara Bridges notes that, while tremendous diversity of racial/ethnic groups characterizes the populations serviced at Alpha Hospital, "providers, staff, and administrators" spoke of their patients in "cultural terms" that were, at once, expressly racialized and at the same time officially put forward using the nonracial

terminology of the "average" Alpha patient. Bridges coins the oxymoronic term "deracialized racialist discourse" to refer to the way staff were able to speak race tacitly.

33. Moncur 4; and Cho, "Belly Dance."

34. Melinda Cooper concludes, "The creation of surplus population, of a life not worth the costs of its own reproduction, is strictly contemporaneous with the capitalist promise of more abundant life" (*Life as Surplus*, 60–61). Capitalism concocts a "prophetic, promissory moment" in the future, "accompanied by a simultaneous move to disinvest from . . . and lay waste to whole sectors of unprofitable production [in the present]. A prime target here, Marx suggests, is human life and its costs of reproduction, since 'for all its stinginess, capitalist production is thoroughly wasteful with human material'" (ibid., 60–61).

35. Henri Bergson's *Comedy* (1956).

36. Biologists classify worms (limbless invertebrates) into several phyla, including annelida (segmented worms), platyhelminths (flatworms, including tapeworms), nematoda (roundworms), and acanthocephela (spiny-headed worms that anchor to an animal's intenstinal wall). See http://animal.discovery.com/worms/worm-info.htm.

37. In biology, amphimixis—sexual reproduction by way of the union of gametes contributed by two distinct organisms—is counterposed to automixis—the latter referring to self-fertilization by which many, e.g., hermaphroditic, plants propagate. (Note: hermaphroditic animals often reproduce by way of amphimixis with another hermaphroditic member of their species, an outcrossing opportunity, and use automixis or self-fertilization only under conditions of duress—e.g., when outcrossing opportunities are not available.) In psychoanalysis, amphimixis refers to "the combining of anal and genital eroticism in the development of sexuality." At the juncture of these two fields, Elizabeth Wilson, borrowing from Sandor Ferenczi, uses the term "amphimixis" in a distinct other way, to refer to the shared ontogenetic cellular matter that then differentiates across embryonic development into different organs and tissues.

38. Wilson, "Gut Feminism," 85. On the neurotransmitter serotonin, Elizabeth Wilson notes,
    [T]he vast majority of the body's serotonin . . . is made, stored, and metabolized in the gut, and most of the serotonin in the blood is derived from the gut. Serotonin is thought to be important in a whole range of digestive processes, especially intestinal secretion [and] peristaltic activity. . . . [with] gastrointestinal disruption . . . a common side effect of SSRI medication; correspondingly, pharmaceuticals that regulate serotonin in the gut have been found to be useful in the management of functional gastrointestinal disorders such as irritable bowel syndrome. (*Psychosomatic*, 36)

39. Kirsten Tillisch's 2013 study "shows what has been suspected but until now had been proved only in animal studies: that [stress and other emotional] signals travel [not only from brain to the gastrointenstinal tract but] the opposite way as well" (Champeau, "Changing Gut Bacteria"). Using functional magnetic resonance imaging (fMRI) scans "conducted both before and after the four-week study period [that] looked at . . . women's brains in a state of rest and in response to an emotion-recognition task [of angry or frightened faces]," Tillisch's lab found significant distinctions between the women who had their guts stabilized by commensal bacteria (via oral intake of probiotic yogurt) and those who hadn't. Specifically, having more "probiotic" bacteria in the gut registers as a measurable difference—visualized/assessed by fMRI scans—in the brain activity of both the insula and the somatosensory cortex regions during emotional reactivity tests (Champeau).

40. Wilson, "Gut Feminism," 81.

41. Ibid., 80, quoting Ferenczi.

42. Ibid. Contrasting a "flat" notion of biology, Wilson writes of an alternative model that recognizes that
    archaic, conflicted motivations are native to human physiology. Take for example, the infant nursing at the mother's breast. For Freud this relation is the prototype for oral

sexuality. . . . No doubt [the physiology of this encounter] could be explained as a flat metabolic event: the breakdown of the food and the distribution of those metabolites to tissues in the infant's body. But Ferenczi sees something else. . . . "The human being, in consuming mother's milk and other animal products is after all a lifelong parasite who incorporates the bodies of his human and animal forebears." He calls this phylophagy: "the eating of the entire evolutionary system. . . . [T]he infant . . . is taking in milk and mother and everything that mother has eaten and in turn everything eaten, absorbed, and metabolized by "the whole . . . history of nutrition." (158)

Wilson challenges us to see "physiological process as phylogenetically (affectively, motivationally) alive in this way" ("Another Neurological Scene," 158).

43. In monotremes, there is a singular exit point of both these systems.

44. Quoted in Wilson, *Psychosomatic*, 44. On the theory that living species on land evolved out of original watery environments, Sandor Ferenczi proposes that

amniotic fluid is a sea that was introjected, as it were, into the mother's body, in which . . . the delicate, vulnerable embryo carries out movements and swims. . . . [The vaginal-uterine cavities of] *mothers should actually be seen as symbols or partial substitutes for the ocean not the other way around. First comes la mer, then la mere*. (quoted in Theweleit, 292)

45. Sex workers in Singapore, in fact, requested such reciprocity of care as the price for their enrollment in an experimental use of Tenofovir patented by Gilead Sciences, usually given to those testing serio-positive for HIV, in preventing the contracting of HIV in those not yet having the disease (a strategy called pre-exposure prophylaxis). The sex workers were sought as a population at high risk for exposure to HIV; nonetheless, these women demanded that the risks they bore from participation in the trial be offset by healthcare for thirty years to attend to long-term health effects resulting from the unknown risks of exposing their nonsymptomatic, nonseriopositive bodies to these anti-HIV drugs or for those who contracted HIV during the trial. The sponsoring organizations canceled the drug trial rather than meet this demand. See Cooper 2013.

46. Terada, "Radical Anxiety."

47. My evocation of a "sideways" approach is indebted to Stockton's *Queer Child*. She uses "sideways" to describe a methodology that is "outside and beside" realist, heteronormative history in two ways (9): it uses fiction as a mode of alternative historical contextualization, and it alludes to an affective disposition akin to Freud's *nachtraglichkeit* (retro-causality, afterwardness, belated understanding, deferred effect) whereby "events from the past acquire meaning only when read through their future consequences . . . [which on the individual level puts] past and present ego structures side-by-side, almost cubistically, in lateral spread" (14). Stockton also claims "sideways" movement as an "apt phrase for what recent cognitive science recognizes as the brain's growth (throughout a person's lifetime) through the brain's capacity to make neural networks through connection and extension" (11).

48. "Maodun" "points to paradoxical . . . events that far from being impossible, are routinely familiar," as distinct from the Western notion of contradictions that cancel each other out or cannot "coexist in the same universe" (Eoyang, "Of 'Invincible Spears and Impenetrable Shields,'" 2). "Maodun" is translated as both "dialectics" and "contradiction."

49. Ibid., 3–4.

50. According to Vsevolod Holubnychy, while Mao's dialectical method, like Leninist dialectics, emphasizes "contradiction" as "a universal characteristic of all things," Chinese dialectics is distinguished by an additional emphasis both on "contradiction not between but rather within things, phenomena, and thoughts . . . [and on] the complementarity of opposites a necessary prerequisite for the development of contradictions [hence the movement of history]" ("Mao Tse-tung's Materialist Dialectics," 30). Moreover, while traditional Chinese dialectics "postulated a balance and harmony of opposite inside the contradiction

[with] a repetitive motion along a circulate route [e.g., of temporality] . . . derived from such a balance and harmony," Mao's conception of motion is more helical in that he postulated that "the balance of opposites inside the contradiction [was] not even. . . . [T]his imbalance inside and among the contradictions that brings all the things and phenomena into motion [does so] along a one-way spiral route" (30).

51. According to Lisa Parks, $5.78 billion is the 2013 budget for unmanned drone bombers, with previous years' budgets being $5.4 billion (2010), $4.53 billion (2009), $3.9 billion (2008), and $3 billion (2007), drawn from www.militaryaerospace.com. According to the Center on Budget and Priority Policies, of the $3.6 trillion in total 2011 federal spending,
    20 percent of the budget, or $718 billion, paid for defense and security-related international activities. . . . Another 20 percent of the budget, or $731 billion, paid for Social Security. . . . Three health insurance programs—Medicare, Medicaid, and the Children's Health Insurance Program (CHIP)—together accounted for 21 percent of the budget in 2011, or $769 billion. . . . And about 13 percent of the federal budget in 2011, or $466 billion, went to support programs that provide aid (other than health insurance or Social Security benefits) to individuals and families facing hardship. (see http://www.cbpp.org/cms/index.cfm?fa=view&id=1258)
    Compare these figures to the budget for food stamps or the Supplemental Nutrition Assistance Program: "[In 2011, the U.S.] government spent about $78 billion on SNAP. . . . [Since 2009, SNAP spending has had] a large but temporary growth" because of the 2009 Recovery Act and more U.S. households falling under the borderline poverty levels required to access the program." See http://www.cbpp.org/cms/index.cfm?fa=view&id=2226.

52. Critiquing Gilles Deleuze and Felix Guattari's misogyny directed at aging women and their disdain of companionate relations to domestic animals (i.e., dogs) as opposed to their fetishizing of the pack animal in the wild (i.e., wolves), Donna Haraway (2008) makes much the same point regarding the need for autre-mondialisations (imagining and practicing of the world otherwise) that are from the mud and the everyday rather than attached to the singular event of catastrophe and crisis.

53. R. Lee 2004.
54. Wilson, "Gut Feminism," 75.
55. Ibid., 84.
56. Ibid., 83–84.
57. Ibid., 84.

NOTES TO CHAPTER 4

1. Marcus and Best, "Surface Reading." See also my later discussion of Sedgwick on pp. 241–43.
2. As Margulis and Sagan define them, "sex" refers to "any process [including cosmic irradiation] that recombines genes (DNA) in an individual cell or organism from more than a single source; sex may occur at the nucleic acid, nuclear, cytoplasmic, and other levels," while "reproduction" refers to the process in autopoietic entities resulting in "an increase in the number of live beings" (Margulis and Sagan 1986, 235, 25). Reproduction can occur asexually or sexually; indeed, the authors allude to the process whereby malarial parasites of the genus *Plasmodium* reproduce in multiple fashion while inside a vertebrate red blood cell as exemplary of asexual reproduction (26–27). They use the term "parasexual" to refer to " 'comings together' that are neither" prokaryotic DNA recombinations or eukaryotic variations on meiotic sex (31). They further note that "parasexuality, more than standard sexuality, tends to be an occasional and irregular process, differing widely in the various species that display the phenomenon" (32).
3. My analysis mines the novel's internal argument with the concept of "homogenous empty time" (Anderson) or what Dipesh Chakrabarty calls "the time of history"—time conceived

as a forward-moving linear chronology that liberates humanity from cyclical, religious, seasonal, and reproductive temporalities construed as repetitive (i.e., eternally the same) (Kermode).

4. The reproductive aspects of *The Calcutta Chromosome* have garnered little attention, with the important exception being Diane Nelson's notable 2003 essay in which she asserts that Ghosh's novel presents "non-sexual repro" as an alternative way of knowing and being in the world" ("A Social Science Fiction of Fevers," 249).

5. To relate this back to the last chapter, Cho's performance asks us to conceive of the nexus of America's reproductive infrastructure to include the dissemination of advertising style— and through it a zeitgeist of gross consumption—and an apparatus of military (imperialist) aggression to protect America's way of life.

6. Murphy, "Distributed Reproduction."

7. Nelson, "A Social Science Fiction of Fevers," 247. Attending in particular to the history of U.S. empire accomplished in part through the creation of tropical fantasy spaces through which Asian and Pacific Islander bodies were colonized and incorporated into the "American visual and geopolitical field" (xxviii), Allan Punzalan Isaac's *American Tropics: Articulating Filipino America* employs a similar terminological play with tropics as place and as discursive practice. The American Tropics as place refers to "U.S. territories in and adjacent to the torrid zone," including America Samoa, the Federated States of Micronesia, Guam, the Northern Mariana Islands, the Marshall Islands, Palau, the Caribbean, Puerto Rico, and the U.S. Virgin Islands; as "controlling metaphors," American tropics/tropes bespeak discourses of "imperial tutelage and containment that separate the primitive from the civilized, chaos from order, property from the proper" (2).

8. Nelson, "A Social Science Fiction of Fevers," 247.

9. Schulze-Engler, "Strange Encounters," 177–78.

10. Cooper and Waldby 2014 updates this history by looking at how in the contemporary moment, neoliberal risk societies enlist bodies for experimental "risk-bearing" labor for medical experimentation in ways both evocative of but also distinct from colonial dynamics.

11. Nelson, "A Social Science Fiction of Fevers," 257 and 247, quoting Bruno Latour.

12. See, for instance, U.S. secretary of state Hilary Clinton's recent prediction in 2012 that water security arises as the global issue of the next decade at http://www.bloomberg.com/news/2012-03-21/u-s-intelligence-says-water-shortages-threaten-stability.html.

13. Foucault, *Order of Things*, 128–38.

14. Patton, "Introduction: Foucault after Neoliberalism," xvi–xvii.

15. Ibid., xvii.

16. The Asian Americanist literary critical field has yet to develop a theory of the cosmological (and cross-species) aspects of its literary narratives and poetics/rhetorics, perhaps because of desires to stress the modern rather than the ancient, Eastern, and mystic. Yet, at the same time, Asian Americanist critique has rarely examined the physical body in isolation from its contextual milieu—even as that milieu has been taken primarily as driven by social and economic dynamics rather than also ecological, cosmological, and evolutionary ones.

17. I refer here to variants of American feminism of the late 1970s and early 1980s building on Nancy Chodorow's *Reproduction of Mothering* and Carol Gilligan's expansion after her, regarding the distinct modes of "empathy" characteristic of girls more so than boys ("Woman's Place").

18. The female mosquito's reproductive robustness too depends on the vertebrate, "blood being a necessary requirement at different stages in the life cycle of a female mosquito [such as] ovarian development and egg laying" (Rogier and Hommel, "Impact Malaria").

19. Ibid.

20. Ibid.
21. "The polymorphism of Plasmodium populations is considerable and it has been evaluated that, on average, a malarial infection in humans represents 3.9 parasite populations" (ibid.).
22. Greg Bear's *Blood Music* literalizes that realization when the intelligent white blood cells gain consciousness that the cosmos/world of their maker's (Vergil Ulam)'s body is nested in another cosmos.
23. Haraway, *When Species Meet*, 17.
24. Ibid., 15.
25. Gk. *khimaira*, a fabulous monster with a lion's head, a goat's body, and a serpent's tail.
26. Haraway, *When Species Meet*, 32.
27. Hartsock, "The Feminist Standpoint," 229, quoting Adrienne Rich.
28. Ibid., 230.
29. E. Cohen, *A Body Worth Defending*, 4.
30. Ibid., 72–73.
31. As Heather Paxson puts it with regard to the raw-milk cheese industry, "Whereas Pasteurianism in the realm of food safety has suggested a medicalization of food and eating, post-Pasteurians want to invest in the potentialities of collaborative human and microbial cultural practices" ("Post-Pasteurian Cultures," 17).
32. Ibid.
33. My concept of the chimeracological harmonizes somewhat with Timothy Morton's framing of queer ecology. Rejecting both the incessant "Mother Nature" metaphors and "masculine memes" of environmentalism, Timothy Morton radically defines a "queer ecology" as one that rejects organicism entirely and stresses "unfathomable intimacies" that "cannot be totalized" as the story of evolutionary biology ("Queer Ecology," 274, 280, 270). In other words, though he doesn't cite Margulis, implicit in Morton's argument is a critique of the teleological perspective that looks back at queer moments of chimeric, nonconsilient intimacies (conjoinings that are neither quite "sex acts" nor quite "failed eatings" but simply queer intimacies) as they result in eventual symbiogenesis (the evolution of a new species in nature). Queer, in other words, would stress less the "sym" of biosis that are selected in the end for "survival," and more the proliferating perverse contacts that are unfathomable in and across human and nonhuman biomes, some of which necessarily are not selected in evolution and die off.
34. Foucault quoted by Kang in *Compositional Subjects*. On the Asian regard for silence's significance in contradistinction to the Western privileging of voice and logocentrism, see Cheung's *Articulate Silences*.
35. See Hondagneu-Sotelo's *Domestica* and Parreñas's *Servants of Globalization*.
36. Here I make an argument that departs slightly from Hardt and Negri, who instead call caretaking immaterial not because it's not publicly valued but because its product (which they identify as "social networks" and which Gayle Rubin in her inaugural "The Traffic in Women" essay called "kinship") is immaterial:

    Affective labor is better understood by beginning with what feminist analyses of "women's work" have called "labor in the bodily mode." Caring labor is certainly entirely immersed in the corporeal, the somatic, but the affects it produces are nonetheless immaterial. What affective labor produces are social networks, forms of community, biopower. (*Empire*, 293)
37. One implication is that immaterial labor must be materialized—aka made visible or voiced in terms of value production. However, Ghosh's novel complicates that investment in the material as equivalent with the visually or vocally *manifested* sign. One must recall the novel's emphasis on the positive value of silence, which is another way of saying that immaterial or latent effects are happening but inaccessible to our knowledge. Put another way, part of the product of reproductive labor cannot be acknowledged within the very terms

of material production, for "what is produced [by such affective labor]" is, namely, the illusion of unique individuality transcendant of a person's utility to processes of commodity-production and capitalism (Vora 2012, 691).

38. Urmila's bodily labors in the performance of hospitality—to feed and host the family's guests—at first appears in conflict with her waged information-communications work. It is the time constraint of having "to leave within the hour if she was to be on time for the press conference" that has her buy the fish from (Laakhan/Lutchman masquerading as) a fish seller who miraculously knocks on her door. Through this plot twist, and as if in dramatization of Hardt and Negri's grouping both analytic/symbolic labor and caretaking in the umbrella category of "immaterial labor," the affective labor of cooking fish transmutes into information work, for the old newspaper (from 1898!) that spoiled the fish contains reportage from the past crucial to Murugan's research on tropical medicine and malaria (Urmila and Murugan team up in the search). The immaterial labor of symbol analysis, first appearing as the wrapping or outer covering for that which will serve to feed the family, overtakes the latter as the narrative focal site of interest. More simply put, textuality triumphs as cooking labor disappears.

39. Hardt and Negri, *Empire,* 290–94.

40. Hardt and Negri distinguish three types of immaterial labor, the first being that which transforms industrial manufacture through information technology—e.g., by way of just-in-time production—making manufacturing into a service industry; the second referring to the immaterial labor of "analytical and symbolic tasks" from computer programming to systems analysis to data entry; and the third being "affective labor" (understood through "woman's work") and involving "the production and manipulation of affect and requir[ing] (virtual or actual) human contact, labor in the bodily mode" (*Empire,* 289–94).

41. Cooper 2012 distinguishes between the express reasons given by phase one clinical subjects in the United States (largely males from the margins of society) and phase two clinical subjects (largely white middle-class females) for their participation in these trials. Phase one subjects are expressly motivated by economics—the money to be earned by "volunteering" for testing (Cooper finds agency in their attempt to game the system by lying about washing-out periods). In contrast, while the phase two female medical subjects are often looking to mitigate healthcare costs, their primary reasons for participation are altruistic: their labor, crucial to the findings of the drug trial, will help future patients. The latter motive, in other words, remains on an affective continuum with the gifts of communal caretaking that have been called domestic labor; whereas the risk-bearing work of men (who supply the predominant population of phase one clinical trial labor) appears historically "new." See also Cooper and Waldby's *Clinical Labour.*

42. However, there is one narration of a woman sinking into the riverbed that is a dramatized, visceral account of something like somatic transformation and passage to another form *and* this passage is framed as a story retold by Urmila, who first hears it from the nationally renowned author Phulboni. While Urmila frames this story as one of a woman bathing, it is of a woman sinking into damp mud of a weed-rich pond, her foot slipping and her body falling into the depthless murk, as if drowning. She literally becomes entangled in the lowest banks of the pond. What rescues her from this watery death is her grabbing hold of a seed stone and arising into the air again (229). While not a high-tech portrait of cross-species assemblage, this mundane merging of the vertebrate into the ecology of the pond (with its abundant plant, minerals, aquatic life, and mud) has affinities to the chimeracological.

43. Even if we were given the positive contours of Ava(n)tar's merging with Tara—and here I allude to Ghosh's sprinkling his narrative with wordplay and spliced entities—we would have only an avatar(a), rather than *the* polymorphism that could stand in for the entire chimeracological chain.

44. To be sure, the Lamarckian notion of inheriting acquired traits has not been revived whole-sale as much as there has been a reassessment of what the abuse of Lamarck has wrought—a denial of "nongenetic contributions to biological form" and an approach to biological processes that denies or understates interactionism between entity and its surrounds or, put another way, "begins with inert raw materials [that] require a mindlike force [e.g., genetic codes] to fashion this matter into a functioning animal-machine. This approach is at odds with what we know about physics and chemistry" (Oyama, *The Ontogeny of Information*, 33–34).

45. Of a part with the carving up of things—the localization of agency rather than the embed-ded view emphasizing cascades of interaction (any initiating agent of an action can be said to be reacting to a prior action)—is the fetish of genes/genomes—chromosomes—as the key to life. As Susan Oyama wrote in 1985,

    What we are moving toward is a conception of a developmental system, not as the read-ing off of a preexisting code, but as a complex of interacting influences, some inside the organism's skin, some external to it, and including its ecological niche in all its spatial and temporal aspects, many of which are typically passed on in reproduction either because they are in some way tied to the organism's (or its conspecifics') activities or characteristics or because they are stable features of the general environment. (39)

46. Mrs. Aratounian heads a plant nursery; in her first encounter with Urmila, she advises Urmi (rather brusquely) on the basics of horticulture (Urmila has hidden behind a bunch of chrysanthemums and knocked them over): "That's a plant, not a dog . . . [and] it doesn't want to be petted" (63). Interestingly, while dogs are symbols of docile companions who've evolutionarily adapted to human preferences, one variety of the chrysanthemum—the plant Mrs. Aratounian warns against petting—is cultivated for its pyrethrins, contained in "the seed cases," and used as a natural insect repellant. The pyrethrins of chrysanthemums, in other words, inhibit female mosquitoes from biting, thereby allowing for the controlling of conditions in which *Plasmodium* parasites might transfer and coassemble in vertebrates.

47. Lowe, *Immigrant Acts*, 21.

48. Thanks to Deboleena Roy for her insights on mangala and her Bengali dictionary. In *Cal-cutta Chromosome*, Ghosh himself comments on the regional variations in the pronuncia-tion of names as they "travel" from place to place and are also Anglicized.

49. Heiland, "Approaching the Ineffable," 128. John Dennis "characterized sublimity as 'an invincible force, which commits a pleasing rape upon the very soul of the reader" (quoted in Heiland, 133)

50. Oyama, *The Ontogeny of Information*, 26–27.

NOTES TO CHAPTER 5

1. Amelia Jones.

2. Holly Hughes and David Roman's anthology collects Uyehara's *Hello (Sex) Kitty* under the umbrella of queer solo performance, a "democratic" art form because of its small budgets ("nearly anyone can do it and nearly everyone does" [*O Solo Homo*, 1]), which was also demonized by Congress so that by 1997 the National Endowment for the Arts pulled fund-ing for individual artists. Hughes makes the case for queer performance as "rooted . . . in a particularly American tradition of . . . witnessing history in the first person," and Roman frames queer solo performance as "one of the few areas in public culture that is immedi-ately understood as multiracial, cogendered, and multisexual" (1).

3. Founding members of the SNNG, in addition to Uyehara, include Akilah Oliver, Laura Meyers, and Danielle Brazell. The lasting effect on Uyehara of this collaboration may be her indebtedness to what troupe member Akilah Oliver calls "flesh memory [or] the multiplic-ity of languages and realities that our flesh holds. . . . [I]t's the way we re-invent scenarios

... worlds and ... images to transcribe what we see, what we feel, what we think. It's a language that's activated in our bodies" (Oliver in interview with Coco Fusco, "Sacred Naked Nature Girls").

4. Uyehara's work harmonizes more with a "crip" deconstructive approach to normativity than with a devotion to limning in depth the expressive subjectivity of "actual disabled persons." See McRuer; and Davis, *Bending Over Backwards* and *Enforcing Normalcy*. On caring for those with dementia, see also J. Taylor, "On Recognition."

5. Mahmood, *The Politics of Piety*, 28.

6. Tango and flamenco dancers collaborated with Uyehara on previous artworks, for instance, a 1998 Helsinki commission where the artist was charged with creating a "specific work around concepts of city space in globalized culture" (128). Part of that commission involved tango dancers who opened the performance's reflections on learning how to swim. When this story on swimming was later incorporated in the retrospective show *Maps of City and Body* premiering at Highways in 1999, the director Chay Yew eliminated the tango dancers, a directorial decision to which Uyehara took exception (*Maps of City and Body*, 132–33).

7. The title of this sequence may function as a performance artist's insider joke, referring to the fantastically successful performance piece by Spaulding Gray, *Swimming to Cambodia* (1987).

8. Where page numbers are provided, I refer to the text of Uyehara's performances published in *Maps of City and Body* (Kaya Press, 2003). However, I also rely on my experience of seeing the live performance of *Big Head* in March 2003, as well as a six-minute reel of clips from this show. I also give direct quotes, without page numbers, when referring to the video-recorded performance (in its entirety) of Uyehara's 1999 Highways production of *Maps of City and Body*.

9. The retold memory equivocates on the harmfulness (or not) of the mutual touching between Elle and Denise. To be clear, I do not claim that Uyehara understates the harm of pedophilia. In those italicized commands, "You are mine / Don't tell anyone / Don't make a sound," the game teaches an adult code of possession—of sexual aggression as a means of making a girl into an object. The *Dragnet* soundtrack that completes the ambience of this lesson hints at how the law chases after other crimes (of property) and simply misses or cannot see the domestic scenario (the bedroom) as a site of predation.

10. Davis, *Enforcing Normacy*, 41–49. Mitchell and Snyder, while challenging authoritative interpretations authorized in narratives of disability, also refuse to offer noninterpretation, not narrating, as *the* positive alternative. They position themselves against "the dismissive critical stance that narrative merely replays retrograde politics of disability" (*Narrative Prosthesis*, 164). They also assert that "literature makes disability a socially lived, rather than a purely medical, phenomenon. Disabled characters fill the pages of literary narrative even as disabled people in society are locked away or sequestered from view. This characteristic intimacy with disabled characters in literature makes our stories a rare exception to the exclusions encountered by disabled people in their lives" (166).

11. "Bad Girl" and "Queen of Hearts" were both disco hits, the first by Donna Summers and the second by Carol Williams.

12. Chaudhuri, *Staging Place*, 56.

13. Nikolas Rose and others frame the more pastoral forms of governmentality exemplified in the individual prenatal consult and the "will to health" as on a continuum with the extermination eugenics of the past (Rose, "The Politics of Life Itself," 5–6, 9–10). On contemporary "genetics" including stem cell therapies and mo-cell lines as part of this eugenic continuum, see also Mitchell and Snyder's *Cultural Locations of Disability*; and L. Davis's *Bending Over Backwards*, 20.

14. Mahmood, *The Politics of Piety*, 28–29, with reference to Foucault.

15. Ibid., 28.

16. Caring connotes protectiveness: "Caring is an attitude that suggests constant worry and apprehension about dangers and failures. . . . Caring also carries duties and evaluations" (Margalit, *Ethics of Memory*, 36). I thank Jack Halberstam for suggesting Margalit as a key interpretive partner to Uyehara's performances.

17. Margalit surmises that "ethics might turn out . . . to be less like a litmus test and more like a wine tasting, with its constant comparisons to good examples. Ethics seems to be more suitable to what I have called e.g., philosophy, and morality for i.e., philosophy" (38–39); he earlier calls "e.g., philosophers" illustrators and "i.e., philosophers" explicators (ix). I take Margalit here to mean that questions of morality are those postulates and norms (supposedly) universally applicable; whereas ethics are those thick, knotty, complex, and contingent situations that must be decided on the basis of the particular circumstances on the ground. Fiction and narratives are often prized precisely because they show how characters struggle with supposedly "universally" applicable morals and norms that fail to guide them or guide them incorrectly in specific situations. We prize good stories precisely for their examples of how rich complexity cannot be reduced to the one-to-two-line norm.

18. "Because it encompasses all humanity, morality is long on geography and short on memory. Ethics is typically short on geography and long on memory" (ibid., 8).

19. One more item in Margalit's disquisition that remains worth remarking upon: in his elaboration on caring as an attitude that meets the demands of others for sustained attention, he again mentions a possible gendered difference in the performance of such care only to dismiss that difference as immaterial ultimately to his argument: "What we find hard is the attention that is implied by caring. Women may be better at dividing their attention than men, and thus more able to care for others than men, as Carol Gilligan used to argue. But even Mother Teresa lacked the resources to pay attention to everyone" (33). I will return to this point about the gendered difference in what Margalit calls care, but which Teresa Brennan usefully recasts by way of (external and internal modes in) the "transmission of affect" to synthesize or fill in a performative component to this discussion of ethics, memory, and affect.

20. Palumbo-Liu's definition of "ethics" is left to readerly inference; at one point he speaks of "an ethical self [that] is 'always already' 'accountable' to an other, already constituted in relation to an other or its trace" (2012, 177, citing Levinas and Nancy). In other words, for this Asian Americanist literary critic, "ethics" and "morality" are both terms referring to mnemonically rich (storied) feelings of obligation to remote others. This thickness or thickish-ness to memory and obligation contrasts medical "ethics" governing the circulation of biomaterials (as limned by L. Cohen 1999 and discussed in the introduction) and environmental/business ethics that tries to outsource waste (socialize waste costs and privatize gain), specifically exemplified by an infamous memo by Larry Summers cited by Palumbo-Liu. These latter types of ethics look to procedural or calculative formulas to achieve a justice—or equilibrium—derived from market models. See also Thompson's *Good Science*.

21. Video recording of *Maps of City and Body*.

22. According to J. Taylor, "social death is visited upon those institutionalized with dementia because in a world where sociality and friendship is solidified by reciprocity (the exchange of gifts, calls, attention, care, etc.), those with ADRD are thought incapable of reciprocal returns on the care (e.g., conversation, being with, tender touches) that "temporarily able-brained" friends deliver in their visits to those with ADRD ("On Recognition," 28).

23. Love, *Feeling Backward*, 5–6.

24. Nancy Mairs's memoir of living with multiple sclerosis, in fact, equates suicidal thoughts, following upon more diminished physical capacities as the disease progresses, as a sign of depression and hence mental illness. She does so to question whether it will ever be a rational decision for her to euthanise herself, even as those pastorally eugenic in

orientation—aka those unsympathetic to or avoiders of disability—would seem to want her to do so.

25. According to dance theorist Susan Foster, rather than being synonymous with choreography or its execution, dance is best conceived as a mode of heightening attention to "the body's unending ability to yield up new moves or to have its movement seen or experienced in a new way" ("Walking and Other Choreographic Tactics," 127–28). Kinesthetics promises a mode of physical responsiveness—bodily animation—that might occur sideways to rational hermeneutics, a sensual switch into a different register of encounter.

26. Mitchell and Snyder, *Narrative Prosthesis*, 56–60; italics in original.

27. See Chambers-Letson's "Imprisonment/Internment/Detention" for a history of internment and detention.

28. Exploring "the ways in which mobility of the body is crucial to the building of new cultural stories" (Kochar-Lindren, "Towards a Communal Body of Art," 218), the Brazilian director Augusto Boal's community-based political theater famously used techniques such as Image Theater—a facilitator/jokester picks a subject (in the spect-act circle) and asks the others to present their image of that subject with their bodies—and Forum Theater, in which

> the scene is performed once to present the model of the story, and then is played again as a type of contest in which audience members can yell "stop" and insert themselves into the dramatic storyline in an effort to change the outcome. The original players work to take the story to its original outcome; the new players try to change the outcome. (223)

29. *Big Head* plays a recorded interview with Shady Hakim in which he recounts that his uncle's friend, a Coptic Christian Egyptian mistaken for Muslim, was killed in his grocery story on Sept. 15, 2001:

> [Then] the American flag started popping up everywhere. And every time I would drive on the freeway and see a flag . . . I would wonder, what does that mean to that person? Does that flag mean they want me dead? . . . You're almost driving with your head down because you're not sure what the person next to you is thinking. (Uyehara, *Maps of City and Body*, 39–41)

Flag-waving, an ostensible patriotic act, also thoughtlessly injures, with auto-mobility figured as an aggressive exercise of agency presumed to be under one's muscular control (foot to the pedal, hand maneuvering the wheel).

30. See Hobjin and Sager for defense budget figures as well as Office of Management and Budget 2012 press release on Homeland Security.

31. *Big Head* incorporates the voice of LuLu Emery, who says,

> I'd like them to remember the power of grassroots activism. No matter how little you are, how insignificant you are, you still have a say, and whatever you say will have an effect. And even if you talk to your next-door neighbor and educate him about whatever it is—about your country, about your rights, about peace issues, no matter what—you don't have to be this famous person, you don't have to be an artist, you don't have to be an author, you don't have to be a poet, you can be this average person. (41)

32. Within the performance, Uyehara introduces the letters from her great-uncle Masamori Kojima by voicing the text of one of them, while also moving her hand alternatingly over her heart and up in the air in the two poses (current and past) of the pledge of allegiance. The letter Uyehara selects refers to another absent letter, one written by "Dear Fred"—the addressee of Kojima's letter. Fred's missive urges Kojima and others to " 'not for one minute let the American public forget the Nisei or the Issei. Write a continual flow of letters out into the world' " (32). Uyehara expressly compares her one-woman show to the act of "typing a letter to send out into the world" (performance notes, 69).

33. See Christine Balance's *Tropical Renditions* (forthcoming) for an astute analysis of the phatic social qualities of karaoke in Asian diasporic communities.

34. See video at http://deniseuyehara.com/archives/91.
35. The clay used in the preamble to *Big Head* is brown-red (according to the stage directions). If indeed Uyehara used the same material to film her claymation sequences, brownness— as a stable sign of racial difference/color—is itself suspended, in that Uyehara projects a blue light across both her own body and the claymation film, so that the effect is to render the clay figure a dark grey.
36. For instance, Chinese Americans and Korean Americans announced their ethnic difference from the Japanese during World War II in acts of ethnic disidentification. The beating of this South Asian man and his family by East Asians reveals the fragile ways in which those of South Asian and Southeast Asian (versus East Asian) descent have been unevenly incorporated into the pan-ethnic "Asian American" racial identity and political coalition. See Grewal, "The Postcolonial," on this point.
37. In her performance notes, Uyehara details her reaction upon first hearing this news of Sundeep's beating: "Standing in my living room after reading about this, I created a *dance in response.* As I moved, I thought about how we Asian Americans are just as susceptible to beating our neighbors in xenophobic rage as anyone else. The Vincent Chin case echoed in my head. . . ." (67; italics added).
38. Quite early in the show, Uyehara shapes red clay into various figures so crude as to be unidentifiable to the audience. (Her performance notes indicate they are of a rocket ship, a heart, and a human.) My argument here is that the end products (and their communicative significance for the audience) remain less important than the devotion to this repertoire of molding clay. This repertoire of squeezing, balling, bending, and indenting the material flashes forward to the performer's use of the clay man film projected into the theater space, and flashes back to the process at her kitchen table through which Uyehara made that clay man sequence. Meta-performatively, the past, present, and future repertoires of impressing clay with historical events (or moments in time) instantiate the work of the "live" show.
39. Grotowski recommended the use of simple raw materials as props, as part of an effort to protest the lush, bourgeois conventions of realist stage settings.
40. Brennan, *The Transmission of Affect*, 87.
41. Uyehara, *Maps of City and Body*, 35.
42. M. Cheng, review of *Big Head*, 519.
43. Uyehara, *Maps of City and Body*, 42.
44. "Kindness," Brennan writes, "is the refusal to pass on or transmit negative affects and the attempt to prevent the pain they cause others. . . . [It] is another way of describing the protective attitude that stands between another and the experience of negative affects" (*The Transmission of Affect*, 124).
45. Brennan's framework harmonizes with Ed Cohen's on the foundational myth of bodily boundaries and defensive immunity as health. Citing the phenomenon of the menstrual periods of women living in proximity (or not in proximity but exposed to smells from those women) cycling in synchronization. Through this evidence, Brennan stresses that science understands that the "environment in the form of other people changes human endocrinology. . . . That otherwise good science holds back from this conclusion testifies to the power of the illusion of self-containment" (73).
46. "The rhythmic aspects of behavior at a gathering are critical in both establishing and enhancing, a sense of collective purpose and a common understanding. This can be done consciously, whereas chemical entrainment works unconsciously . . . word and images are matters of vibration, vibrations at different frequencies, but vibrations" (Brennan, *The Transmission of Affect*, 70–71).
47. Taylor, "On Recognition," 47.
48. Davis, *Bending Over Backwards*, 4–5.
49. Ibid., 25.

50. Fassin, "Another Politics of Life," 47–48.

51. For the apt phrase "proleptic desire," I'm indebted to Lowell Gallagher. Here, I define pro-leptic desire as a kind of time sickness, as the needing to be ahead, the leading beat, that which—in a paranoid vein—predicts and defends against bad surprises. Proleptic desire very much accords with Vincanne Adams, Michelle Murphy, and Adele Clarke's outline of "anticipation."

52. In her research on how to give voice to those with Alzheimer's disease and related dementia (ADRD), Anne Davis Basting headed Time Slips, a project involving caregivers, staff at eldercare facilities, students, and people with ADRD in collaborative creative workshops to tell stories of those with cognitive disorders. The resulting composite genre emphasized not "one independent self, but [several] relational selves" ("Dementia," 209) offering an alter-native to "linear autobiographies . . . defined by [their] control of memory" (204). Whether or not we accept Basting's claim that "[p]eople with ADRD are an extreme example of a self that is relational, formed through interaction with others [with] family, friends, and care providers [having to] supply memories of the long-term and immediate past" (203), her framing of their non-normate "time-slips" as affording a positive enhancing quality— demanding intimate "thick" social relations—remains thought-provoking.

53. Calling disability "really a socially driven relation to the body . . . propelled [in modernity] by economic and social factors . . . to control and regulate [it]" (*Enforcing Normalcy*, 3), Lennard Davis proposes a countering notion of dismodernism: "[Dismodernism] aims to create a new category based on the partial, incomplete subject whose realization is not autonomy and independence but dependency and interdependence. . . . Impairment is the rule and normalcy a fantasy. . . . The watchword of dismodernism could be: Form follows dysfunction" (Davis, *Bending Over Backwards*, 30–31, 27).

NOTES TO CHAPTER 6

1. I am grateful to Banu Subramaniam for her suggestion on comigration and am inspired by her own work deconstructing discourses of so-called invasive plant and animal species (kudzu, carp, Asian long-horned beetle, but, interestingly, not the "Georgia" peach also originally from Asia, i.e., China) as they bespeak xenophobic disdain for Asian life taking hold on American shores. Along with Karen Cardozo, Subramaniam offers the concept of "invited invasions" to name the conditions whereby plants and animals from Asia, "circuits of flora and fauna" (akin to the travel of African slaves and their foodstuffs to the "New World") were channeled to the United States "at the behest of the hosts" (Cardozo and Subramanian 6). They are interested in the historical and material particularities whereby some "Asian/American formations" become constructed as "desirable" and others as deserving vigilance as to their potential damaging effects on the environment (14–15).

2. In considering the marking out of microscopic *though no less biological* differences as grounds of emergent forms of raciology, I am emphasizing a certain continuity in the mundane and extraordinary ways in which early-twenty-first-century metropolitan society segregates and slots for the rubbish heap ill, diseased, aging biologies (and even microscopic scales of their selves) and the practices that are less-debated as instances of racism (e.g., black slave plantation labor, Chinese coolie plantation labor, Japanese Ameri-can internment, sterilization surgeries on Latina women). However, I would not go so far as to nominate as a "racist" enslavement the putting to work of one's own chimeric bio-logical materials as they reside endogenously within the body, even as speculative fiction such as Ghosh's and Bear's novels lead to those limit-testing kinds of considerations as food for thought.

3. State policies are themselves limited or deliberately obfuscating when they speak about the nation's problems in terms of foreigner and native, instead of in terms of the U.S. econo-my's producing jobs "that only third world workers find attractive":

Since the 1950s, undocumented immigrants from Mexico and Latin America have provided much of the low-wage labor in agriculture, construction, hotels, restaurants, and domestic services in the . . . United States. . . . The result is an officially disavowed and yet unofficially mandated, clandestine movement of illegal immigration, which addresses the economy's need for low-wage labor but whose dehumanization of migrant workers is politically contradictory. (Lowe, *Immigrant Acts*, 21)

4. See especially chapter 4's treatment of undocumented babysitting.
5. Prashad, *Everybody Was Kung Fu Fighting*, 10.
6. Ibid.
7. Ibid., 4.
8. Gilroy, *Against Race*, 25.
9. Gilroy: "The Nazi period constitutes the most profound moral and temporal rupture in the history of the twentieth century and the pretensions of its modern civilization. Remembering it has been integral to the politics of 'race' for more than fifty years, but a further cultural and ethical transition . . . is irreversibly under way" (ibid.).
10. See Dr. Preserved Porter and his slave Fortune in Connecticut as recounted by Marilyn Nelson's *Fortune's Bones* and as further elaborated in the work of critic P. Gabrielle Foreman and the histories of black, poor, and devalued bodies for medical dissection.
11. Margulis, *Symbiotic Planet*, loc. 1590. The erudite Lynn Margulis, through her interest in cytoplasmic genes (DNA found outside the cell nucleus) and cellular organelles, found herself confounded by the disciplinary split between those who studied animals and those who studied plants, those who studied whole organisms and those who studied molecular biology. Turning the tide against such divisions in focalization and thereby apprehending similarities in microbial life and cytoplasmic components such as mitochondria and chloroplasts, Margulis convincingly hypothesized that these organelles interior to the cell wall—including the nucleus itself—were at some point formerly free-standing bacterial organisms. Margulis proposes that evolution occurs by way of serial endosymbiogenesis, the sharing of habitat and eventual merger of different organisms that then form a new species, as they reproduce in this new merger. The engines of biological creativity are the bacteria, with humans as simply a later endosymbiogenetic formation of serial astomasistic events.
12. See storm of coverage regarding the actress Angelina Jolie's announcement regarding her medical decision to undergo preemptive radical double mastectomy ("My Medical Choice").
13. See Vandana Shiva on farmer suicides consequent upon the Green Revolution in India. See *Seeds of Plenty* for a historical fiction on the disruptions to local communities of Nigeria consequent upon the green revolution—U.S. farm aid—in the latter half of the twentieth century.
14. Lowe and Lloyd, *The Politics of Culture*, 15.
15. Bataille inverted classical economics and its assumption of scarcity; instead, Bataille characterized cultures and governments not by the efficient management of economic resources (against looming potential or real scarcities) but by the manner in which they expend cultural surpluses. Kosalka notes that Bataille differentiates the cultures he analyzes (those of Tibet, the Aztecs, and early Islam) "by an initial choice of gift, of the way the excess wealth the culture produces is expended" (Kosalka, "Georges Bataille and the Notion of Gift"). See David Staples's "Women's Work" for an analyses of Bataille's distinction between the "general" and "restricted" economies, the latter tied to the logic of accumulation, and the former tied to the gratuitous expenditure of surplus.
16. See also Sobchack's excellent use of the literary example in her outlining of the phenomenological encounter of being reduced to the visible or epidermal outline ("Is Any Body Home?").

17. Along these lines and with respect specifically to refugee literature as represented by Nam
Le's *The Boat*, Asian Americanist critic Donald Goellnicht has also figured ethnic writing as
enjoining the writer and reader to the difficult ethical work of imagining, recognizing, and
suffering with, despite not knowing, the refugee. This is an ethics that "does not demand
knowledge . . . but rather keeps the reader open to other possibilities. Ethical response . . .
demands empathy and compassion even in the face of lack of comprehension, an affective
reaching out that carries the viewer beyond self to recognize and identify with suffering
and vulnerability while leaving aside pride and the pity" (Goellnicht, "Ethnic Literature's
Hot," 216).

18. See Londa Scheibinger's historicization of Linnaeus's substituting the term "mammal"
for other possibilities (biped, pilosi). She traces Linneaus's investment in the lactating
mammaries—which characterize only half the population of mammals, the female half—
as driven by his ideological investment in maternal lactation and discouragement of wet-
nursing in the upper classes.

19. In *The Posthuman*, Braidotti's aim is to place her prior articulations of "nomadic subjectivity" in relation to several other quarters of posthuman or antihumanist (but crucially not
inhumane) schools of thinking: "[P]hilosophical anti-humanism must not be confused
with cynical and nihilistic misanthropy" (6). Nomadic subjectivity, she claims, "promotes
an ethical bond of an altogether different sort from the self-interests of an individual
subject. . . . A posthuman ethics for a non-unitary subject proposes an enlarged sense of
inter-connection between self and others, including the non-human or 'earth' others" (49);
this "posthuman recomposition of human interaction . . . is not the same as the reactive
bond of vulnerability, but is an affirmative bond that locates the subject in the flow of relations with multiple others" (50).

20. In contrast to the approach of Martha Nussbaum and the universalist philosophers and
political theorists emphasizing increased precarity as that which unites humans to other
species and to the earth, Braidotti's "posthuman theory" proclaims "ethical relation on
positive grounds of joint project and activities, not on the negative or reactive grounds of
shared vulnerability" (190) and "the key notion in posthuman nomadic ethics is transcendence of negativity" (191).

21. See Cooper, *Life as Surplus*, especially chapters 4, 5, and 6.

22. According to Didier Fassin, *zoe* (bare/biological life) is (now) our most sacred form of
protected life: mere life, rather than life conforming to a particular political path (one
upholding, e.g., a democratic capitalist ideology rather than a communist/socialist feminist
one) becomes the state's concern. Human rights rather than the progress of the free world
become that which rationalizes grants of asylum, foreign policy, and military mobilization.
As suggested by Bridges, the fetus makes fleshy and concrete the rather amorphous idea
of "life"; it is by way of Court decisions regarding the fetus (from *Roe* to *Casey* to *Carhart*)
that we might track the state's increasing political interest or claims over *zoe* ("Writing an
Ethnography of Life").

23. As drawn out by Denise Ferreira da Silva, the temporary and partial avoidance of reduction to instrumentalized vitality provides the (white) subject the signifying conditions
for ascension to modern ethical subjectivity. Racial subjection remains crucial to the very
ontological construction of the ethical modern (Euro-American) subject precisely because
this subject can only ignore her place as part of biological life—i.e., as *zoe* regulated or
"outer-determined" by natural laws—by way of contrasting her condition to the diminished choices (the being enmired in necessity) of the non-European, minority, or indigenous subject. The enhanced degree of freedom from outer-determination enjoyed by the
ethical subject, in other words, comes by way of asserting and/or actualizing the lesser or
wholly lacking freedom of those from the nonelect populations.

24. Lowe, *Immigrant Acts*, 22.
25. Joseph Jonghyun Jeon and Timothy Yu, for instance, characterize what we think of as the epitome of abstract formal experimentation in poetry and conceptual art (i.e., the avant-garde) as very much part of the repertoire in which Asian American artists have reflected upon race.
26. Jeon, *Racial Things,* xx.
27. By way of a quote from Langer, Ngai defines aesthetic objects as ones in which we (briefly) set aside our direct (instrumental) pleasures in them to make them into also beautiful (or affectively endowed) objects of our concern (*Ugly Feelings*, 85):

    > Santayana regarded beauty as pleasure objectified—the spectator's pleasure is "projected" into the object that caused it. . . . What the picture has is our projected, i.e., objectified pleasure. But why is subjective pleasure not good enough? Why do we objectify it and project it into [the form] of "beauty," while we are content to feel it directly, as delight, in candy and perfumes and cushioned seats. . . . We project the [pleasurable] feeling that the object inspires to create a distance between ourselves and that feeling. But why are we compelled to separate ourselves from the feeling that the object elicits? Precisely because our feeling has made the object into an object of concern. . . . It is precisely this combination of steps—an affective engagement that itself prompts distancing—that constitutes the object as an aesthetic object: to introduce such a distance into our affective relationships to candy and perfume would be to make them aesthetic objects as well. (Ngai, *Ugly Feelings*, quoting Langer, 95)

28. However, deflecting an act of dehumanization is not equivalent to a rehumanization, but only a negation of a negation. That is, one could deflect one's commodification (that dehumanization) through turning oneself, metaphorically speaking, into a wood sprite or a disentangleable organism in a micro-ecology. These latter acts are not returns to "being human" aka rehumanization, even as they are deflections of commodification. In other words, this tactic settles for one form of negation from *bios*—aesthetic reification—to deflect another negation from *bios*—economic or biomedical reification. Moreover, we might consider how strategies of deflecting dehumanization—as opposed to rehumanizing the worker (see my earlier discussion of reproductive labor in chapter 4)—comprise the avatars of reproductive labor's agency in the twenty-first century.
29. Braidotti, *The Posthuman*, 107.
30. My recourse to Critchley's work and the importance of sublimation to ethics is indebted to Crystal Parikh's paper presented at the April 2013 Association for Asian American Studies conference. Errors in the rehearsal of Critchley's argument with respect to sublimation and comedy are my own.
31. Drawing on psychoanalysis, Critchley writes,

    > [T]he ethical subject is . . . *hetero-affectively* constituted. It is a split subject divided between itself and a demand that it cannot meet, a demand that makes it the subject that it is [ethical, i.e., bounded to its specific notion of good], but which it cannot entirely fulfill. The sovereignty of my autonomy is always usurped by the heteronomous experience of the other's demand. The ethical subject is a *dividual*. (10–11)

    Additionally, Critchley does not distinguish ethics from morals in the way Margalit does. He uses a Levinasian definition of ethics as "infinitely demanding."
32. Diagnostically, Critchley treads familiar ground, rehearsing sentiments proposed by Nietzsche: if ethics is "infinitely demanding," how does the ethical subject not devolve into bad consciousness or "conscience vivisection" and "self-torture" (Critchley 69, quoting Nietzsche)?
33. Critchley uses the psychoanalytic definition of "sublimation" as "the satisfaction of a drive insofar as that drive is deflected from its aim or goal in finding a new object" (71).

34. See Robin Kelly, "The U.S. v. Trayvon Martin"; and Cheryl Harris, "Whiteness as Property."
35. My work on Uyehara further develops the thread on ethics and morality expressly engaged in chapter 4 (Ghosh) with its herald in chapter 2 (Yu) spoken of in terms of sentimental witnessing of another's suffering.
36. Joshua Foa Dienstag's notion of modernity is tied to the idea of the measurability of time, and the measurability of all sorts of phenomena that previously seemed to exceed contouring as calculable, measurable, and hence exchangeable (commodifiable) entities.
37. "All the algae, slime molds, ciliates, and many other obscure microbial organisms" form the protoctists (Margulis, *Symbiotic Planet*, loc. 714–19).
38. Ibid., loc. 1034–36.
39. To my mind, most valuable about the evolutionary picture that Margulis maps, called SET phylogeny (serial endosymbiosis theory) is (1) its crediting the work of fusion or symbiosis as much as branching in evolution, and (2) its visualization of the foundation and continuing agency of bacteria (prokarya) and protoctists (the first species) in the emergence of the larger groupings we call kingdoms. That is, where Linnean classification catalogues resemblance through one to four key characteristics *within group* (e.g., mammals are hairy, possess three boned ears, are viviparous) but solidifies, ultimately, the main distinction of plant, animal, fungi, and microorganisms, SET phylogeny stresses a "coming together, . . . [a] merging of cells of different histories and abilities. . . . Cellular interliving, an infiltration and assimilation far more profound than any aspect of human sexuality, produced everything from spring-green blooms and warm, wet mammalian bodies to the Earth's global nexus" (ibid., locs. 459–64).
40. Ibid., 259.
41. Ibid., locs. 80–85.
42. The question of race is presupposed in the phrasing "acting white," which less offensively might be phrased "acting immune," that is, dis-obliged and unhospitable toward microbes but not toward people of color and vice versa. The latter phrasing (acting immune) may indeed be the more normative critical paradigm ushered in through the next fifty years of the twenty-first century. However, in my argument that the turn of the twenty-first century is not a *post*-race era but a *race-post-race* era, it seems all the more important to articulate the continuing salience of geopolitical, racialized idioms (a billion Chinese, acting white) in familiarizing and defamiliarizing phobic impulses in relation to the microbial scale of interorganismal and endo-organismal relations. Counterintuitively, the impetus to avoid using the phrase "acting white" as a synonym for empiric acts of expansion, coupled with dis-obligation from those roiled by these contacts, may indicate how much we still live in an era protecting the privileges of whiteness.
43. Adamowicz speaks of the surrealist image as a "limit-form of analogy": "[W]hereas in traditional metaphors the two semes brought together can be reduced to a single isotope by the presence of common semantic markers, in the surrealist metaphor the intersection is often minimal or apparently absent" (81); "[S]urrealist analogy is not grounded in prior links, to be deciphered upstream of the image; analogical links on the contrary are projective, forging new semantic realities" (82).
44. Stockton, *The Queer Child*, 13, 4.
45. Ibid., 11.
46. In the selected work of Tompkins edited by Sedgwick and Adam Frank, Tompkins covers "interest-excitement," "enjoyment-joy," "surprise-startle," "distress-anguish," "shame-humiliation and contempt-disgust," "anger," and "fear-terror."
47. Sedgwick, *Touching Feeling*, 94.
48. Ibid., 146.
49. Ibid., 145–46.

NOTES TO THE TAIL PIECE

1. The comedic recourse to the scatalogical, according to Joachim, has been an express vehicle for making Terreform's "open network ecology" appealing, not to other theorists and like-minded environmental nerds who need no convincing but to "the Homer Simpsons of the world." See Joachim, "Post-Sustainable."

2. Addressing the art-lab practices of Oron Catts and Ionat Zurr's *Disembodied Cuisine*—that is, food "cultured" *in vitro*, Allison Carruth raises the issue of whether *in vitro* processes can render their (meat) products "victimless": "Can any food be considered victimless?" ("Culturing Food," 9), which we can modify here to ask as well whether any habitat materials can be considered victimless.

3. The term "Hox" derives from a "180 base-pair sequence in homeotic genes" dubbed the "homeobox" (or "Hox" for short) that translate into a sixty-protein sequence (aka "home-odomain")—usually a transcription factor that binds to and thereby controls or regulates the actions of other genes (Carroll, "Imitations of Life," 62). The expression and regulation of the proteins indexed to Hox genes—a transcription and regulation also dependent on environmental conditions—is responsible for either the normal or the mutational development of anatomical structures such as the eyes and legs, etc.

4. Lawrence Goldstein, distinguished professor in the Department of Cellular and Molecular Medicine and the Department of Neurosciences at UC–San Diego School of Medicine, as well as the director of the UC–San Diego Stem Cell Program, at http://www.youtube.com/watch?v=QyoZuxHhvvE.

5. The cell culture platform often consists of "a standard host cell, expression vector, transfection and selection methods, cell culture media and culture techniques with appropriate process control, and scale-up methodologies" (Pacis et al., 1).

6. See Pacis et al.; for the intellectual and manual labor involved in growing cell cultures, see, for instance, this lab protocol at Rice ("Feeding Cells" part of the "BIOE342 Tissue Culture Laboratory Protocol") .

7. Which laboring bodies can we re-entangle into this picture? Is it too obvious to inquire as to the racial or geopolitical backgrounds of all those Harvard lab assistants forming the "infrastructures of reproduction" at the hidden core of this vascular, multinucleated urban-ism? And, of course, what about the bodies (not simply the cells) whose landscapes provide the places to relocate these pig bladders—will it be decaying urban housing projects with their primarily African American denizens?

8. I am indebted here to Anne Cheng's extraordinary discussion in *Second Skin* of modern-ist skins, clothing, and built environments, which she links to the term "cladding," as well as her essay on "Modernism" in *The Routledge Companion to Asian American and Pacific Islander Literature*, edited by Rachel Lee.

BIBLIOGRAPHY

Aaronson, Philip. "Smooth Muscle." In *The Oxford Companion to the Body*, edited by Colin Blakemore and Shelia Jennett. Oxford: Oxford University Press, 2001.

Adamowicz, Elza. *Surrealist Collage in Text and Image: Dissecting the Exquisite Corpse*. New York: Cambridge University Press, 1998.

Adams, Cecil. "Who Is Jimmy, and Why Does He Crack Corn?" *Straight Dope* (October 30, 1998), http://www.straightdope.com/columns/read/1288/who-is-jimmy-and-why-does-he-crack-corn.

Adams, Rachel. *Sideshow U.S.A.: Freaks and the American Cultural Imagination*. Chicago: University of Chicago Press, 2001.

Adams, Vincanne, Kathleen Erwin, and Phouc V. Le. "Governing through Blood: Biology, Donation, and Exchange in Urban China." In *Asian Biotech: Ethics and Communities of Fate*, edited by Nancy N. Chen and Aihwa Ong. Durham, NC: Duke University Press, 2010. 167–89.

Adams, Vincanne, Michelle Murphy, and Adele E. Clarke. "Anticipation: Technoscience, Life, Affect, Temporality." *Subjectivity* 28, no. 1 (2009): 246–65.

Agamben, Giorgio. *Homo Sacer: Sovereign Power and Bare Life*. Translated by Daniel Heller-Roazen. Stanford, CA: Stanford University Press, 1998.

Ahmed, Sara. *The Cultural Politics of Emotion*. New York: Routledge, 2004.

Alarcón, Norma. "The Theoretical Subject(s) of *This Bridge Called My Back* and Anglo-American Feminism." In *Making Face, Making Soul/Haciendo Caras: Creative and Critical Perspectives*, edited by Gloria Anzaldúa. San Francisco: Aunt Lute Books, 1990. 356–69.

"All about Secret." Proctor & Gamble, http://www.secret.com/deodorant-history.aspx.

Anderson, Benedict. *Imagined Communities: Reflections on the Origin and Spread of Nationalism*. New York: Verso, 1983.

Balance, Christine. *Tropical Renditions: Popular Music and Performance in Filipino America*. Durham, NC: Duke University Press, forthcoming.

Baldwin, James. *The Fire Next Time*. New York: Dial Press, 1963.

Barboza, David. "China Turns Out Mummified Bodies for Displays." *New York Times*, August 8, 2006. Accessed August 30, 2013, http://www.nytimes.com/2006/08/08/business/world business/08bodies.html?pagewanted=all&_r=0.

Bascara, Victor. *Model Minority Imperialism*. Minneapolis: University of Minnesota Press, 2006.

Basting, Anne Davis. "Dementia and the Performance of Self." In *Bodies in Commotion: Disability and Performance*, edited by Carrie Sandahl and Philip Auslander. Ann Arbor: University of Michigan Press, 2005. 202–13.

Bear, Greg. *Blood Music*. 1986. London: Orion, 2001. Kindle edition.

Beck, Ulrich. *Risk Society: Towards a New Modernity*. Thousand Oaks, CA: Sage, 1992.

Bergson, Henri. "Laughter." In *Comedy*, edited by Wylie Sypher. Baltimore, MD: John Hopkins University Press, 1956. 60–190.

Berlant, Lauren. *The Queen of America Goes to Washington City: Essays on Sex and Citizenship*. Durham, NC: Duke University Press, 1997.

Bernier, Francois. "A New Division of the Earth." Translated by Janet L. Nelson. *History Workshop Journal* no. 51 (Spring 2001): 247–50.

Bliss, Catherine. *Race Decoded: The Genomic Fight for Social Justice*. Stanford, CA: Stanford University Press, 2012.

Blumenbach, Johann Friedrich. *On the Natural Varieties of Mankind*. 1781. New York: Bergman, 1969.

Boal, Augusto. *Theatre of the Oppressed*. Translated by Charles McBride and Maria Odilia Leal McBride. New York: Theatre Communications Group, 1985.

Bolnick, Deborah A., et al. "The Science and Business of Genetic Ancestry." *Science*, October 19, 2007, 399–400.

Braidotti, Rosi. "Bio-power and Necro-politics" (2007), http://www.hum.uu.nl/medewerkers/r.braidotti/files/biopower.pdf.

———. *The Posthuman*. Cambridge, England: Polity, 2013.

Brennan, Teresa. *The Transmission of Affect*. Ithaca, NY: Cornell University Press, 2004.

Breton, André. *Manifestoes of Surrealism*. Ann Arbor: University Michigan Press, 1969.

Bridges, Khiara M. *Reproducing Race: An Ethnography of Pregnancy as Site of Racialization*. Berkeley: University of California Press, 2011.

———. "Writing an Ethnography of Life." Presentation at the Life (Un)Ltd Symposium, Center for the Study of Women, UCLA. May 11, 2012.

Briggs, Laura. "Foreign and Domestic: Adoption, Immigration, and Privatization." In *Intimate Labors: Cultures, Technologies, and the Politics of Care*, edited by Eileen Boris and Rhacel Parreñas. Stanford, CA: Stanford University Press, 2010. 49–62.

———. *Somebody's Children: The Politics of Transracial and Transnational Adoption*. Durham, NC: Duke University Press, 2012.

Brodwin, Paul E. *Biotechnology and Culture: Bodies, Anxieties, Ethics*. Bloomington: Indiana University Press, 2000.

Brown, Bill. *A Sense of Things: The Object Matter of American Literature*. Chicago: University Chicago Press, 2003.

Buell, Frederick. *National Culture and the New Global System*. Baltimore, MD: Johns Hopkins University Press, 1994.

Bukatman, Scott. "Terminal Penetration." In *The Cybercultures Reader*, edited by David Bell and Barbara Kennedy. New York: Routledge, 2000. 149–74.

Bull, Malcolm. "Vectors of the Biopolitical." *New Left Review* 45 (2007): 7–25.

Bulosan, Carlos. *America Is in the Heart*. 1943. Seattle: University of Washington Press, 2000.

Butler, Judith. *Bodies That Matter: On the Discursive Limits of "Sex."* New York: Routledge, 1993.

———. *Gender Trouble: Feminism and the Subversion of Identity*. New York: Routledge, 1989.

———. *Precarious Life: The Powers of Mourning and Violence*. London: Verso, 2004.

Byrd, Jodi. *The Transit of Empire*. Minneapolis: University of Minnesota Press, 2011.

Callon, Michael. "Some Elements of a Sociology of Translation: Domestication of the Scallops and the Fishermen of St. Brieuc Bay." In *The Science Studies Reader*, edited by Mario Biagioli. New York: Routledge, 1999. 67–83.

Cardozo, Karen, and Banu Subramaniam. "Assembling Asian/American Naturecultures: Orientalism and Invited Invasions." *JAAS* 16, no. 1 (February 2013): 1–23.

Carney, Judith A., and Richard Nicholas Rosomoff. "Botanical Gardens of the Dispossessed." In *In the Shadow of Slavery: Africa's Botanical Legacy in the Atlantic World*. Berkeley: University of California Press, 2009. 123–38.

Carroll, Rachel. "Imitations of Life: Cloning, Heterosexuality, and the Human in Kazuo Ishiguro's *Never Let Me Go*." *Journal of Gender Studies* 19, no. 1 (2010): 59–71.

Carruth, Allison. "Culturing Food: Bioart and in Vitro Meat." *Parallax* 19, no. 1 (January 2013): 88–100.

Case, Sue-Ellen. "Towards a Butch-Femme Aesthetic." *Discourse* 11, no. 1 (Fall/Winer 1988–89): 55–71.

Chakrabarty, Dipesh. "The Time of History and the Times of the Gods." In *The Politics of Culture in the Shadow of Capital*, edited by Lisa Lowe and David Lloyd. Durham, NC: Duke University Press, 1997. 35–60.

Chambers, Claire. "Networks of Stories: Amitav Ghosh's *The Calcutta Chromosome*." *ARIEL* 40, nos. 2–3 (2009): 41–62.

———. "Postcolonial Science Fiction: Amitav Ghosh's *The Calcutta Chromosome*." *Journal of Commonwealth Literature* 3, no. 1 (2003): 57–72.

Chambers-Letson, Joshua. "Imprisonment/Internment/Detention." In *The Routledge Companion to Asian American and Pacific Islander Literature*, edited by Rachel Lee. New York: Routledge, 2014.

Champeau, Rachel. "Changing Gut Bacteria through Diet Affects Brain Function, UCLA Study Shows." *UCLA Newsroom* (May 28, 2013), http://newsroom.ucla.edu/portal/ucla/changing-gut-bacteria-through-245617.aspx.

Chan, Sewell. " 'Bodies' Show Must Put Up Warnings." *New York Times* (City Room section), October 1, 2008, http://cityroom.blogs.nytimes.com/2008/05/29/bodies-exhibit-must-put-up-warnings/?_r=0.

Chaudhuri, Una. *Staging Place: The Geography of Modern Drama*. Ann Arbor: University of Michigan Press, 1995.

Chen, Mel Y. *Animacies: Biopolitics, Racial Mattering, and Queer Affect*. Durham, NC: Duke University Press, 2012.

Chen, Tina. *Double Agency: Acts of Impersonation in Asian American Literature and Culture*. Stanford, CA: Stanford University Press, 2005.

Cheng, Anne Anlin. *The Melancholy of Race: Psychoanalysis, Assimilation, and Hidden Grief*. New York: Oxford University Press, 2001.

———. "Modernism." In *The Routledge Companion to Asian American and Pacific Islander Literature*, edited by Rachel Lee. New York: Routledge, 2014.

———. *Second Skin: Josephine Baker and the Modern Surface*. New York: Oxford University Press, 2011.

Cheng, Meiling. *In Other Los Angeleses: Multicentric Performance Art*. Berkeley: University of California Press, 2002.

———. Review of Denise Uyehara's *Big Head*. *Theater Journal* 55, no. 3 (October 2003): 518–19.

Cheung, King-Kok. *Articulate Silences: Hisaye Yamamoto, Maxine Hong Kingston, and Joy Kogowa*. Ithaca, NY: Cornell University Press, 1993.

Chin, Frank. "Backtalk." In *Counterpoint*, edited by Emma Gee, et al. Los Angeles: Asian Amerian Studies Center, UCLA, 1976. 556–57.

———. "Confessions of a Chinatown Cowboy." *Bulletin of Concerned Asian Scholars* 4.3 (Fall 1972): 58–70.

Cho, Margaret. "Belly Dance." *Margaret Cho* (blog) (June 13, 2005), http://www.margaretcho.com/2005/06/13/belly-dance.

———. *Cho Revolution*. Live concert at the Wiltern, Los Angeles, CA, May 2, 2003.

———. *I Have Chosen to Stay and Fight*. New York: Riverhead Books, 2003.

———. *I'm the One That I Want*. DVD. Performed by Margaret Cho in 1999. New York: Winstar TV & Video, 2001.

———. *I'm the One That I Want*. Book. New York: Ballantine Books, 2001.

———. *Notorious C.H.O.* Live concert at the Universal Ampitheater, Los Angeles, CA, September 12, 2001.

Chodorow, Nancy. *The Reproduction of Mothering: Psychoanalysis and the Sociology of Gender*. Berkeley: University of California Press, 1999.

Chow, Rey. *The Protestant Eth(n)ic and the Spirit of Capitalism.* New York: Columbia University Press, 2002.

———. *Writing Diaspora: Tactics of Intervention in Contemporary Cultural Studies.* Bloomington: Indiana University Press, 1993.

Choy, Catherine Ceniza. *Empire of Care: Nursing and Migration in Filipino American History.* Durham, NC: Duke University Press, 2003.

———. *Global Families: A History of Asian International Adoption in America.* New York: New York University Press, 2013.

———. "Race at the Center: The History of American Cold War Asian Adoption." *Journal of American–East Asian Relations* 16, no. 3 (2009): 1–20.

Chua, Amy. *Battle Hymn of the Tiger Mother.* New York: Penguin Books, 2011.

Chuh, Kandice. *Imagine Otherwise: On Asian Americanist Critique.* Durham, NC: Duke University Press, 2003.

Clough, Patricia. Introduction to *The Affective Turn: Theorizing the Social.* Edited by Patricia Clough. Durham, NC: Duke University Press, 2007.

Cohen, Ed. *A Body Worth Defending: Immunity, Biopolitics, and the Apotheosis of the Modern Body.* Durham, NC: Duke University Press, 2009.

Cohen, Lawrence. "Given Over to Demand: Excorporation as Commitment." *Contemporary South Asia.* 21.3 (2013): 318–332.

———. "Operability: Surgery at the Margin of the State." In *Anthropology in the Margins of the State*, edited by Veena Das and Deborah Poole. Santa Fe, NM: School of American Research Press, 2004. 165–90.

———. "The Other Kidney: Biopolitics and Beyond." *Body and Society* 7, nos. 2–3 (2001): 9–29. Rpt. in *Commodifying Bodies*, edited by Nancy Scheper-Hughes and Loïc Wacquant. London: Sage, 2002. 9–29.

———. "Where It Hurts: Indian Material for an Ethics of Organ Transplantation." *Daedalus* 128, no. 4 (Fall 1999): 135–65.

Coole, Diana, and Samantha Frost, eds. *New Materialisms: Ontology, Agency, and Politics.* Durham, NC: Duke University Press, 2010.

Cooper, Melinda. "Double Exposure: Sex Workers, Biomedical Trials, and the Dual Logic of Public Health." *The Scholar and the Feminist* 11, no. 3 (Summer 2013), http://sfonline.barnard.edu/life-un-ltd-feminism-bioscience-race/double-exposure-sex-workers-biomedical-prevention-trials-and-the-dual-logic-of-global-public-health.

———. *Life as Surplus: Biotechnology and Capitalism in the Neoliberal Era.* Seattle: University of Washington Press, 2008.

———. "The Work of Experiment: Clinical Trials and the Production of Risk." Paper presented at Life (Un)Ltd: A Symposium on Feminism, Race, and Biopolitics, Center for the Study of Women, UCLA. May 11, 2012.

Cooper, Melinda, and Catherine Waldby. *Clinical Labour: Human Research Subjects and Tissue Donors in the Global Bioeconomy.* Durham, NC: Duke University Press, 2014.

Critchley, Simon. *Infinitely Demanding: Ethics of Commitment, Politics of Resistance.* New York: Verso, 2007.

Cuvier, Georges. *The Animal Kingdom: Arranged in Conformity with Its Organization.* Translated and abridged by H. M'Murtire. New York: Carvill, 1832.

Darwin, Charles. *The Origin of the Species by Means of Natural Selection; or, The Preservation of Favored Races in the Struggle for Life* and *The Descent of Man.* New York: Modern Library, 1936.

Davis, Lennard J. *Bending Over Backwards: Disability, Dismodernism, and Other Difficult Positions.* New York: New York University Press, 2002.

———. *Enforcing Normalcy: Disability, Deafness, and the Body.* London: Verso, 1995.

———. "From Culture to Biocultures." *PMLA* 124, no. 3 (2009): 949–51.

Davis, Rocio, and Sue Im Lee, eds. *Literary Gestures: The Aesthetic in Asian American Writing.* Philadelphia: Temple University Press, 2005.

Derrida, Jacques. "Hospitality." Translated by Barry Stocker and Forbes Morlock. *Angelaki* 5, no. 3 (2000): 3–18.

deSouza, Allan. *Divine.* 2008. *AllandeSouza.com.* Photograph. 11 April 2014.

———. *Redactions.* 2010/11. *AllandeSouza.com.* C-Prints. 11 April 2014.

———. *Terrain.* 1999–2000. *AllandeSouza.com.* C-prints. 11 April 2014.

———. *Threshold.* 1996–1998. *AllandeSouza.com.* Photographs and C-prints. 11 April 2014.

Dienstag, Joshua Foa. *Pessimism: Philosophy, Ethic, Spirit.* Princeton, NJ: Princeton University Press, 2006.

Dimock, Waichee. *Residues of Justice: Literature, Law, Philosophy.* Berkeley: University of California Press, 1997.

Diprose, Rosalyn. "Women's Bodies between National Hospitality and Domestic Biopolitics." *Paragraph* 32, no. 1 (2009): 69–86.

Doyle, Rich. *Darwin's Pharmacy: Sex, Plants, and the Evolution of the Noösphere.* Seattle: University of Washington Press, 2011.

Dreger, Alice. *Hermaphrodites and the Medical Invention of Sex.* Cambridge, MA: Harvard University Press, 1998.

Duden, Barbara. *The Woman beneath the Skin: A Doctor's Patients in Eighteenth-Century Germany.* Cambridge, MA: Harvard University Press, 1998.

Duster, Troy. "The Molecular Reinscription of Race: Unanticipated Issues in Biotechnology and Forensic Science." *Patterns of Prejudice* 40, no. 4–5 (2006): 427–41.

Edelman, Lee. *No Future: Queer Theory and the Death Drive.* Durham, NC: Duke University Press, 2004.

Eng, David, and David Kazanjian, eds. *Loss: The Politics of Mourning.* Berkeley: University of California Press, 2002.

Engels, Frederick. "The Origin of the Family, Private Property, and the State." 1884. In *The Marx-Engels Reader,* second edition, edited by Robert C. Tucker. Princeton, NJ: Princeton University Press, 1978. 734–59.

Eoyang, Eugene. "Of 'Invincible Spears and Impenetrable Shields': The Possibility of Impossible Translations." *LEWI Working Paper Series* no. 49. Hong Kong: David C. Lam Institute for East-West Studies, 2006.

Erdrich, Heid. E. *Cell Traffic: New and Selected Poems.* Tucson: University of Arizona Press, 2012.

Esposito, Roberto. *Bios: Biopolitics and Philosophy.* Translated by Timothy Campbell. Minneapolis: University of Minnesota Press, 2008.

Fabian, Johannes. *Time and the Other: How Anthropology Makes Its Object.* New York: Columbia University Press, 2002.

Fadiman, Anne. *The Spirit Catches You and You Fall Down: A Hmong Child, Her American Doctors, and the Collision of Two Cultures.* New York: Farrar, Straus, and Giroux, 1997.

Fassin, Didier. "Another Politics of Life Is Possible." *Theory, Culture, Society* 26, no. 5 (2009): 44–60.

Fausto-Sterling, Anne. "The Five Sexes: Why Male and Female Are Not Enough." *Sciences* 33, no. 2 (March/April 1993): 20–25.

"Feeding Cells." BIOE342-Tissue Culture Laboratory Protocol at http://www.ruf.rice.edu/~bioewhit/labs/bioe342/protocols.html.

Felski, Rita. "Context Stinks!" Public lecture at the Mellon Seminar Series "Cultures in Transnational Perspective," UCLA, October 20, 2011.

———. *The Uses of Literature.* Malden, MA: Blackwell, 2008.

Ferguson, Roderick A. *Aberrations in Black: Toward a Queer of Color Critique.* Minneapolis: University of Minnesota Press, 2003.

Fiedler, Leslie. *Freaks: Myths and Images of the Secret Self.* New York: Simon & Schuster, 1978.

Finkler, Kaja. "Family, Kinship, Memory, and Temporality in the Age of the New Genetics." *Social Science & Medicine* 61, no. 5 (2005): 1059–71.

Foreman, P. Gabrielle. "The Doctors' Fortune: A Traffic in Black Bodies and Bones." From "The Art of DisMemory: Historicizing Slavery in Poetry, Performance, and Material Culture." Unpublished manuscript, 2013.

Foster, Susan Leigh. "Movement's Contagion: The Kinesthetic Impact of Performance." In *Cambridge Companion to Performance Studies*, edited by Tracy C. Davis. Cambridge: Cambridge University Press, 2008. 46–59.

———. "Walking and Other Choreographic Tactics: Danced Inventions of Theatricality and Performativity." *SubStance* 98/99, 31, nos. 2–3 (2002): 125–46.

Foucault, Michel. *Birth of the Clinic: An Archaeology of Medical Perception*. New York: Random House, 1973.

———. *Discipline and Punish: The Birth of the Prison*. Translated by Alan Sheridan. New York: Vintage Books, 1979.

———. *The History of Sexuality*. Vol. 1, *An Introduction*. Translated by Robert Hurley. New York: Random House, 1978.

———. *The History of Sexuality*. Vol. 2, *The Use of Pleasure*. Translated by Robert Hurley. New York: Random House, 1985.

———. *The Order of Things: An Archaeology of the Human Sciences*. New York: Random House, 1970.

François, Anne-Lise. "'O Happy Living Things': Frankenfoods and the Bounds of Wordsworthian Natural Piety." *Diacritics* 33, no. 2 (2003): 42–70.

Fretz, Eric. "P.T. Barnum's Theatrical Selfhood and the Nineteenth-Century Culture of Exhibition." In *Freakery*, edited by Rosemarie Garland Thomson. New York: New York University Press, 1996. 97–107.

Fu, Qifeng. *The Art of Chinese Acrobatics*. Beijing: Foreign Languages Press, 1985.

Fullwiley, Duana. "The Molecularization of Race: Institutionalizing Racial Difference in Pharmacogenetics Practice." *Science as Culture* 16, no. 1 (2006): 1–30.

Fusco, Coco. "Sacred Naked Nature Girls." *BOMB* 52, Summer 1995. Accessed August 30, 2013, http://bombsite.com/issues/52/articles/1884.

Garland Thomson, Rosemary. *Extraordinary Bodies: Figuring Physical Disability in American Culture and Literature*. New York: Columbia University Press, 1995.

Gellner, Ernest. *Nations and Nationalism*. Ithaca, NY: Cornell University Press, 1983.

"Genetics and Genomics Timeline." *Genome News Network*, at http://www.genomenewsnetwork .org/resources/timeline/timeline_overview.php.

Ghosh, Amitav. *The Calcutta Chromosome*. New York: Harper Perennial, 2001.

———. *The Hungry Tide: A Novel*. New York: Houghton Mifflin, 2005.

Ghosh, Bishnupriya. "On Grafting the Vernacular: The Consequences of Postcolonial Spectrology." *Boundary 2* 3, no. 2 (2004): 197–218.

Gilligan, Carol. "Woman's Place in the Man's Life Cycle." In *A Different Voice: Pyschological Theory and Women's Development*. Cambridge, MA: Harvard University Press, 1982. 5–23. Rpt. in *The Second Wave: A Reader in Feminist Theory*, edited by Linda Nicolson. New York: Routledge, 1997. 198–215.

Gilroy, Paul. *Against Race: Imagining Political Culture beyond the Color Line*. Cambridge, MA: Belknap Press of Harvard University Press, 2002.

———. *Postcolonial Melancholia*. New York: Columbia University Press, 2005.

Goellnicht, Donald. "'Ethnic Literature's Hot': Asian American Literature, Refugee Cosmopolitanism, and Nam Le's *The Boat*." *Journal of Asian American Studies* 15, no. 2 (June 2012): 197–224.

Grewal, Inderpal. "The Postcolonial, Ethnic Studies, and the Diaspora: The Contexts of Ethnic Immigrant/Migrant Cultural Studies in the U.S." *Socialist Review* 24, no. 4 (1994): 45–74.

Ha, Nathan. "Diagnosing Erotic Preferences: Kurt Freund, Penile Plethysmography, and Late-Twentieth-Century Sexology." Unpublished manuscript.

Hagedorn, Jessica. *Dogeaters*. New York: Penguin, 1990.

Halberstam, Judith. *Female Masculinity*. Durham, NC: Duke University Press, 1998.

Halpin, Jenni G. "Gift Unpossessed: Community as 'Gift' in *The Calcutta Chromosome*." *ARIEL* 40, nos. 2–3 (2009): 23–39.

Haraway, Donna J. "A Manifesto for Cyborgs: Science, Technology, and Socialist Feminism in the Last Quarter." *Socialist Review* 80 (March/April 1985): 65–107.

———. *Modest_Witness@Second_Millenium.FemaleMan©_Meets_OncoMouse™: Feminism and Technoscience*. New York: Routledge, 1997.

———. *Primate Visions: Gender, Race, and Nature in the World of Modern Science*. New York: Routledge, 1989.

———. *Simians, Cyborgs, and Women*. New York: Routledge, 1991.

———. *When Species Meet*. Minneapolis: University of Minnesota Press, 2008.

Hardt, Michael. Foreword to *The Affective Turn: Theorizing the Social*. Edited by Patricia Clough. Durham, NC: Duke University Press, 2007.

———. "The Withering of Civil Society." *Social Text* 45 (Winter 1995): 27–44.

Hardt, Michael, and Antonio Negri. *Empire*. Cambridge, MA: Harvard University Press, 2000.

Harris, Cheryl. "Whiteness as Property." *Harvard Law Review* 106 (June 1993): 1710–91.

Hart, Hugh. "Art of Urgency: A New Performance Work Focuses on the Plight of Arab Americans." *Los Angeles Times*, February 18, 2003.

Hartmann, Heidi. "The Unhappy Marriage between Marxism and Feminism." In *Women and Revolution*, edited by Lydia Sargent. Boston: South End Press, 1981. Rpt. in *The Second Wave: A Reader in Feminist Theory*, edited by Linda Nicholson. New York: Routledge, 1997. 97–172.

Hartmann, Saidiya V. *Scenes of Subjection: Terror, Slavery, and Self-Making in Nineteenth-Century America*. New York: Oxford University Press, 1997.

Hartsock, Nancy. "The Feminist Standpoint." In *Discovering Reality: Feminist Perspectives on Epistemology, Metaphysics, Methodology, and Philosophy of Science*, edited by Sandra Harding and Merill B. Hinnitikka. New York: Kluwer Academic, 1983. Rpt. in *The Second Wave: A Reader in Feminist Theory*, edited by Linda Nicolson. New York: Routledge, 1997. 241–60.

Hayles, N. Katherine. *How We Became Posthuman*. Chicago: University of Chicago Press, 1999.

Hayot, Eric. "The Asian Turns." *PMLA* 124, no. 3 (May 2009): 906–17.

———. "Chinese Bodies, Chinese Futures." *Representations* 99, no. 1 (Summer 2007): 99–129.

———. *The Hypothetical Mandarin: Sympathy, Modernity, and Chinese Pain*. New York: Oxford University Press, 2009.

Heiland, Donna. "Approaching the Ineffable: Flow, Subliminity, and Student Learning." In *Literary Study, Measurement, and the Sublime*, edited by Donna Heiland and Laura J. Rosenthal. New York: Teagle Foundation, 2011. 115–32.

Hird, Myrna. "Digesting Difference: Metabolism and the Question of Sexual Difference." *Configurations* 20, no. 3 (2012): 213–37.

Ho, Jennifer, and Jim Lee, eds. Special Issue on "The State of Illness and Disability in Asian America." *Amerasia Journal* 39, no. 1 (2013).

Hobjin, Bart, and Erick Sager. Defense Budget figures. Federal Reserve Bank of New York publication, 2007.

Hochschild, Arlie. *The Managed Heart: The Commercialization of Human Feeling*. 1983. Second edition Berkeley: University of California Press, 2003.

———. *The Second Shift*. New York: Avon, 1997.

Holland, John. *Emergence: From Chaos to Order*. New York: Basic Books, 1998.

Holubnychy, Vsevolod. "Mao Tse-tung's Materialist Dialectics." *China Quarterly* 19 (September 1964): 3–37.

Hondagneu-Sotelo, Pierrette. *Domestica: Immigrant Workers Cleaning and Caring in the Shadows of Affluence*. Berkeley: University of California Press, 2007.

Huang, Zhe-bin, and Yo-zhi Gao. "Mackay the Unforgettable 'Black-Bearded Foreigner.'" *Want China Times* (December 6, 2010), http://www.wantchinatimes.com/news-subclass-cnt.aspx?id=20101206000044&cid=1503.

Hughes, Holly, and David Roman, eds. *O Solo Homo: The New Queer Performance*. New York: Grove, 1998.

Huttunen, Tuomas. "The Ethics of Representation in the Fiction of Amitav Ghosh." PhD diss, University of Turku, Finland, 2011.

Inoue, Todd. "Take These Tea Leaves and Shove 'Em: Denise Uyehara Gets in Touch with Her Inner Kitty in 'Hello (Sex) Kitty.'" Review. *Metroactive* Arts section (Silicon Valley, CA), March 7–13, 2002, http://www.metroactive.com/papers/metro/03.07.02/uyehara-0210.html.

Isaac, Allan Punzalan. *American Tropics: Articulating Filipino America*. Minneapolis: University of Minnesota Press, 2006.

Ishiguro, Kazuo. *Never Let Me Go*. New York: Random House, 2005.

Jain, Sarah Lochlann. "Living in Prognosis: Toward an Elegiac Politics." *Representations* 98 (Spring 2007): 77–92.

Jeon, Joseph Jonghyun. *Racial Things, Racial Forms: Objecthood in Avant-Garde Asian American Poetry*. Iowa City: University of Iowa Press, 2012.

Jerng, Mark C. *Claiming Others: Transracial Adoption and National Belonging*. Minneapolis: University of Minnesota Press, 2010.

———. "Giving Form to Life: Cloning and Narrative Expectations of the Human." *Partial Answers: Journal of Literature and the History of Ideas* 6, no. 2 (2008): 369–93.

Joachim, Mitchell. "Post Sustainable: The Future of Socio-Ecological Cities." Cooper Union Institute for Sustainable Design symposium on "Urban Planet: Emerging Ecologies" (video-recording), April 10, 2012, http://cooper.edu/events-and-exhibitions/events/urban-planet-emerging-ecologies.

Jolie, Angelina. "My Medical Choice." *New York Times*, May 14, 2013, http://www.nytimes.com/2013/05/14/opinion/my-medical-choice.html?_r=0.

Jones, Amelia. *Body Art/Performing the Subject*. Minneapolis: University of Minnesota Press, 1998.

Juo, Jennifer. *Seeds of Plenty*. CreateSpace Independent Publishing Platform, 2013.

Jung, Moon-Ho. *Coolies and Cane: Race, Labor, and Sugar in the Age of Emancipation*. Baltimore, MD: John Hopkins University Press, 2008.

Kang, Jerry. "Thinking through Internment: 12/7 and 9/11." In *Asian Americans on War and Peace*, edited by Russell C. Leong and Don T. Nakanishi. Los Angeles: UCLA Asian American Studies Center Press, 2002. 55–62.

Kang, Laura Hyun Yi. *Compositional Subjects: Enfiguring Asian/American Women*. Durham, NC: Duke University Press, 2002.

Kelly, Robin. "The U.S. v. Trayvon Martin: How the System Worked." *Huffington Post*, August 16, 2013. Accessed August 16, 2013, http://www.huffingtonpost.com/robin-d-g-kelley/nra-stand-your-ground-trayvon-martin_b_3599843.html.

Kermode, Frank. *The Sense of an Ending: Studies in the Theory of Fiction*. New York: Oxford University Press, 2000.

Kim, Claire J. "Objects, Methods, and Interpretations: Imperial Trajectories, Haunted Nationalisms, and Medical Archives in Asian American History." *Journal of Asian American Studies* 14, no. 2 (2011): 93–219.

Kim, Daniel. *Writing Manhood in Black and Yellow: Ralph Ellison, Frank Chin, and the Literary Politics of Identity*. Stanford, CA: Stanford Unniversity Press, 2005.

Kim, Jodi. *Ends of Empire: Asian American Critique and the Cold War*. Minneapolis: University of Minnesota Press, 2010.

Kingston, Maxine H. *The Woman Warrior: Memoirs of a Girlhood among Ghosts*. 1976. New York: Random House, 1989.

Kirshenblatt-Gimblett, Barbara. "Objects of Ethnography." In *Exhibiting Cultures: The Poetics and Politics of Museum Display*, edited by Ivan Karp and Steen D. Lavine. Washington, DC: Smithsonian Press, 1990. 387–443.

Kochar-Lindren, Kanta. "Towards a Communal Body of Art: The Exquisite Corpse and Augusto Boal's Theatre." *Angelaki* 7, no. 1 (2002): 217–26.

Kondo, Dorinne K. *About Face: Performing Race in Fashion and Theater*. New York: Routledge, 1997.

———. "(Re)Visions of Race: Contemporary Race Theory and the Cultural Politics of Racial Crossover in Documentary Theatre." *Theatre Journal* 52, no. 1 (March 2000): 81–107.

Kosalka, David R. "Georges Bataille and the Notion of Gift." *Kagablog*, June 9, 2008, http://kaganof.com/kagablog/2008/06/09/georges-bataille-and-the-notion-of-gift.

Koshy, Susan. "The Fiction of Asian American Literature." *Yale Journal of Criticism* 9, no. 2 (1996): 315–46.

———. "Morphing Race into Ethnicity." *Boundary* 2 28, no. 1 (2001): 153–94.

Kunzle, David. "The Art of Pulling Teeth." In *Fragments for a History of the Human Body, Part Three*, edited by Michel Feher with Ramona Naddaff and Nadia Tazi. New York: Zone, 1989. 28–89.

Kuppers, Petra. *The Scar of Visibility: Medical Performances and Contemporary Art*. Minneapolis: University of Minnesota Press, 2007.

Lai, Larissa. "Ham." *Automaton Biographies*. Vancouver, BC: Arsenal Pulp Press, 2009. 85–122.

Landecker, Hannah. *Culturing Life: How Cells Became Technology*. Cambridge, MA: Harvard University Press, 2010.

———. "Food as Exposure: Nutritional Epigenetics and the New Metabolism." *Biosocieties* 6 (2011): 167–94.

———. "Immortality, in Vitro: A History of the HeLa Cell Line." In *Biotechnology and Culture: Bodies, Anxieties, Ethics*, edited by Paul E. Brodwin. Bloomington: Indiana University Press, 2000. 53–72.

Laqueur, Thomas. *Making Sex: Body and Gender from Greeks to Freud*. Cambridge, MA: Harvard University Press, 1990.

Latour, Bruno. *Pandora's Hope: Essays on the Reality of Science Studies*. Cambridge, MA: Harvard University Press, 1999.

———. *We Have Never Been Modern*. Translated by Catherine Porter. Cambridge, MA: Harvard University Press, 1993.

Lee, Chang Rae. *Native Speaker*. New York: Riverhead Books, 1995.

Lee, Christopher. *The Semblance of Identity: Aesthetic Mediation in Asian American Literature*. Stanford, CA: Stanford University Press, 2012.

Lee, Esther Kim. "Between the Personal and the Universal: Asian American Solo Performance from the 1970s to the 1990s." *JAAS* 6, no. 3 (October 2003): 289–312.

Lee, Rachel. "Introduction to Life (Un)Ltd: Feminism, Bioscience, Race." *The Scholar and the Feminist* 11, no. 3 (Summer 2013), http://sfonline.barnard.edu/life-un-ltd-feminism-bioscience-race/introduction/0.

———. "'Where's My Parade?' Margaret Cho and the Asian American Body in Space." *TDR: The Drama Review* 48, no. 2 (Summer 2004): 108–32.

Lee, Robert. *Orientals: Asian Americans in Popular Culture*. Philadelphia: Temple University Press, 1999.

Lee, Sue Im. "The Aesthetic in Asian American Literary Discourse." In *Literary Gestures: The Aesthetic in Asian American Writing*, edited by Rocío Davis and Sue Im Lee. Philadelphia: Temple University Press, 2005. 1–16.

Lee, Yoon Sun. "Type, Totality, and the Realism of Asian American Literature." *Modern Language Quarterly* 73, no. 3 (September 2012): 415–32.

Leyendecker, G., et al. "Uterine Peristaltic Activity and the Development of Endometriosis." *Annals of the New York Academy of Sciences* 1034 (December 2004): 338–55.

Li, Yiyun. *The Vagrants*. New York: Random House, 2009.

Lifsher, Marc. "Dissecting Source of Cadavers." *Los Angeles Times*, January 25, 2008.

Lim, Shirley Geok-lin, et al., Introduction to *Cross Wire: Asian American Literary Criticism* (special issue of *Studies in the Literary Imagination* 37, no.1). Atlanta: Georgia State University Press, 2004.

Linmark, R. Zack. *Rolling the R's*. 1995. New York: Kaya, 2006.

Love, Heather. *Feeling Backward: Loss and the Politics of Queer History*. Cambridge, MA: Harvard University Press, 2009.

Lowe, Lisa. *Immigrant Acts: On Asian American Cultural Politics*. Durham, NC: Duke University Press, 1996.

Lowe, Lisa, and David Lloyd, eds. *The Politics of Culture in the Shadow of Capital*. Durham, NC: Duke University Press, 1997.

Lye, Colleen. *America's Asia: Racial Form and American Literature, 1893–1945*. Princeton, NJ: Princeton University Press, 2004.

———. "Asian American 1960s." In *The Routledge Companion to Asian American and Pacific Islander Literature and Culture*, edited by Rachel Lee. New York: Routledge, 2014.

———. "In Dialogue with Asian American Studies." *Representations* 99 (Summer 2007): 1–12.

MacKenzie, Donald. *Material Markets: How Economic Agents Are Constructed*. New York: Oxford University Press, 2009.

Mahmood, Saba. *The Politics of Piety: The Islamic Revival and the Feminist Subject*. Princeton, NJ: Princeton University Press, 2011.

Mairs, Nancy. *Waist-High in the World: A Life among the Non-Disabled*. Boston: Beacon, 1996.

Manderson, Lenore. "Public Sex Performances in Patpong and Explorations of the Edges of Imagination." *Journal of Sex Research*. 29, no. 4 (1992): 451–75.

Mansfield, Becky. "Race and the New Epigenetic Biopolitics of Environmental Health." *BioSocieties* 7 (2012): 352–72.

Marcus, Sharon, and Stephen Best. "Surface Reading: An Introduction." *Representations* 108, no. 1 (Fall 2009): 1–21.

Margalit, Avishai. *The Ethics of Memory*. Cambridge, MA: Harvard University Press, 2002.

Margulis, Lynn. *Symbiotic Planet: A New Look at Evolution*. Amherst, MA: Sciencewriters, 1999. Kindle edition.

Margulis, Lynn, and Dorion Sagan. *Acquiring Genomes: A Theory of the Origin of the Species*. New York: Basic Books, 2008.

———. *The Origins of Sex: Three Billion Years of Genetic Recombination*. New Haven, CT: Yale University Press, 1986.

Martin, Emily. "Working across the Human and Animal Divide." In *Reinventing Biology: Respect for Life and the Creation of Knowledge*, edited by Lynda Birke and Ruth Hubbard. Bloomington: Indiana University Press, 1995. 261–75.

Massumi, Brian. *Parables for the Virtual: Movement, Affect, Sensation*. Durham, NC: Duke University Press, 2002.

Mathur, Suchitra. "Caught between the Goddess and the Cyborg: Third-World Women and the Politics of Science in Three Works of Indian Science Fiction." *Journal of Commonwealth Literature* 39, no. 3 (2004): 119–38.

Mbembe, Achille. "Necropolitics." Translated by Libby Meintjes. *Public Culture* 15, no. 1 (2003): 11–40.

McLuhan, Marshall, and Quentin Fiore. *The Medium Is the Massage*. Berkeley, CA: Gingko, 2001.

McRuer, Robert. *Crip Theory: Cultural Signs of Queerness and Disability.* New York: New York University Press, 2006.

"Melissa Etheridge Calls Angelina Jolie's Double Mastectomy a 'Fearful' Choice." *Huffington Post*, June 18, 2013, http://www.huffingtonpost.com/2013/06/18/melissa-etheridge-angelina-jolie -double-mastectomy-fearful_n_3458853.html.

Mitchell, David T., and Sharon Snyder. *Narrative Prosthesis: Disability and the Dependences of Discourse.* Ann Arbor: Unviersity of Michigan Press, 2001.

———, eds. *Cultural Locations of Disability.* Chicago: University of Chicago Press, 2006.

Moncur, Laura. "Margaret Cho's 'F**K It' Diet." *Starling Fitness*, January 28, 2005, http://www .starling-fitness.com/archives/2005/01/28/margaret-chos-fk-it-diet.

Morton, Timothy. "Queer Ecology." *PMLA* 125, no. 2 (March 2010): 273–82.

Müller, Andreas, et al. "Modulation of Uterine Contractility and Peristalsis by Oxytocin in Estrogen-Primed Non-Pregnant Swine Uteri." *European Journal of Medical Research* 11, no. 4 (May 2006): 157–62.

Murphy, Michelle. "Distributed Reproduction, Chemical Violence, and Latency." *Scholar and Feminist* 11, no. 3 (Summer 2013), http://sfonline.barnard.edu/life-un-ltd-feminism -bioscience-race/distributed-reproduction-chemical-violence-and-latency.

———. *Seizing the Means of Production: Entanglements of Feminism, Health, and Technoscience.* Durham, NC: Duke University Press, 2012.

Muñoz, José Esteban. *Disidentifications: Queers of Color and the Performance of Politics.* Minneapolis: University of Minnesota Press, 1999.

Nelson, Diane M. "A Social Science Fiction of Fevers, Delirium, and Discovery: *The Calcutta Chromosome*, the Colonial Laboratory, and the Postcolonial New Human." *Science Fiction Studies* 30, no. 2 (2003): 246–66.

———. "'Yes to Life = No to Mining': Counting as Biotechnology in Life (Ltd) Guatemala." *Scholar and Feminist* 11, no. 3 (Summer 2013), http://sfonline.barnard.edu/life-un-ltd-feminism -bioscience-race/yes-to-life-no-to-mining-counting-as-biotechnology-in-life-ltd-guatemala.

Nelson, Marilyn. *Fortune's Bones: The Manumission Requiem.* Asheville, NC: Front Street Press, 2003/2004.

Ngai, Sianne. *Our Aesthetic Categories: Zany, Cute, Interesting.* Cambridge, MA: Harvard University Press, 2012.

———. *Ugly Feelings.* Cambridge, MA: Harvard University Press, 2005.

Nguyen, Viet Thanh. *Race and Resistance: Literature and Politics in Asian America.* New York: Oxford University Press, 2002.

Nicholson, Linda. "Interpreting Gender." In *Social Postmodernism: Beyond Identity Politics*, edited by Linda Nicholson and Steven Seidman. Cambridge: Cambridge University Press, 1995. 39–67.

Nigam, Sanjay. *Transplanted Man.* New York: HarperCollins, 2002.

Ninh, erin Khuê. *Ingratitude: The Debt-Bound Daughter in Asian American Literature.* New York: New York University Press, 2011.

Office of Management and Budget at the White House. "Homeland Security," http://www.white house.gov/omb/factsheet_department_homeland.

Omi, Michael. "'Slippin' into Darkness': The (re)Biologization of Race." *Journal of Asian American Studies* 13, no. 3 (2010): 343–58.

Oyama, Susan. *The Ontogeny of Information: Development Systems and Evolution*, second edition. Durham, NC: Duke University Press, 2000.

Ozeki, Ruth. *My Year of Meats.* New York: Penguin, 1998.

Pacis, Efren, et al. "Systematic Approaches to Develop Chemically Defined Cell Culture Feed Media." *BioPharm International* 23, no. 11 (Nov. 1, 2010) at http://www.biopharminternational .com/biopharm/article/articleDetail.jsp?id=695161.

Palumbo-Liu, David. *Asian/America: Historical Crossings of a Racial Frontier*. Stanford, CA: Stanford University Press, 1999.

———. *The Deliverance of Others: Reading Literature in a Global Age*. Durham, NC: Duke University Press, 2012.

———. "Rational and Irrational Choices: Form, Affect, and Ethics." In *Minor Transnationalism*, edited by Shu-mei Shih and Francoise Lionnet. Durham, NC: Duke University Press, 2005.

Parikh, Crystal. "'I Don't Really Know What That Means': Autism and the Ethics of Asian American Sublimation." Paper presented at the Annual Meeting of the Association for Asian American Studies, Seattle, WA, April 2013.

Park, Josephine Nock-Hee. *Apparitions of Asia: Modernist Form and Asian American Poetics*. New York: Oxford University Press, 2008.

Parks, Suzan-Lori. "Elements of Style." *The America Play and Other Works*. New York: Theatre Communications Group, 1995. 6–18.

———. *Venus*. New York: Theatre Communications Group, 1990.

Parreñas, Rhacel Salazar. *Servants of Globalization: Women, Migration, and Domestic Work*. Stanford, CA: Stanford University Press, 2001.

Patton, Cindy. "Introduction: Foucault after Neoliberalism; or, The Clinic Here and Now." In *Rebirth of the Clinic: Places and Agents in Contemporary Health*, edited by Cindy Patton. Minneapolis: University of Minnesota Press, 2010. ix–xx.

Paxson, Heather. "Post-Pasteurian Cultures: The Microbiopolitics of Raw-Milk Cheese in the United States." *Cultural Anthropology* 23, no. 1 (2008): 15–47.

Phelan, Peggy. "Reconsidering Identity Politics, Essentialism, and Dismodernism." In *Bodies in Commotion: Disability and Performance*, edited by Carrie Sandahl and Philip Auslander. Ann Arbor: University of Michigan Press, 2005. 319–26.

———. *Unmarked: The Politics of Performance*. New York: Routledge, 1993.

Prashad, Vijay. *Everybody Was Kung Fu Fighting: Afro-Asian Connection and the Myth of Cultural Purity*. Boston: Beacon, 2001.

Pratt, Mary-Louise. *Imperial Eyes: Travel Writing and Transculturation*. New York: Routledge, 1992.

Puar, Jasbir. *Terrorist Assemblages: Homonationalism in Queer Times*. Durham, NC: Duke University Press, 2007.

Rajan, Kaushik Sunder. *Biocapital: The Constitution of Postgenomic Life*. Durham, NC: Duke University Press, 2006.

Reardon, Jenny, and Kim Tallbear. "'Your DNA Is Our History': Genomics, Anthropology, and the Construction of Whiteness as Property." *Current Anthropology* 53, no. S5 (April 2012): S233–45.

Reddy, Chandan. *Freedom with Violence: Race, Sexuality, and the US State*. Durham, NC: Duke University Press, 2011.

Reissman, Catherine Kohler. *Narrative Methods for the Human Sciences*. Thousand Oaks, CA: Sage, 2008.

Richards, Robert J. "Biology." *From Natural Philosophy to the Sciences: Writing the History of Nineteenth-Century Science*. Ed. David Cahan. Chicago: University of Chicago Press, 2003. 16–48.

Riddell, Adaljiza Sosa. "The Bioethics of Reproductive Technologies: Impacts and Implications for Latinas." In *Chicana Critical Issues* Ed. Norma Alarcón, et al. Berkeley: Third Woman Press, 1993. 183–96.

Riggs, Damien W., and Clemence Due. "Gay Men, Race Privilege, and Surrogacy in India." *Outskirts: Feminisms along the Edge* (May 2010), http://www.thefreelibrary.com/Gay+men,+race+privilege+and+surrogacy+in+India.-a0230416790.

Roach, Joseph. *Cities of the Dead: Circum-Atlantic Performance*. New York: Columbia University Press, 1996.

Roberts, Dorothy. *Fatal Invention: How Science, Politics, and Big Business Re-create Race in the Twenty-First Century*. New York: New Press, 2012.

———. *Killing the Black Body: Race, Reproduction, and the Meaning of Liberty.* New York: Vintage, 1998.

Rogier, Christophe, and Marcel Hommel. "Impact Malaria." Accessed July 20, 2012, http://en .impact-malaria.com/iml/cx/en/layout.jsp?scat=746866F9-2FEE-4C5E-9770-A544EE462C14.

Roof, Judith. *The Poetics of DNA.* Minneapolis: University of Minnesota Press, 2007.

Rose, Nikolas. "Politics and Life." In *The Politics of Life Itself: Biomedicine, Power, and Subjectivity in the Twenty-first Century.* Princeton, NJ: Princeton University Press, 2007. 41–76.

———. "The Politics of Life Itself." *Theory, Culture & Society* 18, no. 6 (2001): 1–30.

———. "Race in the Age of Genomic Medicine." In *The Politics of Life Itself: Biomedicine, Power, and Subjectivity in the Twenty-First Century.* Princeton, NJ: Princeton University Press, 2007. 155–86.

Rose, Nikolas, and Carlos Novas. "Biological Citizenship." In *Global Assemblages.* Ed. Aihwa Ong and Stephen J. Collier. Malden, MA: Blackwell, 2005.

Roughgarden, Joan. *Evolution's Rainbow: Diversity, Gender, and Sexuality in Nature and People.* Berkeley: University of California Press, 2009.

———. *The Genial Gene: Deconstructing Darwinian Selfishness.* Berkeley: University of California Press, 2009.

Roy, Deboleena. "Asking Different Questions: Feminist Practices for the Natural Sciences." *Hypatia* 23, no. 4 (Fall 2008): 134–57.

———. "Cosmopolitics and the Brain: The Co-Becoming of Practices in Feminism and Neuroscience." In *Neurofeminism: Issues at the Intersection of Feminist Theory and Cognitive Science.* Eds. Robyn Bluhm, Anne Jaap Jacobson, and Heidi Maibom. New York: Palgrave Macmillan, 2012. 175–92.

———. "Should Feminists Clone? And If So, How?" *Australian Feminist Studies* 23, no. 56 (2008): 225–47.

Rubin, Gayle. "The Traffic in Women: Notes on the 'Political Economy' of Sex." In *Toward an Anthropology of Women*, edited by Rayna Reiter. New York: Monthly Review Press, 1975. 157–210.

Rydell, Robert W. *All the World's a Fair.* University of Chicago Press, 1984.

Saldanha, Arun. "Reontologising Race: The Machinic Geography of Phenotype." *Environment and Planning D: Society and Space* 24, no. 1 (2006): 9–24.

Sandahl, Carrie, and Philip Auslander, eds. *Bodies in Commotion: Disability and Performance.* Ann Arbor: University of Michigan Press, 2005.

Savigliano, Marta. *Tango and the Political Economy of Passion.* Boulder, CO: Westview, 1995.

Schechner, Richard. "Performers and Spectators Transported and Transformed." *Kenyon Review* 3, no. 4 (1981): 83–113.

Schechner, Richard, and Victor Turner. *Between Theater and Anthropology.* Philadelphia: University of Pennsylvania Press, 1985.

Scheibinger, Londa. "Why Mammals Are Called Mammals: Gender Politics in Eighteenth-Century Natural History." *American Historical Review* 98, no. 2 (April 1993): 382–411.

Scheper-Hughes, Nancy. "Commodity Fetishism in Organs Trafficking." In Scheper-Hughes and Wacquant, eds., *Commodifying Bodies.* London: Sage, 2002. 31–62.

———. "The Last Commodity: Post-Human Ethics and the Global Traffic in 'Fresh' Organs." In Aihwa Ong and Stephen Collier, eds., *Global Assemblages: Technology, Politics, and Ethics as Anthropological Problems.* Hoboken, NJ: Wiley-Blackwell, 2004. 145–67.

Scheper-Hughes, Nancy, and Loic Wacquant, eds. *Commodifying Bodies.* London: Sage, 2002.

Schulze-Engler, Frank. "Strange Encounters or Succeeding Dialogues." In *The Fuzzy Logic of Encounter*, edited by Sunne Juterczenka and Gesa Mackenthum. Göttingen: Waxmann, 2009. 173–83.

"Science Museum of Minnesota to Welcome New *Body Worlds* and *The Cycle of Life* Exhibition." 2012 Press Release. http://www.bodyworlds.com/en/media/releases_statements/2012.html.

Sedgwick, Eve Kosofsky. *Touching Feeling: Affect, Pedagogy, Performativity.* Durham, NC: Duke University Press, 2003.

Sedgwick, Eve Kosofsky, and Adam Frank, eds. *Shame and Its Sisters: A Silvan Tomkins Reader.* Durham, NC: Duke University Press, 1995.

Shah, Nayan. *Contagious Divides: Epidemics and Race in San Francisco's Chinatown.* Berkeley: University of California Press, 2001.

———. *Stranger Intimacy: Contesting Race, Sexuality, and the Law in the North American West.* Berkeley: University of California Press, 2011.

Shimakawa, Karen. *National Abjection: The Asian American Body Onstage.* Durham, NC: Duke University Press, 2002.

Shimizu, Celine Parreñas. *The Hypersexuality of Race: Performing Asian/American Women on Screen and Scene.* Durham, NC: Duke University Press, 2007.

Shinn, Christopher. "On Machines and Mosquitoes: Neuroscience, Bodies, and Cyborgs in Amitav Ghosh's *The Calcutta Chromosome.*" *MELUS* 33, no. 4 (2008): 145–66.

Shiva, Vandana. *Staying Alive: Women, Ecology, and Development.* London: Zed Books, 1989. Rpt. Women Unlimited/Kali for Women, 2009.

Shohat, Ella, ed. *Talking Visions: Multicultural Feminism in a Transnational Age.* New York: New Museum and MIT Press, 1998.

Silva, Denise Ferreira da. *Towards the Global Idea of Race.* Minneapolis: University of Minnesota Press, 2007.

Skloot, Rebecca. *The Immortal Life of Henrietta Lacks.* New York: Crown, 2010.

Smith, Andrea. "Queer Theory and Native Studies: The Heteronormativity of Settler Colonialism." *GLQ* 16, nos. 1–2 (2010): 42–68.

So, Christine. *Economic Citizens: A Narrative of Asian American Visibility.* Philadelphia: Temple University Press, 2009.

Sobchack, Vivian. "Is Any Body Home? Embodied Imagination and Visible Evictions." In *Carnal Thoughts: Embodiment and Moving Image Culture.* Berkeley: University of California Press, 2004. 179–204.

Sohn, Stephen Hong, and John Blair Gamber. "Currents of Study: Charting the Course of Asian American Literary Criticism." *Studies in the Literary Imagination* 37, no. 1 (Spring 2004): 1–16.

Spillers, Hortense J. "Mama's Baby, Papa's Maybe: An American Grammar Book." *Diacritics* 17, no. 2 (1987): 64–81.

Spivak, Gayatri. *The Post-Colonial Critic: Interviews, Strategies, Dialogues.* New York: Routledge, 1990.

Squier, Susan. "Life and Death at Strangeways: The Tissue-Culture Point of View." In *Biotechnology and Culture: Bodies, Anxieties, Ethics,* edited by Paul E. Brodwin. Bloomington: Indiana University Press, 2000. 27–52.

———. *Liminal Lives: Imagining the Human at the Frontiers of Biomedicine.* Durham, NC: Duke University Press, 2004.

Staples, David. "Women's Work and the Ambivalent Gift of Entropy." In *The Affective Turn: Theorizing the Social,* edited by Patricia Ticineto Clough with Jean Halley. Durham, NC: Duke University Press, 2007. 119–50.

Steinfatt, Thomas. *Working at the Bar: Sex Work and Health Communication in Thailand.* Westport, CT: Greenwood, 2002.

"Stem Cell Basics." *National Institutes of Health.* Last modified June 7, 2012, http://stemcells.nih .gov/info/basics/pages/basics4.aspx.

Stern, Alexandra Minna. *Eugenic Nation: Faults and Frontiers of Better Breeding in Modern America.* Berkeley: University of California Press, 2005.

———. "Sterilized in the Name of Public Health: Race, Immigration, and Reproductive Control in Modern California." *American Journal of Public Health* 95, no. 7 (2005): 1128–38.

Stockton, Kathryn Bond. *The Queer Child; or, Growing Sideways in the Twentieth Century*. Durham, NC: Duke University Press, 2009.

Stuurman, Siep. "Francois Bernier and the Invention of Racial Classification." *History Workshop Journal* 50 (Autumn 2000): 1–21.

Subramaniam, Banu. *Ghost Stories for Darwin: The Science of Variation and the Politics of Diversity*. Urbana-Champagne: University of Illinois Press, 2014.

Sumida, Stephen. "*All I Asking for Is My Body*." In *A Resource Guide to Asian American Literature*, edited by Sau-ling Cynthia Wong and Stephen H. Sumida. New York: Modern Language Association, 2001. 130–39.

Tajima-Peña, Renee. "'Más Bebés?': An Investigation of the Sterilization of Mexican-American Women at Los Angeles County–USC Medical Center during the 1960s and 70s." *Scholar and Feminist Online* 11, no. 3 (Summer 2013).

Tallbear, Kim. "An Indigenous Ontological Reading of Cryopreservation Practices and Ethics (and Why I'd Rather Think about Pipestone)." Paper delivered at the American Anthropological Association, San Francisco, 2012, and archived at http://www.kimtallbear.com.

———. "Genomic Articulations of Indigeneity." *Social Studies of Science*, August 1, 2013, 465–83.

———. *Native DNA: Tribal Belonging and the False Promise of Genetic Science*. Minneapolis: University of Minnesota Press, 2013.

Taylor, Diana. *The Archive and Repertoire: Performing Cultural Memory in the Americas*. Durham, NC: Duke University Press, 2007.

Taylor, Janelle. "On Recognition, Caring, and Dementia." In *Care in Practice: On Tinkering in Clinics, Homes, and Farms*, edited by Annemarie Mol, Ingunn Moser, and Jeannette Pols. Bielefeld, Germany: Transcript Verlag, 2010.

Terada, Rei. "Radical Anxiety." Public lecture hosted by the English Department, UCLA, January 31, 2013.

Thacker, Eugene. *The Global Genome: Biotechnology, Politics, and Culture*. Cambridge, MA: MIT Press, 2005.

Theweleit, Klaus. *Male Fantasies*. Vol. 1, *Women, Floods, Bodies, History*. Trans. Chris Turner, et al. Minneapolis: University of Minnesota Press, 1987.

Thieme, John. "The Discoverer Discovered: Amitav Ghosh's *The Calcutta Chromosome*." *Studies in Indian Writing in English*, volume 2, edited by Rajeshwar Mittapalli and Pier Paolo Piciucco. New Delhi: Atlantic, 2001. 170–83.

Thompson, Charis. "Asian Regeneration? Nationalism and Internationalism in Stem Cell Research in South Korea and Singapore." In *Asian Biotech*, edited by Aihwa Ong and Nancy N. Chen. Durham, NC: Duke University Press, 2010. 95–117.

———. *Good Science: The Ethical Choreography of Stem Cell Research*. Cambridge, MA: MIT Press, 2013.

———. *Making Parents: The Ontological Choreography of Reproduction*. Cambridge, MA: MIT Press, 2005.

Thrall, James H. "Postcolonial Science Fiction? Science, Religion, and the Transformation of Genre in Amitav Ghosh's *The Calcutta Chromosome*." *Literature & Theology* 23, no. 3 (2009): 289–302.

Trauner, Joan B. "The Chinese as Medical Scapegoats in San Francisco, 1870–1905." *California History* 57, no. 1 (1978): 70–87.

Truong, Monique. *The Book of Salt*. New York: Houghton Mifflin, 2003.

"The Unparallelled Success." Gunther von Hagen's *Body Worlds* website at http://www.bodyworlds.com/en/exhibitions/unparalleled_success.html. Accessed April 25, 2014.

Uyehara, Denise. *Big Head*. Live Performance at Highways Theater, Santa Monica, CA, March 2003.

———. "Denise Uyehara Demo." *Denise Uyehara*. Publicity video. Accessed April 18, 2011, http://www.deniseuyehara.com/about/vidphotos.html#introvideo.

Uyehara, Denise. "'Hate Crime' scene from *Big Head*." Video. Accessed April 7, 2014, http://vimeo.com/8755970.

———. *Hello (Sex) Kitty*. London, 1995.

———. "Lost and Found, I." Los Angeles, 1997.

———. "Lost and Found, II." Helsinki, 1998.

———. *Maps of City and Body*. Video Recording of Performance at Highways Theater, Santa Monica, CA, November 1999.

———. *Maps of City and Body: Shedding Light on the Performances of Denise Uyehara*. New York: Kaya Press, 2003.

———. *Senkotsu (Mis)Translation*. Performance at Barnsdall Art Park, Los Angeles, 2009.

Vaughn, Christopher. "Ogling Igorots: The Politics and Commerce of Exhibiting Cultural Otherness, 1898–1913." In *Freakery*, edited by Rosemarie Garland Thomson. New York: New York University Press, 1996. 219–33.

Vickers, Nancy. "Members Only." In *The Body in Parts: Fantasies of Corporeality in Early Modern Europe*, edited by David Hillman and Carla Mazzio. New York: Routledge, 1997. 3–21.

Vora, Kalindi. "Indian Transnational Surrogacy and the Commodification of Vital Energy." *Subjectivity* 28 (2009): 266–78.

———. "Limits of Labor: Accounting for Affect and the Biological in Transnational Surrogacy and Service Work." *South Atlantic Quarterly* 111, no. 4 (Fall 2012): 681–700.

———. "Medicine, Markets, and the Pregnant Body: Indian Commercial Surrogacy and Reproductive Labor in a Transnational Frame." *Scholar and Feminist* 9, nos. 1–2 (Fall 2010–Spring 2011), http://sfonline.barnard.edu/reprotech/vora_01.htm.

Wailoo, Keith, Alondra Nelson, and Catherine Lee, eds. *Genetics and the Unsettled Past: The Collision of DNA, Race, and History*. Piscataway, NJ: Rutgers University Press, 2012.

Wald, Priscilla. "American Studies and the Politics of Life." *American Quarterly* 64, no. 2 (2012): 185–204.

———. *Contagious: Cultures, Carriers, and the Outbreak Narrative*. Durham, NC: Duke University Press, 2008.

Waldby, Catherine, and Robert Mitchell. *Tissue Economies: Blood, Organs, and Cell Lines in Late Capitalism*. Durham, NC: Duke University Press, 2006.

Wang, Ping. *Aching for Beauty: Footbinding in China*. Minneapolis: University of Minnesota Press, 2000.

Wang, Zhengbao. *The Art of Chinese Acrobatics*. Beijing: Foreign Languages Press, 1982.

Wei, William. *The Asian American Movement*. Philadelphia: Temple University Press, 1993.

Williams, Raymond. *Marxism and Literature*. New York: Oxford University Press, 1977.

Wilson, Elizabeth A. "Another Neurological Scene." *History of the Present: A Journal of Critical History* 1, no. 2 (2011): 149–69.

———. "Gut Feminism." *differences: A Journal of Feminist Cultural Studies* 15, no. 3 (2004): 66–94.

———. *Psychosomatic: Feminism and the Neurological Body*. Durham, NC: Duke University Press, 2004.

Woloch, Alex. *The One vs. the Many: Minor Characters and the Space of the Protagonist in the Novel*. Princeton, NJ: Princeton University Press, 2003.

Wong, Sau-ling. *Reading Asian American Literature: From Necessity to Extravagance*. Princeton, NJ: Princeton University Press, 1993.

Wynbrandt, James. *The Excruciating History of Dentistry: Toothsome Tales & Oral Oddities from Babylon to Braces*. New York: St Martin's, 1998.

Yamamoto, Hisaye. "Wilshire Bus." In *Seventeen Syllables and Other Stories*. New Brunswick, NJ: Rutgers University Press, 1998. 34–39.

Yamanaka, Lois Ann. *Blu's Hanging*. 1997. New York: HarperCollins, 2002.

———. *Heads by Harry*. 1999. New York: HarperCollins, 2000.

———. *Saturday Night at the Pahala Theater*. Honolulu, HI: Bamboo Ridge, 1993.

Yamashita, Karen Tei. *Tropic of Orange*. Minneapolis, MN: Coffee House Press, 1997.

Yu, Cheng-Chieh. *Bowl Problems*. 1999. Live performance at the Roy and Edna Disney/Calarts Theater (REDCAT), Now Festival, July 2004.

———. *Hood, Veil, Shoes*. Performed by the Sun-Shier Dance Theater of Taiwan. Live performance at the Dance Theater, Glorya Kaufman Hall, January 18, 2008.

———. *My Father's Teeth in My Mother's Mouth*. 2000. Live performance at the LA Women's Theater Festival, LA Theater Center, Los Angeles, 2003.

———. Personal Conversation with Rachel Lee, July 22, 2004.

———. "She Said He Said, He Said She Said," in *Trade*. Live performance at Highways, Santa Monica, CA, November 20, 2005.

Yu, Timothy. *Race and the Avant-Garde: Experimental and Asian American Poetry since 1965*. Stanford, CA: Stanford University Press, 2009.

Yun, Lisa. *The Coolie Speaks: Chinese Indentured Laborers and African Slaves in Cuba*. Philadelphia: Temple University Press, 2008.

Zhan, Mei. "Civet Cats, Fried Grasshoppers, and David Beckham's Pajamas: Unruly Bodies after SARS." *American Anthropologist*, New Series 107, no. 1 (2005): 31–42.

INDEX

Abjection, 63, 117, 164, 261n20; national, 83; racial, 220, 271n12

Acrobatics, 66, 96, 101, 215; as Chinese national culture, 70–74, 94; age/aging, 72; Li Tong Hua Acrobats, 70

Adams, Vicanne, 215, 276n29, 288n51

Adoption, 62, 176; birth parents, 104; moral, 103, 275n11; as neoliberalization of child welfare, 104; plenary, 104; reproductive justice, 97, 101–102; trafficking, 105; transnational/transracial, 97, 102–105, 275n9

Aesthetics, 31, 78, 192, 233, 244, 246, 252; acrobatics, 71–72; feminist, 72; and form, 4, 10, 12, 20, 50, 261n20, 267n24; objects/objectification, 228–29, 291n27; pulsing/peristaltic, 100, 123; and racial critique, 213, 225–33; rehumanization, 229, 291n28; as sublimation, 229–31; theory, 228

Affect, 4, 20, 29, 161, 163, 233, 258, 263n43; and aesthetics, 31, 228, 270n56, 291n27; affective labor, 110, 129, 141, 145, 151–52, 158, 192, 213, 219–21, 226, 281n36, 282nn37–38, 282n40; affective moderation, 74; affective trauma, 205; and agency, 21–27; alien/alienable, 73, 220; anticipatory, 215, 276n29; of anxiety, 108, 221; relation to biopower/biopolitics, 59, 108, 201–202, 221; and critical disposition, 209, 231, 241–43, 264n64, 278n47; circulation of, 7, 30, 195, 205, 264n64; and cognition, relation to, 24, 152, 200, 255; as energy, 195; embodiment/feeling, 24–25, 84; relation to ethics and memory, 41, 158, 164, 175, 198, 209, 285n19, 290n17, 291n31; gendered, 195–96, 208, 215, 226; impersonal, 116; negative, 192–95, 200, 204, 208–209, 242, 287n44; positive, 242; relation to race, 56, 59, 236–37; as social/environmental/atmospheric, 200–201, 205, 207, 209;

"structures of feeling," 124; subcategories of, 24, 261n20; sublime/surrealist, 27, 153, 158–59

Agamben, Giorgio, 28, 47, 266n2

Agency, 4, 25, 33, 63, 96, 101, 110, 155, 160, 199, 224, 239, 282n41, 283n45; Asiatic, 219, 227, 264n58; avatar of, 4, 21, 23, 95, 264n56, 291n28; biopolitical, 101, 225; of capital, 263–64n55; cellular, 58, 121; in characterization, 235; and citizenship, 22, 29; critical, 202, 243; of gut, 101, 118, 121; human/humanistic, 38, 123, 144, 169, 192, 218, 223, 231; in matter, 33, 201, 233; nonhuman, 50, 240, 292n39; operability, 22, 95; in organ donation/transplantation/trafficking, 21–23, 264n56; queer, 121; suspended/limited, 18, 24, 27, 259n2, 264n58

Ahmed, Sara, 200

Alarcon, Norma, 32

American studies, 36

Anagnost, Ann, 105

Anatomopolitics, 40, 45–46, 67, 69, 114, 116, 185

Animal studies, 47, 142, 277n39

Anthropocentrism, 143, 159, 162, 212, 231, 235, 237, 244; in aesthetics, 19, 229

Anthropomorphic aperture, 14–15, 21, 30, 38

Asian American, 30, 42; aesthetic quality, 4; body/body politic, 4, 8, 31, 95, 101; cultural production, 8–10, 24, 26, 35, 40, 47–48, 50, 52, 63, 238; as discursive construct, 8–9, 11–12; pan-ethnic community, 193

Asian Americanist critique, 3, 5–7, 20, 49, 107, 129, 220, 259n2–3, 261n20; biological/biopolitical/biosocial approach, 12, 28, 30, 35–38, 56–57, 63, 77, 211–12, 223, 255, 260n13; on cultural production, 226; feminist, 130; and fragmentation of, 8, 260n9; on melancholia, 226, 261n20; and

Health (*continued*)
 assessments, 46, 54; will to, 29, 63, 69, 76,
  80, 83, 103, 108, 114, 162, 266n8, 284n13
 HeLa, 18, 93; biomaterial labor/bioslavery,
  19, 262n35; racialization of 16–17. *See also*
  Cell lines; Lacks, Henrietta
Heteronormativity, 34, 174, 180, 278n47;
 family/kinship, 100, 103, 105, 121, 169;
 heteronormative reproduction, 34
Hird, Myrna, 35
Hmong, 44, 62
Homophobia, 112–13
Humanism, 5, 20, 222, 254; antihumanism, 223, 290n19; humanistic agency/
 autonomy, 38, 230–31, 239; humanist
 approaches, 7, 12, 21, 30–31, 239, 260n15;
 humanist subject, 4, 7, 23, 37–38, 201;
 humanist values/concerns, 19, 162; post-
 humanist, 218, 233, 265n72. *See also*
 Posthuman
Humor, 243; in *My Father's Teeth*, 67, 75; as
 political critique, 108, 121; and racial justice, 225, 229–33

Identity politics, 157, 163, 208, 265n78
Immigration, 43–44, 222, 288–89n3; Asian,
 42, 275n11; Angel Island, 42; legal restric-
 tions, 270n17, 272n2, 275n11
Immunity, 200, 210, 292n42; biopolitics, 201,
 207; defensive, 142, 287n45; immunology,
 12, 265n72; materialization/fetishization
 of, 223–24; natural healing, 142; theory, 64
Indigenous, 50, 86, 102, 214, 217, 222, 248,
 250, 268n34, 269n44, 270n55; epistemology, 212, 224; medical subjects, 131, 133;
 Native American dispossession, 188, 204;
 tribal sovereignty, 50
Infertility, 40, 65, 97, 102
Intimacy, 6, 29, 62, 64, 234, 281n33, 284n10;
 in affective labor, 221; cross-species, 52;
 in dance, 165; "hetero," 34; "homo"/queer,
 34, 281n33
In vitro fertilization (IVF), 34, 130
Ishiguro, Kazuo, 28, 48, 59–61, 63, 162, 211,
 269n45

Jain, Sarah Lochlann, 31, 221
Jeon, Joseph Jonghyun, 12, 228, 261n20,
 291n25
Jerng, Mark, 48; on *bios*, 47, 50, 211, 269n45
Joachim, Mitchell, 246–48, 293n1

Kang, Laura Hyun Yi, 35, 259n2, 272n17
Kim, Claire J., 42–43
Kim, Jodi, 48, 221; on Cold War, 45, 111; on
 reproductive justice, 97; on transnational
 adoption, 102
Kinesthetics, 26, 75, 161, 184–85, 232–33, 235,
 258; choreography, 92, 160, 171, 196, 198,
 211; in dance/performance, 80, 90–92,
 160, 165–66, 179, 183, 192, 194, 197–99, 208,
 286n25; of gut, 101; kinesthetic imagination, 67; kinesthetic memory, 179; literary
 aesthetics, 155, 158; masculine, 92; micro-
 kinetics, 198, 200. *See also* Dance
Kingston, Maxine Hong, 48
Kinship, 11, 34, 172, 268n34, 281n36; adoptive, 175; biological, 91; incest, 34; normative, 105; non-nuclear/queer troubling of,
 34, 103–104, 211. *See also* Adoption
Koshy, Susan, 9, 23, 59

Labor, 80, 216, 219, 222, 239–40, 247–48,
 276n27, 293n6; affective, 110, 129, 141,
 145, 151–52, 213, 221, 226, 281–82n36–38,
 282n40; alienated, 18–20, 36, 150, 228,
 262n39; Asiatic, 43, 81, 96; bioavailable, 51;
 biomaterial, 19, 259–60n8, 263n43; cellu-
 lar/metabolic, 141, 150, 222; domestic, 101,
 149–50, 282n41; experimental, 128–129,
 134, 216, 280n10, 282n41; feminized, 81,
 215, 226; flexible, 205; gendered division
 of, 152, 195, 266n1; immaterial/invisible,
 129, 143, 149–52, 215, 263n43, 281–82n37–
 38, 282n40; immigrant, 43, 98–99, 214,
 248; informational, 127, 151; nativist, 219;
 organizing, 2; plantation, 43–44, 288n2;
 prostitution/sex work, 110, 114; racialized,
 156, 213–15, 220; reproductive, 104–105,
 128, 141, 150, 213, 215, 281–82n37, 291n28;
 slave, 217–18, 248–49, 288n2; stratification, 40, 148; surplus, 217; theory of race,
 213–16; transnational, 6, 20; wage, 150,
 214, 288–89n3. *See also* Caretaking; Coolie
Lacks, Henrietta 16–19, 28, 262n35. *See also*
 HeLa
Lai, Larissa, 50–52
Landecker, Hannah, 20, 30, 208; on HeLa,
 16–18; on metabolism, 276n30
Laqueur, Thomas, 33
Lateral reading, 25–27, 118, 123–24, 278n47.
 See also Sideways approach; Transversal
Lee, Chang Rae, 46

Rachel C. Lee is Associate Director of the Center for the Study of Women, Associate Professor of English and Gender Studies, and Faculty Affiliate of the Institute for Society and Genetics at the University of California–Los Angeles. She is the author of *The Americas of Asian American Literature: Gendered Fictions of Nation and Transnation* (1999), coeditor of the volume *Asian America.Net: Ethnicity, Nationalism, and Cyberspace* (2003), and editor of the *Routledge Companion to Asian American and Pacific Islander Literature* (2014).